nourishingmeals

nourishingmeals

365 WHOLE FOODS, ALLERGY-FREE RECIPES FOR
HEALING YOUR FAMILY ONE MEAL AT A TIME

Alissa Segersten
Tom Malterre, MS, CN

HARMONY
BOOKS · NEW YORK

Published in the United States by Harmony Books, an imprint of the Crown Publishing Group,
a division of Penguin Random House LLC, New York.
crownpublishing.com

Harmony Books is a registered trademark, and the Circle colophon is a trademark of
Penguin Random House LLC.

A previous edition of this work was published in the United States by Whole Life Press,
Bellingham, WA, in 2012.

Library of Congress Cataloging-in-Publication Data

Names: Segersten, Alissa, author. | Malterre, Tom, author.
Title: Nourishing meals : 365 whole foods, allergy-free recipes for healing your family one meal at a time /
Alissa Segersten, Tom Malterre.
Description: New York : Harmony Books, [2016] | Includes bibliographical
references and index.
Identifiers: LCCN 2016003320 (print) | LCCN 2016016115 (ebook) |
ISBN 9780451495921 | ISBN 9780451495938 ()
Subjects: LCSH: Gluten-free diet—Recipes.
Classification: LCC RM237.86 .S44 2016 (print) | LCC RM237.86 (ebook) |
DDC 641.5/639311—dc23
LC record available at https://lccn.loc.gov/2016003320

ISBN 978-0-451-49592-1
eBook ISBN 978-0-451-49593-8

Printed in the United States of America

Book design by Debbie Glasserman

Insert photographs by Alissa Segersten
Cover design by Debbie Glasserman
Cover photographs by Alissa Segersten

10 9 8 7 6 5 4 3 2 1

First Harmony Book Edition

This book is dedicated to
my Grandmother Marie,
for nourishing my mother
so she could nourish me.
—ALISSA

This book is dedicated to
all parents who
relentlessly seek out
what is best for their children,
and to all children
who deserve an opportunity
to experience life to the fullest.
—TOM

Contents

Acknowledgments

Most important, I'd like to thank my five children for putting up with all the recipe testing and computer work that went into this book. They helped taste-test each recipe, clean the kitchen when it was a big mess, and sometimes assisted with more than their fair share of house duties. I'd also like to put in a special mention to my oldest daughter, Lily, who prepared breakfast, lunch, and dinner many times when I was too busy writing, plus helped test so many of the recipes in this book!

I also want to give a big thank-you to my editor, Donna Loffredo, and the entire team at Harmony for helping me to create such a beautifully revised second edition of this book! I am so grateful for your insights and recommendations. You all have been so wonderful to work with.

Thank you to all of my recipe testers; your honest feedback was much appreciated. I'd also like to give special mention to a few people who tested nearly every recipe in this book: Mary Jensen, Linda Stiles, and my mom, Deb Segersten.

Finally, I'd like to thank my parents for being my constant cheerleaders; my mom for flying halfway across the country to help out so many times; my friend Jenna Anderson for her honest feedback in previewing some of the chapters; our personal assistant, Dot, for her constant work keeping our business and house organized; and Tom for collaborating with me on this project.

Alissa

First and foremost, I find it imperative to acknowledge Ali for her intuitive genius in creating and preparing new recipes faster than any other human I have ever witnessed. Our children, Lily, Grace, Sam, Ben, and Camille, deserve medals for their patience while we worked through crazy schedules. HUGE kudos and thanks to our parents—you are our lifeboats! Thank you for coming out to help so many times while I traveled to medical conferences.

There are many researchers and clinicians I would love to thank for inspiring me along the way, but I'd like to give a special mention to a few: Bruce Ames for his eloquent theories on nutritional deficiencies. Dr. Don Huber and Jeffrey Smith for their diligence, intelligence, and wit in informing us all about the negative effects of GMOs. Dr. Stephen Genuis for bringing awareness to how environmental exposures and nutrient deficiencies are partnering to change our immune systems. The Autism Research Institute faculty, clinicians, and staff who are putting together the pieces of environment, genetics, and nutrition into the puzzle of neurological decline in our children. I would also like to thank the Institute for Functional Medicine for their thorough training in evidence-based medicine that looks at all facets of life to find nourishment.

Tom

Preface

Tom and I met in nutrition school at Bastyr University, in Washington state, in the year 2000. We were both passionate young students wanting to help improve the lives of people through the power of food and plant medicine. He was sold after the first bite of a nourishing, whole foods meal I prepared for him.

A year after graduating with my Bachelor of Science degree in Nutrition, I began a personal-chef service in Seattle, Washington, called Whole Life Nutrition. It quickly grew, and I began serving many families throughout the Seattle area nourishing meals specifically tailored to their dietary needs and health goals. It was exhilarating to see so many positive changes as a result of some simple, but powerful dietary changes. The idea to write a cookbook that would share those simple yet powerful changes with even more people began to form in my mind, which ultimately became our first book, *The Whole Life Nutrition Cookbook*. Eventually, Tom graduated with his Master of Science in Nutrition and became a Certified Nutritionist. Tom had been passionate about the power of food as medicine since he was a ten-year-old boy. We merged our passions and he joined Whole Life Nutrition—it was only natural to bring together nourishing meals and nutritional counseling to help better the health of both people and the planet.

In the early days of running our nutrition practice, Whole Life Nutrition, we saw fewer cases of food sensitivities, allergies, autoimmune conditions, and other disorders in children. In recent years, though, we started to see more cases of ADHD, autism, eczema, nut and soy allergies, digestive disorders, gluten sensitivities, and seasonal allergies. We wanted to know why the incidence of these conditions was rising so quickly, so we looked to science for answers.

We found many connections between our immune system and our environment. Toxins from our food, water, and air are damaging our body's ability to recognize food. We kept coming back to the need to eat a gluten-free, organic whole foods diet that is rich in plants, especially cruciferous vegetables, to maintain optimal health, prevent disease, and heal food allergies.

After a few years of recommending gluten-free diets, we noticed that many people were beginning to consume more processed gluten-free foods, thinking that "gluten-free" means healthy. This led us to refine our education and cooking skills even further to help others remember that it is optimal to maintain a diet based on organic whole foods and to leave the processed gluten-free products on the grocery store shelves.

This book offers over 365 gluten-free whole food recipes—one nourishing recipe for every day of the year. These recipes are the tools for building a life of good health. We know it's hard to make changes in your busy life. So, we just ask that you swap one meal a day for one of the healing and nourishing meals in this book. One meal a day is enough to make a difference, and it will help you fill your toolkit with favorite go-to recipes, developed through experimentation and trial. Maybe for the first swap you just trade your sandwich bread for a nori wrap; maybe you'll make your salad dressing from scratch, which takes almost no time at all. Maybe it's snacking on carrot sticks instead of chips. By the end of a year, you'll have laid a foundation for raising healthy, resilient children.

7 Steps to Sustainable Dietary Change

If you are feeling overwhelmed, but are ready to begin making changes to your family's diet, then start with one simple change every few weeks or every few months—whatever feels most sustainable. Here is an order of operations we often recommend—see if it works for you. Oftentimes, it's better to begin by adding new things to an existing diet instead of removing individual foods or large food groups. The idea is *restorative nourishment*, which can gently and gradually nurture the system until some of those unhealthy foods and habits naturally fade away. Then you may begin experimenting to see how you and your family feel without gluten or dairy. These steps help make the process lasting and sustainable.

1. Add More Vegetables. You know it, I know it, we all know that vegetables play an integral role in health and wellness, but sometimes it can be tricky to get your children excited about eating their veggies! This book is loaded with tips—covering from pregnancy through childhood—on how to help deal with and prevent picky eating behaviors so your whole family can enjoy plant-rich meals. Check the "Salads and Vegetables" chapter for delicious recipes and helpful tips. Some of my favorite ways to help my children get the vegetables they need is to make them a green smoothie everyday (see the "Smoothies" chapter for recipes); serve a plate of cut celery, cucumbers, and carrots along with a bowl of Herb and Olive Oil Hummus (page 343) as a snack in the afternoon or before dinner, if they are hungry. I also like to add finely chopped dark leafy greens, such as kale or collards, to pasta sauces, soups, and stir-fries.

2. Make Your Own Salad Dressings. If you are going to be enjoying more salads and vegetables, then what better way to enjoy them than with a homemade salad dressing? Once you begin making dressings from scratch, you'll wonder why you ever bought them—the flavors and pureness of homemade dressings are simply unmatched by anything you can buy. I like to keep two jars of different dressings on hand in my fridge at all times. You can use the weekend to create your dressings—they literally take just minutes to prepare. It's important to remember, though, that my recipes use extra-virgin olive oil, which partially solidifies at refrigerated temperatures. The dressings you find in the grocery store use refined vegetable oils that stay in a liquid state when cold, which is great for marketing but not so great for your health. I usually take one of my homemade dressings from the fridge and place it on the back of my stove while I cook dinner, or place it in a bowl of warm water until dinner is ready, then shake well and serve it.

3. Replace Processed Grain Foods with Whole Grains. What does this mean? Look around your kitchen and in your pantry. Do you have breakfast cereal, packaged crackers and cookies, bags of pretzels, and bags of sandwich bread? You might find that you have more energy, more resistance to colds and flus, and better skin—and you also might begin to notice better behavior in your children—if all these processed grain foods are removed and replaced with whole grains or grain-free alternatives. For example, you can swap the dry cereals at breakfast for warm whole-grain cereals (try the Cream of Rice Cereal, page 76) topped with Raw Almond Milk (page 451) or raw cream and blueberries, or replace the dry cereal with nourishing grain-free pancakes (try the Fluffy Cashew Pancakes, page 95); or substitute with a protein-rich meal like the Chicken Breakfast Sausages (page 91) and a smoothie. Your child's teacher will probably notice a big difference in your child's alertness and attentiveness in school during the late morning hours—the time of day when there's usually a big blood sugar crash in the children who ate a refined, sugary breakfast. At dinnertime, replace the bread or rolls with a bowl of warm cooked quinoa, millet, or rice. You might notice more stable blood sugar, fewer cravings, and better bowel movements. Consider keeping processed foods out of your house to avoid temptation or put them away for occasional treats.

4. Start Making Homemade Bone Broths. When you feel that your family is eating more salads and vegetables, and you have removed some of the processed foods, begin a weekly routine of cooking a large pot of bone broth. You can freeze the broth in quart jars or even ice cube trays to have ready-made broth on hand. Remember to label and date the broth! I've checked my freezer plenty of times and wondered, *Is this turkey broth? Chicken broth? Beef broth*? Use your homemade broth instead of those store-bought broths. I also like to use bone broth as the base for all my soups and stews. The broth is also delicious warmed and served in a mug with breakfast, instead of that cup of coffee. See the "Soups and Stews" chapter for some nourishing bone broth recipes.

5. Add Fermented Foods. Our children devour a jar of lacto-fermented vegetables so quickly that I can hardly keep up! Why is this? Because they taste so good—salty, tangy, and crunchy. They are a great alternative to chips or crackers when you are craving something salty and crunchy! Fermented foods are full of beneficial bacteria that nourish the gut microbiome. In fact, a healthy microbiome is one of the most important determinants of health, as well as helpful in preventing food allergies and nutrient deficiencies. (You'll learn more about this in the chapters that follow.) Fermented foods include items like sauerkraut, kefir, beet kvass, naturally fermented pickles (made with a salt brine instead of vinegar), miso, kimchi, kombucha, and fermented vegetables. Go to the "Preserving the Harvest" chapter for some tasty fermented vegetable recipes. Our children's favorites include the Dilly Radishes (page 475), Pickled Carrots and Cauliflower (page 476), and the Raw Sour Dill Pickles (page 477). Try making a jar a week, perhaps on the same day as you prepare your pot of bone broth and your homemade salad dressings.

6. Go Organic! If you have been using this book for a few months, the chances are that your kitchen is already stocked with organic ingredients. Even so, we encourage you to take some extra steps to ensure that at least 95 percent of your food is organic. What does this mean? You can go to page 4 to learn more about the importance of organics, but in a nutshell it means you'll be consuming foods that are free of harmful pesticides, fungicides, and GMOs. There is a great body of research connecting these substances to a host of diseases—conditions you may be trying to cure or control right now, such as cancer, diabetes, allergies, thyroid disorders, and autoimmune diseases. Begin by purchasing organic meats, eggs, and dairy products (if you eat them) from your local health food store, as these foods can harbor environmental toxins. Explore if there are local farmers in your area who offer pastured and organic meats and eggs; sometimes you can buy direct from a farmer and also get a better price. Then move on to your fruits and vegetables. Look up the Dirty Dozen list on www.ewg.org for the most contaminated fruits and vegetables—the ones you really need to start buying organic immediately. Most whole grains and legumes are surprisingly full of herbicide residues if they're not organic, as farmers generally spray a crop of grains or beans an additional time just before harvesting; this often is called a "pre-harvest desiccant." Luckily, organic grains and legumes do not cost much more than their nonorganic counterparts, so it is fairly easy to make this switch. Lastly, consider upgrading some of the items you may use less frequently, like condiments or nuts and seeds.

7. Go Gluten-Free. So, you've probably already been adding more vegetables to your diet, you've eliminated processed grain foods (most of the gluten in your diet, I bet), and you've been making bone broths and nourishing soups and stews, eating fermented vegetables, and in the process have been lessening your exposure to toxic substances. Now it's time to see how you feel if you eliminate the gluten from your family's diet. You may be surprised to find this at the end of our list of recommendations, but experience has taught us that not everyone needs to go gluten-free. The earlier six steps are more important to begin with, and can unleash fantastic improvements in your family's overall health and well-being. But there's one caveat now: If you or your child is experiencing a health problem such as eczema, a digestive disorder, an autoimmune condition, or autism, we *highly recommend* that you begin removing all sources of gluten (as well as dairy) from your family's diet as soon as possible! With that said, we suggest that everyone eliminate gluten from his or her diet for four to twelve weeks as a test. This change in diet takes 100 percent commitment and plenty of kitchen skills (which you probably have by now if you have been using this book for several months). Oftentimes, a person's mysterious, nagging symptoms simply disappear once gluten also disappears. Others might experience a general sense of increased alertness and well-being. Regardless of the results, everyone can benefit from a reduction in his or her gluten consumption. You will learn more about gluten in the "Why Gluten-Free?" chapter. We also have plenty of tips for helping you go gluten free; see our website, www .WholeLifeNutrition.net, and my blog, www.NourishingMeals.com. Note: Every recipe in this book is gluten-free, so when you are ready to eliminate gluten from your family's diet, you will be able to plan your weekly meals using these recipes and easy meal ideas.

There is no one right way when it comes to diet. We all face different health issues, requiring different diets at different times in our lives. The key is to remain open and alter your current diet when you see fit. With this book, our hope is to offer a wide variety of recipes, from plant-based main dishes to nourishing grain-free desserts, so that no matter what your current diet is, there is a recipe idea for you. Remember that implementing new dietary changes can involve a process. It can take time for your brain and body to adjust—just going gluten-free can be a huge transition! This is okay; it is important to set your own pace, so you don't get overwhelmed.

It may seem challenging sometimes to eat nourishing food; but it's easy with the right tools, recipes, and mind-set. But you're in good company. There are thousands of other individuals and families embarking on that same journey as yours. We encourage you to go online to share your photos, recipes, tips, and stories—you'll benefit from the collective wisdom of the community and you'll feel you're part of a cultural movement to return to a nourishing way of eating. Use the hashtags #nourishingmeals and #onemealaday to share your journey on social media and connect with others.

Many of us are looking for ways to nurture our children so they not only survive but also thrive in this world. Nourishing our children with real food—meals that are whole foods–based and organically grown—may offer them the best chance to thrive. This cookbook will be an invaluable resource for supporting your family in health for years to come.

Introduction

We all want the best for our children. We want them to grow into strong, healthy, capable adults, but today our children face more obstacles than ever before. As of 2010, as many as one in every 68 U.S. children—one in every 42 boys—is afflicted with autism; and a 2015 government survey states that one in every 45 children from the ages of 3 through 17 has been diagnosed with autism spectrum disorder. Additionally, one in every 13 children now suffers from food allergies. With the current trends in diet choices, by the year 2050, one in three adults born after the year 2000 will develop type 2 diabetes. And ADHD rates are at an all-time high; childhood cancers are increasing as well. The incidence of peanut allergies has quadrupled over the last decade; obesity rates continue to climb; and more and more adults and children suffer from a host of autoimmune conditions.

Humans are amazingly adaptable creatures who should be able to eat and flourish regardless of whatever is in our environment, from high-starch diets to meat-based foods. But what if our environment is so out of balance that it can no longer support healthy development? What if the majority of our foods are so denatured that they no longer do what they are supposed to for our bodies?

This is the time we live in—a time when corporate goals take precedence over human health and the health of our planet. Humans have, for tens of thousands of years, lived in small tribes or clans that worked the land—honored it—because they knew that by supporting the land, they supported themselves. When we don't support and cultivate what gives us life, we contribute to our own demise and the degeneration of our species.

Consuming denatured, highly processed foods full of chemical residues is the cultural norm these days, but realize that this food system was set in place only recently. It was in the 1930s that we began consuming processed foods, so only a few generations have experienced the impact of this radical shift. Our great-grandparents ate seasonal whole foods—not altered in any way—and did not have the pollution we see today. With each succeeding generation, though, our diets have become further and further removed from nature. Chemical use in agriculture became widespread after World War II; natural and organic farming methods were replaced with fertilizers, insecticides, and pesticides. The 1950s saw a boom in processed foods, mainly as a result of the introduction of the supermarket. No longer did people go to the butcher for their meat, the baker for their bread, or the grocery for their vegetables. Convenient canned and packaged foods were in! Our grandparents and parents got to ride the wave of resilience passed down from previous generations. They could handle a certain amount of processed foods and environmental toxicity without seeing the effects on health that we do today.

Our bodies are subjected to more environmental chemicals than ever before, while consumption of highly processed foods continues to climb and eating genetically engineered foods has become commonplace. This environment is changing the way our genes are being expressed, causing damage to our guts, creating chronic inflammation, and contributing to a rise in food and environmental allergies such as we have never seen before.

True nourishment is possible, however, when we educate ourselves about foods that heal and prevent disease. For many people, eliminating gluten from their diets can help heal their bodies by lowering the amount of inflammation, healing the intestines, and allowing for proper nutrient absorption—actions that are especially important for growing children and women who are pregnant or trying to conceive. An estimated one in every 133 people has celiac disease, though the total number of people reacting to gluten is much higher when you include incidences of gluten sensitivities and intolerances. Gluten is ubiquitous in our food supply, and only by removing it completely from our diet do we begin to heal from its adverse effects. It is easy to get on the gluten-free bandwagon and begin relying on processed gluten-free versions of your old favorites, but that isn't what will bring about the healing and improved long-term health, and it can often perpetuate the cycle of malnourishment. It is important to work toward a diet that is full of *healing whole foods*.

By eating foods in their whole, natural state, organic and free of genetically modified organisms (GMO), we retrain our bodies to act in a way they were meant to act. That is, the phytochemicals from fruits and vegetables signal our cells to produce more natural antioxidants. Healthy fats provide our cell membranes the compounds needed to communicate with each other and keep inflammation in check. Complex carbohydrates from starchy vegetables and whole grains give us clean-burning energy that won't raise blood sugar levels too quickly. Protein from grass-fed animals, as well as beans, nuts, and seeds, gives us the building blocks to repair and build new cells—critical functions for someone healing after celiac disease and other nutrient-deficiency disorders.

Let us be grateful for the rise in food sensitivities, because they have been a reminder to get back to basics: to eat whole foods, to cook from scratch, and to consume more vegetables. They tell us to look toward the environment and realize that our immune system is working overtime to rid our bodies of toxins. They remind us that we are as much a part of the solution as we are of the problem—but that doesn't have to be the case.

foundationsofhealth

Why Whole Foods?

The definition of the word *whole* is "a thing that is complete in itself." When we eat foods in their whole form, we get all the nutrients, carbohydrates, proteins, and fats contained therein in perfect balance. These compounds act synergistically to orchestrate all the reactions in our bodies. When some nutrients are missing, though, the body cannot function properly; and when many nutrients are missing for an extended period of time, the body can become diseased. Obesity, chronic inflammation, food allergies, infertility, and many other diseases stem from the body's being starved of essential nutrients—nutrients that are lacking in a diet of processed foods.

FOOD IS A SIGNALING SUBSTANCE

It is easy to lose sight of the reasons we eat. We feel hungry, and immediately we think of calories—of eating to fill up. The real reasons our bodies need food go beyond the ingestion of calories, though. Food, by nature, is a signaling substance.

The chemical composition of food—its vitamins and phytochemicals—sends signals to our cells designating how the genes will express themselves; this means that every time we eat, we are telling our bodies which genes to turn on and which genes to turn off. Did you know that there is more gene expression within two hours of eating than at any other time of the day? This is the fascinating world of nutrigenomics—the idea that food is information, not merely calories.

Processed Foods and Gene Expression

With an understanding of gene expression, you can see that when you eat a diet of processed foods full of chemicals and devoid of nutrients, you are telling your genes to "turn on" for certain diseases you may be predisposed to. On the other hand, when you eat a whole foods diet rich in plants, the opposite is possible.

Research has indicated that a plant-rich whole foods diet can communicate to your genes in a way that may prevent and/or alter disease progression. For example, a child could have the genetic makeup that predisposes him to type 1 diabetes. With a diet of processed foods devoid of nutrients and high in gluten, dairy, sugar, and nonfood constituents, he could develop this disease in childhood. If the mother has a gluten-free, dairy-free, nutrient-dense diet from the time of conception, the baby would more likely not develop diabetes.

If you want to lower the risk of developing allergies and disease, then you can change the way your genes are being expressed by eliminating all processed foods and eating a nutrient-dense, organic whole foods diet.

WHAT CONSTITUTES A PROCESSED FOOD?

There is a lot of debate about what actually constitutes a "processed food." In reality, there is a continuum of processing of foods that ranges from naturally preserved foods (like home-canned tomatoes or frozen berries), to completely denatured foods (such as high fructose corn syrup). Foods that undergo minimal processing can still be nutritious; these include extra-virgin olive oil, virgin coconut oil, and raw apple cider vinegar. Highly processed foods include man-made pseudo-foods such as artificial sweeteners and hydrogenated oils. Additionally, processed foods often have nonfood constituents, like bleaching agents, solvents, and alkalizing agents, as well as often being fortified with synthetic vitamins. For our purposes here, processed foods are those that are *highly* processed—that is, those that are entirely man-made or have had parts removed or added, such as the refining of corn into high fructose corn syrup or the bleaching and enriching of white flour.

What's in a Chicken Sandwich?

Take an unassuming grilled chicken sandwich with lettuce, tomato, and melted cheese—something you might choose when dining out. Let's throw in a side of fries and a diet soda. Seems pretty straightforward, right?

What you don't see are the large amounts of chemicals that were used on the genetically engineered grains or the arsenic that was added to the feed the chicken ate, whose meat now contains those chemicals, and the antibiotics that were added prophylactically to its feed. You don't see the pesticide residues on the lettuce or tomato—chemicals that are never tested for human safety. You don't see rBGH, a genetically engineered hormone that was injected into the cows to produce more milk and is now in that cheese.

What about the toxic combination of artificial sweeteners and caffeine in your soft drink? It has neuroexcitatory toxins that can kill brain cells and cause migraines and joint pain. How about a little sodium acid pyrophosphate to maintain color, or dimethylpolysiloxane to prevent foaming in your fries? Unfortunately, these chemicals are in most seemingly "natural" fries when you dine out.

Let's not forget the bun. Not only is it made from refined wheat—white flour—that can be highly inflammatory, but it also most likely contains ingredients you can't pronounce. If you wouldn't keep a jar of these unpronounceable ingredients in your kitchen cabinet, then they don't belong in your diet.

Loss of Nutrients

Not only are many processed foods full of genetically engineered ingredients and unnatural chemicals, but they are high in calories and low in nutrients. A diet of processed foods essentially starves your body while at the same time causing weight gain, as the body, in its innate wisdom, keeps demanding more food in order to get the necessary vitamins, minerals, fats, and amino acids.

When a food item is processed, such as with the polishing of brown rice to make white rice, many essential nutrients and fibers are lost that could be used by the body for properly digesting the grain. In the late 1800s, a Japanese doctor made the connection between the disease beriberi and a diet consisting mainly of polished, or white, rice. This marked the discovery of thiamine, or vitamin B_1. Thiamine is found in the outer portion of rice, or the bran; this portion is removed when brown rice is polished into white rice. Thiamine and also biotin help the body utilize its blood sugar by bringing glucose into the powerhouse of the cell—the mitochondria—to be burned for energy. Yet thiamine and biotin are just two of the nutrients that get stripped away during processing. Furthermore, consuming white rice causes the blood sugar to spike, as the fiber that slows down the release of sugar into the blood stream has been removed. In essence, the majority of helpful vitamins, minerals, and phytochemicals that were present in the outer portion of the brown rice kernel are lost when the rice is polished.

Remember that it's fine to eat a small amount of white rice on occasion, such as with other nourishing foods like pastured meats, bone broth, and vegetables. The healthy combination can balance out the negative effects of the lost nutrients in the bran and germ of the rice. I like to combine brown rice with cooked dried beans and vegetables, or serve organic white jasmine rice on occasion with meat and poultry—sometimes brown rice feels too heavy to eat with meat, and white rice can be just the thing to accompany it.

Eating a diet of refined, processed foods over time can deplete the body of essential nutrients that it needs to function properly. However, eating something refined on an occasional basis shouldn't cause much harm if the body is well nourished from an otherwise whole foods diet. If you are currently eating a diet heavy in processed foods, though, start out with the easy swaps, like trading bread for brown rice, or fruit juice for an apple or orange; also, consider replacing one of your present meals a day with one of the recipes in this book. Over time, you'll gravitate to the whole foods and save the processed foods for occasional treats.

HEALTHY WHOLE FOODS

Whole foods are naturally more calming and nourishing than processed foods. Why is this? It's because a whole food is something you can imagine growing or living in nature, like kale, chicken, eggs, fish, almonds, carrots, millet, olives, apples, strawberries, brown rice, or avocados. These foods have not been processed, enriched, or denatured in any way. They contain a perfect balance of nutrients—just as nature intended. Basing your diet on whole foods, and using small amounts of minimally processed foods like olive and coconut oils, whole-grain gluten-free flours, and natural sweeteners, you'll most likely see a dramatic improvement in your and your children's overall health.

Eat a Plant-Rich Diet

A plant-rich diet is one that focuses on foods such as vegetables, fruits, whole grains, legumes, nuts, and seeds. Animal foods, while very nutrient dense, make up a smaller proportion of your diet. Compared to all other food types, plants provide the body with the most gene-signaling molecules.

You've heard the architectural expression, "Form follows function." In nature, form *equals* function. Plants package themselves in their whole forms for brilliant reasons: the tougher outer portions are barriers against potential threats, such as sudden temperature changes, bacteria, fungi, or insects, and they contain important chemicals that act as natural antioxidants, microbial deterrents, and insecticides. It so happens that these very same plant chemicals

offer numerous beneficial effects to the human body. Phenols, such as catechins, ellagic acid, and tannins, as well as pectin and other soluble fibers, are protective against forms of cancer, with some of these compounds even binding readily to heavy metals and radioactive particles from the environment, allowing for proper excretion from the body. When the exteriors of these plants are broken or stripped during processing, many of the protective compounds are lost. But when you base your diet on whole plant foods, you get an abundance of phytochemicals, antioxidants, vitamins, and minerals, which signal your genes to keep the immune system calm and the body healthy.

THE IMPORTANCE OF ORGANICS

A review published in 2010 found organic foods to contain higher levels of vitamin C, iron, and magnesium, as well as more of the important antioxidant phytochemicals like carotenoids, flavonoids, and anthocyanins. The higher mineral level is logical, considering that organic farmers continuously add organic material to the soil to nurture the fruits, vegetables, and grains they grow, as well as the animals that eat those crops. If you talk with an organic farmer, you will quickly learn how important soil quality is for higher yields, better flavor, and insect and disease control. They all acknowledge that well-fed plants are naturally more resistant to disease and harmful insects.

Chemical Use Changes How Plants Behave

Conventional farmers use chemical fertilizers, pesticides, herbicides, and fungicides that may persist in the soil and the environment for upward of 50 years. Not only do these chemicals get into the food we eat, but they also enter our water, air, and soil, harming the delicate balance of beneficial insects, aquatic life, soil microorganisms, and other living things that inhabit the farms. These chemicals can change the ability of those crops to interact well with the environment, including how they handle the soil microorganisms, harmful insects, competitive plants, and other natural stressors. These stressors are important because they force the plants to produce protective chemical compounds. Anytime you stress a plant, it forces that plant to defend itself and become "stronger." For example, when the sun strikes a plant, with UV radiation, the plant will produce natural sunscreens like carotenoids and flavonoids. When insects nibble on the leaves of a broccoli plant, the plant can produce natural insecticides, such as the sulforaphane found in the cruciferous family of vegetables. If these same cruciferous vegetables are conventionally farmed and periodically sprayed with pesticides, they are not as likely to produce these natural substances.

The Impact of Chemical Farming

The chemical pesticides that farmers use are likely to negatively impact all who consume them, whether insect or human. And why wouldn't they? That is exactly what they are engineered to do. Research done in California found that the children of mothers living within 500 meters of commercial field sites using the highest levels of organochlorine pesticides had a 6.1 times higher risk of having autism. Numerous studies examining the pesticide exposure of neonates have determined that the negative impact on brain function and intelligence measures increases as pesticide levels rise. One study showed a lowering of IQ by seven points by the age of seven, in those with the highest exposures to pesticides.

Organic Is the Most Nourishing Choice

Children who eat a conventional diet are continually exposed to pesticides. One study examined the urinary levels in children of two commonly used agricultural pesticides—malathion and chlorpyrifos. Measured before, during, and after the children ate a five-day organic diet, the study showed that pesticide levels were elevated before the organic diet, and again when the children returned to a conventional diet. During the organic diet, however, the urinary levels of these two pesticides were almost undetectable.

Clearly, buying and eating organic food are of utmost importance in decreasing the amount of chemicals we are exposed to—not only for our children but also for everyone else, especially those living near commercial farms. Ideally, this diet change should begin before a child is even conceived, as the preconception time and the last two trimesters of pregnancy are the most vulnerable periods for chemical exposure. Remember: plants grown in nutrient-rich soil contain more vitamins, minerals, and phytochemicals than their conventionally grown counterparts. These natural nutrients keep our bodies functioning properly, help us grow resilient children, and protect us all from disease.

Why Gluten-Free?

Food is made up of thousands of large molecules that need to be broken down into smaller molecules so they can be taken into the body and used for fuel—as a facilitator of many reactions—or is incorporated into cell structures. This process of *digestion and absorption* can be altered by numerous factors, one of which may be the food itself. And this food may be gluten. People react differently to the ingestion of gluten. For some, the reaction may be an IgE-mediated gluten allergy, while for others it is a tearing down of the intestinal lining otherwise known as *celiac disease*. Others can have adverse symptoms known broadly as a *gluten sensitivity reaction*. Though not everyone will experience these serious reactions, everyone is likely to have a gluten-initiated *leaky gut* after consuming gluten. It's important to note, of course, that people who are very healthy, have low stress levels, who have an optimal nutrient status (including good levels of vitamin D), and have well-functioning immune and digestive systems with a diverse population of beneficial microbes in their guts—a healthy microbiome—will experience fewer adverse effects after gluten consumption.

Some people with celiac disease or a gluten sensitivity can immediately feel the effects of eating something containing gluten, usually bloating and digestive upset; others may have "silent" symptoms that range from infertility to osteoporosis. For example, it is possible to have celiac disease but have no symptoms other than iron-deficiency anemia. There are just too many possible ways that gluten can cause harm. So even if you do not have a gluten sensitivity or celiac disease, your digestion and overall health may well benefit from a gluten-free diet.

You can begin a gluten-free diet by swapping some of your favorite gluten-filled cookies or muffins with our gluten-free and grain-free versions in this book. You can eliminate the bread at dinner in favor of more vegetables, and possibly a bowl of cooked quinoa or rice. Instead of toast for breakfast, try some of the breakfast suggestions on pages 72–106, as they don't revolve around bread. Indeed, you may find that you have more energy and feel better by reducing your gluten consumption.

COMMON SYMPTOMS OF GLUTEN INTOLERANCE

Digestive

- Abdominal pain
- Bloating
- Diarrhea
- Constipation
- Fat malabsorption
- Multiple nutrient deficiencies
- Irritable bowl syndrome
- Crohn's disease
- Ulcerative colitis

Skin & Hair

- Acne
- Dermatitis herpetiformis
- Eczema
- Hair loss

Bone

- Osteoporosis
- Osteopenia
- Dental cavities
- Dental enamel defects

Endocrine

- PCOS
- Thyroid disorders
- Addison's disease
- Diabetes (Type II)
- Weight loss
- Weight gain
- Infertility
- Recurrent miscarriages
- Stunted growth in children

Autoimmune

- Rheumatoid arthritis
- Lupus
- Diabetes (type 1)
- Lou Gehrig's disease

Neurologic & Behavioral

- Peripheral neuropathy
- ADHD
- Depression
- Migraines
- Dyslexia
- Loss of memory
- Autism

Blood

- Anemia
- Bleeding gums
- Easy bruising

General

- General weakness and fatigue
- Inability to lose weight
- Chronic fatigue syndrome
- Muscle cramping
- Restless leg syndrome
- Joint pain

WHAT IS GLUTEN?

Gluten is a composite of proteins joined with starch that is found in wheat, spelt, barley, and rye. It is what gives the airy, chewy structure to bread, or what makes some noodles hold together while cooking instead of turning to mush. The two main groups of proteins are gliadins and glutenins. Once broken down into smaller peptides—or chains of amino acids—these proteins, specifically the gliadins, can elicit multiple responses in the intestines. They can cause the release of harmful antibodies and inflammatory chemicals that lead to the destruction of the intestinal lining leading to celiac disease. They can also increase the secretion of inflammatory substances that disrupt the local and systemic inflammatory balance without tearing down the intestines, leading to what was mentioned earlier and is known as gluten sensitivity.

Interestingly, oats contain a protein called avenin, which when broken down during digestion, has a similar peptide structure to the gliadin proteins. This means that it can have a similar effect on the body as gluten has on some people, especially those with celiac disease.

Why Can It Be So Damaging?

Gluten—particularly the gliadin peptides—differs from all other foods, in that its consumption activates the immune cells and stimulates the secretion of a protein called zonulin that is involved in a leaky-gut condition. This can lead to a permeable gut for a short time after eating. In other words, you don't have to have celiac disease or a gluten sensitivity to have a reaction to gluten!

How does this happen? Normally, the intestinal cells are bound to one another by tight junctions, which control what is allowed into the intestinal cells. When the cell barrier is permeable, that regulatory funciton is lost and the contents of the intestinal tract, including bacteria and undigested food proteins, are allowed to pass through the intestinal barrier. This leads to an alert and alarm—or inflammatory—response from the local immune cells, and may ultimately contribute to an increased sensitivity to those food proteins.

Intestinal Degradation

People with celiac disease—essentially a genetic alteration in immune cell function—sustain a permeable gut for an extended period of time after eating gluten-containing foods. This permeability feeds a vicious cycle of both foods and microbes exciting the secretion of inflammatory cytokines by the immune cells. This then leads to atrophy of the villi (the small finger-like projections of the upper intestines), or a tearing down of the lining of the upper intestines. Unfortunately, this cycle can drastically alter both the digestive and the absorptive functions normally carried out in the small intestines.

In addition to celiac disease, though, there are many other factors that can lead to this intestinal degradation. Parasitic infections like giardia, dairy and soy reactions, small-intestinal bacterial overgrowth, and adverse medication reactions (particularly to NSAIDs) may lead to destruction of the villi as well.

NUTRIENT DEFICIENCIES

Without sufficient villi in the small intestines, many nutrients cannot be absorbed properly. This loss of nutrients can have devastating effects on a growing child or a pregnant woman, because the body has such a high nutrient demand during those times. Vitamins such as A, D, B_{12}, and folates; minerals such as iron, iodine, and zinc; amino acids such as tryptophan; and other nutrients like essential fatty acids rely either directly or indirectly on the upper intestinal tract working properly for their utilization by the body.

CROSS-CONTAMINATION

Becoming gluten-free calls for gaining a deeper understanding of our food supply. We need to learn where our food is grown, how it is processed, and where it is stored, transported, and sold. Are our grains being processed in the same facility as wheat is processed? When I am buying bulk sea salt at my local co-op, is there a bin of wheat flour above it that could be contaminating the salt?

Since gluten is everywhere in our food supply, getting it completely out of our diet can be quite challenging. Certain foods such as millet and lentils are usually crop-rotated with wheat or barley in the agricultural fields. Have you ever taken a look at your lentil jar? You will probably find a few whole wheat berries, barley, or spelt. If you don't remove the grains and thoroughly rinse the lentils, you run the risk of consuming a small amount of gluten and not feeling fully well. Indeed, all foods that require processing, however minimal, run the risk of con-tamination if the facility also processes wheat or other gluten-containing grains or flours. The most commonly, possibly contaminated products include coconut flour, coconut sugar, and gluten-free flours like brown rice flour. It is best to contact the manu-facturer to determine if the facility is gluten-free.

Other sources of cross-contamination include, of course, restaurants, grills, and salad bars, as well as your own cutting boards, wooden rolling pins, toasters, pizza stones, and countertops.

Gluten Cross-Contamination in Food

NO RISK

- Fresh meats
- Fresh vegetables
- Most cheeses
- Coconut milk
- Honey
- Fresh eggs
- Fresh fruit
- Cow's or goat's milk
- Almond flour
- Nuts (in the shell) and whole seeds

LOW RISK

- Shelled nuts and seeds
- Dried beans
- Quinoa
- Teff
- Cornmeal
- Masa
- Gluten-free flours
- Coconut sugar
- Oils
- Yogurt
- Nut and seed butters
- Brown rice
- Amaranth
- Sorghum products
- Corn flour
- Coconut flour
- Cane sugar
- Rice noodles
- Vinegars
- Spices

HIGH RISK

- Oats
- Buckwheat
- Processed foods
- Millet
- Lentils

Reduce the Risk of Gluten Cross-Contamination

Oats, millet, buckwheat, and lentils are often crop-rotated in fields with grain crops. There's bound to be some mixing and cross-contamination. Therefore, look for the "Certified Gluten-Free" label on these products before purchasing. For example, I like to purchase 25-pound bags of raw buckwheat groats from Bob's Red Mill, which are organic and have been certified gluten-free. The recipes in this book use flour ground from gluten-free *raw* buckwheat groats.

Why the Rise in Food Allergies and Sensitivities?

No one can argue against the observation that children these days have more food-related problems. The reasons for this rise in food allergies and sensitivities are numerous, ranging from our food and medical culture to our environmental health.

The wheat plant has been hybridized over the years to achieve a higher gluten content. Large-scale conventional farming is the major source of our food supplies. Genetically modified foods (GMOs) pervade our marketplace. Simultaneously, nutrient deficiencies are increasing. Antibiotics are overused. Use of fossil fuels results in environmental toxicity. These modern-day practices have reduced the nutrient content of our food while flooding our bodies with foreign substances. This has all resulted in an imbalanced gut and an overreactive immune system.

Common Symptoms of a Food Allergy or Sensitivity

FOOD ALLERGIES

- Skin (eczema, swelling, hives)
- Respiratory (wheezing, swelling of the throat, repetitive cough)
- Eyes (itching, watering, swelling)
- Gastrointestinal (nausea, vomiting, diarrhea, abdominal pain)
- Anaphylaxis

FOOD SENSITIVITIES

- Skin (acne, eczema, rashes, hives)
- Behavior (hyperactivity, violence, moodiness)
- Sleep (trouble falling asleep or staying asleep)
- Stomach (gas, nausea, bloating, abdominal pain)
- Gastrointestinal (diarrhea, constipation)

POTENTIAL CAUSES OF FOOD ALLERGIES AND SENSITIVITIES

When the body launches an attack against a food we've consumed, or is touched by something found in the environment like pollen or pet dander, the immune system reacts to a particular protein structure. For example, the food substances might be the casein protein in cow's milk, some 15 different proteins in soy products, the albumen in eggs, and certain peptide chains in peanuts. It is also theorized that it is not just these proteins that cause a reaction but also certain starches that attach themselves to the proteins and change the shapes of the proteins, making them unrecognizable to the body.

Some of the things that can damage a person's ability to properly digest, absorb, and recognize foods are:

- Environmental toxins
- Chronic Inflammation
- Imbalanced gut microbiota
- Overuse of antibiotics
- Overuse of nonsteroidal anti-inflammatory drugs
- Gastric acid-blocking medications, especially during infancy
- Leaky gut syndrome
- Low stomach acid
- Pancreatic enzyme insufficiency
- Use of formula in lieu of breastfeeding

- Deficiency of key nutrients for normalizing immune response
- Diet high in processed, denatured foods and refined sugars
- Increase in consumption of reactive foods like gluten, dairy, and soy products
- Consumption of genetically modified foods
- Increase in stress

ENVIRONMENTAL TOXICITY

The primary stance of the immune system is tolerance, or recognizing what is not foreign and leaving it alone. Our immune cells are constantly coming into contact with other molecules, cells, and organisms. It is their job to determine who is friend and who is foe. These days, our immune systems are bombarded with environmental toxins in the form of cleaning supplies, building materials, and many of our foods consumed each day.

Many children have what is described as a toxicant-induced loss of tolerance, or TILT, meaning their bodies are continually exposed to certain chemicals in the home, greater environment, or food they are given to eat, and they reach a point where they cannot tolerate those things anymore. Their bodies begin to malfunction. They develop allergies, food intolerances, and chemical hypersensitivities. They can become sensitive to low levels of diverse and unrelated triggers in the environment, such as more common chemicals, inhalants, or food antigens.

The Toxins in Food

According to U.S. government data, there were 74 billion pounds of chemicals imported into or produced in the United States every day in 2010. That is 250 pounds of chemicals per person per day. This equates to residual toxic chemicals in our air, water, soil, and food. Billions of pounds of pesticides are used on agricultural crops in addition to the air pollutants that settle on the plants and seep into the soil. Many of these chemicals accumulate as they are ingested by animals and travel up the food chain.

Some of the most harmful toxins for humans have been deemed Persistent Organic Pollutants, or POPs, and include the pesticide DDT, which has a 50-year half-life, PCBs from electrical transformers, PBDEs from flame retardants, and dioxins from the manufacture of plastics. These chemicals are often derived from petroleum, and they have been associated with diabetes, asthma, cancer, and thyroid disorders. Because of their chemical makeup, they can stick to fats. In fact, the highest body amounts of these chemicals are often found in the fat, skin, and liver. Trimming beforehand or removing the excess fat from meat after cooking can lower your exposure to some of these compounds. Choosing wild-caught Alaskan salmon will dramatically reduce your PCB exposure, as some farmed salmon has been shown to have up to 40 times the PCBs as their wild-caught counterparts. Research indicates that eating lots of vegetables, seaweeds, and fiber-rich foods (especially brown rice fiber), and keeping your intestinal tract healthy, helps eliminate these compounds from the body. This is one of the main reasons we advocate for a plant-rich diet revolving around organic whole foods.

Other food sources of ingested chemicals include conventionally grown fruits and vegetables such as apples, grapes, celery, strawberries, bell peppers, peaches, spinach, potatoes, blueberries, raspberries, lettuce, and kale. The chemicals commonly sprayed on these foods include glyphosate (Roundup), chlorpyrifos, malathion, and endosulfan. These chemicals disrupt the body's reproductive function, immune function, and mitochondrial function, causing symptoms such as infertility, food allergies, learning disabilities, neurologic problems, poor growth, and gastrointestinal disorders, including low secretion of gastric acid. Thankfully, there is a simple solution for lowering your exposure to these compounds: *eat organic foods*. Multiple research trials have shown lower levels of these chemicals within days of people's going on a strictly organic diet.

If you cannot choose organic foods, then choose wisely. The Environmental Working Group (EWG) has published its Dirty Dozen and Clean 15 lists to let you know which foods are best chosen organic and as of 2015 the lists are as follows:

THE DIRTY DOZEN (BEST TO BUY ORGANIC)

Apples, celery, cherry tomatoes, cucumbers, grapes, nectarines, peaches, potatoes, snap peas, spinach, strawberries, sweet bell peppers and hot peppers, kale, collard greens

THE CLEAN 15 (OKAY TO BUY COMMERCIAL)

Asparagus, avocados, cabbage, cantaloupe, cauliflower, eggplant, grapefruit, kiwi, mangoes, onions, papayas, pineapples, sweet corn, sweet peas (frozen), sweet potatoes

CHRONIC INFLAMMATION

When you get injured or develop an infection like the common cold, your immune system is triggered and a chain of events occurs, called the *inflammatory cascade*. The familiar signs of standard inflammation—heat, pain, redness, and swelling—are the first indications that your immune system is being called into action. These pro-inflammatory compounds signal the white blood cells to do their job and clear out the infection or repair the damaged tissue. When the threat is neutralized, equally powerful anti-inflammatory compounds emerge to begin the healing process. This process keeps the body healthy. But what happens when chronic inflammation occurs?

The Master Switch for Inflammation

The "master switch" that turns on the immune system's alert and alarm signals—inflammation—is called Nuclear Factor Kappa Beta, or NFkB. When levels of NFkB increase, hundreds of pro-inflammatory chemicals are turned on. But when these pro-inflammatory chemicals don't turn off, there's a risk for increased inflammatory disease, which can take the form of heart disease, diabetes, arthritis, and irritable bowel disease. In one study, a fast-food egg-and-sausage breakfast muffin

with two hash browns was shown to cause a dramatic spike—a 500 percent increase—in diners' inflammation response shortly after eating this meal.

Which Foods Cause Inflammation?

Pro-inflammatory foods—foods that contribute to inflammation—are polyunsaturated vegetable oils, meat from grain-fed animals, charbroiled meats, pasteurized cow's milk, sugar, and other highly refined starchy foods. Most vegetable oils, like peanut, safflower, sunflower, corn, and soy, are high in linoleic acid, an omega-6 essential fatty acid the body converts into arachidonic acid, which has a predominantly pro-inflammatory effect. Grain-fed animals produce a high amount of arachidonic acid in their tissues. In contrast, grass-fed animals and wild-caught cold-water fish contain high levels of omega-3 fatty acids, or anti-inflammatory compounds. It has been hypothesized that our prehistoric ancestors ate a diet that balanced omega-6 acids with omega-3 on a ratio of 1:1. Our current ratio is anywhere between 10:1 and 25:1!

Refined sugar and other refined starchy foods with a high glycemic index raise insulin levels and put the immune system into that alert and alarm mode. This is because short-lived hormones in the cells called eicosanoids act as either pro- or anti-inflammatory compounds, depending on their type; when insulin levels are high, the eicosanoids skew toward pro-inflammatory. Additionally, excess sugar in the bloodstream can stick to proteins and change their shape; these misshaped proteins, or advanced glycated end products, also trigger the immune system, causing an increase in systemic inflammation.

Reducing Chronic Inflammation

You can reduce chronic inflammation by eliminating the pro-inflammatory foods we've just mentioned, as well as limiting certain foods that may be causing inflammatory reactions in the gut—gluten and dairy being the most common culprits. Be careful about switching to a diet of processed, packaged gluten-free and dairy-free foods, as these products are often high in sugar and refined starches—such as cornstarch and potato starch, as well as canola oil, all of which contribute to inflammation. Consuming a diet high in anti-inflammatory foods such as raw organic berries and cherries, organic green vegetables like kale and broccoli, soaked raw nuts and seeds, slow-cooked whole grains, cold-water fish like wild-caught salmon, and small amounts of sustainably-raised meats will reduce chronic inflammation by sending signals to the immune system to keep the body calm and balanced. A calm immune system is one that reacts to pathogenic bacteria and viruses, and is less likely to react to food and other substances in the environment, like pet dander and pollen. What's the message? The food we eat either increases or decreases the alert and alarm signals of the body.

LEAKY GUT SYNDROME

As mentioned earlier, in a healthy gut the intestinal cells are linked so as to control what is allowed through to the bloodstream. When there is damage to the gut and the barrier becomes permeable—a situation called *leaky gut*—proteins can pass into the bloodstream, where the immune system recognizes them as foes and attacks them. This leads ultimately to an increase in food allergies, skin rashes, and weight gain, as well as many chronic diseases. Consuming gluten causes leaky gut, even if just for a short time. However, as we said earlier, in a healthy individual who has been eating a diet with adequate nutrients, has normal digestion, limits exposure to toxic chemicals, and maintains a healthy microbiome, leaky gut is not likely to increase the risk for developing disease.

Normal Digestion

The two primary jobs of the intestinal tract are to recognize food particles and call for digestive hormones and enzymes to be released; and to keep foreign molecules like bacteria, yeast, fungi, parasites, and undigested food out of the bloodstream. The intestinal cells do this by binding tightly to one another to form a barrier, and by secreting a protective layer of mucous and a compound called secretory immunoglobulin class A, or SIgA. When all is working well, food enters the stomach and is broken down into smaller parts by acid and churning. The stomach acid begins to destroy any harmful bacteria or fungi present in the food, as well as food lectins. The food then moves into the upper part of the small intestine, where cells recognize the food particles and call for secretions of bile and pancreatic enzymes to break down the fats, proteins, and carbohydrates in the food. It is only then that the food particles can be properly absorbed and utilized by the body.

Compromised Digestion

There are a number of things that can damage the entire digestive process, such as chemicals in the environment and certain foods. The damaging chemicals include heavy metals from amalgam fillings or via fish consumption, air pollution, or vaccines; excess cortisol as a result of chronic stress; repeated antibiotic use; heavy use of acid-blocking medications and over-the-counter anti-inflammatory drugs (NSAIDs); birth control pills; and chlorinated drinking water. Foods that can be quite damaging to the digestive system include gluten, dairy, and sometimes soy products, as well as many processed foods—gluten-free or not—such as meat products, refined carbohydrates, simple sugars, juices, high fructose corn syrup, and alcohol. All of these factors contribute to the degradation of the digestive system and what is known as leaky gut syndrome.

> The primary triggers for a leaky gut include acid-blocking medications, nonsteroidal anti-inflammatory drugs (NSAIDs), stress, high fructose corn syrup, alcohol, high-fat meals, toxins, and gluten.

IMBALANCED GUT MICROFLORA

Our bodies contain more bacteria than we could ever imagine! One gram of microbes in a person's colon, for example, contains more organisms than there are people in the United States! In fact, our entire digestive tract is lined with a wide variety of probiotics—*pro* meaning "for" and *biotic* meaning "life"—or bacteria that support life. These beneficial bacteria are responsible for helping digest our food by breaking down carbohydrates; degrading any anti-nutrients; increasing our mineral absorption; producing amino acids like tryptophan and tyrosine; making B vitamins like folates, biotin, and riboflavin; inhibiting viral, bacterial, or fungal problems; helping modulate the immune system; and degrading, metabolizing, and discarding toxins. In essence, healthy and beneficial bacteria signal the immune system to say: "Everything is okay, stay calm, and don't overreact."

There are a few ways we can get a constant supply of beneficial bacteria, and there are a few ways we can deplete them. To gain beneficial bacteria, eat fermented foods daily; take a high-quality probiotic supplement; and let babies and children play with and eat dirt—yes, that's right, dirt; all these can lead to a collection of flourishing, healthy bacteria in the gut. Antibiotics, acquired either from eating animals that were fed antibiotics or from taking prescription medications; chlorine in the drinking water; using formula instead of breastfeeding; and heavy stress levels can all deplete the amount of beneficial bacteria in the gut.

Birthing and Breastfeeding

When women give birth through the birth canal, they pass on the strains of microflora in their guts to their babies. Cesarean section babies, who don't go through the birth canal, are inoculated with the bacteria in the hospital and acquire it from the nurses who handle them. Because our twins were born via cesarean section, we brought a bottle of high-quality infant probiotic powder to the hospital, which we let them suck off our fingers within an hour after birth. Even if you have an older infant who was delivered by cesarean section, you can still offer probiotics—it's never too late. Look for a company that offers a high-quality probiotic supplement specifically designed for infants. Check our website, www.WholeLifeNutrition.net, for more information and links to recommended companies.

Breastfeeding provides a way for babies to become inoculated right after birth, as beneficial bacteria are also present on the skin surrounding the nipple. Recent research indicates that bacteria from the mother's intestines travels through her bloodstream and into her breast milk. So, not only does the milk have beneficial microbes but it also contains specific foods to feed those microbes. Human mother's milk contains substances called Human Milk Oligosaccharides (HMOs) that cannot be absorbed or used by the infant; these substances are elegantly designed instead to feed specific strains of microbes known to be protective for human infants. Curiously, no other animal species has these specific compounds in the mother's milk—not even cows, goats, or gorillas. It appears that nature has intended for humans to attract certain microbes, assuring our survival.

Fermentation

Traditionally, people have fermented most of their grain flours into sourdough, whether the bread produced was injera from Ethiopia or sourdough rye from northern Europe. They cultivated the wild yeasts present on the grain and in the air. Lactobacilli bacteria also helped in the sourdough process by creating an acidic environment in the starter, which keeps pathogenic bacteria out, helps break down the grain lectins, predigests the carbohydrates, and allows minerals to become more bioavailable by neutralizing phytic acid.

Years ago, fresh, raw milk obtained from cows that ate grass—not grains—was fermented into clabber, kefir, and yogurt, thereby breaking down the lactose and rendering the proteins more digestible. A diet of such grasses creates nutrient-dense milk, full of essential fatty acids and the vitamins K and A.

Similarly, because refrigeration did not yet exist, vegetables were fermented to preserve the harvest. Cabbage was made into sauerkraut, cucumbers into pickles, soybeans into natto, and fruits into vinegars and wines. (See the "Preserving the Harvest" chapter in this book for recipes, as well as the "Get Cultured!" chapter in our book *The Whole Life Nutrition Cookbook*.) People relied on these beneficial microbes present on the vegetables, grains, and dairy to preserve their food, and in doing so they also supported their own health and their body's ability to absorb nutrients. These synergistic interactions between humans, food, and the natural environment are mostly missing in our modern civilization.

Let Them Eat Dirt!

Our modern lifestyle keeps us indoors more today than in our agricultural past, so we don't get much time to interact with our environment. Babies used to crawl around and move about out of doors instead of on synthetic carpeting or vinyl flooring that releases chemicals such as flame retardants and phthalates. Toys used to be made of wood or were simply rocks, sticks, and leaves—and they teamed with beneficial microorganisms. You know that as soon as they can move, babies begin to "sample" everything in their environment, putting it in their mouths! This sampling is nature's way, we think, of ensuring that their guts have a variety of bacteria to help them begin digesting solid foods. So, when you can, go to a pristine and clean environment in the forest, the mountains, or the countryside and give your babies and young children the opportunity to crawl, play, and eat dirt!

The Antibiotics in Our Food

The residual antibiotics in our meat and dairy products are a large contributor to the destruction of good bacteria in our bodies. Most dairy products and meat you buy at the grocery store or eat at a restaurant came from animals that were raised in large factory farms. They were fed a diet of grains and soybeans, which they cannot properly digest; for example, cows are ruminants—meaning they have multiple stomachs for digesting high-cellulose grasses, not grains. This creates a high need for antibiotics to be prophylactically administered in their feed. In fact, over 80 percent of the antibiotics used today are applied to animals! Chickens and eggs are also raised in large factory farms, where the birds live so close together that they get sick easily. Antibiotics, as well as arsenic-based parasitic medications, are prophylactically administered in their feed also; after all, the growers want to keep the profit margins high, so the chickens shouldn't die before slaughter. When you consume these animals or the eggs and milk that came from them, you are also consuming what they ate—that is, you are ingesting small residue amounts of the antibiotics they were administered, and those residues can damage the beneficial flora in your gut.

Prescription Antibiotics

Prescription antibiotics, while lifesaving in some situations, are grossly overused today. Most children have had multiple rounds of antibiotics by the time they are five years old—mainly for ear infections, which are oftentimes preventable with a proper diet. The word *antibiotic* means to go against life. Antibiotics kill both the harmful bacteria that are causing the infection and the good bacteria in the gut.

We have five children, yet have used antibiotics only once with one of them—our first daughter, when she was seven years old. To keep her gut balanced, though, we simultaneously gave her large amounts of probiotics, as well as for weeks afterward. Generally, our children don't get infections that necessitate the use of antibiotics. It is totally possible to raise healthy children!

LACK OF DIGESTIVE ENZYMES

After food has passed from the stomach into the upper intestinal tract, cells located there sample the digested food particles and signal the gallblad-

Microbes Prevent Food Allergies

The most important factor in preventing food sensitivities or allergies in children is . . . microbes! It appears that humans have a sixth sense. That is, the immune system is an entire network of cells that are designed to sample bacteria, viruses, fungi, parasites, and other organisms from the outside world and determine if they are harmful or safe. A more appropriate name for the immune system would be the *microbial-interaction system.*

In the third trimester, a mother starts increasing the number of microbes she carries in her colon. During birth, the head of the baby presses on the cecum and frees some of the microbe-rich fecal matter that has been accumulating in the mother's colon. If the mother is in a natural birthing position, such as squatting or kneeling, the baby will be born toward the mother's anus with its mouth open. Some scientists believe this is not an accident, and is intended to inoculate the newborn with the organisms the mother had been carrying from *her birth* onward. The birth canal also harbors many of the organisms that can be found in the colon.

When there's been a natural childbirth free of antibiotics, the infant will have been exposed to numerous organisms during the birthing process. It appears that nature does everything possible to keep those organisms on and in the human body. The vernix coating on a baby is actually made of prebiotics that attract protective microbes. And breast milk is filled with human milk oligosaccharides—specific foods that elegantly feed a particular organism called *Bifidobacterium infantis.* Science is now demonstrating that this organism can train the immune cells and lessen the possibilities of allergies, eczema, and asthma. It also produces nutrients like B vitamins and amino acids, helps to protect the intestinal lining, and crowds out harmful pathogenic organisms. The more we learn about microbes, the more we realize that we need them for optimal health.

Researchers are even beginning to imply that we should no longer be called "humans," and instead should be called "superorganisms." They say that we do not really complete ourselves until we invite the many different microbes to inhabit our human form. It appears that food allergies, diabetes, obesity, heart disease, autoimmune diseases, brain and mood disorders, and even cancers may be prevented by having a diverse population of beneficial microbes living in us and on us.

der and pancreas to secrete digestive aids, such as bile and pancreatic enzymes, that assist in further digesting the food (breaking it into smaller particles). Disorders of the upper intestinal tract such as celiac disease, dairy and soy enteropathies, and small intestinal bacterial imbalances have been shown to decrease the secretion of these digestive aids. Symptoms of pancreatic enzyme insufficiency include light-colored stools, chronic constipation, undigested food in the stool, and deficiencies of fat-soluble vitamins such as A, D, E, and K, as well as essential fatty acid. A lack of proper digestion can lead to food sensitivities because the larger, undigested food proteins are exposed to the immune system through a leaky gut. And we have discussed earlier how a leaky gut can be initiated through gluten ingestion, stress, antibiotic use, and many other factors.

NUTRIENT DEFICIENCIES

Nutrient deficiencies during pregnancy are passed down to the offspring, and if not rectified with proper diet and supplementation early in childhood, can lead to health issues, including allergies. Additionally, if a person has a damaged upper intestine, then vitamins A, D, zinc, folates, and essential fatty acids are not properly absorbed. These nutrients are used by immune cells to determine how to react to insults and when to stop reacting. If there is a deficiency, then those immune cells can "misbehave" or recognize common food antigens as allergenic.

GMOS AND FOOD ALLERGIES

The research is clear that use and consumption of genetically modified organisms, or GMOs, is leading to more diseases in plants and animals, contributing to an increased use of potentially toxic herbicides and pesticides; additionally, GMOs are not increasing crop yields, and may be increasing people's risk of developing food allergies.

The genetic engineering of food involves inserting or deleting specific genes in plants or animals. The incidence of food allergies has shot up after genetically engineered foods were introduced into the marketplace in 1996. For example, the occurrence of peanut allergies doubled from 1997 to 2002! And there was a 50 percent increase in soy allergies just one year after genetically engineered soy was introduced in 1996. Coincidence?

These genetically engineered foods, often called GM or GMO foods, are in everything these days, from shampoo to cooking oil and clothing. Over 90 percent of our major food and feed crops are now GMOs. The developers and manufacturers have infiltrated the market with GMOs to a point now that the products can be difficult to avoid unless you cook everything at home from 100 percent organic ingredients. Corn, soy, sugar beets, papaya, canola oil, zucchini, and milk (hormones injected into dairy cows) are the most common genetically engineered foods. This means that if you switch to a gluten-free diet, and yet you rely on many of those packaged gluten-free products made with cornstarch and canola oil, you might actually be increasing your intake of GMOs! For everyone's health, it is best to stick with naturally gluten-free whole foods that are organically grown.

GMO Pesticides Found in Pregnant Women and Fetuses

Research carried out by a team at Sherbrooke University Hospital in Quebec found that the toxic *Bacillus thurigiensis* (Bt) insecticide protein Cry1Ab, engineered into GMO crops, was present in the blood serum of 93 percent of pregnant women tested. This Bt toxin was also present in 80 percent of umbilical blood samples taken from fetuses, and in 67 percent of nonpregnant women. The researchers suggest that the most probable source of this toxin is the genetically engineered food consumed as part of a normal diet in Canada. According to the researchers, "to our knowledge, this is the first study to highlight the presence of pesticides-associated genetically modified foods in maternal, fetal and nonpregnant women's blood. 3-MPPA and Cry1Ab toxin are clearly detectable and appear to cross the placenta to the fetus. Given the potential toxicity of these environmental pollutants and the fragility of the fetus, more studies are needed."

No Human Trials

The most frightening thing about genetically engineered foods is that there have been no human trials to test whether these foods are safe for human consumption! In May 2009, the American Academy of Environmental Medicine called for a morato-

The 5-R Program

1. Remove. Removing offending foods is the first step in the healing process. If you never completely remove a food or food group from your diet—like dairy or gluten—you will never know how you feel without it. When testing to see if a particular food or food group works for you, keep it out of the diet completely for at least four weeks, preferably three months. Then put it back in by eating it for three days straight, noting how you feel. This is the process of an elimination diet. For more information, see our book *The Elimination Diet;* also, visit our website, www.WholeLifeNutrition.net, for further information. In addition to excluding certain foods, it is important to consider eliminating your exposure to environmental toxins, such as those found in nonorganic foods, chemicals at the workplace, cleaning supplies in the home such as scented laundry detergents and dryer sheets, personal-care products, and mercury in certain types of fish.

2. Replace. When the gut is not functioning properly, pancreatic enzymes, stomach acid, and bile are often not being produced in sufficient quantities. Taking high-quality digestive supplements and adding food sources of enzymes to your daily diet are essential for the healing process. Food sources of enzymes include raw and sprouted foods, such as sprouted mung beans, broccoli sprouts, fresh pineapple, raw honey, green leafy vegetables, and fermented foods such as sauerkraut and raw kombucha. Foods that stimulate bile and stomach acid production are artichokes and bitter foods, including dandelion leaf, dandelion root tea, chamomile tea, gentian root, fresh ginger, and bitter salad greens.

3. Reinocculate. Start consuming foods rich in probiotics daily, such as raw sauerkraut, homemade coconut kefir, kombucha, cultured vegetables, and raw sour dill pickles (see the "Preserving the Harvest" chapter for recipes). Taking a high-quality probiotic supplement, including soil-based probiotics, may also be very beneficial to reinocculate the gut. Adding prebiotics—foods that feed beneficial bacteria—is also very important; these include sunchokes, asparagus, dandelion greens, onions, garlic, leeks, legumes, buckwheat, quinoa, amaranth, millet, flax seed, and chia seeds.

4. Repair. Consider supplementation of key nutrients to help your body repair itself. Glutamine and glycine are amino acids that help repair the gut lining. Homemade bone broths (see the "Soups & Stews" chapter) offer an easily assimilated source of glutamine and glycine, as well as gelatin in a flavorful form that work together to repair the gut. Raw sauerkraut is another excellent source of glutamine and beneficial bacteria. Other nutrients that may be of benefit are zinc, vitamin D, and essential fatty acids. If you are still not feeling well, you may need to follow a strict diet for a period of time to further assist the gut in repairing, such as the GAPS diet, SCD diet, or a low-FODMAP diet (see our website, www.WholeLifeNutrition.net, for more information).

5. Rebalance. Changing some lifestyle factors, in addition to diet and supplementation, is important in healing the gut. Managing your stress levels will reduce cortisol's damaging effect on the gut. Ensure you are getting at least eight hours of restful sleep per night to help with gastric motility and repair the intestinal lining. Doing some light to moderate daily exercise that you enjoy will also help heal and maintain a healthy gut.

rium on genetically modified (GM) foods, stating: "Avoid GM foods when possible. . . . Several animal studies indicate serious health risks associated with GM food. . . . There is more than a casual association between GM foods and adverse health effects. There is causation. . . . The strength of association and consistency between GM foods and disease is confirmed in several animal studies."

Organ Damage

European researchers at the University of Caen, France, studied data on 90-day feeding trials with rats. They concluded that three varieties of GMO corn that had been approved for consumption by safety authorities in the United States, Europe, and other countries were linked to organ damage in mammals. According to the researchers, these include "adverse impacts on kidneys and liver, dietary detoxifying organs, as well as different levels of damages to heart, adrenal glands, spleen and haematopoietic system."

HEALING THE GUT

To help heal the gut, reduce food sensitivities and allergies, and heal malabsorptive disorders such as osteoporosis and anemia, we suggest you use the 5-R program as outlined by the Institute for Functional Medicine. You'll see the most benefit by following this program for at least three months, though most people usually observe a dramatic shift in health within the first few weeks. For further assistance, consider talking with a trained functional medicine health-care practitioner.

It is important to maintain the most nutrient-dense diet during this 5-R program. When the gut has been damaged for a long time, the body is often depleted in certain nutrients. So, soak or ferment your grains, beans, nuts, and seeds before consuming them (see the "Getting Started" chapter); consume nutrient-dense meats only from organic, pastured, or grass-fed animals; eat large quantities of organic vegetables, both raw and cooked; and keep all processed foods and sugar out of your diet.

raisinghealthychildren

Nourishing Your Growing Child

Feeding your children a whole foods diet that is rich in plant foods helps to nourish and protect them from diseases that can form later on in life. Plants—including vegetables, seaweed, fruits, whole grains, legumes, nuts, and seeds—contain an amazing array of protective compounds that will keep their bodies functioning properly and assist in detoxifying any environmental chemicals they ingest. Yet somewhere between 20 to 50 percent of children in the United States are described by their parents as picky eaters. Picky eating can indeed lead to nutrient deficiencies, poor appetite, cavities, lowered immunity, and obesity. Resolving problems of picky eating while preparing daily nourishing meals will be a way of giving your children the nutrients they need so they have the best chance to grow into vibrant, healthy adults.

Given the opportunity and right environment, children are more likely to choose a diet that is best for them than not. Have you ever noticed how one day your child may gag on a certain food and another day beg for it? This is the innate self-regulation we all have about food. It is governed by our sense of taste and smell. Children who have only been fed processed foods, have undiagnosed sensitivities to gluten and/or casein, who have an imbalance in their gut microflora, who have a zinc deficiency, or who were overfed as infants may have temporarily "lost" this native wisdom and crave only highly refined starchy and sugary foods. In addition, as parents we all too easily focus on how to get our children to eat healthy instead of setting up an environment that supports their innate wisdom to choose foods that nourish. Raising children in such a supportive environment from pregnancy onward will result in a healthy diet that is a normal and natural part of life.

If your children are picky eaters and are suffering the consequences, it's not too late to bring them back to health. The human body is amazingly adaptable. Healing can happen quickly, given the right ingredients and environment.

NUTRITION DURING PREGNANCY

Research shows that during pregnancy, a mother's food preferences and eating patterns have a direct effect on her developing baby—children's food preferences and habits have been linked back to time spent in the womb! Recent studies suggest that mothers who consume particular vegetables during pregnancy (and then later during breastfeeding) have infants who display a quicker acceptance of those vegetables. In the womb, a baby's taste buds begin forming at around five weeks, and by twelve weeks the baby begins to inhale and swallow the amniotic fluid (consisting mainly of water with some carbohydrates, proteins, lipids, and electrolytes). The flavors from the foods the mother is consuming end up in the amniotic fluid (and later in the breast milk as well). The amniotic fluid is the baby's first exposure to flavor!

By consuming a nutrient-dense diet full of healing whole foods, a pregnant woman not only begins to set up her child's future food preferences, but also offers the developing fetus a wide variety of nutrients needed for proper growth. Additionally, by avoiding irritating foods like high fructose corn syrup and gluten, a pregnant woman increases her chances of absorbing sufficient key nutrients needed for the proper growth and development of her baby. The evidence is clear: Our eating habits begin prenatally. Pregnancy is the time to eat a diet that is as clean as possible, loaded with nutrient-dense foods.

THE FIRST THREE YEARS

The first three years of a child's life are critical, as over 100 trillion neuronal connections are forming in the brain that establish lifelong behavioral patterns. By age two or three, most of a child's food preferences have formed, as the brain and taste buds are most malleable during these early years. These food preferences are greatly influenced by the child's immediate surroundings—his family and home life. We've noticed that each of our children's eating habits differs slightly, and all can be linked to what foods we were consuming during their development. For example, we were not drinking green smoothies when our oldest daughter was in this critical three-year period; it wasn't until she was about three and a half years old that we began making them. She still isn't as fond of green smoothies as our younger children are, either. And not only are the food preferences formed during these first three years, but a child's ability to control food intake—when and how much to eat—develops during this time.

The first three years are a time of imitation. What your children see you eat, even when only an infant, will set the stage for later eating habits. Children see right through everything we do; we cannot expect a child to eat a healthy meal if we have just come back from a fast-food restaurant. Children pick up on every nuance of our existence. It is a child's survival mechanism to study what the adults around her are eating before choosing what and how to eat. If it is the norm in your house to make and drink a green smoothie every morning, your young child will naturally want to participate in this ritual. If he sees you in the garden eating carrots just pulled from the ground, he will do the same. Conversely, if he sees you indulging in a bag of potato chips and drinking a soda, he will naturally want to do the same. Even before your child is born, it is best to consider what foods you eat and make changes accordingly. That way you'll be bringing your child into an established environment of healthful food.

Breastfeeding

Breastfeeding is one of the most important things you can do to nourish and protect your new baby against allergies and disease, for both short-term and long-term health. Breast milk contains particular proteins to build up and protect your infant's developing immune system, human milk oligosaccharides that feed the beneficial bacteria in the colon, and fatty acids for proper neural and brain development. Interestingly, while the nutrient composition of breast milk remains relatively constant among different diets, the types of fatty acids that are present change in response to the mother's diet. It has been found that DHA in human milk is significantly higher in women who eat a diet rich in seafood and is lower in those who don't.

Formula doesn't contain many of these protective compounds and is often made from genetically engineered soy oil, corn syrup, and soy or whey protein, along with synthetic vitamins and minerals, and is packed in BPA-lined containers. These substances can contribute to a pro-inflammatory state in the infant's body. Formula feeding combined with a diet high in processed foods can also lead to development of food allergies and sensitivities in some children. But what if you find you can't breastfeed or you have an adopted child? The best option is to obtain pumped milk from several breastfeeding mothers for at least the first year. Or, for babies six months and older, a homemade formula made primarily from raw goat's milk is often used. Lastly, you can try a pure amino acid formula prescribed by a doctor; these formulas don't have any dairy or soy antigens that a baby could react to, but they also don't have the protective compounds found in breast milk.

In addition to being health-protective, breast-

7 Ways to Help your Child THRIVE!

1. Reduce your toxic load before conceiving. If you have lived or worked near a chemical-laden area, taken a lot of medications, consumed high amounts of alcohol, smoked, or eaten a diet of processed nonorganic foods, then you might consider a detoxification or cleansing program using herbs and raw foods for six to twelve months before trying to get pregnant. Reducing your toxic load may increase fertility as well; your ability to absorb key nutrients, such as zinc, is lessened with exposure to toxic chemicals.

2. Decrease your family's chemical exposure. Over 80,000 chemicals are registered for use in the United States, and each year some 700 to 2,000 new ones are introduced for use in foods, drugs, household cleaners, lawn-care products, and personal-care items like shampoos and deodorants. Of this vast number, only five have been banned owing to adverse effects! So, what can you do? Buy organic food! Use eco-friendly cleaning supplies and laundry detergents. Use natural personal-care products. Avoid contact with the toxic phthalates found in soft plastics, baby toys, vinyl flooring, dryer sheets, and plug-in air fresheners. Replace those plastic baby toys with uncoated natural wood toys, any vinyl flooring with wood flooring, and use air fresheners with 100 percent pure essential oils. Consider green building materials when you are remodeling or building a home. Question everything and ask, "Is this safe?"

3. Breastfeed your baby until at least 12 months of age, preferably 24 months or longer. Breast milk promotes the growth of friendly bacteria in your infant's gut, protects his immature immune system by building natural immunity, and promotes brain development through the types of fats found in mother's milk.

4. Go 100 percent gluten-free. Eliminating the gluten from your diet decreases the chances of developing a leaky gut. When someone has a leaky gut, even for a short time after ingesting gluten, large food molecules can enter the bloodstream, causing an adverse reaction to other foods. Gluten, casein, and sometimes soy can limit absorption of certain nutrients; increase inflammation in the body; and can send neuropeptides to the brain that can contribute to behavioral disorders in children.

5. Eat a plant-rich, whole foods diet. A diet high in fresh vegetables and fruits provides the most protection against chronic diseases. Plants are naturally anti-inflammatory, keeping the immune system calm and making it less likely to react to certain foods and/or pet dander. Consuming cruciferous vegetables every day, like broccoli or raw sauerkraut, helps the body naturally rid itself of toxins that have come from the environment or our food. Consuming sea vegetables once a week provides the body with sufficient iodine for proper thyroid function. And clean sources of animal foods provide important amino acids, minerals, and fats.

6. Address nutrient deficiencies. If a child has poor digestion, has not eaten a whole foods diet, is a picky eater, or is constantly getting sick, then she may have certain nutrient deficiencies. Children with ADD and autism usually have multiple nutrient deficiencies because they are either not consuming sufficient nutrients or are not able to absorb or break them down in the gut. Talk with your health-care provider about a "functional" lab analysis to determine what might be going on.

7. Rebalance the gut. If the gut is out of balance—meaning there is an overgrowth of unfriendly bacteria and yeasts, and not sufficient good bacteria—then the chance of inflammation increases, nutrient absorption decreases, lectins and phytates cannot properly be broken down, and brain function might be disturbed from bacterial metabolites and food neuropeptides. A diet high in raw plant foods naturally keeps the gut in good shape. Additionally, serve your children daily portions of fermented foods. These include kefir, homemade yogurt, kombucha, cultured coconut water, cultured vegetables, raw sauerkraut, and raw sour dill pickles. A high-quality probiotic supplement and specific diets for rebalancing the gut can also be beneficial.

feeding can contribute to establishing healthy eating habits. We are all born with an innate control system that alerts us to when we are hungry and to when we have had enough food. Babies who are breastfed on demand without much interference from the mother learn to control their own food intake—which is crucial for preventing overeating behaviors later in life. When breastfeeding, you do not have a visual gauge of how much milk your baby is consuming, which gives the baby full control. When bottle feeding, you do have an idea and, hence, exert external influence. When a mom encourages a baby to finish a bottle, the baby goes beyond its internal satiety cues, which over time can disrupt this innate self-regulation of food intake, possibly leading to overeating later in life.

A natural, drug-free childbirth allows the hormones in the mother's body to make breastfeeding initiation a pleasant experience for both mom and baby. When the mother is stressed or has had a medicated birth, hormones such as oxytocin are inhibited, and the milk supply can take longer to become established. Hiring a doula and having support during childbirth and during the postpartum period help with both the initiation of breastfeeding and the continuance of exclusive breastfeeding during infancy. If you are having a difficult time breastfeeding your new baby, contact a trained lactation consultant, discuss this with your local La Leche League support group, or talk with other

Foods to Increase Milk Production

Pastured chicken, wild-caught salmon, homemade bone broth, sweet potatoes, winter squash, carrots, beets, sweet brown rice, quinoa, oats, lentils, leafy green salads, sea vegetables, nettles, fennel seed, fenugreek, coconut milk, coconut oil, pumpkin seeds, almonds, walnuts, and almond butter.

breastfeeding mothers. Infant craniosacral therapy can be beneficial for dealing with latch issues. We had great success within a few treatments right after the birth of one of our babies.

If you are concerned about your milk supply, remember that the milk doesn't fully come in until about three days after birth. During this time, your baby will be getting small amounts of immune-protective colostrum, often referred to as "liquid gold." There is no need to supplement with formula, even if your baby seems hungry. Babies build up fat stores during the last months of pregnancy, and they use that for energy until the mother's milk is fully established. Once your milk is in, you'll notice that the supply waxes and wanes throughout breastfeeding. Your baby may all of a sudden be constantly hungry, and you might feel that your breasts are always empty. This is normal! I've doubted having enough milk with all my babies when they were between four and six months old. Not by coincidence, formula manufacturers often send out free formula samples during this time! Babies naturally build your milk supply to the amount they need by nursing more often and more frequently. Trust in this natural rhythm, and let the baby feed as long and as often as necessary to build up your supply to meet its needs. If formula or solid foods are introduced, your milk supply will drop. Milk production is an "on demand" cycle: the more you nurse, the more milk is produced. Likewise, skipped feedings will lead to a decrease in milk supply.

Prolonged breastfeeding into the second and third year of life not only protects your child's gut and immune system but also provides your baby with ample nutrients for bone growth. Once your toddler is weaned, there is no reason to introduce cow's milk or dairy-free milk substitutes. Feeding your toddler a plant-based whole foods diet provides ample nutrients for growth, though if you feel that your child would thrive with dairy products (some children really do), then be sure to offer *raw* dairy to lessen the risk of developing an immune response.

Introducing Solid Foods

The standard guidelines for introducing solid foods are that by the time baby is four to six months of age, you should be introducing iron-fortified rice cereal. Humans have survived and thrived for hundreds of thousands of years without manufactured, highly processed baby cereals. In years past, babies were breastfed until they were interested in food. They were then given mashed or pre-chewed bits of whatever the rest of the family were eating.

It is best to avoid rice cereal as baby's first food, for a few reasons. First, rice cereal is highly processed and causes a spike in blood sugar after consumption. This could lead to cravings for processed grain products later on, and may be a contributor to the obesity epidemic. Second, grains are difficult for babies to digest. Salivary and pancreatic amylase are enzymes needed to break the polysaccharide bonds found in grains and form simple sugars for absorption and utilization in the body. Newborn babies don't produce any salivary amylase; production begins only after about three months of age, and in small amounts. Pancreatic amylase isn't produced in large amounts until after two years of age—about the time when the molar teeth fully emerge for chewing—though research does show that pancreatic amylase production can vary in 6- to 24-month-old babies; some babies at six months may be able to properly digest very small amounts of complex starches from cereal grains, while others may not. When you are ready to introduce grains, soak them for 12 to 24 hours, and then slow-cook them; see our "Whole Grains and Noodles" chapter for instructions. You can also serve your older baby or toddler a pancake—called injera, from Ethiopia—made from Gluten-Free Sourdough Starter (page 112). Simply heat a cast-iron skillet over medium heat, add a few teaspoons of coconut oil, and pour in ¼ to ½ cup of starter; cook for 1 to 2 minutes on each side. Fermented flours are highly digestible, a good way to introduce grains into your child's diet, plus their taste buds will develop early to favor soured foods.

Don't babies require supplemental iron from rice

cereal so they don't become anemic? It is true that we do have a worldwide iron deficiency epidemic among infants and toddlers. Upon closer examination, though, it appears that these iron-deficient children were not exclusively breastfed. Exclusive breastfeeding—no supplemental feedings of formula or solid foods—allows the iron in breast milk to be properly absorbed. It is important also to note that fetuses store iron during the last month of a full-term gestation. Exclusively breastfed pre-term babies can become iron deficient during the first six months, since they do not have the same amount of stored iron as full-term babies; therefore, introducing some heme iron sources (like bone broths and pureed red meat) at six months might be beneficial. It is also theorized that since iron competes with zinc, breast milk is naturally lower in iron to allow the zinc to be properly absorbed. Zinc is a mineral needed for optimal development of an infant's nervous and immune systems. Breast milk has adequate zinc as long as the mother is consuming and absorbing enough zinc-rich foods.

The introduction of solid foods can begin around six months of age, but certainly should not be done before, as an infant's digestive system is still developing. For exclusively breastfed babies that were born full-term, solid foods can even wait until nine or twelve months, or until the child is interested in eating. Offer your baby a wide variety of flavors and nutrients with easily digestible fresh, in-season raw or lightly cooked fruit and steamed vegetables. Steer clear of jarred, processed baby foods, instead allowing your child's taste buds to develop a preference for fresh foods. I wouldn't feed anything to my baby that I wouldn't eat myself. Have you tried jarred, strained spinach? Yuck!

These first few months of eating solids are not so much about getting a lot of nutrients in—as milk is still the primary nutrient source— but, rather, are an exploratory phase of flavor, textures, and learning to swallow. Start slowly with just a few flavors and textures, and gradually offer a wider selection during the first three years. This will set the stage for

Great First Foods for Baby

Steamed carrots and winter squash, blueberries, applesauce, sea vegetables, ripe bananas, diced or mashed avocado, mango, sautéed zucchini, roasted turnips, diced fresh watermelon, and peeled diced fresh pears. For an older baby, try slow-cooked organic chicken, wild-caught salmon, finely chopped kale cooked in homemade chicken stock, cooked egg yolk, injera flatbread, cultured vegetables, small amounts of brine from raw sauerkraut, and celery sticks to teethe on.

a lifelong love of nutritious food. On average, it can take up to 10 introductions of a food before a child will accept it into his diet.

Remember that each child develops differently. Our second daughter at seven months refused to eat even a mashed banana, but by eight months she was ready to eat. Our twin boys were interested in food early on, so we started them on solids around six months. Since it was summertime, their first food was pureed raw cantaloupe. They were so interested in food that by the time they were nine months, they were eating more than their toddler sister—a complete salmon dinner! Our youngest daughter started eating solids at about seven and a half months, first with nori seaweed and then a little wild-caught salmon and roasted organic chicken, as these were the foods she was most interested in eating. By the time she was eight months old, she was feeding herself a whole meal of baked wild-caught salmon, steamed broccoli, and frozen blueberries! When our twin boys were a year old, we were offering mixed green salads with a little homemade dressing on top. Since they didn't chew it thoroughly, I am sure they didn't get much nutrition out of it, but now they beg for salads and will eat a whole plate of greens with just about any type of homemade dressing drizzled on top.

Is My Baby Ready for Solid Foods?

- **Can my baby sit unassisted?** If your baby can sit in a high chair without slumping over or leaning to one side, then the risk of choking is lessened and the swallowing reflex is able to properly function.
- **Can my baby hold her head up properly?** Good head control is absolutely critical for proper swallowing and eating.
- **Has my baby's tongue-thrust reflex diminished?** Young infants have something called a tongue-thrust reflex; when an object hits their mouths, such as food or small toys, they automatically push it out of their mouth. By six months of age this begins to diminish, though for some babies it can take up to eight or nine months, and for others it might diminish by five months. If you try to introduce solid foods and your baby continually pushes them out of his mouth, then wait a few weeks and try again—your baby is not yet ready.
- **Does my baby show interest in foods during family mealtimes?** Once you see your baby following forkfuls of food from your plate to your mouth, you'll know that your baby is almost ready to try solid foods. Start by offering tastes of food from your plate—a bite of mashed yams, baked winter squash, a soft carrot from a bowl of chicken soup, a bite of steamed broccoli, or a taste of ripe fruit.

Schedule for Introducing Solid Foods

When you are introducing those first foods, freshly made baby food can be easily prepared from organic fruits and vegetables. Vegetables may be steamed, and then pureed with a small amount of purified water or bone broth to desired consistency. Younger babies need their food fairly thin and watery, while older ones do fine with thicker purees. Soft in-season fruits such as peaches, plums, pears, apricots, cherries, and melons can be blended raw into a smoothie or thick pudding. Grains, which are more difficult to digest than vegetables or fruits, are best introduced after nine months of age, when pancreatic enzymes are more abundantly produced.

The following is an *informal* schedule for introducing solid foods. The simple ability to sit unassisted and swallow foods, and the maturity of a baby's digestive and immune systems, are important determining factors. It appears to be very important that solid foods are completely avoided before six months of age, and it may be unnecessary to start solid foods even at this age. Exclusive breastfeeding may be continued from nine to twelve months. By this age, most babies will be quite eager and ready to eat. When beginning solid food, it is important to watch for reactions such as sneezing, runny nose, eczema, skin rashes, rash around the mouth or diaper area, changes in stools, or changes in personality. If you notice any of these signs, wait to offer that particular food again for another month.

Above all, remember to listen to those motherly intuitions when introducing solid foods. You will know, better than any chart or book, what is best for your baby and at what time. The simple act of observation can give you more information than anything else!

6 to 9 months

Focus on hypoallergenic foods such as steamed, pureed vegetables and soft fruits. Start out with

1 to 2 tablespoons of food per day. Some babies do fine also with most berries at this stage. Frozen berries can be placed into a mesh feeding bag for teething.

- bone broths (simmer vegetables in it and then mash)
- winter squash (including pumpkin)
- yam (sweet potato)
- summer squash (zucchini, pattypan, crookneck)
- avocado
- applesauce
- blueberries
- banana
- prunes
- broccoli
- Jerusalem artichoke (sunchoke)
- turnips
- rutabaga
- carrots
- beets
- parsnips
- cauliflower
- cherries
- apricots
- peaches and nectarines
- plums
- pears
- melons
- green peas

9 to 12 months

Focus on low-allergen foods that help to develop chewing, swallowing, and the pincer grasp—a developmental milestone that enables a child to pick up small objects with the thumb and index finger, which also leads to the correct hold of a pencil for writing properly. Cut soft foods into small pieces to help develop the pincer grasp. Freshly made fruit and green smoothies are particularly nutritious and easy to digest; these can be introduced at nine months. Introduce low-mercury seafood such as wild-caught salmon, herring, and sardines. Be sure to slow-cook meats over a long period of time to break down the proteins into a more digestible form—chicken soup, beef stew, or slow-roasted turkey are great choices. Whole grains are best kept out of the diet until the digestive system is more mature; this can happen anytime between nine months and two years. Many infants lack the capability to properly break down complex starches from whole grains, which can lead to bacterial and yeast overgrowth, as well as other digestive disorders. Soak or sprout your whole grains before cooking them for best digestibility (see the "Whole Grains and Noodles" chapter for more information). White rice does not need to be soaked or sprouted; simply cook with a little extra water for best digestibility. When you try introducing whole grains, watch for signs of digestive discomfort, irritability, and rashes within one to two days. When I introduced homemade brown rice cereal (made from soaked sweet brown rice that was slow-cooked and pureed) to our first daughter when she was about 7½ months old, within hours our happy little girl—who never cried—turned into a crying, uncomfortable baby hardly recognizable to us. This lasted for about 30 hours! I waited a couple more months to introduce grains again, trying quinoa that was ground in a baby food grinder after it was cooked—she digested it wonderfully! No crying or bloated belly this time. I shortly added other grains to her diet, including fermented flour products, and all was well. Just remember to observe your child, and you will know if the food you introduced was tolerated. All babies develop differently—some

Recent research indicates that foods, such as seafood and eggs, which were once thought to be more likely to cause allergies if introduced too early, are actually safe to offer to older babies. The most important factor in the development of food allergies is any imbalance in the infant's microbiome (see page 15 for more information).

are able to handle more grains early on, while others may need to wait until after one year of age.

- egg yolks
- wild-caught salmon
- pastured chicken
- organic turkey
- lamb
- wild game
- grass-fed beef
- onions
- garlic
- potato
- cabbage
- kale (pureed)
- collard greens (pureed)
- lettuce (pureed)
- green smoothies (made without lemon)
- green beans
- raspberries and blackberries
- cranberries (fresh or frozen)
- papaya
- lima beans
- split pea soup
- pumpkin seeds (ground to a powder and added to foods or pumpkin seed butter)
- sunflower seeds (soaked and pureed with food or ground to a powder)
- blackstrap molasses (added to foods in small amounts for extra iron)
- nori seaweed (eaten plain as a snack for extra minerals)
- hemp milk
- virgin coconut oil
- extra-virgin olive oil
- organic pastured butter
- brown and white rice
- millet
- quinoa

12 to 18 months

Focus on foods higher in bulk and calories. Continue to watch for signs of food allergy and sensitivity reactions, as stated previously.

- whole eggs
- citrus
- grapes (cut up)
- spinach
- salads with homemade dressing
- asparagus
- tomatoes
- eggplant
- bell peppers
- strawberries
- hummus (for recipe, see page 343)
- cooked dried beans
- sprouted tofu
- raw goat's milk
- goat's milk yogurt
- goat cheese
- teff
- amaranth
- buckwheat
- wild rice
- flax seeds
- chia seeds

Introducing Potentially Allergenic Foods

Cow's milk, tree nuts, peanuts, gluten grains, corn, and soy products can present problems for some children. If and when you introduce them, make sure they are offered in their most digestible forms. For example, use homemade yogurt or kefir made from raw milk that has been sweetened only with a little maple syrup; tree nuts soaked overnight in water and then blended into a smoothie; gluten grains that are sprouted or fermented into a sourdough starter and made into bread; masa harina for the introduction of corn; and organic soybeans that have been sprouted and made into tofu or fermented into miso, tamari, or tempeh.

18 to 24 months

Focus on foods that are high in protein calories to support growth. Soak any tree nuts overnight in purified water to aid in digestion and chewing.

- corn
- gluten (wheat, spelt, rye, Kamut, barley)
- raw or fermented cow's milk products
- almond butter
- cashew butter
- peanut butter
- almonds
- cashews
- pecans
- Brazil nuts
- walnuts
- pineapple

KEY NUTRIENTS FOR PROPER DEVELOPMENT

Here are some of the nutrients that are key for the proper growth and development of your children, whether still in utero or in the various stages of childhood. If you and your children are consuming a plant-rich whole foods diet, you'll most likely be getting plenty of vitamin C, B vitamins, potassium, beta-carotene, vitamin E, and trace minerals, but a large portion of our population is typically deficient in these or has difficulty absorbing them.

By combining a diet rich in plant foods along with some sustainably raised, organic animal foods, your child will have the best chance of thriving. Remember, the nutrients in whole foods work best synergistically, with the body utilizing them fully, so as long as you and your children are eating a balanced whole foods diet, you're all probably getting what you need.

Omega-3 Fatty Acids

Omega-3 fatty acids lower chronic inflammation; in fact, they are a prime modulator of the inflammatory hormones in the body, and are key to preventing and healing food allergies. Omega-3 fatty acids are also critical in modulating fetal and infant growth and in the development of the central nervous system. In fact, over 18 percent of an infant's brain is docosahexaenoic acid, or DHA!

Here's the actual mechanism: omega-3 fatty acids come from plants as alpha-linoleic acid (ALA), and from animals as DHA and eicosapentaenoic acid (EPA). The ALA can be converted into DHA and EPA in the body, but the process is not very efficient, as it requires numerous co-factors such as zinc, magnesium, and vitamin B_6. When we consume a lot of omega-6 vegetable oils in our diet, the body prioritizes the enzymes to convert those oils into arachidonic acid (AA) instead of using them to convert the EPA to DHA. The take-home message is this: greatly reduce your consumption of these vegetable oils and increase your consumption of DHA and EPA.

To optimize pregnancy outcomes and fetal health, consensus guidelines have recommended that pregnant women consume at least 200 mg of DHA per day. The FDA advises all pregnant women to limit seafood consumption to two 6-ounce servings per week so as to decrease fetal exposure to trace amounts of neurotoxins, but this level of consumption still provides the necessary 200 mg DHA per day as long as you are consuming fish that is rich in EPA and DHA. Alternatives to fish include DHA-enriched eggs, which contain about

150 mg DHA per serving, or fish oil supplements. A new method of fish oil purification, called "Super Critical CO_2 Extraction," has produced some of the cleanest oil products to date, so consider spending the extra money for these if you are concerned about environmental exposure. DHA does not pass easily through the placenta without EPA, so it is of utmost importance to consume fish oil supplements that combine EPA and DHA while you are pregnant.

Signs of Deficiency: Lower growth rate in infants and children, dry skin and dry scaly rashes, decreased wound healing, and an increase in infections.

Contributors to Deficiency: Low dietary intake, high stress levels, high amounts of insulin circulating in the blood, fat malabsorption from celiac disease, and degradation of the small intestine from various factors, including candida overgrowth, heavy antibiotic use, and consumption of gluten.

Food Sources: Salmon, halibut, sardines, pastured eggs, grass-fed beef, leafy greens, walnuts, chia seeds, and flax seeds.

Recipes: Orange Pepper Salmon (page 299), Thai Coconut Fish Sticks (page 304), Kale and Egg Scramble (page 87), Green Chia Smoothie (page 68), Garden Salad with Creamy Herb Dressing (page 205)

Vitamin A

Vitamin A is a class of fat-soluble nutrients that includes retinoids and carotenoids. Retinoids are also known as preformed vitamin A, and they can only be found in animal foods. Carotenoids are found in plant foods, and are also known as provitamin A. Carotenoids need to be converted into vitamin A by the body in order for the body to use it. This process requires numerous reactions and co-factors, including zinc and thyroid hormone (T3).

Vitamin A is needed for normal eyesight function, for reading portions of our DNA, for normal growth and development of cells (including red blood cells), for normal reproduction functions including spermatogenesis, and for supporting normal bone metabolism. It is also essential for balancing immune cell function, which reduces the development of autoimmune diseases.

Signs of Deficiency: Increased incidence of infection, diarrhea, vomiting, night blindness, thyroid dysfunction, and skin disorders such as keratosis pilaris (raised bumps on the back of the upper arms).

Contributors to Deficiency: As a fat-soluble vitamin, vitamin A levels are often compromised in individuals who have fat malabsorption disorders. These include but are not limited to Crohn's disease, celiac disease, cystic fibrosis, Whipple's disease, and other pancreatic and biliary disorders. Carotenoids need to be converted by the body to vitamin A if animal products are not consumed; this process utilizes the thyroid hormone (T3) and zinc. If there is a deficiency in either of these, then there may not be adequate vitamin A. Many other factors may play a role in hindering this conversion, including excessive consumption of alcohol, bacterial imbalances in the intestines, medication interactions, genetic susceptibilities, and digestive disorders.

Food Sources for Retinoids: Beef liver, chicken liver, cod liver oil, shrimp, eggs, and raw cow's milk.

Food Sources for Carotenoids: Sweet potatoes, carrots, pumpkin, spinach, winter squash, collards, and kale.

Recipes: Chicken Breakfast Sausages (page 91), Winter Vegetable Gratin (page 241), Mini Quiches with a Sweet Potato Crust (page 90), Spiced Pumpkin Soup (page 168), Creamed Kale (page 228), Sweet and Spicy Kale Chips (page 371).

Vitamin D

Vitamin D is an essential nutrient for bone formation and proper immune system functioning. When you have adequate vitamin D, you can bind and absorb 30 to 80 percent of any intestinal calcium, whereas a person with a low vitamin D status is lucky to get between 10 to 15 percent absorption. So, which is more practical—taking large amounts of calcium for bone development or efficiently absorbing the calcium that is in your intestines by having adequate vitamin D? Beyond its beneficial effects on bones, higher vitamin D levels have been associated with reducing autoimmune diseases and infections in growing children. Unfortunately, many pregnant women are deficient in vitamin D, and thus their offspring will most likely be deficient in utero and at birth. Breast milk is often a poor source for vitamin D, so a mother's building up her stores prior to and during pregnancy may be of utmost importance.

Research has found that women who supplement with 4,000 IU of vitamin D during pregnancy significantly decreased their risk of pregnancy complications, such as small-for-gestations-age babies, high blood pressure or preeclampsia, and gestational diabetes. A minimum of 4,000 IU a day is required during pregnancy, however, taking 6,000 IU a day was found to get circulating amounts of vitamin D (25-OHD) to levels beneficial for a healthy pregnancy.

Year-round, in areas of the United States below the 35th parallel, vitamin D naturally forms in the skin upon exposure to UVB radiation from the midday sun. In the winter months, years ago the native peoples of the northern latitudes typically consumed animal organ meats and fat—rich sources of vitamin D. Now these foods are too contaminated with environmental toxins to be considered safe. If supplementation is needed to maintain adequate vitamin D levels in you or your child, choose a supplement that is free of artificial preservatives; these preservatives include sodium benzoate, BHT, or BHA, and GMO carrier oils such as soy oil. Nutrition experts have agreed that 1,000 IU per 25 pounds of body weight appears to be a valid formula for meeting the needs of young children. For an infant, use 200 IU per 5 pounds of body weight.

Signs of Deficiency: Rickets, osteoporosis, osteopenia, osteomalacia, elevated parathyroid hormone, bone pain, inflammation, weakness, and fatigue.

Contributors to Deficiency: Lack of sun exposure, use of sunscreen, having dark skin, fat malabsorptive disorders including celiac disease and cystic fibrosis. In infants, low maternal vitamin D status during pregnancy.

Food Sources: Lard, organ meats, fatty fish, mushrooms, eggs.

Recipes: Garlic Ginger Salmon (page 298), Cream of Mushroom Soup (page 164), Basil Zucchini Frittata (page 88).

The best way to get enough vitamin D is to get plenty of sunshine, take a liquid vitamin D–vitamin K supplement in the fall and winter, and reduce your exposure to chemicals. Research has shown that pesticides, certain medications, and BPA can degrade the vitamin D in your body to an inactive form. For more information on this, visit our website, www .WholeLifeNutrition.net.

Vitamin K

There are two types of vitamin K used by the body. Vitamin K_1 (phylloquinone) and vitamin K_2 (menaquinone). Vitamin K_1 is primarily used in clotting functions of the blood; K_2 is used for putting calcium into the bones, which is essential for young children to grow bones and healthy teeth. Vitamin K_1 is primarily found in plants and can be converted into K_2 two different ways. First, certain organs in the body, including the pancreas, testes, and blood vessels, can directly convert K_1 into K_2 (MK4). Second, in the intestines, nonpathogenic *E. coli* bacteria convert K_1 into K_2 (MK7).

Signs of K_1 Deficiency: Easy and pronounced bruising, bleeding gums, nosebleeds, heavy menstrual bleeding, and bleeding in the gastrointestinal tract.

Signs of K_2 Deficiency: Osteoporosis, osteopenia, increased fracturing, and dental cavities.

Contributors of Deficiency: Malabsorptive disorders including celiac disease and cystic fibrosis, bacteria imbalances in the colon, pancreatic enzyme insufficiency, low dietary intake.

Food Sources for K_1: Kale, collards, spinach, brussels sprouts, romaine lettuce, and broccoli.

Food Sources for K_2: Natto, meat, eggs, pastured butter, and raw cheese.

Recipes: Pan-Fried Steak Salad with Sesame Ginger Dressing (page 214), Baby Green Smoothie (page 67), Mini Quiches with a Sweet Potato Crust (page 90), Sautéed Winter Greens with Caramelized Onions (page 230).

Calcium

Calcium is needed to mineralize the teeth and bones in growing children, as well as for aiding muscle contractions and signaling damaged cells to destroy themselves (a process called *apoptosis*). For young girls, the most important time to have adequate calcium intake is during the pre-teen and teenage years, from about nine to nineteen years of age, as this is the peak of bone mass formation. Nutritional emphasis has always been on consuming a lot of calcium in order to have strong bones; however, this is only a small part of a larger picture. It may be that vitamin D and vitamin K deficiencies, as well as chronic inflammation, play a larger role in bone health than does calcium intake.

Signs of Deficiency: Rickets, dental cavities, muscle spasms, tingling and numbness, and bone fractures.

Contributors to Deficiency: An inability to process oxalates, caffeine consumption, excessive animal protein intake, a diet very high in phytic acid, and a high intake of sodium.

Food Sources: Sea vegetables, agar flakes, collard greens, kale, broccoli, sesame tahini, raw almonds, hazelnuts, black-eyed peas, canned salmon or sardines, and raw goat's or cow's milk or fermented dairy like yogurt and kefir.

Recipes: Spicy Black-Eyed Pea Soup (page 181), Raw Breakfast Tacos (page 82), Strawberry Almond Smoothie (page 65), Raw Blueberry Cheesecake (page 405), Raw Kale Salad with Lemon Tahini Dressing (page 220), Overnight Quinoa Hot Cakes (page 100) Baby Green Smoothie (page 67).

Magnesium

Magnesium is one of the most important minerals for the human body. It is a co-factor for over 300 different enzymes needed for proper function of the heart, skeletal muscle, bones, cardiovascular system, nervous system, and digestive system. Magnesium helps regulate blood sugar, maintain normal blood pressure, and keep the bones strong—in fact, over 50 percent of the body's magnesium is found in the bones! One of the reasons magnesium is so essential for human health is that it allows adenosine triphosphate (ATP), the primary energy currency of the cells, to be moved around in the body. Magnesium also acts to block the stimulation of an excitatory receptor in the brain (known as the NMDA receptor) that can lead to increased cases of ADD/ADHD and anxiety. Magnesium is one of the most common nutrient deficiencies in our society.

Signs of Deficiency: Anxiety, insomnia, high blood pressure, muscle cramping, weakness, tremors, headaches, restless leg syndrome, and irregular heartbeat.

Contributors to Deficiency: Stress, kidney disease, malabsorptive disorders, chronic diarrhea, and alcoholism.

Food Sources: Nuts, seeds (pumpkin seeds are highest), legumes, leafy greens, chocolate, and whole grains, particularly oats.

Recipes: Overnight Oatmeal Cinnamon Muffins (page 142), Chocolate Brownie Cupcakes (page 429), Sweet and Spicy Kale Chips (page 371), Cashew Orange Date Balls (page 376), Herb and Olive Oil Hummus (page 343), Raw Kale Salad with Lemon Tahini Dressing (page 220).

Zinc

Unfortunately, mild to severe zinc deficiencies exist worldwide in most people. Women in Third World countries are at highest risk because their overall caloric intake is low and because cereal grains make up most of their diet. Zinc is needed as a co-factor in over 200 body reactions. The zinc keeps the immune system functioning properly, aids in wound healing, helps to make the active form of the thyroid hormone, and is involved in DNA synthesis and cell division. Also, zinc is needed to properly be able to taste and smell things; in fact, one of the most common symptoms of a zinc deficiency in children is picky eating and a loss of appetite. But since the body has no way of storing zinc, we all need a daily supply to maintain optimal health. A recent article found an association between low levels of maternal and infant zinc and the incidence of autism. When you are zinc deficient, you up-regulate the formation of receptors in the small intestine for absorbing zinc; those zinc receptors are not selective for only zinc, however, and will also absorb any heavy metals from the diet, such as cadmium and arsenic from rice or potatoes and root crops grown with chemical pesticides and fertilizers. Therefore, consider purchasing only organic food and make sure to consume a zinc-rich diet.

Signs of Deficiency: Picky eating, growth retardation, mood and behavioral issues, hair loss, poor wound healing, diarrhea, and even Down syndrome. Skin rashes, learning disabilities, lowered immunity,

and infertility are also strongly associated with a zinc deficiency. A zinc deficiency during pregnancy can lead to structural abnormalities and low birth weight in offspring, intrauterine growth retardation, prolonged labor, and learning disabilities in offspring, such as dyslexia.

Contributors to Deficiency: Low zinc intake, food grown in poor soil conditions, undiagnosed celiac disease and gluten enteropathies, damage to the small intestine from candida, high consumption of phytic acid from unfermented or unsoaked cereal grains, and unfermented soy (soy milk, fake meats, soy protein isolate, soy flour). See the "Whole Grains and Noodles" chapter for more details on phytic acid.

Food Sources: Animal sources include venison, beef, lamb, chicken, and turkey. Oysters also have high amounts of zinc, but because of possible mercury contamination, it is not a good idea to eat them. Plant sources include pumpkin seeds and whole grains, but these need to be soaked or fermented for the best bio-availability.

Recipes: Turkey Quinoa Meatballs (page 316), Nori Rolls with Pumpkin Seed–Parsley Pâté (page 361), Grain-Free Chicken Nuggets (page 312), Cream of Mushroom Soup (page 164), Overnight Quinoa Hot Cakes (page 100), Slow-Cooked Beef Stew (page 319).

Iron

Iron deficiency anemia is one of the most common nutritional concerns for most people worldwide, affecting 20 to 50 percent of the global population. Iron is an essential component of hemoglobin, a protein in red blood cells that is used for oxygen transport. In fact, over two-thirds of the iron in our bodies is found in the hemoglobin! Iron is also used for cell growth and differentiation—critical during pregnancy and childhood growth. Requirements for iron nearly double during pregnancy, as it is needed for development of the placenta, for meeting the iron needs of the fetus, for increasing the maternal red blood cell count, and for coping with blood loss at delivery. Iron deficiency anemia during pregnancy increases the risk of low birth weight in neonates. It has also been associated with pre-term labor and premature rupture of the membranes, although some studies give conflicting results. Babies store iron during the last month of pregnancy, which is why pre-term infants are at a much higher risk for becoming anemic. Research demonstrates that when a mother is deficient in iron during pregnancy, the fetus cannot store as much and therefore could become anemic in infancy. Infants born of mothers who are not anemic during pregnancy usually have enough stored iron to last six to eight months.

It is important to note that iron is classified as heme (from animals), or nonheme (from plants). While heme iron is generally better absorbed by most people, it can also be quite toxic in large amounts. This is yet another reason to consume a diet high in plants, with a smaller proportion of animal foods.

Signs of Deficiency: Eating less, gaining weight poorly, paleness, weakness, and tiring easily. Symptoms of iron deficiency in children are not apparent until they are extreme. They may have frequent respiratory and intestinal infections, and may develop pica. Iron deficiency also can lead to impaired development in behavior, cognition, and psychomotor skills.

Contributors to Deficiency: Low intake of vitamin C (needed to absorb iron), undiagnosed celiac disease and gluten enteropathies, damage to the small intestine from candida, high consumption of phytic acid from unfermented or unsoaked cereal grains, and unfermented soy (soy milk, fake meats, soy protein isolate, soy flour). See the "Whole Grains and Noodles" chapter for more details on phytic acid.

Food Sources: Iron is found in high concentrations in all animal tissues, otherwise known as heme iron. Plant sources of iron—or nonheme iron—include nettles, dandelion leaf, broccoli, bok choy, teff, quinoa, sprouted lentils, and tempeh.

Recipes: Slow Cooker Chicken Stew (page 184), Grass-Fed Beef Chili (page 186), Smoked Salmon Salad with Honey Mustard Dressing (page 222), Lentil Minestrone (preferably made with sprouted lentils) (page 174), Green Chia Smoothie (page 68), Gluten-Free Sourdough Bread (page 114), Quinoa and Lentil Salad with Caramelized Onions (page 263).

Iodine

Iodine is primarily used by the body to make the thyroid hormones T3 and T4. These hormones are three and four iodine molecules, respectively, attached to one tyrosine (an amino acid). Zinc and selenium are needed to convert the inactive form of thyroid hormone, T4, into the active form, T3. Did you know that every cell in the human body has receptors for thyroid hormones? Without sufficient thyroid hormones, you cannot properly convert beta-carotene from plants into the active form of vitamin A—something to consider if you are raising a vegan child.

Iodine deficiency is the most frequent cause of mental retardation, as it is needed for brain development during the first trimester of the developing fetus. An iodine deficiency and low thyroid hormones (hypothyroxinemia) have been linked to infertility in women and sperm abnormalities in men. This deficiency can negatively affect cognitive development in children and even cause a severe stunting in physical and mental growth, called *cretinism*. One study found that 63.6 percent of children born to women with hypothyroxinemia developed ADHD. The opposite is also true, in that iodine supplementation during pregnancy can increase head circumference and cognitive functioning in offspring. The World Health Organization has recently raised its recommended iodine levels during pregnancy from 200 to 250 mcg per day.

Signs of Deficiency: Cretinism, cognitive impairment, goiter, multiple miscarriages, hypothyroidism, weakness and fatigue, weight loss resistance, and weight gain.

Contributors to Deficiency: Low dietary intake and consumption of arsenic from nonorganic chicken may interfere with the uptake of iodine by the thyroid gland. Cruciferous vegetables and soy are often avoided by people with thyroid issues, out of fear that their consumption might lead to goiter. After close examination of the literature, it appears that this only occurs in populations that have iodine and selenium deficiencies.

Food Sources: The best sources of iodine are sea vegetables such as kombu, arame, hijiki, dulse, and nori. Fish appears to vary wildly in iodine content. Yogurt, milk, eggs, and strawberries also contain smaller amounts of iodine.

Recipes: Quinoa Salad with Arame and Daikon (page 261), Nori Rolls with Salmon and Mustard Greens (page 362), Homemade Chicken Broth (page 156), Cucumber Arame Salad (page 203), Herb-Roasted Turkey Breast (page 315).

Folate

Folate, or vitamin B_9, is needed by the body to help convert the food that is eaten into energy. It also helps to make RNA, DNA, and red blood cells; that's why the developing fetus needs a continual supply of folate to assist in these processes, especially early on in the first trimester. Additionally, elevated blood homocysteine levels, considered an indicator of folate deficiency, have been associated with an increased incidence of miscarriage, as well as pregnancy complications like preeclampsia and placental abruption. Folate is also used for methylation, or "remodeling," reactions in the human body. For example, methylation of DNA can turn on and off the reading of certain genes, called *epigenetics*, depending on where the methyl group is placed on the DNA strand. This is important for preventing childhood cancers and cardiovascular disease.

A lot of foods are now fortified with folic acid (the synthetic form of folate), like orange juice and all-purpose flour. But did you know that the form of folic acid used to fortify these foods and included in most supplements is not absorbable in a certain percentage of our population? Furthermore, studies show that this synthetic form of folic acid can actually be quite toxic to the human body. That's because this is not a metabolically active form of vitamin B_9 and so it has to be metabolized to different folate forms—folinic acid and 5-methyltetrahydrofolate (5MTHF)—before it can be used by the body. If a person has a lessened ability to transform the synthetic folic acid to a biologically active form, the synthetic folic acids can build up in the body and may be associated with an increased risk of cancer. Therefore, when supplementation is necessary, it makes sense to use folinic acid and 5MTHF exclusively, and to avoid folic acid all together.

Signs of Deficiency: Anxiety, depression, memory issues, headaches, loss of appetite, bleeding gums, elevated homocysteine levels, macrocytic anemia, low birth weight in babies, and colon cancer.

Contributors to Deficiency: Low amounts of gastric acid, heavy use of acid-blocking medications, celiac disease or other causes of irritation of the upper intestinal tract (bacterial overgrowth, parasitic infections, non-celiac food reactions, Crohn's disease), weight-loss surgeries, and alcoholism.

Food Sources: Dark leafy greens, salad greens, legumes.

Recipes: Apple Cider Baked Beans (page 277), Arugula Salad with Shaved Fennel (page 196), Greek Salad with Chickpeas (page 207), Pear Pomegranate Salad with Orange Vinaigrette (page 215), Spring Green Smoothie (page 70).

Vitamin B_{12}

Like folate, vitamin B_{12} is used by the body for methylation ("remodeling") reactions. It also builds new blood cells in the bone marrow and helps to orchestrate all functions of metabolism. Vitamin B_{12} is involved with balancing hormones, digesting food, eliminating waste, and utilizing oxygen. It and folate act synergistically to prevent miscarriage. You cannot properly develop a fetus without sufficient B_{12} and folate. The metabolically active forms of vitamin B_{12} for supplementation are adenosylcobalamin and methylcobalamin.

Signs of Deficiency: Anemia, neurological symptoms such as depression, poor memory, numbness and tingling of the hands and feet, and loss of balance.

Contributors to Deficiency: Low amounts of gastric acid, heavy use of acid-blocking medications, celiac disease or other causes of irritation of the upper intestinal tract (bacterial overgrowth, parasitic infections, non-celiac food reactions, Crohn's disease), weight-loss surgeries, and alcoholism.

Food Sources: Sardines, salmon, lamb, and beef.

Recipes: Sloppy Joes (page 318), Slow-Cooked Beef Stew (page 319), Tandoori Salmon (page 301), Quinoa Salmon Burgers (page 297).

MOVING FROM PROCESSED FOODS TO WHOLE FOODS

Why cook from scratch? It's certainly easier to just go out to eat or pick up a frozen meal. But by preparing your own food, you have control of the quality and freshness of the ingredients—no hidden MSG, flavor enhancers, GMOs, or gluten. Moving away from convenience may take more effort at first, but in the long run you and your family will be healthier as a result.

Changing the Diet

When we look at diet as a continually evolving process, rather than an end goal, making the changes becomes easier. It's okay if you didn't start your child out with a lot of fresh fruits and vegetables, or a green smoothie every day; what's important is that you are making the changes now. If you are feeling overwhelmed at the prospect, then make one new change a week or a month until you adjust. Let's say you start by going gluten-free, then a few months later, you remove all the highly processed foods from your house, and six months later you add a green smoothie twice a week. Maybe a year or two down the line, you begin to soak your grains, soak and dehydrate your raw nuts and seeds, and make sourdough bread. During each step of the way, you know that you are improving your health and the health of your family.

Whatever overall changes you are making now (going gluten-free, going processed food–free), we do recommend that you start now, *today,* by swapping one of your typical meals with a recipe in this book, whether it's breakfast, lunch, dinner, or a snack. It will get you into the groove of cooking from scratch and will start you on your journey toward discovering favorite new flavors for your family.

The younger the children are, the easier it is to make changes. Some parents find that small changes over time are easier, while others feel that a complete kitchen overhaul is needed. Whichever method you choose, stick with it, even when it looks like nothing is working and you feel your child may starve. Don't worry; your children's survival instincts will kick in and they will begin to eat what you offer. If your children are older, involve them in the preparation. It can be fun to look together for new recipes to try, to create a menu plan, and to have them help you shop for groceries. Keeping the process positive and upbeat will go a long way.

My Child Has a Very Limited Diet and Won't Change

Healthy children have healthy appetites, and they want to expand their diets. A child who is a picky eater or who doesn't have an appetite often has a compromised digestive system, is addicted to certain foods, or has nutrient deficiencies—notably zinc—that affect the sense of taste. Sometimes, a child gets comfortable eating only five different foods because he has constant bellyaches and a difficult time digesting food. Often, parents don't even realize their child has a problem because she has always had a compromised digestive tract and doesn't know what it is like to be well. Food sensitivities are often at the root of stomach pain, as well as disinterest in all but a limited variety of foods.

A large percentage of the world's population lacks a particular enzyme called dipeptyl peptidase, or DPP4, that breaks down gluten and casein. The DPP4 can be damaged by mercury, whether from amalgam fillings, vaccines, or environmental toxicity such as produced by coal-burning power plants. If the gluten and casein (which are found in bread, pasta, tortillas, milk, cheese, ice cream, and other dairy products) are only partially broken down, they create partial proteins, or peptides, that are similar to opiates. These peptides act like morphine once they are in the bloodstream, creating a high and then a low, and leading to cravings for more gluten and casein-containing foods, thus perpetuating the cycle. Additionally, incomplete digestion of these proteins damages the villi of the small intestine, potentially causing inflammation, digestive discomfort, malabsorption, and nutrient deficiencies. Remember, a damaged gut lining, or leaky gut, often results in a number of other food allergies and intolerances.

When food is not properly broken down and absorbed, the unfriendly gut bacteria and yeasts feed off of the undigested food particles and grow out of balance. These organisms can cause mood changes and increased cravings for sweet and refined foods. When this occurs, the child's digestive tract becomes so irritated and inflamed that he simply does not want to eat. In this case, you might consider an Elimination Diet (see our website, www .WholeLifeNutrition.net, and our book *The Elimination Diet* for more information), or a specific diet for rebalancing the gut, such as the GAPS diet or Specific Carbohydrate Diet. Supporting the digestive system with enzymes, high-quality probiotics, and amino acid supplements is also very beneficial. We usually recommend an amino acid powder that can be mixed with smoothies for children who need the extra support; you can go to our website for product recommendations. Another great way to offer some of these digestive-supporting nutrients is by

serving raw kombucha, a pleasing fizzy, fermented beverage. Our children consider this "soda" and love to drink it! Homemade bone broths and raw sauerkraut also offer many gut-healing nutrients, and they should be consumed daily for best results. For more information, see "Healing the Gut" (page 18) to help rebalance your child's digestive system.

A zinc deficiency can also be at the root of extreme picky-eating behaviors. Zinc is needed to properly taste and smell things. If a child has an altered sense of taste and smell, she may develop picky eating habits. The body's demand for zinc increases during pregnancy, and zinc deficiencies can be passed down from mother to child. Second, third, and subsequent children are at higher risk if the mother did not consume or absorb enough zinc from her diet. You may want to consider talking to your health-care provider about zinc supplementation until the child's diet contains enough zinc-rich foods.

When digestion is supported and nutrient deficiencies are addressed, do a complete kitchen overhaul: eliminate all gluten and casein foods from your house and any other unhealthy foods lingering in the pantry, refrigerator, and freezer. Start by offering healthier gluten-free, casein-free versions of what the children know and then move on to unfamiliar foods. They may protest, scream, cry, and not eat much for a week or more. This is especially true of a child who is addicted to gluten and casein foods.

Since bacteria in the gut respond to the types of food we eat, there may be a die-off of unfriendly bacteria and yeasts when the diet is drastically changed. This is a good thing. Eventually the child will eat, even if just part of the whole meal. It is easy to give your children whatever they will eat, because of the false notion that something is better than nothing. This just encourages children to continue eating a limited number of foods, many of which lack essential nutrients or are high in sugar. Long-term health and well-being are the goals, not temporary satiation. Children are naturally adaptable and quick to heal, so once the process has begun, you'll begin to see results almost immediately.

Education Is Key

Invariably, children will be exposed to the billion-dollar snack-food industry, whether through TV, school, or friends. Forbidding these foods can backfire and cause binging later on, but if instead your children are educated about what those foods really are, where they come from, and how they injure our bodies, they can make empowered choices about the food they eat.

So, what can we do as parents? If we keep junk food out of our children's diet for as long as possible, their taste buds will be set to prefer healthy foods over junk food later on. We can educate our older children on the importance of eating organic food, non-GMO food, and a healthy diet, giving them the tools to make healthy choices when they are away from home. It is important to make the lesson positive and inspirational, keeping their interest and energy focused on the benefits of eating nourishing meals.

The time to begin educating your children depends on their development. A child's nature is to see the good in the world, and we want to help each one develop in that bubble for as long as possible. Once the child is ready to explore global situations and see how other people live, he will also be ready for detailed information on food and nutrition. For our family, this has seemed to occur between seven and nine years of age. At this time, we discuss the details of organic versus nonorganic food, and how our planet is affected by these different growing methods. We discuss what genetically modified foods are, and what we can do to *not* support that industry. We explain about the factory farming of animals, which is something that can create a lot of fear in young children, so make sure your child is ready for this before delving into it. Other points of discussion can be how eating a diet rich in fruits and vegetables prevents disease—particularly cancer—and how our food choices affect our planet and the

people living on it. Education early on will empower your children to say no to food choices that don't support their individual health and the health and well-being of our planet.

A HOME ENVIRONMENT FOR HEALTH

We are often asked how we get our children to eat a healthy, nourishing diet. We have found that by having only foods available in our home that we are comfortable with our children eating at any point in the day, our children will naturally consume a diet that is good for them. This is the key factor in eliminating food battles. *No food to battle over, no battle.*

Snacking

If our children are hungry for a snack, they reach into the freezer and serve themselves a bowl of frozen organic berries and cherries, they cut up apples and carrots, or they eat whatever fruit we have ripe in our fruit basket. I also keep a few jars of soaked and dehydrated nuts on the counter for them to grab at any time. Occasionally, I have other homemade snacks on hand for them (see the "Snacks and Treats" chapter).

If your children are hungry before dinner and the meal is not quite ready yet, consider offering raw vegetables such as carrot and celery sticks or raw cauliflower and broccoli florets. A small bowl of raw sauerkraut is also a great food to keep them busy. These foods will fill them up slightly for a short time, and then they will actually increase their appetites and digestion for the meal ahead of them.

Snacking before bedtime can be a tricky thing. If your children don't eat a meal, and then ask for a bedtime snack and get it from you, the message they are receiving is that it is okay not to eat dinner. This can set up a cycle whereby the parents work hard to create healthy meals; the children don't eat them, and then they get hungry before bed. Breaking that cycle may be hard at first, but your children will learn to eat dinner as long as they know there won't be any more bedtime snacks.

Family Mealtimes

Food is the source of many family traditions. Family mealtimes nurture connectivity and security among family members. Research shows that children who participate in family meals are more likely to eat a balanced diet full of fresh fruits and vegetables, they are generally happier with higher self-esteem, and they have lower obesity rates.

It is important to begin the family mealtimes during your child's infancy. All our babies snuggled in our arms at the dinner table from the time they were newborns. When they were able to sit up, we put them in a chair that hooked onto the dinner table. Babies who don't yet have teeth and are not eating can be given a raw carrot or celery stick to teethe on. As soon as our first daughter was eating solid foods, we fed her part of our meal. So, if I was making a soup with carrots, she had mashed steamed carrots.

Children learn to love food by eating with us and watching what and how we eat. In fact, parents are the best role models for establishing healthy eating behaviors. Humans are social creatures and want to feel included. If parents prepare and enjoy eating nourishing foods at every meal, children will eventually want to try those same foods—they don't want to feel excluded! Just make sure never to force your children into eating anything—that just sets up a separation between parent and child. A child who is a picky eater can eventually enjoy a diverse array of healthy foods; it may just take some time and patience.

Kids in the Kitchen

Involving your children in the kitchen is key to developing a love of food. This is a wonderful time to have them participate in preparing family meals. Young children, even toddlers, can help set the table and bring dishes of food to the table. They can even participate in planning the meal. As they grocery-shop or garden with you, they begin to know individual ingredients and where food comes from. Having them help prepare a meal creates a lot of excitement and an eagerness to eat the finished product. It may seem to take more energy at first, but it pays off in the long run for everyone to be working as a team.

Children as young as two years old can help with a variety of tasks. When our oldest daughter was about two and a half years old, I gave her a small paring knife and a pile of green beans to trim. I set the pot right next to her for her to fill as she cut them. She was thrilled with this task. By the time she was nine years old, she was cooking entire meals, even creating her own recipes (that actually tasted good).

A three-year-old can keep busy peeling carrots or potatoes while an older child chops the vegetables. We have let all our children cook at the stove from an early age. They have all burned themselves once—and only once. That one time is enough to learn how to safely navigate in front of a hot stove. A three-year-old will love to participate in sautéing vegetables. Older children can help measure ingredients for baking and whisk ingredients together. A child who is reading can read a recipe to you as you cook. If you want to double a recipe, this is the perfect time for a math lesson! Involving your children in the menu planning, grocery shopping, and meal preparation establishes an environment for healthy eating and provides a strong sense of belonging.

What's Served Is Served

We don't make special meals for our children. If they don't like what we make, they don't have to eat. We don't even ask them what they want for breakfast, lunch, or dinner. We just make a meal and serve it. We live in a time of steady food supply. Your child won't go hungry if she doesn't eat much one night or occasionally skips a meal. Usually, there is still something at the table she will eat, like steamed broccoli or cooked quinoa. Just make sure that everything you are serving is nutrient-dense so that your children get the most out of what they do eat.

Sometimes, mealtime battles erupt when parents are overly concerned with what their children are or are not eating. Instead of concentrating on the food

> If you have young children, then consider serving dinner by 5 or 5:30 P.M. If children get tired and over-hungry, chances are they won't eat or will display more picky-eating behaviors.

and who is eating what at your mealtimes, focus on something completely different, such as what each family member did that day. There are so many things to discuss other than the food. This is a time for everyone to slow down and connect with others, so simply relax and know that the children are getting enough food. Most of the time, if children don't eat much for dinner in an evening, they will eat a large breakfast the next morning.

By letting your children set the pace for their eating, you empower them, allowing them to learn how to control their own intrinsic metabolism and eating patterns. If we parents constantly cater to our children's food preferences, we rob them of the opportunity to expand their horizons of likes and dislikes. Some evenings, a child might not be hungry enough to try a new food whereas other times he may be so hungry that he will eat anything.

MAKE IT A LIFESTYLE!

We are all doing the best we can to raise our children, given the information we have and our available resources. The more information you can gather about food and nutrition, the more educated you are to make changes and stick with them. Searching out local health food stores, food co-ops, organic farmers, and online sources of ingredients will make eating nourishing food a lifestyle. By serving and consuming a nutrient-dense whole foods diet, as well as reducing chemical exposure and rebalancing the gut, you'll give your body and those of your children the best chance to not only survive but also to thrive! Our children learn so much from us. Not only do they learn to eat by watching us but they also learn the process of positive change and growth as we all journey through life.

Packing a Healthy Lunchbox

A healthy school lunch is essential for building health and resilience in a growing child. Most hot school lunches don't provide the necessary vitamins, minerals, and phytochemicals in an easily digestible and absorbable form. Plus, they are usually full of chemicals, pesticides, and herbicide residues; are made from GMO ingredients; and may contain too much sodium, refined oils, and refined carbohydrates. Luckily, though, the school-lunch scene is beginning to change as more and more parents and health-care practitioners demand something different for our children.

There are so many ways to quickly pack a school lunch, even without bread! In fact, bread is *not* at all a necessary component of a healthy lunch. It has become so ingrained that we need to have bread for sandwiches that it can be difficult to think of other options. Although a few slices of homemade bread can sure come in handy once in a while, our goal here is to emphasize other lunchbox ideas— ones that are healthy and naturally gluten-free. Visit our website, www.NourishingMeals.com, to print out our colorful "Packing a Healthy School Lunch" chart. Post it on your refrigerator and let your children learn how to pack their own balanced lunches. They will be more likely to eat what they pack themselves.

"GROWING" FOODS

The following ideas are nutrient-dense, "growing" foods our children frequently pack into their lunchboxes. We always have four child-size thermos bottles clean and ready to be used for school lunches. Leftover soups and stews, or cooked beans and a whole grain, can form the foundation of a healthy school lunch.

- Lentil and vegetable soup
- Chicken vegetable soup
- Grass-Fed Beef Chili (page 186)
- Reheated frittata
- Black beans and brown rice
- Curried vegetables and chickpeas over quinoa
- Organic turkey slices and raw cheese wrapped in a lettuce leaf
- Quinoa and bean salad
- Smoked salmon
- Hard-boiled pastured eggs
- Chicken salad wrapped in a lettuce leaf (see page 366)
- Container of homemade hummus (see page 343)
- Nutty granola (see page 80)
- Nori rolls with sticky brown rice, salmon, and carrots
- Quesadilla made from organic refried beans, pastured raw cheese, and organic sprouted corn tortillas

We have a kitchen drawer full of different-size stainless steel and glass containers for our children to pack fresh fruits and vegetables into. It really helps to have a good number of these containers handy to make lunch packing go smoothly. We even have a few very small stainless steel containers for our children to pack dips for apples, carrots, and celery sticks. Go to www.LifeWithoutPlastic.com to shop for healthy plastic-free food storage containers.

Fresh Fruits and Vegetables

We use only organic produce in our house, and we encourage you, for the long-term health of your children, to use only organic produce or produce from farms that use organic farming practices, though they may not be certified as organic.

- Sliced cucumbers
- Carrot sticks
- Celery sticks
- Lettuce leaves
- Napa cabbage leaves
- Apple slices
- Orange slices
- Bananas
- Fresh berries
- Grapes
- Raw Sauerkraut (page 472)
- Raw Sour Dill Pickles (page 477)

High-Quality Fats

High-quality fat is needed for blood sugar stabilization, as well as for proper brain function both in and out of school. It's important to include a small amount in every lunch for your child.

- Mashed avocado with lime and sea salt
- Organic butter from grass-fed cows

- Hard- or soft-boiled eggs from organic, pastured hens
- Raw walnuts
- Raw macadamia nuts
- Coconut oil truffle
- Bone broth heated with cooked beans, fish, rice, or vegetables
- Chia seed and coconut fruit smoothie
- Soaked almond smoothie
- Raw Vanilla White Chocolates (page 389)

Snacks and Treats

Sugar is a stimulant that can lead to hyperactivity and learning impairment in children. Choose a treat made from whole foods that is naturally sweetened. The dessert recipes in this book use small amounts of natural sweeteners, such as coconut sugar, maple syrup, or honey, along with other whole food ingredients to create nutrient-packed sweet treats.

- Raisins
- Dried mango
- Homemade naturally sweetened cookie
- Homemade yogurt topped with berries
- Candied nuts
- Homemade popcorn cooked in coconut oil
- Nut-and-date energy ball

therecipes

Getting Started

What does a kitchen that produces nourishing meals look like? Imagine opening your pantry to find jars of whole grains, dried beans, dried fruits, homemade canned jams, applesauce, canned organic coconut milk, coconut flour, and whole-grain gluten-free flours lining your shelves. A box of potatoes and yams sits on your pantry floor. Imagine opening your refrigerator, also, to find drawers stocked with leafy greens; organic pastured butter and eggs on the door shelf; pure maple syrup, nut butters, and homemade cultured vegetables on the top shelf; organic apples in the bottom drawer; and a leftover pot of soup on the main shelf. In the freezer, you find containers of organic berries and other fruits, organic raw nuts, almond flour, grass-fed meats, and pastured poultry. On your kitchen counter, you see a small bowl of raw almonds soaking, a jar of bubbling gluten-free sourdough starter, a large bowl of dried beans being reconstituted, a jar of lentils sprouting, a small basket of onions and garlic, and a large basket of fresh organic fruit. Next to the stove, you find a small container of unrefined sea salt, a black pepper grinder, a big jar of organic virgin coconut oil, and a bottle of extra-virgin olive oil. Your cabinets are full of fresh organic spices, dried herbs, organic vinegars, and a jar of local raw honey. This is what our kitchen looks like; it's what works for us. Maybe some of these things might work for you, too? Choose one aspect of this kitchen that excites you most, and work on achieving that first. Set a pace of dietary change that feels right to you.

NO CALORIC INFORMATION?

You'll notice that we don't provide caloric information with the recipes. Calories are only a small fraction of the overall picture of health. What's most important is the quality of your food, not the quantity. Your body functions properly when you have all the necessary vitamins, minerals, and phytochemicals in your daily diet. Managing weight can be effortless when you combine regular exercise with a plant-rich, organic, whole foods diet.

But how do we know if we are getting the recommended daily amounts of these nutrients? Here's the thing: we all have this intrinsic, intuitive process with food and when given the opportunity, we choose the exact foods we need, on a daily basis. One day you may crave raw cauliflower, and the next day it may cause you to gag. We've witnessed our children do this, too. Some weeks, all the children want to eat is seaweed, and at other times they want nothing to do with it. Listen to these cues for certain foods—they are telling you what your body really needs. This is far more important than regulating caloric intake.

GUIDE TO INGREDIENTS

The following are commonly used ingredients in these recipes. Most items can be found at your local health food store or can be ordered in bulk online. In fact, to save money, we order many of these products either in bulk through our local food co-op or through online food-buying companies, such as Azure Standard. Their larger quantities of dried foods often come in paper bags, which easily biodegrade, cutting down on waste.

Fresh Organic Produce

Organic produce usually takes up most of the space in our shopping carts and in our refrigerator. We like to purchase perishable vegetables more frequently, like lettuce, parsley, and cilantro. Root vegetables and tubers, such as yams, carrots, potatoes, rutabagas, and beets, can be purchased less frequently because they store for long periods of time. For optimal levels of nutrients, it is best to consume produce that is in season. This way you are consuming the majority of your food from local sources—meaning it didn't have to travel very far to get from farm to plate, and hence it will be fresher. In the spring, look for baby salad greens, kale, collards, asparagus, radishes, strawberries, garlic greens, and peas. In the summer, look for all types of stone fruits, melons, berries, cucumbers, green beans, corn, bell peppers, fresh onions, zucchini, tomatoes, and carrots. In the fall, look for beets, carrots, onions, garlic, broccoli, cauliflower, kale, collards, mustard greens, lettuces, apples, and pears. In the winter, use root crops that you've stored from the fall, such as rutabagas, turnips, potatoes, carrots, celery root, and sweet potatoes, as well as cabbages, onions, and winter squash.

Grass-Fed Meats and Organic Poultry

Most meat you buy at the grocery store or eat in a restaurant contains varying amounts of antibiotic and hormone residues; dyes and other additives; and has often been irradiated. With the rise in consciousness of the way most meat and poultry is mass-produced, people today are choosing sustainably raised animals instead. With this rise in demand, new farms are popping up all over the country. It is likely you have a number of very small farms near you where you can directly buy whole chickens or cuts of beef, pork, or lamb. Ask around for contact information or search websites like www.EatWild.com or www.LocalHarvest.

Animals raised on organic pastureland have meat that is more nutritious and contains a more even balance of omega-3 and omega-6 fatty acids. The animals are usually healthier, having required little or no antibiotics, and their waste has been composted and turned back into the earth, instead of polluting the water supply and nearby farms. Since their meat is more nutrient-dense, you'll find that you don't need to eat as much of it, thereby supporting the environment and everyone's health. Having an extra freezer is ideal for storing meat you buy in large quantities directly from a farm. It is best to use frozen meat within a year of purchasing it.

Eggs

Allergies and sensitivities to eggs are certainly on the rise, but for many, eggs still offer an excellent source of nutrition. Large-scale egg production creates eggs that are far less nutritious than their pastured counterparts. Chickens are often fed genetically engineered grains that have arsenic and antibiotics added to them, so as to keep parasites and disease at bay. Raising backyard egg-laying chickens is becoming quite popular as a healthy source of eggs, when it's possible in your neighborhood. You can also check your local food co-op, farmer's market, or small family farms for pastured eggs—or eggs from chickens that are raised outdoors and fed vegetable scraps and minimal organic grains. Pastured eggs have dark orange yolks and are far richer in nutrients such as vitamins E, D, and A, as well as omega-3 fatty acids. They may cost more than "free range" or organic eggs, but you'll end up saving money in the long run because you won't need to spend as much on expensive vitamin supplements!

Dairy

While some adults and children—especially of northern European decent—can digest dairy products, the vast majority of others cannot, especially those with damaged upper intestines. It is actually quite common for the body to recognize dairy proteins as foreign and to launch an immune attack against them. Dairy products are not a necessary component of a healthy diet, but if you choose to eat them or feed them to your children, it is important to purchase the healthiest forms. Dairy products that undergo a lot of processing, such as through pasteurization and homogenization, are far less digestible and less nutritious than raw or fermented dairy products.

In fact, research shows that pasteurizing milk causes the loss of key nutrients, either through destruction of carrier proteins or destruction of nutrients themselves. Vitamin C, iron, calcium, vitamin A, folate, B_6, and B_{12} are all affected. Homogenization breaks apart larger fat molecules into smaller ones; these smaller fat particles present a dramatically increased surface area onto which allergenic milk proteins can adhere to. With raw milk, many of the antigenic proteins are located inside the casein micelles, whereas in homogenized milk, the amount of exposed antigenic proteins is reported to increase. These small fat particles, with their attached casein proteins, might be a large contributor to the general increase in inflammatory diseases, food allergies, and heart disease.

If possible, find a local source of raw milk that is produced from cows or goats that have been raised on grasses. If you can't find raw milk, the next best thing is to buy fermented organic dairy products from milk that was not homogenized—like "cream on the top" yogurt. It is important to note that many people feel better when they remove dairy from their diets, as their immune systems have often been programmed from a young age to the dairy proteins found in pasteurized milk. This includes the removal of raw milk, too; once the immune system has been programmed, it can be difficult to tolerate any type of dairy. If you are looking for an alternative to cow's milk, check out our "Beverages" chapter for homemade dairy-free milk and kefir recipes.

Gluten-Free Whole Grains

You can find a variety of gluten-free whole grains in the bulk section of your local food co-op or health food store, but you need to be careful about cross-contamination. Some stores are knowledgeable and place the containers of wheat berries and wheat flours away from everything else—but most do not. Flour dust can linger in the air and contaminate surrounding bins. We prefer to order organic quinoa and brown rice in 25-pound bags from Azure Standard. Millet, raw buckwheat groats, and rolled oats need to be purchased from a place that offers certified gluten-free versions, such as Bob's Red Mill. Place your grains in large glass jars and store them in a cool, dark pantry where they will keep for up to nine months.

The optimal way to prepare grains is to soak them for 12 to 24 hours in warm water with the addition of something acidic, such as lemon juice, raw apple cider vinegar, whey, or fermented dairy. Doing this will help neutralize the phytic acid and allow for better absorption of minerals such as iron, zinc, calcium, and magnesium. See the "Whole Grains and Noodles" chapter for details on how to soak and cook whole grains.

Legumes

We buy dried beans in bulk from our local food co-op or in 25-pound bags from Azure Standard. For optimal nutrient availability, it is best to soak the dried beans in warm water for 8 to 48 hours. Soaking them helps to neutralize the phytic acid, as well as eliminate most of the lectins—proteins abundant in uncooked beans and grains that are believed to be natural insecticides. Lectins can sometimes be hard on the digestive tract if not broken down before consuming. Soaking and cooking, as well as having adequate stomach acid and a healthy population of friendly bacteria in your gut, all help to break down the lectins found in beans and whole grains.

To cook soaked dried beans, drain off the soaking water, place the beans in a large pot, and cover with fresh water; add one strip of kombu seaweed. Bring the beans to a boil, then reduce the heat to low and simmer until soft. Most beans take 45 minutes to 2 hours of cooking time. You'll know when they are done if they mash easily in your mouth. Don't add salt or acids, such as vinegar or tomatoes, during cooking, as this can inhibit the beans from cooking properly. We always add salt and acids to beans after they are cooked, and then simmer them for an extra 20 to 30 minutes to allow the flavors to meld.

For a higher protein content and even better nutrient profile you can sprout your beans after soaking and then slow-cook them. This changes the ratio of starches and protein. If you or your child has weak digestion and multiple nutrient deficiency symptoms, then sprouting is the best route to go when preparing dried beans. If you are new to soaking and sprouting beans, then start with lentils—they are one of the fastest legumes to sprout! For more details on cooking legumes, refer to our first book, *The Whole Life Nutrition Cookbook.*

Nuts and Seeds

Raw organic nuts and seeds are best purchased in bulk from your local food co-op or health food store. Make sure the store you are buying from has a high turnover rate; if not, they could be rancid. We prefer to buy 30-pound boxes of raw organic, unpasteurized almonds directly from farms in California. We order 10 pounds of chia seeds at a time, and pour some into a quart jar for our refrigerator and store the remaining seeds in our freezer until ready to use. Other nuts and seeds we buy in bulk though our local food co-op and store them in our freezer until ready to use.

For optimal nutrient availability and digestibility, soak your nuts and seeds in warm filtered water for 8 to 24 hours (less time for seeds, more for nuts), then rinse and drain, and dehydrate at 110 to 115°F until crisp, usually 24 to 48 hours. Check them for doneness by eating a few; if they don't feel crisp, let them dehydrate an hour or two longer. Dehydrated nuts and seeds are slightly crispier and crunchier compared to plain raw nuts and seeds—they make for a delicious and nutritious snack that's perfect for growing children!

Like grains and beans, nuts and seeds contain phytic acid, as well as enzyme inhibitors, which

lock down the enzymes and nutrients until the seed is ready to germinate. By soaking your nuts and seeds in warm water, you are essentially mimicking the process of nature. Dehydrating them makes them "shelf stable" and usable for all recipes that call for raw nuts and seeds. This process creates a highly digestible nut or seed that is rich in live enzymes! We store jars of soaked and dehydrated nuts on our kitchen counter so our children can have access to a quick, nutritious snack, and so we can use them in recipes. They will keep for about a month at room temperature or about six months in the refrigerator. Roasting the nuts and seeds is another way to reduce the phytic acid and enzyme inhibitors, though soaking seems to work more efficiently. The remainder of our nuts and seeds are stored in the refrigerator or freezer until we have time to soak and dehydrate, or to roast them. Note that chia and flax seeds should not be soaked and dehydrated before using, as they create a thick gel when exposed to liquid.

Gluten-Free Flours

Most gluten-free flours can be found at your local health food store or food co-op. They come in small packages and are stocked in the baking section. To reduce wasteful packaging, consider ordering the flours directly from the mill in 25-pound paper bags. You can use a kitchen scale and divvy up the flour among your friends.

If you want to take your health one step further, consider using sprouted gluten-free flours in cookies, bars, and breads, thereby offering even more nutrients than when made with regular whole-grain flours. Sprouted flours can be replaced in equal quantities for non-sprouted flours. For most flours, the flavor does not change with the sprouting, but for some flours, such as sprouted chickpea flour, the flavor gets better with sprouting. Sprouting wakes up the grain for germination, which increases the nutrients, reduces the phytic acid, and changes the starches into a more digestible form. If you are making sourdough breads, rolls, pancakes, and the like, there is no need to buy sprouted flours—making a sourdough starter renders the grain flours digestible with a high nutrient availability. Additionally, when using blanched nut flours or coconut flour, there is no need for soaking or sprouting.

Fats and Oils

Most of our recipes call for either organic virgin coconut oil or organic extra-virgin olive oil. Coconut oil is rich in medium-chain triglycerides, such as caprylic, capric, and lauric acids, which help boost your metabolism and strengthen your immune system. Medium-chain triglycerides (MCTs) are absorbed differently from how long-chain fatty acids are. In fact, in weight-loss trials, there is evidence that diets higher in medium-chain triglycerides can contribute to greater fat loss. Coconut oil is more stable at higher temperatures than olive oil, but we still use olive oil on occasion for roasting veggies.

When purchasing olive oil, look for ones that are labeled "extra virgin" and preferably are organic. A 2004 article in the *Journal of Nutrition* noted that potent plant chemicals in the olive oil—specifically protocatechuic acid and oleuropein—protect blood vessels and cholesterol from oxidative damage by signaling the genes to express more powerful antioxidant enzymes like glutathione reductase and glutathione peroxidase. When comparing types and qualities of olive oils, researchers found that extra-virgin high-quality oils with higher phenolic compounds have a much more profound beneficial effect than the lower-quality, more refined oils.

Some members of our family also use organic pastured butter on occasion. "Pastured" means that the cows graze on grasses instead of eating grains. This makes their milk and butterfat a good source of nutrients such as vitamins A and K_2, allowing proper utilization of both calcium and phosphorous and leading to strong bones and teeth. Nevertheless, given the high levels of environmental toxicity in the world, it is best to limit your consumption of butter—even organic pastured butter—because toxins are found in the highest amounts in the fats of animals. To replace butter in recipes such as those for biscuits and piecrusts, try using organic palm shortening. High-quality organic extra-virgin olive oil, organic virgin coconut oil, and organic palm shortening can all be found at your local food co-op or health food store.

Vinegars

Raw apple cider vinegar and raw coconut vinegar are some of the healthiest vinegars to use. In fact, taking a spoonful before a meal can improve digestion. These are living foods, rich in live enzymes that can help digest your meal. We use vinegar weekly for our homemade salad dressings and also medicinally to steep herbs in.

Wine vinegars can also make a nice addition to your pantry. Adding a tablespoon or two to a finished bean soup can boost flavors without the need for more salt. Be sure to purchase organic wine and apple cider vinegars, as grapes and apples are routinely sprayed with a variety of toxic chemicals.

Water

We recommend using reverse osmosis (RO) water or the Berkey Water Filtration system, or finding a source of natural spring water and driving there weekly with five-gallon glass jugs to fill up. All water used in this book should be pure—not city tap water—filtered or spring water.

Natural Sweeteners

Most natural sweeteners can be found at your local health food store or food co-op. If you live in an area where maple syrup is produced, search out a small local farm and purchase directly from them. Every town has a few beekeepers to buy directly from, too. Look for a place that sells raw honey, as the glycemic index is generally lower and it contains more nutrients. Medjool dates can be an excellent natural sweetener—high in minerals and natural fibers to slow absorption of sugars into the bloodstream. As an alternative to granulated white sugar, we use coconut sugar, another low-glycemic sweetener. For a more detailed look into natural sweeteners, see our "Desserts" chapter.

Tomato Products

Canned tomato products often contain bisphenol A (BPA), a hormone-disrupting chemical that's used to seal the linings of cans. It has been shown that BPA can seep into the food in the can, so it's best to avoid BPA. Instead, we use freshly diced tomatoes in most recipes. We like to freeze whole Roma (plum) tomatoes in the summertime to use during the winter months. Simply let a few thaw on your counter for 10 minutes, then dice them to add to your soups. Also, look for organic tomato sauce and tomato paste packed in glass jars at your local food co-op or health food store—Bionaturae is a brand we like to use.

Coconut Milk

Coconut milk is rich and thick, perfect for making grain-free cakes or puddings and curries. We prefer to make our own coconut milk from dried, shredded coconut. Canned coconut milk is also a good choice, as it is less processed than the milk found in cartons and contains only coconut milk (and usually a small amount of guar gum). To avoid the BPA in cans, though, we use the Native Forest brand.

Chocolate

It's incredibly important to purchase organic chocolate! Cacao plants, from which chocolate is made, are grown in tropical regions by farmers using heavy amounts of damaging pesticides and often employing child labor. Look for the fair-trade organic label when purchasing your chocolate.

I use a few different forms of chocolate for baking and in raw desserts. Dagoba's bittersweet is perfect for baking; I store it in my freezer until I'm ready to use it. I also prefer using raw cacao powder instead of roasted, as it is higher in antioxidants and lower in caffeine. Make sure the company you purchase the cacao power from is gluten-free, to avoid cross-contamination. We also use dark chocolate chips and cacao nibs from gluten-free companies for our baking and special snacks. If you want to avoid soy products, look for a company that doesn't use soy lecithin.

Extracts and Flavorings

You'll notice that some of our recipes call for almond flavoring or vanilla extract. We use organic almond flavoring, which can be found in the baking section of your local health food store or food co-op. A small amount goes a long way! And placing a few organic vanilla beans in a jar of organic vodka and letting that sit for a few months is a way to make homemade vanilla extract. Nonalcoholic vanilla extract is made using a glycerin extract and this is ideal for raw desserts because the alcohol won't get cooked off. Organic raw vanilla powder is another staple ingredient in our spice cabinet—we use it in raw desserts, homemade ice cream, and smoothies to elevate the flavors and add natural sweetness.

Unrefined Sea Salt

Be sure to purchase sea salt that is unrefined. This means that all the minerals are still in the salt. Don't worry about having to get your iodine from commercial salt; the iodine in commercial salt is poorly absorbed by the body, so it's better to get it from natural food sources like seaweed, yogurt, and turkey. Pink Himalayan salt or Real Salt are good choices. For baking, use a fine-grained sea salt; using coarse sea salt will alter the amount of sodium in the recipe. However, I like to use coarse sea salt for sprinkling into a pot of cooking soup or on top of meats before roasting. We also like to use a natural salt seasoning called Herbamare; if you can't find Herbamare in your local grocery, use my recipe for a Homemade Herbed Sea Salt version on page 484. This recipe calls for steeping organic herbs and vegetables in unrefined sea salt, creating a flavorful seasoning that can be used in soups, meat dishes, beans, or whole-grain salads.

Baking Powder

Baking powder is baking soda combined with some acid salts and cornstarch, and so sometimes it can contain gluten and aluminum. Rumford brand is gluten-free and the cornstarch they use is GMO-free. However, you can easily make your own cornstarch-free baking powder simply by mixing two parts arrowroot powder, two parts cream of tartar, and one part baking soda. Place the homemade baking powder in a glass jar and label it!

ESSENTIAL KITCHEN EQUIPMENT

Creating great recipes requires a few specific tools. These tools are all items that I use daily in my kitchen and that I find essential in any working kitchen.

High-Powered Blender

All the recipes in this book requiring a blender were developed using a high-powered blender such as a Vitamix or Blendtec. High-powered blenders can make smooth and creamy homemade "ice cream," frozen fruit smoothies, and green smoothies. These high-powered blenders have strong motors that can blend very thick sauces or fillings to a smooth, creamy consistency. They also work well breaking down tough greens into a pleasant, fine-textured green smoothie. Some of the recipes indicate that a regular blender can be used, while other recipes simply *cannot* be made without a high-powered blender (such as the Raw Blueberry Cheesecake, page 405). We highly recommend obtaining a high-powered blender and considering it an investment in your health.

Immersion Blender

This is a relatively inexpensive hand-held blender that works well for quickly pureeing cream soups or blending a small amount of ingredients, such as salad dressings. I recommend buying a stainless steel immersion blender if you plan to use it for hot soups—otherwise, the plastic will leach chemicals into your hot soup.

Food Processor

For making nut-based truffles or raw nut crusts, a food processor is essential. I also use the food processor to make fish or bean burgers and meatballs, and to mince vegetables. When fitted with the slicing or grating disk, a food processor can also be used to thinly slice or grate a variety of vegetables in very little time. I use a 14-cup Cuisinart Food Processor, although the 11-cup size will work for all of these recipes as well.

Food Dehydrator

A food dehydrator is essential if you are preparing nuts and seeds for optimal digestibility, meaning that they are soaked and then dehydrated before being used in recipes or eaten as a snack. You can also soak, sprout, and dehydrate whole grains, and then grind them into flour. We get the most use out of our dehydrator in late summer and early autumn, when fresh produce is at its peak. Kale chips, dried tomatoes, and homemade fruit leathers are always being made! The Excalibur dehydrator is one of the best on the market, but the American Harvest works just as well and comes with a cheaper price tag. If you are looking to avoid plastic, then the Excalibur is your best bet.

Pots and Pans

I use both stainless steel and cast-iron pots and pans. Many of my recipes suggest using a deep 11-inch skillet—indeed, I find this pan to be one of the most convenient and useful for any number of recipes. I also recommend having a good-quality stockpot, eight-quart capacity or larger. We usually cook our grains in two- or three-quart pots. Small skillets are also very useful. When purchasing stainless steel pans, make sure the bottom has a thick aluminum core. This prevents food, such as whole grains and pancakes, from sticking and burning. We never recommend using nonstick pots and pans. When heated, these pans release toxic gases, some of which have been found to be carcinogenic.

Stoneware Baking Pans

I bake all my muffins and most of my quickbreads using stoneware molds. This type of cookware never sticks, it heats evenly, and it cleans up quickly. I have a stoneware muffin pan, mini-loaf pan (four mini loaves), Bundt pan, cookie sheet, and pizza stone. I use the Pampered Chef brand, which is relatively inexpensive. This type of cookware is earth-friendly, meaning that when the time comes for it to break, it will biodegrade because it is made of uncoated clay.

Glass Baking Pans

For all other baking and roasting, I use glass Pyrex pans. I have a few 9 by 13-inch pans, as well as one 10 by 14-inch pan. The 8-inch square pans work well for baking small cakes and bars. All the pie plates I use are glass as well. I have a few deep-dish and a few regular pie plates in a range of sizes; they are great for roasting small batches of nuts, too.

Stainless Steel Baking Pans

I have a large stainless steel jelly-roll pan for a variety of purposes, from roasting homemade oven fries to baking cookies and flatbreads. The size I use is 11 by 17 inches. I also have a few stainless steel 9-inch round cake pans for baking layer cakes.

Oven Thermometer

Since correct baking temperature is crucial to a successful end product, a simple oven thermometer is essential. They cost around $5. Many ovens, even newer ones, can be off, sometimes by as much as 25 degrees. Use the oven thermometer to adjust the temperature as needed.

High-Quality Knives

Heavy-duty, sharp knives are indispensable for anyone who cooks regularly. I recommend going to your local kitchen store and checking out a few different brands. They should be comfortable for the size of your hand. I like the brand Wusthof. Since good-quality knives can be a bit pricy, try adding just one at a time.

Liquid Glass Measures

I use everything from a 1-cup to an 8-cup liquid glass measure. It is important to always measure your liquid ingredients in a liquid measure, and to measure your dry ingredients in a dry measuring cup. I use the Pyrex brand and always stick with glass. When measuring hot liquids, it is really important to use glass, and not plastic, as the plastic can leach toxic chemicals into your food.

Garlic Press

I use crushed garlic in most of my recipes calling for garlic. I use a heavy-duty stainless steel garlic press; the cheaper ones tend to break easily, creating unnecessary waste. The brand I use and highly recommend is Rosle. This garlic press is so sturdy that you don't need to peel the garlic before putting it into the press, saving a lot of time.

Microplane

This is an indispensable grating tool. I use mine to grate lemon or orange zest, fresh ginger, and nutmeg.

Fine-Mesh Strainer

Along with a few colanders for draining noodles or chicken stock, I use a fine-mesh strainer for rinsing small grains, such as quinoa and amaranth. A fine-mesh strainer also works well for straining the pulp from homemade raw almond milk.

Food Storage

We store all our leftover food in glass storage containers. I also have a number of small stainless steel containers for packing lunches, as well as a few larger ones for food storage. Each child also has his or her own small stainless steel thermos for packing hot soup or warm grains and beans in school lunches.

allergen key

All of the recipes in the following chapters have symbols in the headnotes to let you know which allergens they are free of. It's important for you to check the actual products you use in each recipe for cross-contamination.

Gluten ⬚: All of the recipes in this book are gluten-free. This symbol is simply a reminder that there is no wheat, barley, rye, or spelt in the recipe.

Grains ⬚: The recipe contains no gluten-free grains, such as rice, corn, oats, millet, sorghum, and teff, as well as no pseudo-grains (seeds of plants that act like grains in the body), such as buckwheat, quinoa, amaranth, and wild rice.

Dairy ⬚: The recipe contains no animal milk, such as goat's or cow's milk, nor the products made from them, such as yogurt, kefir, butter, or cheese.

Soy ⬚: The recipe contains no soy products, such as edamame, soy sauce or tamari, soy-based miso, tofu, tempeh, soy milk, or soy flour. Some of my recipes call for coconut aminos or wheat-free tamari; if you are avoiding soy, use the coconut aminos (made from the sap of the coconut palm) as a substitute for the tamari.

Eggs ⬚: The recipe contains no eggs, egg whites, egg yolks, or any products made from them.

Nuts ⬚: The recipe contains no tree nuts, such as almonds or almond flour, cashews, hazelnuts, pistachios, walnuts, or Brazil nuts, as well as no peanuts. Although peanuts are a legume, and not technically a nut, I've grouped them here because many people with tree nut allergies may also react to peanuts, and peanuts are often cross-contaminated with tree nuts, as they are commonly processed on the same machinery.

Nightshades ⬚: The recipe contains no plant products of the nightshade family, including tomatoes, tomatillos, potatoes, eggplant, sweet and spicy peppers, goji berries, golden berries, and spices such as curry powder, paprika, chipotle chile powder, chili powder, red pepper flakes, and cayenne pepper.

smoothies

Do you feel that your children are not eating enough fresh greens? By adding greens like kale, spinach, and collards to a blender with some fresh fruits and water, you can create the most nourishing, healthy green drink that they will love. We began making green smoothies when our second daughter was a baby. She was hooked at nine months, with her first sip. Now our children make their own green smoothies as a snack whenever they are hungry.

Green smoothies are a fantastic way to consume large amounts of raw green leafy vegetables; it's actually difficult to eat enough green vegetables unless you have one every day. As we mentioned in the beginning of this book, adding a green smoothie to each day is a great way to get more fresh vegetables into your family's diet. We use a Vitamix for all our smoothie recipes. This high-powered blender has a two-plus horsepower motor, which effectively breaks down whole foods—including the leaves, peels, and stems—releasing the valuable phytonutrients that grow inside the plant fibers to become fully bioavailable.

Remember that greens (kale, collards, and other raw cruciferous veggies) have compounds in them that ramp up the body's ability to safely remove toxins from the body. Now, more than ever, our children need these foods to help them detoxify after exposure to the ever-increasing environmental chemicals they are exposed to.

INTRODUCING SMOOTHIES TO CHILDREN

Smoothies are one of the best ways to consume concentrated nutrients and fiber, but they are especially so for young children. The earlier you introduce green smoothies, the more likely it is they will enjoy them and be eager to drink them throughout their childhood and beyond. When you are creating these green smoothies for your children, consider color, texture, and flavor. Begin with citrus-free green smoothies for children between eight and ten months of age (some children react to citrus with rashes if introduced earlier than 12 months). Start with a small amount of greens, and then gradually add more.

By starting young, your child will have a natural acceptance of green foods and slightly bitter flavors. If you are introducing green smoothies to an older child, also start slowly. Have your child participate in the making of it, including picking the fruits and greens. This way, he will be more apt to enjoy the finished product.

Sometime between 12 and 24 months is a good time to introduce nuts to your child's diet. When doing so, soak them overnight to aid digestibility and nutrient availability. Soaked nuts form the basis of many of these smoothies; if desired, replace some of the nuts with other nuts or seeds. For example, replace almonds with raw cashews, sunflower seeds, or macadamia nuts.

10 Tips for Making Healthy Kid-Friendly Smoothies

1. Make beautifully colored smoothies! We first taste with our eyes. Keep in mind which colors you are combining. My kids don't mind a brown smoothie, but some children won't drink one that looks unappealing (even if it tastes great). I like to make dark purple smoothies with berries, cherries, oranges, and greens like napa cabbage and a little kale. We love making vibrant green smoothies using pineapple, banana, avocado, and greens like kale and collards.

2. Start with more fruit and less greens! You can make a berry-banana smoothie and add two or three kale leaves without changing the color of the smoothie. Gradually add more greens each time; they will slowly get used to the bitter flavors of the greens and in no time, your children will most likely love all forms of green smoothies.

3. Use creamy fruits! Add a frozen banana and half an avocado to each smoothie. This lends a rich, creamy feel that your kids will love!

4. Add fat! Adding fat to green smoothies not only creates a nice texture but also helps in properly absorbing the carotenoids from the greens! Try nut butters, nut milks, coconut milk, coconut butter, whole milk plain yogurt, kefir, raw cream, fish oil, avocado, chia seeds, or hemp seeds.

5. Add citrus! I like to add the juice from one to two lemons or limes. Not only do the lemons and limes provide a hearty dose of vitamin C and bioflavonoids, but they also help balance the flavor of the bitter greens. If I'm not adding oranges or pineapple, I almost always add fresh lemon or lime juice.

6. Use a high-powered blender! High-powered blenders, such as a Vitamix, thoroughly break down the greens so the smoothie is, indeed, very smooth. A regular blender has a difficult time breaking the fibers, making the texture of the smoothie less desirable for children.

7. Always serve with a straw! As you can see in the videos on our website (www.WholeLifeNutrition.net and www.NourishingMeals.com), our children love to use glass straws when drinking their smoothies. A straw makes everything much more fun!

8. Use a colored or opaque cup for serving! If your children are new to the green color of their smoothies, serve them in colored cups with lids and a straw. We always use glass tumblers, but to start, try a tumbler that is opaque so they can taste the yumminess with their mouths instead of being afraid to sample.

9. Hide the supplements in the smoothies! Smoothies are a great way to "hide" the supplements you are giving your children. When we were working on healing our daughter's gut, we made special smoothies with powdered L-glutamine, probiotics, liquid vitamin D and K, and fish oil. She loved them, yet couldn't taste the supplements. See our website, www.WholeLifeNutrition.net, for more information on making medicinal, healing smoothies.

10. Get creative with leftovers! Leftover smoothies can be either stored in glass jars in the refrigerator or poured into popsicle molds and frozen for a fun treat later on. My children love green smoothie popsicles!

berry orange smoothie

MAKES ABOUT 6 CUPS

During our Pacific Northwest summers, our kitchen is usually filled with a variety of fresh berries. For this smoothie, try using blueberries, strawberries, blackberries, marionberries, or raspberries for a refreshing afternoon antioxidant snack. Pour any leftover smoothie into popsicle molds and freeze for a fun treat later on for your children.

3 cups fresh berries

2 cups fresh orange juice

2 cups ice cubes

Place the berries, juice, and ice into a blender and blend until smooth. Serve immediately.

blueberry cucumber smoothie

FREE OF

MAKES ABOUT 5 CUPS

Serve this ice cold, refreshing smoothie for a late afternoon summer snack. It is thirst quenching and full of powerful antioxidants. It can also be frozen into popsicle molds for a nutritious, kid-friendly snack.

1 large cucumber, chopped

2 cups frozen blueberries

2 cups water

Small handful of fresh mint leaves

Place the cucumber, berries, water, and mint leaves into a blender and blend on high speed for 60 to 90 seconds. Serve immediately.

> **INGREDIENT TIP**
>
> Cucumber peels are packed with nutrients, particularly minerals such as silica, potassium, and magnesium, but sometimes they can be quite bitter; note that blending the cucumbers with the peels intact will come with more bitterness. Younger, fresher cucumbers often have peels that aren't bitter, however. Peel a little off the cucumber and taste before deciding whether or not to use the rest of the peel.

blueberry cherry smoothie

FREE OF

MAKES ABOUT 6 CUPS

This simple smoothie is packed with cell-protective antioxidants. It is naturally sweetened using fruit, and it provides easily assimilated protein from the raw almond milk and chia seeds.

2 cups frozen blueberries

2 cups frozen pitted cherries

1 small banana

2 to 4 tablespoons chia seeds

2 cups Raw Almond Milk (page 451)

Place the fruit, seeds, and almond milk into your blender and blend on high until very smooth. (If not using a high-powered blender, grind the chia seeds in a small electric grinder or coffee grinder before adding them to the smoothie.) Drink immediately or pour into popsicle molds and freeze any leftovers.

> **NUTRITION TIP**
>
> Studies show that consuming blueberries helps balance the gut. Blueberries—specifically the lowbush, or wild, variety—can decrease the risk of a negative reaction to foodborne pathogens while preserving the function of beneficial bacteria in the intestines. These blueberries appear to have a potent antimicrobial effect on foodborne pathogenic bacteria, including *E. coli*, *Salmonella typhimurium*, and *Listeria*, yet the beneficial *Lactobacillus rhamnosus* is spared. Additionally, research has demonstrated that blueberry consumption can lead to an increase in *Bifidobacterium* in the gut.

blueberry kefir smoothie

FREE OF

MAKES ABOUT 2½ CUPS

This smoothie idea came from our good friend Phyllis, a vibrantly healthy woman in her mid-sixties. She makes her own kefir from organic raw goat's milk, and tells me that this smoothie keeps her energized and full until well after lunchtime. You'll love the tangy and sweet flavors. If you don't have any blueberries, try cherries or Italian prune plums instead.

1 cup kefir (from cow's, goat's, or coconut milk)

1 cup fresh or frozen blueberries

½ avocado

1 tablespoon chia seeds

Place the kefir, blueberries, avocado, and chia seeds into a blender and blend until smooth. For a thinner smoothie, add some water, a few tablespoons at a time, until desired consistency is reached.

VARIATION: Replace the blueberries with frozen cherries for a slightly sweeter smoothie.

creamy cashew peach smoothie

MAKES 5 CUPS

This semi-sweet smoothie feels more like a treat than anything else, but it packs in the protein and magnesium. Any leftovers can be poured into popsicle molds and frozen for another time.

1½ cups raw cashews

2 cups water

2 frozen large peaches, chopped

2 to 4 medjool dates, pitted

2 tablespoons chia seeds

1 teaspoon raw vanilla powder, or 1 whole vanilla bean

Place the cashews and water into a high-powered blender and blend until smooth and creamy. Then add the peaches, dates, chia seeds, and vanilla; blend again, pulsing as needed, until the peaches break down and the smoothie is blended and creamy.

NUTRITION TIP

Both mangos and bananas are beneficial for the gut. Mangos are a good source of glutamine—the amino acid that helps repair a damaged gut, especially one healing from celiac disease—and bananas are high in pectin, a substance that helps to normalize movement of waste through the large intestine. Mangos are also an excellent source of cancer-protective pectins, phenols, and enzymes.

mango banana almond smoothie

FREE OF

MAKES 4 TO 5 CUPS

This smoothie is helpful in repairing the gut. We often recommend this recipe for children as part of a gut-healing plan after they have been diagnosed with celiac disease. I prefer to use frozen mango, as it creates a thick, cold creaminess that can't be achieved with fresh fruit. I also use homemade raw almond milk, but you could use coconut milk, hemp milk, or cashew milk, if desired.

2 cups chopped fresh or frozen mango

2 ripe bananas

2 cups Raw Almond Milk (page 451)

Place the mango, bananas, and almond milk into a blender and blend for about 60 seconds, or until all of the mango pieces are broken down and pureed.

VARIATION: Cashew Milk (page 453) can be used in place of the raw almond milk.

orange creamsicle smoothie

FREE OF

MAKES ABOUT 8 CUPS

This smoothie was inspired by a drink served at Thrive, one of our favorite restaurants in Seattle. It's more like a frosty beverage than a thick smoothie, and quite refreshing on a very hot day. If you don't want to use raw almond milk or have a nut allergy, use hemp milk or any other milk of your choice. I prefer freshly squeezed orange juice over store-bought because all the enzymes needed to help digest the sugars remain intact. This can be frozen in popsicle molds for a frosty treat later on.

4 cups Raw Almond Milk (page 451)

2 cups fresh orange juice

2 frozen bananas

1 or 2 handfuls of ice cubes

Place the almond milk, orange juice, and bananas into a high-powered blender and blend for about 60 seconds, or until smooth. Add the ice cubes and blend again.

INGREDIENT TIP

I like to use Valencia oranges for their high juice content.

pecan berry blast

MAKES ABOUT 5 CUPS

This antioxidant and protein-packed smoothie makes an excellent snack or quick breakfast on the run. Note, though, that the pecans and dates have to be soaked for at least 3 hours before using in this recipe.

1 cup raw pecans

2 or 3 medjool dates, pitted

2 tablespoons chia seeds

2 cups water

1 cup frozen blackberries

1 cup frozen blueberries

1 cup chopped frozen plums or raspberries

Place the pecans in a small bowl and cover with some water. Place the dates in a separate small bowl and cover with water; let both soak for 3 to 6 hours. Drain and place into a blender along with the chia seeds and water. Blend until very smooth and creamy. Add the frozen fruit and blend again until completely smooth, adding more water if a thinner smoothie is desired. Serve immediately.

NUTRITION TIP

Choosing organic wild blueberries over the conventional cultivated blueberries makes a difference! One study revealed that organic wild blueberries had 33 percent more antioxidant activity, over 35 percent more anthocyanins, and 40 percent more phenolic content than their conventional cultivated counterparts.

strawberry almond smoothie

FREE OF

MAKES ABOUT 6 CUPS

It is important to plan ahead when you want to make this smoothie because the almonds need to be soaked overnight. Before I go to bed, I briefly plan out the next day and consider if I need to soak any nuts or beans. It takes only a few minutes to get the nuts out and pour water over them. You want to give them eight to ten hours of soaking time. In the morning, I drain off the soaking water and rinse well in a colander. For this recipe, use any frozen or fresh fruits you have on hand in place of the strawberries, if desired.

1 cup raw almonds, soaked for 6 hours or overnight

1½ to 2 cups water

2 to 3 cups fresh or frozen strawberries

1 teaspoon raw vanilla powder, or 1 whole vanilla bean

1 tablespoon raw honey (optional)

Rinse and drain the soaked almonds. Place the almonds and 1½ cups water into a high-powered blender or a blender fitted with a sharp blade and blend until very smooth, 30 to 60 seconds. Then add the strawberries, vanilla, and honey (if using); blend again until smooth, adding the remaining water, if necessary. Serve immediately.

VARIATION: Replace the strawberries with fresh or frozen Italian prune plums.

raw cacao hemp seed smoothie

FREE OF

MAKES ABOUT 2½ CUPS

This smoothie makes a great nutritious dessert or a sweet afternoon energizing drink, and is another great option for freezing as popsicles. It is free of nuts and high in plant-based protein. Additionally, hemp and chia seeds are excellent sources of omega-3 fatty acids. Raw cacao is very high in antioxidants—even more so than regular cocoa powder. The pear can be replaced with one frozen banana, if desired; just add a bit more water to compensate for the water that would be in the pear.

½ cup raw hemp seeds

1 cup water

1 tablespoon chia seeds

1 ripe pear, cored and chopped

3 to 4 tablespoons raw cacao powder

2 to 3 tablespoons coconut nectar or raw honey

1 teaspoon raw vanilla powder, or 1 whole vanilla bean

Place the hemp seeds and water into a blender. Blend until ultra smooth and creamy, about 60 seconds, then add the pear, 3 tablespoons cacao powder, 2 tablespoons nectar, and the vanilla powder. Blend again until smooth. Taste and add the remaining cacao and coconut nectar, if needed. Blend again. Serve immediately, or pour into popsicle molds and freeze.

> **NUTRITION TIP**
>
> Pears are an excellent source of soluble fiber. The fiber acts as a sponge to mop up toxins that have been released from the liver via the bile and excreted into the intestinal tract.

baby green smoothie

FREE OF

MAKES ABOUT 3 CUPS

This recipe is designed for older babies and younger children who are just getting used to green smoothies. Most babies will be ready for their first cup of smoothie between eight and ten months. Children's taste buds develop during the first three years of life, so establishing healthy eating habits in infancy is important. The flavor of this smoothie is very mild and slightly sweet.

1 ripe pear, cored

1 large frozen banana

2 cups water

2 large kale leaves

Small handful of fresh mint leaves

Place the pear, banana, water, kale, and mint leaves into a blender and blend on high until smooth. Serve immediately, or pour into a glass jar and store in the refrigerator for up to 24 hours.

NUTRITION TIP

Kale is an outstanding source of vitamin K_1, with 1 cup having over 1,000 percent of the recommended daily value. Recent research has pointed to the importance of vitamin K_2 in maintaining optimum calcium balance in the body. Vitamin K_2 is formed from dietary K_1 in reactions with beneficial bacteria in the intestines. When there's enough vitamin K_2 in the body, it allows the protein osteocalcin to deposit calcium in the bones (in the osseous tissue) and allows another protein, matrix gla (MGP), to clean up calcium from soft tissue areas—critical for the development of strong bones and teeth. In essence, when vitamin K is low, the body is less likely to put calcium where it's needed and will leave it where it's not needed.

green chia smoothie

MAKES 2 CUPS

Adding chia seeds to your morning smoothies boosts the protein and fat content, which helps stabilize blood sugar and make the smoothies feel more like a meal, with actual staying power. The coconut water in this smoothie helps it be a great pre- or post-workout drink. Coconut water is very high in potassium, but if you need to replace electrolytes after your workout, add a pinch of sea salt to replace the lost sodium.

1 tart apple, cored
1 large mango
3 or 4 large kale leaves
3 handfuls of baby spinach

1 small cucumber
Juice of 1 lime
2 to 3 tablespoons chia seeds
2 to 3 cups water or coconut water

Place the apple, mango, kale, spinach, cucumber, lime juice, and chia seeds into a high-powered blender. Add the 2 cups water and blend until smooth and creamy, adding the remaining cup of water if a thinner consistency is desired. Serve immediately.

VARIATION: Instead of adding all the coconut water, freeze some of it in ice cube trays and add the coconut ice cubes after you have blended the other ingredients. Blend again for a refreshing, cool drink in the summertime.

ginger berry green smoothie

FREE OF

MAKES ABOUT 8 CUPS

This recipe uses low-fructose fruits, as some people have a difficult time digesting fructose. Apples and pears, which are in many of our smoothie recipes, are very high in fructose. Mandarin oranges, blueberries, and strawberries are lower in fructose and therefore good to use here in place of the apples and pears. Adding the avocado boosts the body's absorption of the beneficial carotenoids in the greens. It also slows digestion of the smoothie, which helps maintain blood sugar levels and keeps you feeling satisfied longer.

3 cups water

2 tablespoons chia seeds

½ cup fresh lemon juice

A 2-inch piece of fresh ginger, peeled

2 cups frozen strawberries

1 cup frozen blueberries

Sections of 1 mandarin orange

1 avocado

½ bunch collard greens

½ bunch kale

Add the water, chia seeds, lemon juice, and ginger to a high-powered blender. Blend on high until the chia seeds are pureed. Then add the strawberries, blueberries, and orange sections. Blend again until smooth and creamy. Add the avocado, collards, and kale and blend until combined.

> **NUTRITION TIP**
>
> Does it make a difference if the blueberries are organic, raw, cooked, juiced, dried, or frozen? Yes! The antioxidant effect of blueberries is similar in fresh, frozen, and dried blueberries, but cooking or pasteurizing the juice decreases the amount of some important components. For example, one study found 64 percent higher levels of antioxidant anthocyanidin levels in fresh blueberries compared to blueberry juice.

spring green smoothie

FREE OF

MAKES ABOUT 6 CUPS

The first vegetables of spring happen to be the bitter greens, making this a season of cleansing. You may be able to harvest many of these early spring greens right in your own backyard: dandelion greens, nettles, bittercress, and lamb's quarters. Bitter greens stimulate the liver to get rid of stored toxins from the winter. We let our kale, collard, and sorrel plants die back in the winter, then when the weather is warm enough—usually in late winter here—the greens begin to grow again.

2 ripe apples, cored

2 ripe pears, cored

Juice of 1 lemon

2 to 3 cups water

1 cup sorrel leaves

2 cups chopped kale or collard greens

½ cup fresh nettles

½ cup dandelion leaves

Place the fruit, lemon juice, and 2 cups water into a high-powered blender and blend until smooth. Add in the greens and blend again until very smooth, adding the remaining cup of water, if necessary, to reached desired consistency.

> **KITCHEN TIP**
>
> Don't forget to use gardening gloves when handling fresh nettles!

super antioxidant smoothie

FREE OF

MAKES 5 TO 6 CUPS

This smoothie is a great way to introduce greens into your child's diet without overwhelming her with the color "green." Start with a little spinach and then add more as her taste buds adjust. You can even add a few drops of liquid stevia to sweeten the mix if you would like a sweeter flavor. I think the consistency is best if some of the fruit is frozen.

1 ripe peach, cut into chunks

1 ripe apple, cored and cut into chunks

3 Italian prune plums, or 1 large plum

1 cup fresh or frozen blueberries

1 cup fresh or frozen blackberries

4 cups packed spinach leaves

2 cups water

Place the fruit, spinach, and water into a blender and blend on high until smooth. Store any unused portions in a glass jar and keep in the refrigerator for up to 2 days.

breakfast

Most of us grew up with breakfast that included some form of refined wheat, dairy, eggs, and sugar. Starting your morning with these foods—whether in the form of cereal with milk, pancakes from a mix made with milk and eggs, or some sort of fast-food breakfast item—causes the day to begin not only with a sharp rise in blood sugar levels but also an increase in inflammation in the body. Research shows that children who eat a healthy breakfast are better able to concentrate, behave, and learn in school. Here are a variety of healthy breakfast options—such as Kale and Egg Scramble, Raw Breakfast Tacos, Overnight Quinoa Hot Cakes, and Nutty Grain-Free Granola—that allow everyone to wake up and begin the day with energy.

STARTING THE DAY WITH A HEALTHY BREAKFAST

Research shows that only about 40 percent of Americans actually eat breakfast—cold cereal with milk being one of the most popular choices. Starting the day with something high in refined carbohydrates and sugar, like cold cereal, causes a dramatic spike in blood sugar. When there is a high amount of circulating blood sugar in the body, inflammatory chemicals are released. This can cause the immune system to become confused and attack things entering the system that wouldn't otherwise cause a problem—like certain foods, pollen, and pet dander—thereby creating allergies or sensitivities to compounds in the food and the environment.

Let's Rethink Breakfast

If your child has mood swings, learning disabilities, is hyperactive, or is ravenously hungry within an hour or two of eating, it might be time to rethink breakfast. Serving complex carbohydrates with protein and fat is essential first thing in the morning. Scrambled eggs with sourdough bread and raw sauerkraut or warm beans and sticky brown rice in broth are good choices. A whole-grain pancake made with coconut oil topped with almond butter and fresh berries is another great choice. A small piece of pan-fried grass-fed beef with salad greens can also be a nutrient-dense breakfast providing essential protein, minerals, vitamins, and fats for proper growth and brain function. Fruit, nut, and green smoothies can be a good option for people with strong digestion, as cold foods can be hard on a weak digestive system. I'm always amazed by how long our children can go on a green smoothie made from blueberries, avocado, apple, chia seeds, amino acid powder, lemon juice, and kale!

Starting the day with nutrient-dense foods that won't cause a blood sugar roller-coaster will help keep inflammation in check, thereby reducing the chances that your children will develop food allergies or sensitivities. Prioritizing a healthy breakfast also helps to strengthen their immune systems, protect their digestive health, and increase their cognitive functioning.

What About Skipping Breakfast?

It is commonly known that starvation is a major stressor of the body—it increases the secretion of the stress hormone cortisol. In other words, skipping breakfast stresses you out. Stress has been associated with numerous health disorders that may, in certain individuals, cause an increase in weight as well. Many people believe that skipping meals

10 Quick and Healthy Breakfast Ideas

1. Two poached or fried eggs served with a leftover cooked grain, such as quinoa, and a fermented vegetable, such as raw sauerkraut.

2. Steamed yams, scrambled eggs, and fresh greens.

3. A quick salad of lettuce, sprouts, and hard-boiled eggs. Drizzle it with a mixture of lemon juice and olive oil, and season with salt and pepper.

4. A nutritious nut-and-fruit smoothie. Soak the nuts overnight, then blend with your favorite fruits.

5. Green smoothie along with a slice of toasted gluten-free bread that's spread with sunflower seed butter or almond butter.

6. Leftover cooked quinoa topped with fresh blueberries, raspberries, chopped walnuts, and a dollop of dairy or nondairy yogurt.

7. Sliced organic sausages and sautéed plantain slices, along with raw sauerkraut.

8. Quesadilla made with refried beans, raw cheese (optional), and two gluten-free tortillas (try organic sprouted corn tortillas, Plantain Tortillas, page 357, or Brown Rice Tortillas, page 355). To cook, add a little coconut or olive oil to a heated 11-inch skillet on the stove; cook each side for about 90 seconds, then cut into wedges using a pizza cutter.

9. A bowl of cooked beans, cooked brown rice, and avocado topped with lime juice and salt.

10. Last night's leftover dinner!

is a good idea because of the misconception that weight is all about "calories in and calories out." But this is not how the body works.

If we do not regularly receive signals from our food, then our cells have to adapt and alter their function. When there is a drop in fuel intake, for instance, lean muscle cells are forced to turn off and another type of cell takes over with calorie management: the fat cell. Prolonged fasting that occurs from sleeping and then skipping breakfast increases the body's insulin response, which in turn leads to fat storage. People who skip breakfast are often overweight, stressed out, have low energy, and do not sleep well.

Research shows that eating meals frequently throughout the day keeps your cells constantly burning energy. Lean muscle cells need fuel to stay active. If you supply fuel evenly throughout the day, then the muscles can remain healthy and productive. Eating a balanced breakfast first thing in the morning usually decreases the total amount of food eaten in a day, significantly decreases late afternoon and evening snacking, and boosts overall metabolism.

cream of rice cereal

MAKES 4 TO 6 SERVINGS

We like to make this simple breakfast for busy weekday mornings. We buy the rice already sprouted—it looks and cooks just like regular rice, but it's much healthier! (You can use regular brown rice in this recipe, too.) The rice grinds up in seconds and can then cook unattended on the stove for 5 to 10 minutes while we prepare a green smoothie and make sure the kids have packed themselves a good lunch. If you have a small family, you may want to cut this recipe in half. We like to top the cereal with ground raw almonds, frozen blueberries, and a sprinkling of coconut sugar for a simple, nutritious breakfast.

2 cups sprouted brown rice

8 cups water, or more as needed

¼ teaspoon sea salt

OPTIONAL TOPPINGS

Ground raw almonds

Coconut sugar or maple syrup

Ground cinnamon

Frozen blueberries or raisins

1. Place the brown rice into a coffee grinder or high-powered blender and grind into a very fine meal—not as fine as flour, but not as coarse as cornmeal, either. (We use the dry container of our Vitamix to grind the rice and then the almonds for the topping.)

2. Place the 8 cups water into a 3-quart saucepan and heat over medium until warm. Pour in the ground rice, whisking immediately so it doesn't clump up. Turn up the heat and bring the cereal to a boil, stirring constantly. Reduce the heat to medium or medium-low, cover, and simmer for about 10 minutes. Remove the cover and whisk the cereal occasionally, adding more water, if necessary,

depending on desired thickness. Cook for a few more minutes, then remove from the heat. The cereal will thicken as it cools.

3. Scoop the cereal into serving bowls and serve with your favorite toppings.

> **INGREDIENT TIP**
>
> We like to use either Lundberg brand sprouted brown basmati rice or Planet Rice sprouted short-grain rice, both of which work well in this recipe. The California-grown organic rice is of a high quality that does not carry with it the concerns of high levels of arsenic and cadmium, as do some of the Asian and midwestern U.S. rice. Soaking and sprouting the rice lessens the risk for arsenic exposure even more.

rice and nut milk porridge

FREE OF

MAKES 3 TO 4 SERVINGS

Leftover brown rice can be mixed with milk and heated on the stove to create a quick, nutritious breakfast—perfect for busy mornings! I use either freshly made Cashew Milk (page 453) or Creamy Macadamia Nut Milk (page 454). If you eat dairy products, then replace the nut milk with raw cow's or goat's milk. We like to top the cereal with ground raw almonds, a little coconut sugar, and frozen blueberries.

3 to 4 cups cooked short-grain brown rice

2 cups nut milk or your favorite unsweetened milk

Pinch of sea salt

Few dashes of pure maple syrup (optional)

OPTIONAL TOPPINGS

Ground raw almonds or walnuts, or raw hemp seeds

Coconut sugar or maple syrup

Frozen blueberries or blackberries

Ground cinnamon

1. Place the rice, milk, salt, and maple syrup, if using, in a small pot and cook over medium-low heat, stirring occasionally, for 5 to 7 minutes, or until thickened and warmed through. Add a little water if the mixture is too thick, and stir.

2. Scoop into serving bowls and sprinkle with your favorite toppings.

> **NUTRITION TIP**
>
> Whole grains, such as brown rice, quinoa, and millet, are considered complex carbohydrates. This means they provide a steady, slow release of sugar into your bloodstream, keeping you energized for hours.

quinoa currant porridge

FREE OF

MAKES 4 SERVINGS

The cinnamon in this recipe creates a slightly sweet porridge without needing to add any sweetener. I like to use homemade almond milk, though any unsweetened nondairy milk will do. If you use a thicker milk, such as coconut milk or whole raw cow's milk, you may need to add a little extra water. Note that the quinoa is soaked overnight before using the next morning.

1 cup quinoa, soaked overnight
4 cups milk
¼ cup dried currants
1 teaspoon ground cinnamon
Pinch of sea salt

TOPPINGS
Chopped nuts
Raw hemp seeds
Fresh raspberries

1. Drain and rinse the quinoa in a fine-mesh strainer. Place the quinoa, milk, currants, cinnamon, and salt in a 2-quart pot. Bring to a boil over high heat, reduce the heat to medium-low, cover, and simmer for 20 to 25 minutes, or until thick and creamy.

2. Serve warm. Sprinkle each bowl with the chopped nuts, raw hemp seeds, and raspberries.

pumpkin pie granola

FREE OF

MAKES 5 TO 6 CUPS

Homemade granola is one of the easiest things to make. Your children can help measure and stir the ingredients and then patiently wait for the pan to come out of the oven. Serve this granola over your favorite dairy or nondairy yogurt. It can also be added as a special treat to your child's lunchbox. Store the granola in a large glass jar for up to two weeks in your pantry.

DRY INGREDIENTS

3 cups gluten-free rolled oats

2 cups raw pumpkin seeds

1 tablespoon pumpkin pie spice

½ teaspoon sea salt

WET INGREDIENTS

½ cup melted coconut oil

½ cup pure maple syrup

½ cup pumpkin puree

1 teaspoon vanilla extract

OPTIONAL ADDITIONS

½ to 1 cup dried currants

½ to 1 cup chopped dried apples

1. Preheat the oven to 300°F. In a large bowl, combine the dry ingredients. In a smaller bowl, whisk together the wet ingredients. Pour the wet into the dry and mix well.

2. Pour the mixture onto a large rimmed baking sheet or into two 9 by 13-inch pans. Spread evenly into a single layer. Bake for 45 to 60 minutes, or until slightly golden, stirring two or three times during baking. Remove granola from oven, and stir in the currants and chopped dried apples, if using. Let the pan sit on the counter until the granola is completely cooled; it will crisp up as it cools.

KITCHEN TIP

I often have freshly baked winter squash stored in my refrigerator during the fall and winter months. To use baked squash or pumpkin that is not pureed, measure ½ cup of the cooked flesh and add it to a blender along with the wet ingredients. Blend until smooth and pour over the dry ingredients on the baking sheet, then bake as directed.

nutty grain-free granola

FREE OF

MAKES 4 TO 5 CUPS

This grain-free granola is packed with protein and healthy fats. With just a smidgen of sweetener to help hold it together and to boost flavors, this treat is great sprinkled over your favorite dairy or dairy-free yogurt. Top it off with fresh berries or diced bananas.

1 cup raw almonds

1 cup raw pecans

1 cup raw walnuts

½ cup raw sunflower seeds

½ cup raw pumpkin seeds

2 to 3 tablespoons chia seeds

2 teaspoons ground cinnamon

¼ teaspoon grated nutmeg

¼ teaspoon sea salt

¼ cup pure maple syrup

¼ cup melted coconut oil

½ to 1 cup dried cranberries or raisins

1. Preheat the oven to 300°F. Line a large baking dish, rimmed baking sheet, or jelly-roll pan with parchment paper.

2. Place the nuts into a food processor fitted with the "s" blade. Process until you have a chunky, coarse meal. Pour into a medium bowl. Add the seeds, cinnamon, nutmeg, and salt. Stir together to evenly distribute the spices and salt. Add the maple syrup and coconut oil and mix using a large spoon. Spread in the baking dish and bake for 35 to 40 minutes, or until slightly golden. Remove from the oven and stir in the cranberries. Let cool completely in the dish, then transfer to a glass jar and store for up to 2 weeks.

NUTRITION TIP

Soaking the nuts and seeds overnight and then dehydrating them until crisp not only makes them more digestible but also allows their nutrients to become more bioavailable. You can do this before using them in this granola recipe, but it's not necessary. See the "Getting Started" chapter for details.

KITCHEN TIP

Lining the baking dish or sheet with parchment paper keeps the granola from burning.

fruit and avocado bowls with hemp seeds

MAKES 2 SERVINGS

On days when we want a lighter breakfast, we make fruit-and-nut bowls along with a green smoothie. Any fruit combination works, but the avocado-mango duo is quite luscious! You'll want to eat this right after it is made, as it will spoil quickly.

1 ripe pear, cored and chopped

1 large mango, cubed

1 large avocado, cubed

Juice of ½ lemon or lime

¼ cup raw hemp seeds

2 tablespoons chia seeds

Handful of chopped raw macadamia nuts or sprouted sunflower seeds (optional)

Place the fruit and avocado in a small serving bowl and toss together. Add the juice and toss again. Sprinkle the hemp and chia seeds over the top and add a sprinkle of macadamia nuts or sunflower seeds, if desired. Serve and enjoy right away!

raw breakfast tacos

MAKES 4 TO 6 SERVINGS

This is my go-to recipe when we have a busy morning. If I make the filling the night before, all I need to do in the morning is slice an avocado and a mango and put everything into a lettuce leaf. I like to use romaine lettuce or napa cabbage leaves for the "taco shell," but any variety of lettuce will work. I include the whole chile, seeds and all, because I like things really hot. However, if you don't want the filling too spicy, or are serving this to young children, remove the seeds before adding the chile to the food processor. Note that the nuts are soaked for at least eight hours before use.

FILLING

1 cup raw walnuts, soaked for 8 to 10 hours

3 to 4 Brazil nuts, soaked for 8 to 10 hours

3 green onions, trimmed

Handful of fresh cilantro

1 hot chile, such as serrano or jalapeño, seeded if desired

Juice of 1 small lime

½ teaspoon sea salt or Herbamare, or as needed

FOR SERVING

4 to 6 lettuce leaves

Sliced avocado

Sliced mango

Lime wedges

1. Drain and rinse the nuts. Place them into a food processor fitted with the "s" blade and add the green onions, cilantro, chile, lime juice, and salt. Pulse until the mixture is smooth. Taste and add more salt, if necessary.

2. To assemble the tacos, place a few dollops of the filling into each lettuce leaf and top with avocado and mango slices. Serve with the lime wedges.

bean and rice breakfast bowls

MAKES 2 TO 3 SERVINGS

This is another favorite recipe of ours to make for just about any meal, but it does serve as a very nutritious, energizing breakfast. It can be prepared quickly if you don't have much time in the morning, as long as you have cooked rice and beans on hand. Cooked quinoa also works great. The sauerkraut adds a nice salty-sour flavor and some crunch. It is also full of beneficial microorganisms that balance the gut flora and aid in digesting the grains and beans.

2 cups cooked short-grain brown rice
1 cup cooked black beans
1 large avocado, diced
½ cup Raw Sauerkraut (page 472)
Sea salt or Herbamare

OPTIONAL ADDITIONS
Chopped mustard greens
Baby arugula
Thinly sliced green onions

Divide the rice, beans, avocado, and sauerkraut equally between two or three bowls. Sprinkle each with a little salt to taste. Top with any optional additions you desire. Serve immediately.

black bean and potato breakfast burritos

FREE OF

MAKES 4 TO 6 BURRITOS

The first time I made this recipe, my children all sat down for breakfast and at first bite said, "Mom, these are so good, you just have to put them in your new cookbook!" They happily devour these every time I make them. To speed the preparation a little, make a big batch of the filling the night before and then reheat what you need in the morning. The filling will last for up to five days stored in the refrigerator.

FILLING

2 to 3 tablespoons extra-virgin olive oil

1 small onion, minced

1 teaspoon dried marjoram or oregano

¼ teaspoon chipotle chile powder

1 teaspoon sea salt or Herbamare

2½ cups diced potatoes (in ¼-inch cubes)

2 cups cooked and drained black beans

½ cup chopped fresh cilantro

FOR SERVING

4 to 6 gluten-free tortillas, warmed (see Tip), or blanched collard greens, baby arugula, or mixed greens

Guacamole

Salsa

Sour cream

1. Heat an 11- or 12-inch skillet over medium heat. Add the olive oil and then the onion; sauté for about 5 minutes, or until softened. Add the herbs, chile powder, and salt; sauté for 30 seconds more. Add the potatoes and sauté for about 10 minutes, or until starting to soften. Add the beans, cover, and cook until the beans are heated through and the potatoes are soft, a few more minutes. Turn off the heat and add the cilantro.

2. Place about ½ cup filling in the center of each heated tortilla, then add any additional ingredients as desired. Fold in the sides of the tortilla and roll up to seal, then serve.

VARIATION: For a nightshade-free recipe, replace the potatoes with sweet potatoes, winter squash, or rutabaga. Replace the chipotle chile powder with freshly ground black pepper.

KITCHEN TIP

To warm the tortillas, steam them one at a time over the filling as it cooks or over a pot of boiling water on the stove, fitted with a wire rack; steam each tortilla for about 60 seconds.

breakfast potatoes

FREE OF

MAKES 4 TO 6 SERVINGS

Our family loves these breakfast potatoes, though we only make them on weekends because they are a little more time-consuming to prepare. Serve them with poached eggs or cooked black beans and sautéed greens for a balanced meal.

1 to 2 tablespoons extra-virgin olive oil or coconut oil

1 red onion, diced

3 pounds red or yellow potatoes, cut into ¼-inch cubes

1 red bell pepper, cored, seeded, and diced

Herbamare or sea salt

Freshly ground black pepper

Snipped fresh chives (optional)

Heat an 11- or 12-inch skillet over medium. Add about 1 tablespoon of the olive oil, then the onion; sauté for 5 minutes. Add the potatoes and sauté for 10 more minutes, keeping them moving in the pan and adding more oil if necessary so they don't stick. Add the bell pepper and sauté a few minutes more. Cover the skillet and cook for 5 to 10 more minutes, or until the potatoes are soft. Remove the lid and cook a few minutes to let any excess liquid cook off. Season to taste with salt and pepper. If desired, sprinkle with the chives.

VARIATION: For a nightshade-free version, replace the potatoes with diced rutabaga, celery root, or sweet potatoes, and omit the bell pepper.

> **KITCHEN TIP**
>
> Using a well-seasoned cast-iron skillet to cook the potatoes will keep them from sticking. Cast-iron skillets are inexpensive and a great addition to your kitchen!

winter vegetable hash

Before refrigeration, people used to store their fall harvests in root cellars, especially their cabbages and their root vegetables and tubers, such as carrots, parsnips, celery root, turnips, beets, rutabaga, sunchokes, and onions. Along with their homemade vegetable ferments, these were the vegetables they had available during the colder months in northern climates. For this hash, use any combination of winter vegetables. I like to use part rutabaga, part carrot, and part winter squash for a simple, flavorful combination. Serve with poached eggs or cooked beans for a hearty breakfast. You can store any leftovers in your fridge for up to five days, and then reheat as needed.

8 cups grated winter vegetables (see Tip)

¼ cup extra-virgin olive oil, butter, or coconut oil

1 small onion, minced

1 teaspoon Herbamare or sea salt

Freshly ground black pepper

Combine the winter vegetables in a bowl. Heat an 11- or 12-inch skillet, preferably cast iron, over medium. Add some of the olive oil and onion; sauté for 1 minute. Add the grated vegetables, and sauté for a few minutes, adding the remaining oil as needed to keep the mixture from sticking to the pan. Cover the skillet and cook for 10 minutes, stirring once after 5 minutes, then uncover and sauté until cooked through, about 15 minutes total. Add the Herbamare and pepper to taste, and sauté 1 minute more. Serve hot.

KITCHEN TIP

If you are using potatoes, grate them and place in a large bowl filled with cold water. Stir around a bit to loosen the starches, then strain through a clean towel, squeezing out all the moisture. If you are using winter squash, peel it first. Use the grating disk on your food processor to quickly grate your winter vegetables or use the "s" blade to finely chop the vegetables in batches.

kale and egg scramble

FREE OF

MAKES 2 TO 4 SERVINGS

This tasty and nourishing recipe was a staple breakfast food during many of my pregnancies. It is quick to prepare and can easily be made on a busy weekday morning. I like to serve it with the Breakfast Potatoes (page 85) and a spoonful of raw cultured vegetables to maximize digestion.

4 teaspoons butter or coconut oil

2 cups finely chopped kale

1 to 2 tablespoons water, if needed

4 large organic eggs

Sea salt and freshly ground black pepper

Hot sauce (optional)

1. Heat a 10-inch skillet over medium; this helps keep the food from sticking. Add 2 teaspoons of the butter, then the kale and sauté for about 5 minutes, adding a tablespoon or two of water if needed to help the kale soften.

2. While the kale is cooking, crack the eggs into a bowl and whisk. Push the kale to the side of the skillet and add the remaining butter. Add the eggs and scramble into the kale. Cook for about 2 minutes, turning constantly. Remove from the heat and season to taste with salt and pepper. I usually drizzle my portion with hot sauce.

NUTRITION TIP

Eggs are a great source of choline and phosphatidylcholine, which are beneficial for proper nerve and brain function. It is estimated that 90 percent of the U.S. population may be choline deficient, with the elderly and pregnant women the most susceptible to deficiencies.

basil zucchini frittata

MAKES 4 TO 6 SERVINGS

Frittatas are basically baked omelets. They are usually made by first lightly sautéing the vegetables in an ovenproof skillet, then beaten eggs are added and the skillet is finished off in the oven. I don't like overcooked zucchini, so I simply add the raw zucchini slices to a pie plate along with the basil, and then add the eggs and bake it in the oven. You can do it either way. I also like to make this recipe for a quick, nutritious lunch in the summertime, often with a bowl of cooked quinoa or a green salad.

Extra-virgin olive oil or butter, for cooking

1 zucchini, thinly sliced

½ cup thinly sliced fresh basil

6 large organic eggs, lightly beaten

Sea salt and freshly ground black pepper

¼ cup grated Parmesan cheese (optional)

1. Preheat the oven to 375°F. Lightly oil a 9-inch pie plate or ovenproof 10-inch skillet. Place the zucchini slices on the bottom of the pie plate, sprinkle with the basil, then add the beaten eggs. Sprinkle with salt and pepper. Add the grated Parmesan cheese, if using.

2. Bake for about 25 minutes, or until cooked through. Slice and serve.

roasted squash and corn frittata

FREE OF

MAKES 4 TO 6 SERVINGS

This recipe is perfect for lazy weekend breakfasts or large family brunches in early autumn, when fresh corn and squash are in abundance. If corn is out of season, use about 1½ cups frozen organic corn. Serve this with Baby Arugula Salad with Zucchini Lime Dressing (page 198) and Buckwheat Cinnamon Rolls (page 130) for a hearty weekend brunch.

1½ cups peeled and cubed butternut squash

1 tablespoon extra-virgin olive oil, plus more for cooking

Pinch of sea salt

3 or 4 green onions, trimmed and cut into rounds

1 or 2 small jalapeño peppers, seeded and diced

2 ears fresh corn, kernels cut from the cob

½ teaspoon Herbamare or sea salt

6 large organic eggs, lightly beaten

¼ to ½ cup crumbled cotija cheese or feta (optional)

1. Preheat the oven to 350°F. Toss the squash in the 1 tablespoon olive oil and sprinkle with salt, then place in an 8-inch square baking dish. Roast for about 35 minutes, or until tender. Let cool slightly.

2. Meanwhile, lightly grease a 9-inch deep-dish pie plate with some olive oil. Place the green onions, jalapeños, and corn in the pie plate. Sprinkle with the Herbamare. Add the roasted squash and gently toss. Pour the eggs over the vegetables, then sprinkle with the cheese, if using. Bake for 25 to 30 minutes, or until the frittata is cooked through. Slice and serve.

KITCHEN TIP

Use leftover roasted squash from a previous meal to cut the prep time in half.

---

mini quiches with a sweet potato crust

This recipe makes a large enough batch that you can reheat some as needed for breakfasts throughout the week; store the extras in a covered glass container for up to five days. I reheat mine in a small, covered skillet with a few tablespoons of water. Use any combination of vegetables, herbs, and cheese. Some of my favorites are chive, asparagus, and feta; broccoli, jalapeño, onion, and cilantro; and cauliflower, mushroom, and spinach. You can add crumbled cooked bacon or sausages, too, if desired. The "crust" is made from grated sweet potato, but other starchy vegetables work as well, such as red potatoes, parsnips, or rutabaga.

1 sweet potato, peeled and grated
1 tablespoon extra-virgin olive oil
2 cups diced vegetables
10 large organic eggs
¼ cup water or raw cream
½ teaspoon Herbamare or sea salt
Freshly ground black pepper

OPTIONAL ADDITIONS
Thinly sliced fresh basil
Chopped fresh cilantro
Grated raw organic cheddar cheese

1. Preheat the oven to 325°F. Grease a 12-cup muffin pan with a little butter or coconut oil. Divide the grated sweet potato among the muffin cups and evenly press into the bottoms of each.

2. Heat a 10-inch skillet over medium. Add the olive oil, then the diced vegetables and sauté for about 5 minutes to soften. Divide the vegetables evenly among the 12 muffin cups.

3. Crack the eggs into a medium bowl and add the water; whisk well, then pour over the vegetables. Season with the salt and pepper. Sprinkle on the basil, cilantro, and cheese, if using. Bake for about 35 minutes, or until cooked through. Use a knife to gently nudge the "quiches" out of the muffin cups. Serve hot.

INGREDIENT TIP
Omit the dairy and any nightshade vegetables, such as bell peppers, in the filling if you need the recipe to be dairy-free and nightshade-free.

chicken breakfast sausages

FREE OF

MAKES 8 SAUSAGE PATTIES

You can make this recipe ahead of time, form the patties, and then either freeze or refrigerate them before cooking; take one or two out at a time to cook as needed. Uncooked sausages will last up to two days in the refrigerator or six months in the freezer. Serve with a green salad and a cup of herbal tea for an energizing breakfast. You can also serve these for dinner, sandwiched between two romaine lettuce leaves and with your favorite fixings!

1½ pounds boneless, skinless chicken thighs

¼ to ½ cup organic fresh chicken livers (optional)

1 tart apple, cored and peeled

5 green onions, trimmed and cut into 1-inch pieces

¼ cup packed fresh sage leaves

2 to 3 teaspoons pure maple syrup

1 to 2 teaspoons fennel seeds

1 teaspoon Herbamare or sea salt

½ teaspoon freshly ground black pepper

¼ teaspoon red pepper flakes (optional)

Extra-virgin olive oil, for cooking

1. Rinse the chicken and chicken livers (if using), pat dry, and set aside. Place the apple, green onions, sage, maple syrup, fennel seeds, Herbamare, pepper, and red pepper flakes (if using) into a food processor fitted with the "s" blade; pulse a few times to mince. Add the chicken and livers, and process until the chicken is ground and the mixture starts to form a ball. It does not take long, only about 30 seconds.

2. With oiled hands, form the mixture into about 8 patties and set on a plate or baking sheet. Heat a large cast-iron skillet over medium-low, then add about 1 tablespoon oil. Add 4 of the patties to the skillet and cook for 4 to 5 minutes on each side, or until cooked through. Repeat with remaining patties, then serve.

> **INGREDIENT TIP**
> Omit the red pepper flakes if you need this recipe to be nightshade-free.

date-glazed banana donuts

FREE OF

MAKES 12 TO 16 DONUTS

These grain-free baked donuts are light and not too sweet; the glaze helps them feel more like a treat. Serve them with Chicken Breakfast Sausages (page 91) and a few spoonfuls of Raw Sauerkraut (page 472) for a hearty breakfast or brunch.

DRY INGREDIENTS

3 cups packed blanched almond flour

1 cup arrowroot powder

2 teaspoons baking powder

¾ teaspoon baking soda

½ teaspoon sea salt

WET INGREDIENTS

½ cup organic palm shortening

1½ cups mashed ripe banana (from about 4 large bananas)

¼ cup honey

4 large organic eggs

2 teaspoons vanilla extract

DATE GLAZE

6 large medjool dates, pitted

6 tablespoons boiling water

4 tablespoons coconut oil

3 tablespoons raw cashew butter

½ teaspoon vanilla extract

Pinch of sea salt

1. Preheat the oven to 350°F. Place the dry ingredients into a food processor and pulse until combined. Add the shortening and pulse again to combine. Add the remaining wet ingredients and process until the batter is smooth and combined.

2. Spoon the batter into donut pans. You can fill them about three-fourths of the way for medium donuts or all the way for larger donuts. Bake for 20 to 25 minutes, depending on donut size, or until cooked through. Cool on a wire rack.

3. To make the glaze, add the dates and boiling water to a small bowl. Let soak for about 15 minutes, then pour the dates and water into

a high-powered blender. Add the coconut oil, cashew butter, vanilla, and salt. Blend on high until ultra-smooth and creamy, a minute or two. Spread the glaze onto the warm donuts and serve.

KITCHEN TIP

Use either cast-iron donut pans or silicone-coated steel donut pans for this recipe. It's really important to avoid all nonstick cookware and bakeware! Most nonstick bakeware contains perfluorooctanoic acid, or PFOA. This toxic compound is beginning to get phased out, but is still present in much of the bakeware still being used. PFOA affects thyroid function, blood sugar regulation, and body weight and is an endocrine disruptor (which means that it can increase your risk of hormone-related cancers like breast cancer). We highly recommend getting rid of all nonstick bakeware and replacing it with safe alternatives like stoneware or stainless steel.

coconut banana breakfast cake

FREE OF

MAKES 8 SERVINGS

Our children think that having cake for breakfast is quite a treat, although this is not your typical cake. It is high in protein and low in sugar. In fact, it is completely free of any sweetener other than mashed ripe bananas! Since this cake is made with coconut flour, you will not be able to replace the eggs with an egg substitute. Serve this with sliced fresh bananas and a dollop of sunflower butter or peanut butter.

DRY INGREDIENTS

½ cup coconut flour

¾ teaspoon baking soda

½ teaspoon sea salt

WET INGREDIENTS

1 heaping cup mashed ripe banana (from about 3 large bananas)

⅓ cup coconut oil

6 large organic eggs

1. Preheat the oven to 350°F. Oil a 9-inch round cake pan with a little coconut oil.

2. In a medium bowl, whisk together the dry ingredients. Place the wet ingredients into a blender and blend until smooth and creamy. Pour the wet ingredients into the dry and whisk together. Pour the batter into the cake pan and bake for approximately 40 minutes. Let the pan cool for about 10 minutes, then turn out the cake onto a large plate. Serve warm or at room temperature.

NUTRITION TIP

To make coconut flour, the coconut meat is dried, defatted, and then finely ground into a powder. Coconut flour is very high in fiber; in fact, about 58 percent of its carbohydrates are fiber! Because of this, coconut flour absorbs a lot of liquid. If you are not accustomed to consuming coconut flour, you may want to drink an extra glass or two of water before or after a meal containing coconut flour.

zucchini almond pancakes

FREE OF

MAKES 10 TO 12 PANCAKES

I like to make these savory grain-free, protein-packed pancakes on a summer morning before we head out for the day. Combined with a green smoothie, they create an energizing breakfast! They store well in the refrigerator, but if you prefer to make a smaller batch, just halve the recipe. Top each pancake with a dollop of sour cream or Cashew Sour Cream (page 336) and chopped parsley, if desired.

4 large organic eggs

3 cups grated zucchini

¾ to 1 cup blanched almond flour

½ cup minced onion

½ to 1 teaspoon Herbamare or sea salt

Freshly ground black pepper

Extra-virgin olive oil or butter, for cooking

1. Mix the eggs, zucchini, flour, onion, Herbamare, and pepper in a medium bowl. Let sit briefly; the batter will thin as it sits.

2. Heat a 10-inch stainless steel or cast-iron skillet over medium-low. When hot, add about 1 tablespoon olive oil, then drop the batter by ¼ cup measures into the hot skillet. Cook for a few minutes on one side, then turn and cook the other side. Keep the pancakes warm while you repeat with the remaining batter, adding a little oil to the skillet before cooking each one.

> **KITCHEN TIP**
>
> A well-seasoned cast-iron skillet keeps pancakes from sticking to the bottom of the pan and is especially useful in this recipe.

fluffy cashew pancakes

FREE OF

MAKES ABOUT 8 PANCAKES

Try these light and fluffy grain-free pancakes for breakfast served with fresh berries and pure maple syrup. They also make a great snack for children and toddlers while hiking or running errands! This recipe requires a high-powered blender to make the batter.

1 cup raw cashews

½ cup water

4 large organic eggs

1 tablespoon pure maple syrup

½ cup arrowroot powder

¼ cup coconut flour (see Tip on page 93)

¾ teaspoon baking powder

¼ teaspoon baking soda

¼ teaspoon sea salt

Coconut oil or butter, for cooking

1. Heat a 10-inch cast-iron skillet over low to medium-low. Place the cashews and water into a high-powered blender and blend until very smooth and creamy. Add the eggs and maple syrup, and blend again. Add the arrowroot powder, coconut flour, baking powder, baking soda, and salt; blend again using variable speeds to combine ingredients. You may need to stop and scrape down the sides of the blender and then continue.

2. Add a few teaspoons of coconut oil to the hot skillet, then pour the batter by ⅓ cup measures into the skillet. Use a spoon or the back of a measuring cup to spread the batter out in the pan. Cook for about 90 seconds on one side, then turn and cook 90 seconds more on the other side.

KITCHEN TIP

The trick here is to have a thoroughly heated skillet that isn't too hot; the pancakes will burn if the skillet is too hot or not cook all the way through if it is too cool.

grain-free banana almond pancakes

MAKES 8 TO 10 PANCAKES

These high-protein pancakes can be made in a snap by combining all the ingredients in a blender. A food processor works well, too. The key to cooking these without burning is to use a well-heated cast-iron pan. I cook my pancakes on low heat, after letting the pan heat for about 5 minutes. Serve these pancakes topped with fresh berries and Whipped Coconut Cream (page 443) for a decadent yet healthful breakfast.

6 large organic eggs

1 large ripe banana

2 tablespoons melted coconut oil or butter

1 tablespoon pure maple syrup or honey

2 cups almond flour

2 tablespoons coconut flour (see Tip on page 93)

½ teaspoon baking soda

½ teaspoon sea salt

Coconut oil or butter, for cooking

1. Heat a 10- or 11-inch heavy-bottomed skillet over low to medium-low. Place all the ingredients except the cooking oil into a blender or food processor and blend until smooth.

2. Add a teaspoon or two of the coconut oil to the pan and pour in the batter by ¼ to ⅓ cupfuls.

Cook for 90 seconds on one side, then turn and repeat on the other side. Keep pancakes warm while you repeat with the remaining batter, adding a little coconut oil before cooking each pancake.

plantain crepes

Green plantains are a low-glycemic source of easily digestible starch. In fact, traditional cultures in tropical regions around the world rely on plantains as their source of carbohydrates. I have found that it is best to use green plantains that are just barely starting to ripen; they should have a small amount of yellow on the skin. These unripe plantains can be peeled using a paring knife. Simply slice off the two ends, then run the knife down one of the ridges, slicing until you hit flesh, then along another ridge. Use a butter knife or spoon to lift the peel off of the flesh. You can then use the knife to scrape any flesh off of the remaining peel. I like to chop the plantains into chunks before adding them to the blender. Omit the maple syrup if you plan on using these crepes with savory fillings. The crepes can be kept in an airtight container in the refrigerator for up to a week.

2 large greenish-yellow plantains, peeled and chopped

3 large organic eggs

½ cup water

¼ teaspoon sea salt

1 tablespoon pure maple syrup (optional)

Coconut oil or butter, for cooking

1. Place the plantains, eggs, water, salt, and maple syrup, if using, into a blender and blend until smooth. Heat a 10-inch cast-iron skillet over medium-low. (I like to heat two pans at a time so I can get the crepes done faster.) Add about a teaspoon of coconut oil, and then pour in a tenth of the batter. Gently move the pan to spread the batter and cook for about 60 seconds on each side.

2. Transfer the crepe to a plate and keep warm while you repeat with the remaining batter, adding about ½ teaspoon to 1 teaspoon coconut oil before making each crepe.

sourdough buckwheat crepes

FREE OF

MAKES 6 TO 8 CREPES

We love the flavor of soured buckwheat flour, and so do our children. We like to make these and set out different fillings for each person to make his or her own crepe. Our favorite fillings are sautéed apples with cinnamon; Vanilla Plum Butter (page 481); homemade blueberry-honey jam; sautéed spinach and caramelized onions; and fresh peach slices with almond butter. Note that the flour mixture needs to ferment for 48 hours before you begin this recipe.

1 cup raw buckwheat flour (see Tip)

1 cup water

2 teaspoons cultured coconut water or kefir

3 large organic eggs, lightly beaten

2 tablespoons melted butter or coconut oil, plus more for cooking

1 to 2 tablespoons coconut sugar or pure maple syrup

¼ teaspoon sea salt

1. Place the flour and water into a quart jar and add the coconut water; whisk well. Place a towel over the top of the jar and set in an undisturbed part of your kitchen for 48 hours. When the mixture is ready, it should be bubbly and smell slightly sour.

2. Pour the buckwheat mixture into a medium bowl and whisk in the eggs, 2 tablespoons butter, 1 tablespoon coconut sugar, and the salt. Taste and add the remaining sugar, if desired.

3. Heat a 10-inch skillet over medium to medium-low. Add a little butter, then add about ⅓ cup of the batter and spread it out by moving the pan in a swirling motion. Cook for about 1 minute, then carefully flip using a very thin, wide spatula. Cook for about 20 seconds on the other side. Remove and keep warm while you repeat with the remaining batter, adding a little butter before cooking each crepe. Serve warm.

> **KITCHEN TIP**
>
> To grind fresh buckwheat flour, place 2 cups raw buckwheat groats in a high-powered blender and blend until you have a fine flour. You can do this in a coffee grinder as well, ½ cup at a time. I buy organic raw buckwheat groats from Bob's Red Mill, which is also certified gluten-free. The typical buckwheat flour sold in the stores is made from *roasted* buckwheat groats, and will *not* work in the recipes in this book.

quinoa and mung bean dosas

FREE OF

MAKES 8 TO 10 DOSAS

Dosas are traditional Indian pancakes or crepes made from soaked and fermented whole grains and beans. Making dosas is a two-part process: you soak the grains and beans overnight, then you blend them into a batter and let it ferment. This is one of the most digestible ways to prepare grains and beans—a perfect way to introduce them to older babies and young toddlers! I use quinoa and mung beans in this recipe, but you can use brown basmati rice, millet, black beans, adzuki beans, lentils, or chickpeas. Serve one for breakfast along with sautéed greens and a dollop of yogurt or Spicy Peach Chutney (page 348). They also pair well with curried vegetables or a lentil dal for dinner.

DAY 1
1½ cups quinoa
¾ cup dried mung beans
1 tablespoon raw apple cider vinegar

DAY 2
1½ cups water
1 teaspoon sea salt
1 teaspoon cumin seeds

Coconut oil, for cooking

1. Rinse the quinoa through a fine-mesh strainer. Place it in a small bowl along with the beans, raw apple cider vinegar, and warm water to cover. Make sure there is at least an inch of water covering, as the quinoa and beans will expand quite a bit during soaking. Let them soak for 6 to 12 hours, or up to 24 hours.

2. Drain and rinse the beans and quinoa. Add to a blender along with the water and salt; blend on high until smooth and creamy. Add the cumin and blend on low speed to incorporate. Pour the mixture into a large (2-quart) mason jar or bowl, cover with a kitchen towel, and let ferment for 24 to 48 hours. It will turn slightly sour and a little bubbly.

3. When ready to cook, heat a cast-iron skillet over medium heat. When hot, add a few teaspoons of coconut oil. Pour about ½ cup batter into the hot skillet, spreading it into a thin pancake in a circular motion using the back of a spoon. Cook for about 2 minutes. The dosa will pull easily from the bottom of the pan when cooked; if it is sticking, leave it there for another 30 seconds or so, then flip and cook for about 1 minute on the other side.

4. Place the cooked dosa on a plate and keep warm. Continue making the dosas with the remaining batter, adding a little coconut oil each time. Serve warm.

overnight quinoa hot cakes

FREE OF

MAKES 10 TO 12 PANCAKES

Griddle cakes, hot cakes, pancakes—they are all the same thing: a whole-grain flour mixture usually made into a thin batter with milk and eggs. Back in the day when raw milk soured naturally owing to a lack of refrigeration, and farm-fresh eggs were outside your back door, pancakes were made to incorporate ingredients that needed to be used up. Soaking your grains overnight in some sort of acidic liquid begins to break down the phytic acid and release some of the grain's minerals. Feel free to substitute other whole grains.

DAY 1

½ cup quinoa

½ cup buckwheat groats

½ cup gluten-free rolled oats

1 cup plain kefir or yogurt (cow's, goat's, or coconut milk)

½ cup water

DAY 2

2 large organic eggs

1 tablespoon pure maple syrup or honey

¾ teaspoon baking soda

¼ teaspoon sea salt

OPTIONAL ADDITIONS

Ground cinnamon

Chopped ripe banana

Chopped nuts

Fresh or frozen berries

Butter or coconut oil, for cooking

1. The night before, place the quinoa, groats, and oats into a bowl and pour the kefir and water over them; stir to combine. Set a plate over the bowl and leave it on the counter overnight or for 8 to 10 hours.

2. In the morning, pour the mixture into a blender. Add the eggs, maple syrup, baking soda, and salt. Blend until smooth. Stir in any of the optional additions.

3. Heat a cast-iron or stainless steel skillet over medium-low heat. Add a little butter to the pan and drop the batter by ¼ cup measures. Cook for 60 to 90 seconds on each side. Remove and keep warm while you repeat with the remaining batter, adding a bit of butter before cooking each batch.

> **NUTRITION TIP**
>
> Buckwheat groats are high in phytase, the enzyme that breaks down the phytates in the grain. Rolled oats contain very little phytase. By combining the two grains in the kefir overnight, the phytase from the buckwheat helps break down the phytates in the oats, allowing for better mineral absorption overall.

baby banana pancakes

MAKES 6 MEDIUM PANCAKES (KID-SIZE) OR 12 SMALL ONES (BABY-SIZE)

This egg-free pancake recipe is perfect for babies about nine months or older. I prefer to use sprouted brown rice flour in this recipe because it is easier to digest and does not interfere with mineral absorption—something very important for growing babies! (I buy sprouted rice flour from a company called Planet Rice.) These pancakes are best served with a little bit of fat, which helps keep blood sugar levels balanced. Try a dollop of pastured butter, coconut butter, or sunflower seed butter. My children like to spread almond butter on top of each one!

DRY INGREDIENTS

1 cup sprouted brown rice flour

¼ cup arrowroot powder

1 teaspoon baking powder

¼ teaspoon sea salt

WET INGREDIENTS

¾ cup mashed ripe banana (about
   2 bananas)

½ cup hot water

2 tablespoons melted coconut oil

1 tablespoon pure maple syrup

Coconut oil, for cooking

1. Heat two cast-iron skillets over medium-low. In a medium bowl, whisk together the flour, arrowroot powder, baking powder, and salt. In another small bowl, whisk together the banana, hot water, coconut oil, and maple syrup. Immediately pour the wet mixture into the dry and whisk together, so the hot water warms the flour mixture; this is how the batter binds together without eggs, gluten, or gums.

2. Add about 1 tablespoon coconut oil to each hot skillet. Pour in ¼ to ½ cup batter into each and spread out with the back of the measuring cup or a spoon. Cook for about a minute on each side. Remove and keep warm while you continue making the pancakes with the remaining batter, adding a bit more coconut oil before each batch. Note: be generous with the oil, as egg-free pancakes can stick to the pan without enough oil.

apple cinnamon teff pancakes

FREE OF

MAKES ABOUT 10 PANCAKES

As summer begins to fade into autumn, my children begin asking for these pancakes in the morning. I like to make a simple apple-cinnamon topping for them by simmering for about 10 minutes one sliced apple in a little water with a few dashes of maple syrup and a pinch of ground cinnamon. Put a spoonful of this topping on each pancake with a few tablespoons of chopped walnuts, and you have a fall treat.

DRY INGREDIENTS

2 cups dark brown teff flour

½ cup tapioca flour

1 tablespoon ground cinnamon

2 teaspoons baking powder

¾ teaspoon baking soda

½ teaspoon sea salt

WET INGREDIENTS

2 cups hemp milk or water

½ cup unsweetened applesauce

2 large organic eggs, lightly beaten

3 tablespoons melted coconut oil or butter

3 tablespoons pure maple syrup, plus more
   for serving if desired

Coconut oil, for cooking

Warm apple topping (optional; see
   Headnote)

1. Whisk together the flours, cinnamon, baking powder, baking soda, and salt in a medium bowl. Add the milk, applesauce, eggs, oil, and maple syrup. Whisk until smooth.

2. Heat a 10-inch skillet over medium-low. Add a few teaspoons of coconut oil. When the pan is hot, use a ½-cup measure to pour the batter into the pan. Cook for 60 to 90 seconds on one side, then flip and cook for 30 to 60 seconds more on the second side. Remove and keep warm while you make the remaining pancakes, adding about ½ teaspoon oil before cooking each pancake. Serve with additional maple syrup or warm apple topping, if desired.

buckwheat hazelnut pancakes

FREE OF

MAKES ABOUT 10 PANCAKES

I like to serve these healthy pancakes with warm Blueberry Syrup (page 105). I use Bob's Red Mill hazelnut meal, but you could try grinding your own raw hazelnuts to a very fine meal, if desired. Use any other milk you like in the batter. Serve the pancakes with some organic sausages and sautéed greens for a balanced breakfast.

Coconut oil or butter, for cooking

DRY INGREDIENTS

1¾ cups raw buckwheat flour (see Tip on page 98)

1½ cups hazelnut meal

1½ teaspoons baking powder

¾ teaspoon baking soda

½ teaspoon sea salt

WET INGREDIENTS

2 cups almond milk or hemp milk

2 large organic eggs

2 to 3 tablespoons pure maple syrup

2 to 3 tablespoons melted butter or coconut oil

1. Heat a cast-iron skillet over medium-low. Add a little coconut oil to the pan also to heat.

2. Whisk together the flour, hazelnut meal, baking powder, baking soda, and salt in a medium bowl. Add the almond milk, eggs, maple syrup, and melted butter and whisk together again. Use a ½-cup measure to pour the batter into the hot pan. Cook the pancake for 30 to 60 seconds on each side, adjusting the heat if needed. Remove from the pan and keep warm while you cook the remaining pancakes, adding a little more coconut oil before each pancake.

whole-grain waffles

FREE OF

MAKES ABOUT 8 WAFFLES

This gluten-free waffle is crispy on the outside and soft on the inside, just as a waffle should be. The waffles can be frozen and then reheated in a toaster, or toaster oven, for convenience. To make breakfasts even easier, plan a day to mix up a few batches of the dry ingredients and store them in separate sealed containers, then place the directions and list of wet ingredients on each container. Any type of milk can be used in this recipe; I usually use homemade Hemp Milk (page 452), but almond milk or raw cow's milk works as well!

Coconut oil or melted butter, for waffle iron

DRY INGREDIENTS
1 cup teff flour
¾ cup tapioca flour
½ cup brown rice flour
½ cup sorghum flour
½ cup millet flour
½ cup quinoa flour
1 tablespoon baking powder

2 to 4 teaspoons ground cinnamon
1 teaspoon baking soda
½ teaspoon sea salt

WET INGREDIENTS
3 large organic eggs
6 tablespoons melted coconut oil or butter
4 tablespoons pure maple syrup
2½ to 3 cups hemp milk

1. Heat the waffle iron. Coat it lightly with some coconut oil or butter.

2. In a large bowl, whisk together the dry ingredients. In a separate bowl, whisk together the eggs, coconut oil, maple syrup, and 2½ cups milk, then combine with the dry mixture. Whisk well.

3. Pour some of the batter onto the waffle iron and make one waffle following the manufacturer's instructions. If it seems too dry, add the remaining milk to the batter. Continue to cook the waffles, keeping them warm while you do.

blueberry syrup

FREE OF

MAKES ABOUT 1½ CUPS

Either fresh or frozen blueberries work in this recipe. To vary the recipe, use blackberries, raspberries, or strawberries—or a mix of all of them. Serve this syrup with freshly made pancakes or drizzled over a slice of cake as an alternative to frosting. Store any leftover syrup in a glass jar in the refrigerator for up to ten days. The syrup will solidify a little in the fridge, so it needs to be reheated before using.

1 cup fresh or frozen blueberries

¾ cup water

2 to 3 tablespoons honey or pure maple syrup

1 tablespoon arrowroot powder

Place the berries, water, honey, and arrowroot powder into a blender and blend on high until smooth. Pour the liquid into a small saucepan and heat over medium until little bubbles form. Reduce the heat just slightly and continue to cook while whisking until thickened and clear. Note: It takes only about 5 minutes; just remember to keep whisking. Serve this syrup hot over pancakes or waffles.

VARIATION: In place of the arrowroot, I sometimes use kudzu starch, which is very healing to the intestines. Use ½ tablespoon kudzu in place of 1 tablespoon arrowroot.

nut butter syrup

MAKES ABOUT ½ CUP

I like to mix maple syrup or honey with a creamy nut butter to sneak in a little extra protein and fat into our children's breakfasts. Use organic sunflower butter, almond butter, or cashew butter. Don't heat the syrup, or it will thicken considerably.

¼ cup creamy nut butter

4 to 6 tablespoons pure maple syrup or honey

In a small bowl, whisk together the nut butter and maple syrup. Use a spoon to scoop it out and drizzle over hot pancakes or waffles.

NUTRITION TIP

Pure maple syrup is more than just glucose and sucrose; it is full of antioxidant phenolic compounds that are beneficial for health and longevity. In fact, it has been found to contain over 26 phytochemicals! Maple syrup is made by boiling down the sap of the sugar maple tree, thereby concentrating its beneficial nutrients.

breadsandmuffins

When you are transitioning to a gluten-free diet, having bread and muffin recipes that mimic the flavor and texture of wheat-based products can be so helpful and comforting. I have worked over the years to create healthy and simple gluten-free baking recipes that are nourishing—and best of all, they taste great. They aren't meant to be consumed every day—no matter how nutritious the ingredients are, eating a diet based on baked goods won't benefit your health. We prefer to revolve our diet around vegetables, whole grains, beans, nuts, fruits, wild-caught fish, and pastured meats. With the exception of sourdough bread, baked gluten-free treats are prepared only a few times a month in our home.

If you're a lover of baked goods, I recommend that you make one batch of gluten-free breads or muffins on the weekend, and eat them throughout the week for a super-easy swap-a-day.

GLUTEN-FREE BAKING BASICS

If you are new to gluten-free baking you might find the number of different flours and different baking methods here a bit overwhelming. Once you have a little practice, though, you'll get the hang of it, and baking gluten-free will become second nature. Keep in mind that your gluten-free baking won't be completely free of gluten if you are also using wheat flour in your kitchen. Flour dust can linger in the air for a day or more, and it can land on countertops, dishes, and cooking utensils. It takes only a minute amount of gluten to cause a reaction in a gluten-sensitive person. So, it is best to keep the kitchen gluten-free for sensitive family members.

Whole-Grain Flours

Many gluten-free products and recipes rely on white rice flour, potato starch, and tapioca flour combinations. These refined flours and starches are devoid of many natural fibers, vitamins, minerals, and phytochemicals, and they can cause a sharp rise in blood sugar. For people with functioning blood sugar regulation, this can mean a large spike in insulin production, with a subsequent quick drop in the level of circulating sugar (a condition called hypoglycemia), which may lead to fatigue, foggy thinking, anxiety, and cravings for sweets. For others with dysfunctional blood sugar regulation, this may lead to extended elevated levels of blood sugar and insulin, leaving the individual susceptible to increased inflammation and at increased risk for developing numerous chronic diseases.

In my recipes, I rely on either whole-grain gluten-free flours or grain-free flours, and I use as little starch as possible—or none at all. My favorite flours are sprouted brown rice and buckwheat, but I also use coconut, almond, sorghum, millet, and teff flours, and I like to mix in ground nuts whenever possible to add flavor and protein.

It saves quite a bit of money and packaging if you buy your flours in bulk (see "Resources and Recommendations"). If you don't use your gluten-free flours frequently, it is best to store them in glass jars in your refrigerator. Otherwise, store them in your pantry for quick access. If you buy 25 pounds of flour at a time, freeze three-quarters of it and store the rest in your pantry or refrigerator.

Milk

The protein in milk provides structure and flavor to baked goods. You'll notice that my recipes simply call for "milk." We generally don't have cow's milk in our house, except for some occasional fresh, local raw cream, so for us this means homemade hemp milk, almond milk, cashew milk, or coconut milk. If you'd prefer, any other type of animal milk can be used with good results, such as fresh cow's or goat's milk. I also use "banana milk" on occasion, which is made by blending a ripe banana with a few tablespoons water until it's thin and milky. See the "Beverages" chapter for homemade dairy-free milk recipes.

Natural Sweeteners

The only refined cane sugar I have in the house is for making cultured drinks like kombucha. I prefer to use sweeteners that retain the beneficial phytochemicals, vitamins, and minerals that help metabolize the sugar. Coconut sugar is one we commonly use. It is a granulated sweetener that has a glycemic index of about 35, and comes from the dehydrated sap of the coconut palm. If you do not have coconut sugar, you can replace it with another granulated sweetener, such as Sucanat (whole cane sugar). Raw local honey, pure grade B maple syrup, and coconut nectar are my choice in liquid sweeteners. Other natural sweeteners that can be used are mashed bananas, applesauce, pureed ripe peaches, yacón syrup, and stevia. For a more detailed look into natural sweeteners, see our "Desserts" chapter.

Healthy Fats

Adding fat to baked goods provides tenderness, moisture, and flavor. I use coconut oil, organic palm shortening, organic pastured butter, and olive oil, but I prefer to use virgin coconut oil for the majority of my baking recipes.

Occasionally I use melted butter in a recipe instead of coconut oil. When purchasing butter, look for one labeled "pastured." This means that the animals grazed on their natural diet of grasses instead of being fed corn and soybeans (which are commonly genetically engineered).

Olive oil can also be used on occasion for quickbreads and muffins if you want a break from everything tasting like coconut, though it isn't as stable when heated as coconut oil is. Organic palm shortening is best used when you need a saturated fat, such as for biscuits, scones, and piecrusts. I never use butter substitutes or refined oils such as canola or safflower. These fats are highly refined, most often genetically engineered, and can transform into trans fats during high-heat cooking.

Natural Binders

You'll notice that my recipes don't contain any xanthan gum. This is because xanthan gum isn't a real food. Xanthan gum is an ingredient commonly used in gluten-free baking to help bind ingredients, provide elasticity, and hold moisture. It is a hydrocolloid, meaning it forms a gel in the presence of water. Xanthan gum is most often produced using corn, though it can also come from wheat, dairy, or soybeans. Labeling laws don't require manufacturers to list where it has come from, but be aware that xanthan gum is created from the excrement of the bacterium *Xanthomonas campestris,* which normally grows on rotting vegetables, such as broccoli, and creates a sticky substance. Food manufacturers use corn syrup to feed the bacteria, then they dry the excrement and sell it as powder.

Instead of xanthan gum, I use—alone or in combination—ingredients such as chia seeds, flax seeds, and psyllium husks. Chia and flax help bind ingredients while psyllium holds moisture. Together, these ingredients work in a similar fashion to xanthan gum. Using eggs also helps bind gluten-free flours.

There isn't an exact science or perfect ratio for replacing xanthan gum. I have found that experimentation is the best bet. Oftentimes it is simply easier and more effective to create a new recipe using ground seeds and psyllium rather than try to replace the xanthan gum in an old recipe.

10 Tips for Successful Gluten-Free Baking

1. High Altitude Adjustments. When baking my recipes at high altitude, you might find slightly different results. We live at sea level in a moist climate, so my gluten-free flours retain a little more moisture compared to ingredients stored in very dry climate. Recipes baked at a high altitude often rise much faster with baking powder or baking soda, and can turn out denser, drier, and a tad more crumbly than recipes baked at sea level. If you live at high altitude, you may need to decrease the baking powder and baking soda by ⅛ to ¼ teaspoon per teaspoon called for, while increasing the liquids by 2 to 4 tablespoons per cup of liquid called for.

2. Measuring. When measuring, be sure not to pack down your flours. I usually just scoop my flours out of the jar and then gently level them off. Always use dry measuring cups for the dry ingredients and liquid measures for the liquid ingredients.

3. Varying Oven Temperatures. Oven temperatures can vary widely—sometimes by as much as 50 degrees!—so be sure to buy an oven thermometer and stick it in the oven to get a correct reading.

4. Preheat your oven! If you wait to preheat your oven until after your dry and wet ingredients are mixed, the rising agents—baking soda and baking powder—will begin to react, and you might end up with a denser muffin or quickbread than you wish. Always preheat your oven before you begin mixing the ingredients.

5. Stoneware for baking. I suggest investing in stoneware baking pans for these baking recipes. I use stoneware from Pampered Chef. It works beautifully for gluten-free baked goods. I use a stoneware muffin pan, mini-loaf pan, Bundt pan, and pizza stone.

6. Glass loaf pans. I like to bake my yeast breads in glass Pyrex bread pans. All of the bread recipes in this chapter were tested using this type of pan.

7. Grind your own flour or purchase from a grain mill? Gluten-free grain flours, other than oats and buckwheat, are best bought from a company that specializes in grinding flour. Even a Vitamix has a difficult time getting a fine enough flour with hard grains such as brown rice or teff. See the "Resources and Recommendations" chapter for product and brand recommendations.

8. Making your own buckwheat flour. You'll notice that many of my recipes call for freshly ground, or "raw," buckwheat flour. This type of flour is made by grinding raw buckwheat groats in a coffee grinder, grain grinder, or high-powered blender for a minute or so until a fine powdery flour forms. It is a soft grain and grinds quite easily. This flour is very different from the strong-flavored roasted buckwheat flour found in grocery store aisles. The mild taste of raw buckwheat flour is quite pleasing. Store-bought buckwheat flour made from roasted buckwheat groats absorbs a lot of liquid in baked goods, so you won't have the same results if you use it. I like to grind a large amount of raw buckwheat groats at once and then store the flour in a glass jar in my pantry. Be sure to use certified gluten-free buckwheat, as most buckwheat you find in the bulk bins from your local health food store is cross-contaminated with gluten!

9. Using chia and flax seeds. Chia seeds and flax seeds are high in omega-3 fatty acids that can spoil quickly if not stored in the refrigerator. Use your coffee grinder, small electric grinder, or Vitamix to grind chia and flax seeds into a fine meal. Store them separately in glass jars in your refrigerator for up to a week. Since they tend to clump up when they are ground, I use a small sifter to sift the measured amount needed into the recipe. Chia seeds and flax seeds are not interchangeable in equal amounts. Chia seeds have about twice the binding power of flax, so you would need to use about twice as much ground flax in a recipe calling for ground chia seeds.

10. Using psyllium. Whole psyllium husks and psyllium husk powder are two different things. Read the recipe carefully and use the correct one. As soon as you whisk warm water into the psyllium husk, it will begin to swell immediately. You need to be ready with your dry ingredients, otherwise the mixture will become too thick to work with.

GLUTEN-FREE SOURDOUGH STARTER

This starter recipe can be used to make the recipes on the following pages or to create your own variations of breads, rolls, muffins, or pancakes.

About the Sourdough Process

Wild yeasts are abundant on whole-grain flours. Traditionally, bread was made by cultivating the wild yeasts present on the grain or in the air—you couldn't just go to a store and buy baker's yeast back then. Wild yeasts become active when the environment is right; they prefer an acidic environment. I have found that adding a little apple juice on the first day of the starter helps get the fermentation process going, though this is not always necessary. After about 48 hours, you should see a bit of bubbling. Oftentimes the first microbes to grow are the ones that prefer a more neutral pH; they eat up some of the starches in the flour and produce acids as a by-product. As the environment becomes more acidic, the wild yeasts wake up, usually when the pH drops below 4.

It usually takes at least seven days to create a viable starter. If your house is cool, it may take ten days. Generally, starters should not be used for baking until they are at least a week old, so that the wild yeasts have proliferated enough to be able to raise the bread. You'll find that after about a month or two, your starter will create a better textured and flavored bread than it did at a week old.

Types of Flours Needed

You can use any gluten-free flour for your starter. I prefer to start with teff flour, and then add any combination of millet, brown rice, sorghum, quinoa, amaranth, and buckwheat flours. Using buckwheat in your starter causes it to become considerably thicker, so you will need less flour when making the bread. If I add too much buckwheat flour and the starter becomes too thick, I usually just thin it out with extra water.

Filtered Water

Always use filtered water for making your sourdough starters. Chlorine in city water can inhibit microbial activity, and we certainly don't want that when making a sourdough starter!

Making the Starter

Day 1: Place 1 cup whole-grain gluten-free flour, 1 cup water, and 2 tablespoons apple juice in a large wide-mouthed half-gallon or gallon glass jar; whisk to blend. Place a thin dishtowel or cloth napkin over it, and place it into an undisturbed warm spot in your kitchen.

Day 2: After 24 hours, add ½ cup flour and ½ cup filtered water; whisk to blend.

Day 3: After 24 hours, add another ½ cup flour and ½ cup water; whisk to blend. By now you should be seeing a lot of bubbling and noticing a distinct sour smell.

Day 4 and Beyond: Feed your starter the same flour-water mixture every 12 to 24 hours—12 if your kitchen is very warm, 24 if your kitchen is cooler. After every feeding, you should see the starter become very active, and then rise and fall within a 12-hour period. Make sure to feed your starter when you see very few bubbles and a layer of dark liquid on top. This liquid is called *hooch,* and is an alcohol by-product of fermentation; it means your starter is starving and needs to be fed! Some people like to pour it off, while others stir it back in before feeding it. I've done it both ways, with good results.

Making a starter is not an exact science. It is about tuning in to those lovely little microbes in your jars. Once you do it a few times, you'll gain a better understanding of the cues that determine when to feed it and when to wait.

Keep feeding your starter every 12 to 24 hours, and by day 7, you should have a viable starter to bake bread with. As your starter grows larger in volume, you will need to start feeding more flour and water at every feeding. By the time I have about half to three-fourths of a gallon of starter, I usually begin feeding it 1 cup of flour and 1 cup of water at each feeding.

Using Your Starter

When your starter is ready to use, measure out the amount needed for your bread recipe and then add 1 cup gluten-free flour and 1 cup filtered water. You can keep your starter going by feeding it every 12 hours with a mixture of ½ cup gluten-free flour plus ½ cup filtered water. This way you can use it every few days to make breads or rolls. If you see a lot of crusting on the jar, then pour it into a clean jar every week.

Taking a Break

If you go on vacation, or don't plan on using your starter for a while, just stick it in the refrigerator with a lid on and feed it equal amounts of flour and water every 2 to 3 weeks. When you're ready to use it again, place the jar on your counter and begin to feed it every 12 hours.

gluten-free sourdough bread

FREE OF

MAKES 1 LOAF

Sourdough bread baking is an art, not an exact science. Each loaf I make yields slightly different complex and unique flavors. The best time to use your starter for bread baking is a few hours after you feed it—when it is in its "active and bubbly" stage. Use this beautiful, nutritious loaf for sandwiches or as a complement to your main meal.

4 cups Gluten-Free Sourdough Starter (page 112), active and bubbly

½ cup warm water, or more as needed

2 teaspoons sea salt

2 tablespoons extra-virgin olive oil

2 tablespoons pure maple syrup

4 tablespoons ground chia seeds

4 tablespoons whole psyllium husks

1 to 1¾ cups whole-grain gluten-free flour, or more as needed

¼ cup tapioca flour or arrowroot powder

1. Place the sourdough starter in a medium bowl. Whisk in the warm water, salt, olive oil, and maple syrup. Whisk in the ground chia and psyllium husks. Let the mixture rest for no more than 2 minutes, then add the flours. Use a fork to mix the ingredients. The dough should feel slightly wet and sticky, but stiff enough to hold shape. If the dough is too dry, it won't rise properly; add a little more water if it feels dense and dry. If it is too wet, add a little extra flour; it should feel wetter than yeast-risen recipes.

2. Place the dough into an oiled 9 by 5-inch loaf pan and smooth the top with your fingers. Place a plastic produce bag or piece of parchment paper over the dough and set it in a warm spot to rise

for 3 to 6 hours. I usually set it on top of my refrigerator or in a warm, sunny spot in my house. To help the dough rise a bit faster, I sometimes set the loaf in a pan of warm water. Warm rising should only take about 3 hours. If your kitchen is very cool, though, the rising time may take up to 8 hours. You should see the dough *almost* double in size during rising.

3. Preheat the oven to 375°F. Bake the bread for 60 to 75 minutes, or until the crust is golden. Let cool for about 10 minutes, then remove from the pan and continue to cool on a wire rack.

sourdough buckwheat burger buns

FREE OF

MAKES 8 BUNS

These sourdough buns are soft and spongy. Use them for sandwiches, burgers, or as an accompaniment to a meal. We like to serve them with the Sloppy Joes (page 318) and some sort of lacto-fermented vegetable. It makes a nice, cozy wintertime meal.

3 cups Gluten-Free Sourdough Starter (page 112), active and bubbly

½ cup warm water, or more as needed

1½ teaspoons sea salt

2 tablespoons extra-virgin olive oil, plus a little extra for bun tops

1 tablespoon pure maple syrup

2 tablespoons ground chia seeds

2 tablespoons whole psyllium husks

1 cup raw buckwheat flour (see Tip on page 98)

¼ cup tapioca flour or arrowroot powder

1. Place the sourdough starter in a medium bowl. Whisk in the water, salt, olive oil, and maple syrup. Then whisk in the ground chia and psyllium husks. Let the mixture rest for about 2 minutes. Slowly add the flours until the dough thickens. Use a fork to mix well. The dough should feel slightly wet and sticky, like thick cake batter. If it feels dense and dry, then add more water, a little at a time, until it lightens up. If the dough is too dry, it won't rise properly and you will have hockey pucks instead of burger buns!

2. Line a baking sheet with parchment paper. Place 8 oiled English muffin rings on the sheet. Scoop

out dough with a spoon and evenly distribute it among the rings. Drizzle a little olive oil over the top of each bun (this will keep the tops from drying out during rising and baking). Place a plastic produce bag or another piece of parchment paper over and set the baking sheet in a warm, sunny spot to rise for 3 to 6 hours, or until doubled in size.

3. Preheat the oven to 350°F. Bake the buns for about 35 minutes. Wait about 10 minutes and then pop the buns out of the metal rings. Cool the buns on a wire rack before slicing in half.

wholesome burger buns

FREE OF

MAKES 6 BUNS

Use these buns to create a nutritious hamburger with grass-fed beef, salmon patties, or vegan veggie burgers. Our children like to make hummus, cucumber, and sprout sandwiches with the buns and pack them into their school lunches. After the buns have cooled, cut them in half and freeze some for later use.

WET INGREDIENTS

2 cups warm water (105 to 110°F)

1 tablespoon active dry yeast

1 tablespoon pure maple syrup

½ cup ground golden flax seeds

¼ cup whole psyllium husks

DRY INGREDIENTS

1¼ cups raw buckwheat flour, or more as needed (see Tip on page 98)

1 cup teff flour

¾ cup tapioca flour

1½ teaspoons sea salt

Extra-virgin olive oil

Sesame seeds

1. Place the water in a small bowl. Add the yeast and maple syrup, then whisk and let rest until foamy and bubbly. Add the flax seeds and psyllium husks; quickly whisk together.

2. In a large bowl, combine the flours and salt, whisking well. Add the yeast mixture to the flour mixture and combine using a wooden spoon until the dough comes together. The dough might feel a little sticky; add a few additional tablespoons of buckwheat or tapioca flour, and knead the dough in the bowl until it forms a ball.

3. Lightly oil a large baking sheet or glass baking dish with olive oil. Form the dough into 6 equal balls, then slightly flatten each between the palms of your hand. Place on the baking sheet and brush each bun with olive oil, then sprinkle with sesame seeds. Let rise in a warm place for 45 to 60 minutes. If your spot is very warm, the buns may need only about 30 minutes of rising time.

4. Preheat the oven to 350°F. Bake for about 30 minutes. Use a spatula to take the buns off the baking sheet. Place on a wire rack to cool, and when cooled, cut each bun in half using a serrated knife and serve.

grain-free burger buns

FREE OF

MAKES 6 BUNS

These hamburger buns contain no yeast, which means no rising time! They are easy to make and they bake quickly. Serve them with grass-fed beef burgers or our favorite, the Sloppy Joes (page 318). Store any leftover buns in a sealed container on your counter for up to three days. These buns are best sliced in half and toasted lightly before serving.

1½ cups raw cashew butter

4 large organic eggs

3 tablespoons extra-virgin olive oil

¾ teaspoon sea salt

¾ teaspoon baking soda

1½ teaspoons raw apple cider vinegar

1 to 2 tablespoons sesame seeds, for topping

1. Preheat the oven to 350°F. Line a large baking sheet with parchment paper and place 6 oiled English muffin rings on it.

2. Put the cashew butter, eggs, olive oil, salt, and baking soda into a food processor and process until smooth. Add the vinegar and process again to combine. Divide the batter evenly among the muffin rings. Sprinkle each with sesame seeds.

3. Bake the buns for 20 to 25 minutes. Cool for about 10 minutes, then run a knife around the inside edges of each muffin ring to release the bun. Cut the buns in half and serve.

everyday sandwich bread

FREE OF

MAKES 1 LOAF

This is the bread recipe our children like best. I've substituted nearly all the flours with good results. For example, I often use just 2 to 2½ cups of sprouted brown rice flour in place of the sorghum flour, brown rice flour, and millet flour (keeping the almond and tapioca flours in the mix). The bread remains moist and ready to eat without needing to toast it. It is great for sandwiches or hot out of the oven!

WET INGREDIENTS

2½ cups warm water (105 to 110°F)

1 tablespoon active dry yeast

2 tablespoons pure maple syrup

2 tablespoons extra-virgin olive oil

⅓ cup ground chia seeds

⅓ cup whole psyllium husks

DRY INGREDIENTS

1 to 1½ cups sorghum flour

1 cup brown rice flour

1 cup tapioca flour

¾ cup blanched almond flour

½ cup millet flour

1½ teaspoons sea salt

1. Place the warm water in a bowl or a 4-cup liquid glass measure. Add the yeast and maple syrup, and whisk together. Let rest for 5 to 10 minutes to activate the yeast. The mixture should get foamy or bubbly. If not, dump it out and start over.

2. While the yeast is activating, mix 1 cup of the sorghum flour with the other flours and salt in a large bowl. Lightly oil a 9 by 5-inch loaf pan.

3. When the yeast is bubbly, whisk in the olive oil, ground chia seeds, and psyllium husks into the yeast mixture. Let stand for about 1 minute to let the chia and psyllium release their gelatinous substances; whisk again.

4. Pour the yeast mixture into the flour mixture and stir with a large wooden spoon until thick.

Turn out the dough onto a floured wooden board. Add the remaining sorghum flour, a little at a time (¼ to ½ cup), until the dough holds together and isn't too sticky. Form the dough into an oblong, and place in the bread pan. Cover with a damp towel or piece of waxed paper, and place in a warm spot to rise. I like to place the bread pan in another larger pan of warm water. Let the dough rise for 1 hour, or until nearly doubled in size. The rising time will depend on the temperature of the air around the dough.

5. Preheat the oven to 375°F. Bake the loaf for 55 to 60 minutes, or until the top is lightly golden and a nice crust has formed. Let the loaf cool in the pan for 10 to 20 minutes, then release it with a knife and turn the loaf over to cool on a wire rack.

dark teff sandwich bread

FREE OF

MAKES 1 LOAF

Most people think this tastes a lot like whole wheat bread. We love it for making sandwiches or for toast in the morning.

WET INGREDIENTS

2½ cups warm water (105 to 110°F)

1 tablespoon active dry yeast

2 tablespoons pure maple syrup

⅓ cup ground chia seeds

⅓ cup whole psyllium husks

DRY INGREDIENTS

3 to 3½ cups teff flour

½ cup tapioca flour or arrowroot powder

1½ teaspoons sea salt

2 tablespoons extra-virgin olive oil

1. Place the warm water in a bowl or 4-cup liquid glass measure. Add the yeast and the maple syrup; whisk together. Let rest for 5 to 10 minutes to activate the yeast. The mixture should get foamy or bubbly. If not, dump it out and start over.

2. While the yeast is activating, mix 3 cups of the teff flour with the tapioca flour and salt in a large bowl. Oil a 9 by 5-inch loaf pan.

3. When the yeast is activated, whisk in the olive oil, ground chia seeds, and psyllium husks into the yeast mixture. Let stand for about 1 minute to let the chia and psyllium release their gelatinous substances; whisk again.

4. Pour the yeast mixture into the flour mixture and stir together with a large wooden spoon until thick. Turn out the dough onto a floured wooden board. Add more teff flour, a little at a time, until

the dough holds together and isn't too sticky. Form the dough into an oblong and place in the loaf pan. Cover with a damp towel or piece of waxed paper, and place in a warm spot to rise, about 1 hour or until nearly doubled in size. (I like to place the bread pan in another larger pan of warm water.) The rising time will depend on the temperature of the air around the dough.

5. Preheat the oven to 375°F. Bake the loaf for 55 to 60 minutes, or until the top is lightly golden and a nice crust has formed. Let the pan cool for 10 to 20 minutes, then release the bread with a knife and turn it over. Cool on a wire rack.

VARIATION: If I reduce the teff flour and replace it with sorghum flour, our children call this "gluten-free wheat bread." I use 2 cups sorghum flour, 1½ cups teff flour, and ½ cup tapioca flour, then I knead in some extra teff or sorghum flour until the dough isn't sticky.

buckwheat cinnamon raisin bread

FREE OF

MAKES 1 LOAF

Our family enjoys this bread so much that I need to make a two loaves at a time. For best storage, slice the bread once it has cooled, wrap in a paper bag and then in a plastic bag, and then freeze. This way you can take a slice or two out of the freezer for toast whenever needed. I usually keep one loaf on the counter and freeze the other. This bread makes great almond butter and jam sandwiches for school lunches!

WET INGREDIENTS

2½ cups warm water (105 to 110°F)

1 tablespoon active dry yeast

4 tablespoons pure maple syrup

2 tablespoons extra-virgin olive oil

⅓ cup ground chia seeds

⅓ cup whole psyllium husks

DRY INGREDIENTS

3½ to 4 cups raw buckwheat flour (see Tip on page 98)

½ cup arrowroot powder

2 tablespoons ground cinnamon

1½ teaspoons sea salt

½ to 1 cup raisins

1. Place the warm water in a bowl or 4-cup liquid glass measure. Add the yeast and maple syrup, then whisk together. Let rest for 5 to 10 minutes to activate the yeast. The mixture should get foamy or bubbly. If not, dump it out and start over.

2. While the yeast is activating, mix 3½ cups of the buckwheat flour with the arrowroot powder, cinnamon, salt, and raisins in a large bowl. Oil a 9 by 5-inch loaf pan.

3. When the yeast is activated, whisk in the olive oil, ground chia seeds, and psyllium husks into the yeast mixture. Let stand for about 1 minute to allow the chia and psyllium to release their gelatinous substances; whisk again.

4. Pour the wet mixture into the flour mixture and stir together with a large wooden spoon until thick.

Turn out the dough onto a floured wooden board. Add more buckwheat flour, a little at a time, until the dough holds together and isn't too sticky. Don't add too much flour, or the dough will become very dense; it should still be slightly sticky. Form the dough into an oblong, and place in the loaf pan. Cover with a damp towel and place in a warm spot to rise for an hour, or until nearly doubled in size. (I like to place the bread pan in another larger pan of warm water.) The rising time will depend on the temperature of the air around the dough.

5. Preheat the oven to 375°F. Bake the bread for about 60 minutes, or until the top is lightly golden and a nice crust has formed. Let the pan cool for 10 to 20 minutes, then release the loaf with a knife and turn it over. Cool on a wire rack.

rosemary sea salt breadsticks

FREE OF

MAKES ABOUT 10 BREADSTICKS

I like to fix a batch of this dough and give it to my children to knead and make shapes. It's a relaxing after-school activity for them, and they help contribute to the evening meal! Use this recipe for breadsticks or omit the fresh rosemary and form the dough into balls to make dinner rolls. You can sprinkle the tops with sesame seeds or add seeds—such as sunflower, pumpkin, flax, and poppy—to the dough. This recipe is versatile. Have fun with it!

WET INGREDIENTS

2 cups warm water (105 to 110°F)

1 tablespoon active dry yeast

1 tablespoon pure maple syrup

2 tablespoons extra-virgin olive oil

½ cup ground golden flax seeds

¼ cup whole psyllium husks

DRY INGREDIENTS

1¼ cups brown rice flour, or more as needed

1 cup teff flour, or more as needed

¾ cup tapioca flour or arrowroot powder

2 to 3 tablespoons chopped fresh rosemary

1½ teaspoons sea salt

1. Place the warm water in a bowl or 4-cup liquid glass measure. Add the yeast and maple syrup, whisk together. Let rest for 5 to 10 minutes to activate the yeast. The mixture should get foamy or bubbly. If not, dump it out and start over.

2. While the yeast is activating, mix the flours, rosemary, and salt in a large bowl. Oil a baking sheet.

3. When the yeast is activated, whisk in the olive oil, ground flax seeds, and psyllium husks into the yeast mixture. Let stand for 2 to 3 minutes to let the flax and psyllium release their gelatinous substances. Whisk again.

4. Pour the wet mixture into the flour mixture and stir together with a large wooden spoon until thick.

Turn out the dough onto a floured wooden board. Add more flour, a little at a time, until the dough holds together and isn't too sticky. Divide the dough equally into 10 balls. On the floured board, roll each ball into a long log, then place the logs on the baking sheet. Put the baking sheet in a warm place to rise for 45 to 60 minutes. (I like to place it on top of a large pan filled partly with water that is set on the stove over low heat.)

5. Preheat the oven to 375°F. Bake the breadsticks for 30 to 35 minutes. Cool for about 10 minutes, then serve with a homemade marinara sauce or a good olive oil for dipping.

farmhouse seed bread

FREE OF

MAKES 1 LOAF

This artisan bread reminds me of a hearty seeded whole wheat bread. If you have a corn allergy, replace the cornmeal with almond meal. I have made this bread with many different flour combinations, so feel free to experiment, though this is my favorite for flavor and texture. The bread gets its crusty crust from being baked on a pizza stone with a pan of water on the lower oven rack. The steam from the water helps form the crust. The bread will be a little gummy hot out of the oven, so let it cool a bit before cutting into it. Slice and serve with a good-quality olive oil for dipping. It is also delicious spread with either almond butter or hummus!

WET INGREDIENTS

2½ cups warm water (105 to 110°F)

1 tablespoon active dry yeast

2 tablespoons pure maple syrup

2 tablespoons extra-virgin olive oil, plus more for drizzling

⅓ cup ground chia seeds

⅓ cup whole psyllium husks

DRY INGREDIENTS

1 cup teff flour, or more as needed

1 cup sorghum flour, or more as needed

½ cup sweet rice flour

½ cup organic cornmeal (see Tip)

¼ cup uncooked millet

¼ cup raw sunflower seeds

2 tablespoons poppy seeds

2 tablespoons flax seeds

1½ teaspoons sea salt

1. Place the warm water in a bowl or 4-cup liquid glass measure. Add the yeast and maple syrup, then whisk together. Let rest for 5 to 10 minutes to activate the yeast. The mixture should get foamy or bubbly. If not, dump it out and start over.

2. While the yeast is activating, combine the flours, cornmeal, millet, seeds, and salt in a large bowl. Line a baking sheet with parchment paper.

3. When the yeast is activated, whisk in the olive oil, ground chia seeds, and psyllium husks into the yeast mixture. Let stand for about 1 minute to

let the chia and psyllium release their gelatinous substances; whisk again.

4. Pour the wet mixture into the flour mixture and stir together with a large wooden spoon until thick. Add more teff and sorghum flours, a little at a time, kneading them in until the dough holds together and isn't too sticky. Form the dough into a ball, place on the baking sheet, and place in a warm spot to rise for an hour, or until doubled in size. (I like to place the baking sheet over a pot of warm water.) The rising time will depend on the temperature of the air around the dough.

5. Preheat the oven to 375 °F. Place a pizza stone (or stoneware baking sheet) on the middle rack to heat up. Put a shallow wide pan of water on the bottom rack of the oven—I usually use a 9 by 13-inch glass pan filled three-fourths of the way with water. Drizzle the top of the risen bread with a little olive oil. Lift the bread and the parchment paper onto the pizza stone in the oven. Bake for 55 to 60 minutes. Remove from the oven and let cool 30 to 60 minutes before cutting into it. The texture of this bread will be perfect once cooled.

VARIATION: For an olive-rosemary bread, omit the seeds and add 1 cup sliced pitted Kalamata olives and 2 to 4 tablespoons chopped fresh rosemary.

INGREDIENT TIP

I use Arrowhead Mills cornmeal because it is the only brand I have found to be both organic and certified gluten-free.

chia dinner rolls

FREE OF

MAKES 6 TO 8 ROLLS

Serve these hearty rolls with a baked chicken dinner or a vegetable bean soup. Because of the amount of chia seeds, the dough will feel a little different from my other bread recipes. The tendency will be to add more flour, but try not to. The dough should remain slightly sticky.

WET INGREDIENTS

2 cups warm water (105 to 110°F)

1 tablespoon active dry yeast

2 tablespoons plus 1 teaspoon pure maple syrup

3 tablespoons extra-virgin olive oil or melted butter

DRY INGREDIENTS

3 cups sorghum flour, plus more as needed

1 cup ground chia seeds

1½ teaspoons sea salt

Milk, for brushing rolls (optional)

1. Place the water in a small bowl. Add the yeast and the 1 teaspoon maple syrup, then whisk and let rest until foamy and bubbly. Add the oil and remaining 2 tablespoons maple syrup, and whisk together again. Oil a 9 by 13-inch baking pan.

2. In a large mixing bowl, combine the flour, chia seeds, and salt. Add the yeast mixture and whisk together until thickened, working quickly so it doesn't form lumps. Turn out onto a well-floured wooden board and knead for a few minutes, incorporating more flour as necessary until the dough is no longer very sticky—but be careful not to add too much flour. (I usually add ½ to 1 cup more flour.) Divide the dough into 6 to 8 equal balls and place in the pan. Cover with a cloth or parchment paper and let rise in a warm place for 1 hour.

3. Preheat the oven to 350°F. Brush the tops of the rolls with milk, if desired. Bake for 30 to 40 minutes.

KITCHEN TIP

To help the rolls rise, place the pan into a larger pan filled partly with very hot water. You can also set the pan atop a pot of heated water.

NUTRITION TIP

Baking with chia seeds improves the texture of the final product; and foods made with chia seeds slow the release of carbohydrates into the bloodstream.

almond herb pizza crust

FREE OF

MAKES ONE 12- TO 14-INCH PIZZA CRUST

Use the Easy Homemade Pizza Sauce (page 329) and your favorite toppings to make healthy gluten-free pizza! If you don't have sprouted brown rice flour, then use regular stone-ground brown rice flour—they both work great!

WET INGREDIENTS

¾ cup warm water (105 to 110°F)

1 package active dry yeast (2¼ teaspoons)

1 teaspoon pure maple syrup

1 tablespoon extra-virgin olive oil, plus more for baking

DRY INGREDIENTS

1½ cups packed blanched almond flour

1 cup sprouted brown rice flour

¾ cup arrowroot powder or tapioca flour

2 to 3 teaspoons dried Italian herbs

¾ teaspoon sea salt

1. Place the warm water in a small bowl or 1-cup liquid glass measuring cup. Add the yeast and maple syrup. Whisk together, then let stand until the mixture gets foamy and bubbly. Then whisk in the olive oil.

2. In a medium bowl, combine the flours, herbs, and salt. Pour the yeast mixture into the flour mixture and stir together using a wooden spoon. Form the dough into a ball, cover the bowl, and let rise in a warm spot for about 45 minutes.

3. Preheat the oven to 375°F. Oil a pizza stone or baking sheet with a little olive oil. Punch down the dough and place in the center of the stone. Drizzle a little more olive oil over the top of the dough so a rolling pin doesn't stick to it. Roll out the dough into a thin crust, about ¼ inch thick. (You can also press the dough into a flat circle using your hands.) Bake for 15 to 20 minutes, then remove from the oven and add your favorite toppings. Return the pizza to the oven and bake for another 10 to 15 minutes, or until the toppings are cooked to your liking. Alternatively, if you want flatbread or to spread raw toppings onto the crust (and not bake it a second time), bake for approximately 25 minutes total.

yeast-free buckwheat pizza crust

FREE OF

MAKES ONE 12- TO 14-INCH PIZZA CRUST

Use this yeast-free recipe to make your favorite pizza. I like to lightly roast a variety of vegetables while the crust is cooking—try red onions, zucchini, mushrooms, and red bell peppers. Use the Pumpkin Seed Pesto (page 339) and a little organic feta cheese or Macadamia Nut Cheese (page 338) as a topping.

DRY INGREDIENTS

2¼ cups raw buckwheat flour (see Tip on page 98)

½ cup tapioca flour

½ teaspoon sea salt

½ teaspoon baking soda

¼ teaspoon garlic powder

WET INGREDIENTS

1 cup warm water

¼ cup extra-virgin olive oil, plus extra for baking

1 tablespoon pure maple syrup

1 tablespoon raw apple cider vinegar

1. Preheat the oven to 375°F. In a medium bowl, combine the dry ingredients, whisking well. In another bowl, combine the wet ingredients. Pour the wet into the dry and whisk until the dough gets stringy. The dough will be thinner, more like cake batter. If it is too thick to whisk, add a tad more water.

2. Oil a 12 by 15-inch stoneware baking sheet or a large pizza stone generously with olive oil. Scoop out the dough (it will begin to thicken as it sits) and, with oiled hands, work the dough into a thin layer covering most of the stone. You may need to drizzle on a little extra olive oil on top of the dough or on your hands to prevent sticking. (I use a 12 by 15-inch baking sheet, though if you use a larger sheet, you'll get a thinner, crispier crust.) Bake the crust for 15 to 20 minutes, or until it is just slightly golden on top. If you like it crispier, leave it in the oven a little longer.

3. Top your crust with your favorite sauce and toppings, then bake for approximately 10 more minutes.

whole-grain pizza crust

FREE OF

MAKES ONE 12- TO 14-INCH PIZZA CRUST

Pizza is so versatile. You can make a simple vegetable pizza and serve small slices as a party appetizer or load on the toppings for a full meal. This is a thin crust with a crispy bottom and a slightly chewy center. I bake it on my 15-inch round pizza stone. Sometimes we fully bake the crust and then add a layer of pesto, fresh baby spinach, sliced cherry tomatoes, and a few dollops of Cashew Sour Cream (page 336) and serve it fresh.

WET INGREDIENTS

1 cup warm water (105 to 110°F)

1 package active dry yeast (2¼ teaspoons)

2 teaspoons pure maple syrup

2 tablespoons ground chia seeds

¼ cup extra-virgin olive oil, plus more for baking

DRY INGREDIENTS

1 cup teff flour, or more as needed

1 cup brown rice flour

½ cup tapioca flour

1 teaspoon sea salt

1. Place the water in a small bowl or a 2-cup liquid glass measure. Add the yeast and maple syrup. Whisk together, then let stand until the mixture gets foamy and bubbly. Whisk in the ground chia seeds and olive oil until the mixture thickens and a thin gel forms.

2. In a medium bowl, whisk together the dry ingredients. Pour the wet mixture into the dry, and stir together using a wooden spoon. Knead the dough a few times while it is still in the bowl. Add more flour if the dough seems sticky. Form the dough into a ball, cover the bowl, and let rise in a warm spot for about 1 hour.

3. Preheat the oven to 400°F. Oil a pizza stone or baking sheet with about 1 tablespoon of olive oil. Punch down the dough and place in the center of the stone. Drizzle a little more olive oil over the top of the dough so the rolling pin doesn't stick to it. Roll out into a thin crust, about ¼ inch thick. Bake the crust for about 15 minutes, then remove from the oven and top with your favorite toppings. Bake for another 10 minutes, or until the toppings are cooked to your liking. (If you want to use your crust as flatbread or spread raw toppings onto it, bake for approximately 20 minutes total.)

coconut flour flatbreads

FREE OF

MAKES 4 SMALL FLATBREADS

This simple bread recipe is nice to make once in a while if you are following a grain-free or low-carb diet. It is quite filling and the texture is very bread-like. Serve it with your main meal or use two of them to make a sandwich. They are also delicious slathered with homemade jam and sunflower seed butter!

½ cup ground golden flax seeds

½ cup hot water

2 tablespoons melted coconut oil or extra-virgin olive oil, plus more for baking

1 tablespoon raw apple cider vinegar

6 tablespoons coconut flour

¼ teaspoon sea salt

¼ teaspoon baking soda

OPTIONAL ADDITIONS

Sliced Kalamata olives

Chopped fresh rosemary

Snipped fresh chives

Sesame seeds; for topping (optional)

1. Preheat the oven to 350°F. Line a baking sheet with parchment paper.

2. In a food processor fitted with the "s" blade, combine the ground flax seeds and hot water; pulse a few times. Let rest for about 3 minutes to thicken. Add the 2 tablespoons oil and the vinegar and process again to combine. Add the coconut flour, salt, and baking soda and process until the dough has formed a ball. Add any optional ingredients at this time and pulse to combine.

3. Use wet hands to form 4 balls. Flatten the balls into individual flatbreads. Place on the baking sheet and brush with oil and sprinkle with sesame seeds, if desired.

4. Bake for 30 to 35 minutes, flipping each flatbread half way though baking, until cooked through. Cool completely, then serve.

pita bread

FREE OF

MAKES FIVE 6-INCH PITA BREADS

These simple, yeast-free pita breads can be made in just minutes. Make pita sandwiches or serve with soup, curried stews, or as a crust for individual pizzas. I like to fill them with Asian Chicken Salad (page 195) or Sweet Potato Falafels (page 294) and cultured vegetables and lettuce. My daughters like to stuff them with turkey, lettuce, and sliced Raw Sour Dill Pickles (page 477) for their school lunches. If you are not using them right away, layer the pitas between sheets of waxed paper and store in a sealed container. They may also be frozen.

WET INGREDIENTS

1¼ cups warm water

6 tablespoons ground golden flax seeds

2 tablespoons extra-virgin olive oil

1 tablespoon raw apple cider vinegar

DRY INGREDIENTS

1½ cups sorghum flour

½ cup sweet rice flour, or more as needed

½ teaspoon sea salt

½ teaspoon baking soda

1. Preheat the oven to broil (550°F). Line one or two baking sheets with parchment paper. Position your oven rack so it is in the center of the oven, not directly underneath the broiler.

2. Combine the warm water and ground flax seeds in a medium mixing bowl. Let rest for about 5 minutes to thicken. Whisk in the olive oil and apple cider vinegar.

3. Add the dry ingredients to the wet and use a fork to mix well. You should be able to form a ball of dough that is neither too sticky nor too dry. If the dough seems sticky, add a little more sweet rice

flour; I sometimes add up to ¼ cup more flour. If the dough seems too dry, add a dash of water. Divide the dough into 5 equal pieces. Using wet hands, roll each piece in the palms of your hands into a ball. Flatten each ball with your hands until 5 to 6 inches in diameter and place on the baking sheet. If your sheet is large enough you should be able to fit all of them on it.

4. Bake for 10 to 12 minutes, flipping each flatbread after 6 or 7 minutes, until they are puffed slightly and golden around the edges. Let cool, and then slice them in half and, if need be, cut into the bread to form a pocket.

buckwheat cinnamon rolls

FREE OF

MAKES ABOUT 10 ROLLS

Cinnamon rolls have always been a favorite of mine. I have fond childhood memories of making homemade cinnamon rolls with my mother. Kids love to help sprinkle the cinnamon and sugar into the filling and then spread a frosting onto the baked rolls. We use the Dairy-Free Cream Cheese Frosting (page 441).

DRY INGREDIENTS

4 cups raw buckwheat flour, or more as needed (see Tip on page 98)

1 cup tapioca flour, or more as needed

1 tablespoon baking powder

1 teaspoon sea salt

½ teaspoon baking soda

WET INGREDIENTS

1 cup mashed cooked white sweet potato (about 1 small potato)

1 cup unsweetened applesauce

⅓ cup pure maple syrup

⅓ cup melted coconut oil

FILLING

¼ to ½ cup softened coconut oil or butter

½ to ¾ cup coconut sugar

2 to 4 tablespoons ground cinnamon

1. Preheat the oven to 350°F. Oil two 8- or 9-inch round cake pans.

2. In a large bowl, combine the dry ingredients and mix well. Place the wet ingredients into a high-speed blender and blend until very smooth and creamy. Pour the wet mixture into the dry and combine using a wooden spoon. Add more buckwheat flour, a tablespoon or so at a time, until the dough forms a ball.

3. Generously flour a work surface using a little more buckwheat or tapioca flour. Turn out the dough onto the floured surface, then sprinkle the top with a little more flour if it is still too sticky. Roll out the dough into a large rectangle using a floured rolling pin. Spread with the softened coconut oil. (Don't use melted coconut oil or another oil, as it will leak out and make it

impossible to roll and hold the shape.) Sprinkle with the sugar and cinnamon. Begin to roll from the long end toward you. If the dough is sticking, coax it up with a large, thin spatula coated with flour. When you have a long roll, slice it with a serrated knife, and place the slices into the pans. Bake for about 30 minutes.

> **NUTRITION TIP**
>
> Buckwheat has many nutritional benefits. It helps to maintain blood glucose levels and has been shown to be beneficial for diabetics. It is high in the flavonoid rutin, which helps to prevent disease through its antioxidant effects. It is also a rich source of magnesium. Magnesium acts as a co-factor for over 300 enzymes in the human body! All reactions that involve ATP, the energy currency of our cells, depend on magnesium.

coconut flour biscuits

FREE OF

MAKES 10 TO 12 BISCUITS

These low-glycemic, grain-free biscuits are simple and quick to prepare! Serve them with organic bacon and sautéed kale for breakfast, or with a bean and vegetable stew for dinner. You can also cut this recipe in half and use it to top the Chicken Pot Pie (page 311).

DRY INGREDIENTS

1 cup coconut flour

1 teaspoon baking soda

¼ teaspoon sea salt

WET INGREDIENTS

½ cup butter or organic palm shortening

6 large organic eggs

1 cup milk (see Tip)

1. Preheat the oven to 375°F. Lightly grease a large baking sheet with coconut oil.

2. Place the dry ingredients into a food processor and pulse a few times to incorporate. Add the butter, and process until fine crumbs form. Add the eggs and milk; process until smooth. The dough will look watery and thin at first. Just turn off the food processor and let the dough rest for a few minutes to thicken up.

3. Drop the batter to form 10 to 12 biscuits onto the baking sheet. Lightly reshape the biscuits with your hands, if desired. Bake for 20 to 25 minutes.

> **INGREDIENT TIP**
>
> For the milk, I prefer to use homemade cashew cream, but any type of thick, rich milk will work, such as coconut milk or raw cream.

pumpkin scones

MAKES 8 SCONES

There is nothing more scrumptious than spiced pumpkin scones and hot tea on a chilly autumn morning. If you can tolerate dairy, then replace the shortening with cold organic unsalted butter and use either cow's or goat's milk. I usually make my own cashew milk for these or use unsweetened Hemp Milk (page 452).

1 cup sorghum flour

½ cup sweet rice flour

4 tablespoons maple sugar or coconut sugar

2 teaspoons baking powder

½ teaspoon sea salt

1 teaspoon ground cinnamon

½ teaspoon ground ginger

¼ teaspoon grated nutmeg

6 tablespoons organic palm shortening

2 tablespoons ground chia seeds

2 tablespoons hot water

6 tablespoons cold pumpkin puree

½ cup cold hemp milk, almond milk, or coconut milk

OPTIONAL TOPPINGS

Milk

Maple sugar

1. Preheat the oven to 425°F.

2. Place the flours, sugar, baking powder, salt, and spices in a medium bowl and whisk together. Add the shortening, cutting it in with your fingers or a pastry cutter. I use my fingers until coarse crumbs are formed.

3. Place the ground chia seeds and hot water into a small bowl and immediately whisk together with a fork. Add the pumpkin and milk; whisk again. (Sometimes I add the ground chia, water, pumpkin, and milk to my blender and blend on high to puree them.) Add the pumpkin mixture to the flour mixture and quickly mix with a fork or spoon until just combined. Only mix the dough until it comes together, or you will end up with a doughier scone rather than a flakey one. The dough should be slightly sticky.

4. Turn the dough out onto a lightly floured cutting board and pat into a circle of about 1 inch thickness. Do not overwork the dough. With a large, sharp knife cut the dough into quarters and then into eighths so you have 8 triangles. Brush the tops with milk and sprinkle with maple sugar, if desired. Place on an ungreased baking sheet and bake for approximately 15 minutes, or until lightly golden.

apple-almond muffins

FREE OF

MAKES 1 DOZEN MUFFINS

This recipe is versatile. You can replace the apple with diced peaches or pears, add different spices such as cardamom and nutmeg, and replace some of the brown rice flour with another flour such as millet or sorghum flour. These muffins are perfect straight out of the oven with a cup of hot apple cider. They will also stay moist for days. My children beg me to make these muffins any time of year!

DRY INGREDIENTS

1½ cups sprouted brown rice flour

1½ cups blanched almond flour

1 tablespoon psyllium husk powder

1 tablespoon baking powder

1 to 2 teaspoons ground cinnamon

½ teaspoon baking soda

½ teaspoon sea salt

WET INGREDIENTS

1 cup hemp milk or almond milk

½ cup unsweetened applesauce

½ cup coconut sugar

¼ cup melted coconut oil or extra-virgin olive oil

1 ripe apple, cored and diced

1. Preheat the oven to 350°F. Grease a 12-cup muffin pan or line with paper liners.

2. In a large bowl, whisk together the dry ingredients. In a smaller bowl, whisk together the wet ingredients. Pour the wet ingredients into the dry and whisk until smooth. Since this batter is egg-free, it will be slightly thicker than a muffin batter made with eggs. Fold in the diced apple.

3. Fill each muffin cup to the top with batter. You may want to smooth the tops with wet fingers before baking. Bake for approximately 30 minutes. Cool the muffins on a wire rack.

apricot-almond quinoa muffins

FREE OF

MAKES 1 DOZEN MUFFINS

I wanted to create a muffin that was high in protein but didn't rely entirely on nut flours, and this is what I came up with. I often make these muffins at night, after the children are in bed, so that breakfast is on the counter when they wake up. Serve with a green smoothie for a quick, nutritious breakfast or bedtime snack. These muffins are also wonderful gifted to a new mom just after birth.

DRY INGREDIENTS

1 cup teff flour

1 cup quinoa flakes

½ cup blanched almond flour

½ cup tapioca flour

2 tablespoons ground chia seeds

2 tablespoons ground flax seeds

2 teaspoons baking powder

½ teaspoon baking soda

½ teaspoon sea salt

WET INGREDIENTS

1 cup unsweetened applesauce

½ cup hemp milk or almond milk

⅓ cup extra-virgin olive oil

⅓ cup pure maple syrup

2 large organic eggs, lightly beaten

¼ cup creamy roasted almond butter

2 teaspoons vanilla extract

1 cup chopped dried apricots

1. Preheat the oven to 350°F. Oil a 12-cup muffin pan or line with paper liners.

2. In a large bowl, whisk together the dry ingredients. In another mixing bowl, whisk together the wet ingredients. Pour the wet into the dry, and whisk together until the batter thickens. Fold in the apricots. Spoon the batter into the muffin cups, filling each to the top. Bake for 30 to 35 minutes. Cool on a wire rack.

banana buckwheat muffins

FREE OF

MAKES 12 TO 18 MUFFINS

This egg-free muffin is light and airy, perfectly sweet with ripe bananas in every bite. By using freshly ground buckwheat flour from raw groats, you create a muffin that is tasty without a strong buckwheat flavor. A high-powered blender can turn raw buckwheat groats into soft flour in two minutes or less! Add one of these muffins to your child's lunchbox for a healthy treat! Store any leftovers in an airtight container for up to three days.

DRY INGREDIENTS

2¼ cups raw buckwheat flour (see Tip on page 98)

¼ cup tapioca flour or arrowroot powder

2 teaspoons baking powder

½ teaspoon baking soda

½ teaspoon sea salt

WET INGREDIENTS

2 cups mashed ripe bananas (from 4 or 5 large bananas)

½ cup coconut sugar

⅓ cup melted coconut oil

2 teaspoons vanilla extract

¾ to 1 cup hemp milk or almond milk

1. Preheat the oven to 350°F. Grease a 12-cup muffin pan or line with paper liners.

2. In a large bowl, whisk together the dry ingredients. In a medium bowl, combine the bananas, coconut sugar, coconut oil, vanilla, and ¾ cup of the milk. Whisk together well. If the batter seems too thick (it will thicken as it rests for a few minutes), add as much of the remaining milk so the batter will easily fall off of a spoon but not so much that the batter is runny and thin. How accurately you measure your dry ingredients will affect how much liquid you need. Pour the wet ingredients into the dry, and whisk together.

3. Fill each muffin cup up with batter for 12 muffins or about three-fourths for 18 muffins. Bake for 20 to 25 minutes. Cool on a wire rack.

blueberry teff muffins

FREE OF

MAKES 1 DOZEN MUFFINS

These super-nutritious, dark, whole-grain muffins are an absolute favorite at our house. My children devour them as they come out of the oven, and then ask to take one in their lunchbox the next day. If you don't have blueberries on hand, use diced apples and a few teaspoons of cinnamon. Raspberries or blackberries also work well. Freeze any leftover muffins once they are cooled for up to six months, or store in an airtight container for up to three days.

DRY INGREDIENTS

2 cups teff flour

½ cup tapioca flour

2 teaspoons baking powder

½ teaspoon baking soda

½ teaspoon sea salt

WET INGREDIENTS

2 tablespoons ground chia seeds

¼ cup hot water

2 large organic eggs, lightly beaten

½ cup coconut sugar

½ cup unsweetened applesauce

⅓ cup melted coconut oil or extra-virgin olive oil

1 cup hemp milk, almond milk, or coconut milk

1 to 2 teaspoons grated orange zest

1 cup fresh or frozen blueberries

1. Preheat the oven to 350°F. Grease a 12-cup muffin pan or line with paper liners.

2. In a large bowl, whisk together the dry ingredients. In a medium bowl, add the ground chia seeds, pour the hot water over them, and quickly whisk together until a thick slurry forms. Add the eggs, coconut sugar, applesauce, coconut oil, milk, and orange zest. Whisk together well. Pour the wet ingredients into the dry, and whisk together. Fold in the blueberries.

3. Scoop the batter into the muffin cups, filling each all the way. Bake for 30 minutes. Cool on a wire rack.

carrot almond muffins

MAKES 1 DOZEN MUFFINS

These muffins are grain-free and more of a savory muffin than a sweet one. They are high-protein and low-glycemic, perfect for a quick breakfast on the go. If you would like to omit the sweetener, replace it with more applesauce. You can also add ¼ teaspoon of liquid stevia, if you prefer, to add more sweetness without the sugar. Use a food processor fitted with the "s" blade to finely grind the almonds. Most of them should be very fine and powdery, with some small chunks that don't grind up completely.

DRY INGREDIENTS

2½ cups finely ground raw almonds (from 2 cups nuts)

¼ cup ground golden flax seeds

1 teaspoon baking soda

½ teaspoon sea salt

½ teaspoon ground cinnamon

WET INGREDIENTS

2 cups grated carrots

¼ cup extra-virgin olive oil or melted coconut oil

¼ cup honey or pure maple syrup

¼ cup unsweetened applesauce

4 large organic eggs, lightly beaten

1. Preheat the oven to 350°F. Line a 12-cup muffin pan with paper liners.

2. In a large mixing bowl, mix the ground almonds with the other dry ingredients. Add the wet ingredients to the dry and whisk together. Spoon the batter into the muffin cups, filling each to the top. Bake for about 30 minutes. Cool on a wire rack.

coconut raspberry muffins

FREE OF

MAKES 1 DOZEN MUFFINS

Combining fresh raspberries, coconut flour, and eggs creates a flavorful, light grain-free muffin. Plus, with so few ingredients, this recipe can be whipped up in very little time. You can replace the raspberries with huckleberries, blackberries, blueberries, or finely diced fresh peaches, if desired. I have found that whisking the coconut flour with the wet ingredients creates a lumpy batter, so it is best to use a food processor to mix the wet and dry ingredients.

WET INGREDIENTS

6 large organic eggs, lightly beaten

¼ cup unsweetened applesauce

¼ cup honey or pure maple syrup

¼ cup melted coconut oil or butter

1 teaspoon vanilla extract

½ teaspoon almond flavoring

DRY INGREDIENTS

½ cup coconut flour

1 teaspoon baking soda

½ teaspoon sea salt

1 cup fresh or frozen raspberries

1. Preheat the oven to 350°F. Line a 12-cup muffin pan with paper liners.

2. Place the wet ingredients into a food processor fitted with the "s" blade and process until smooth. Add the dry ingredients and process again until combined. Scoop the batter into the muffin cups, filling them about halfway. Drop the raspberries on top of the batter of each muffin and gently press into the batter. Bake for 25 to 30 minutes. Remove the muffins from the tin and let cool on a wire rack, or enjoy them warm, spread with butter and honey.

date and walnut cinnamon-swirl muffins

FREE OF

MAKES 1 DOZEN MUFFINS

These cozy little muffins are perfect paired with a cup of hot spice tea on a chilly winter day. Serve them as a healthy treat on Christmas morning or as part of a spring brunch. I like them best topped with Dairy-Free Cream Cheese Frosting (page 441).

CINNAMON SWIRL

½ cup raw walnuts

½ cup medjool dates, pitted

1 tablespoon coconut oil or butter

2 to 3 teaspoons ground cinnamon

¼ cup coconut sugar (optional)

WET INGREDIENTS

6 large organic eggs, lightly beaten

¼ cup unsweetened applesauce

¼ cup honey or pure maple syrup

¼ cup melted coconut oil or butter

DRY INGREDIENTS

½ cup coconut flour

1 teaspoon baking soda

½ teaspoon sea salt

1. Preheat the oven to 350°F. Line a 12-cup muffin pan with paper liners.

2. Place the walnuts into a food processor fitted with the "s" blade and process until very finely ground and pasty. Add the dates, coconut oil, and cinnamon; process again until you have a smooth, thick paste. Add the coconut sugar and pulse until combined. Remove the cinnamon swirl mixture from the food processor and set aside.

3. Rinse out the food processor. Add the wet ingredients, and puree until smooth. Add the dry ingredients and process again until combined. Scoop the batter into the muffin cups, dropping a heaping spoonful of the cinnamon swirl on top of each, then use a knife or spoon to fold it in.

4. Bake the muffins for about 30 minutes. Remove the muffins from the tin and let cool on a wire rack. Cool completely if you plan on frosting them.

hazelnut banana muffins

FREE OF

MAKES 1 DOZEN MUFFINS

A luscious smell fills the kitchen when these muffins are baking. They are high in protein and low in sugar. Eat one with a green smoothie for a protein-packed breakfast or share them with your children for a healthy after-school snack. If you don't want to make your own hazelnut meal, then check your local health food store. Bob's Red Mill is a good brand.

DRY INGREDIENTS

3 cups hazelnut meal

2 tablespoons ground chia seeds

¾ teaspoon baking soda

½ teaspoon sea salt

WET INGREDIENTS

4 large organic eggs, lightly beaten

1 cup mashed banana (about 2 bananas)

¼ cup honey

¼ cup melted coconut oil or butter

2 teaspoons vanilla extract

1. Preheat the oven to 325°F. Grease a 12-cup muffin pan or line with paper liners.

2. In a large bowl, whisk together the dry ingredients. In a small bowl, crack the eggs and whisk them, then add the remaining wet ingredients and whisk together. Pour the wet mixtue into the dry and whisk again. Scoop the batter into the prepared muffin cups. Bake for about 30 minutes. Let cool in the pan for 5 to 10 minutes, then remove and place on a wire rack to cool completely. They are fragile while still warm but will hold together when cooled.

INGREDIENT TIP

To make your own hazelnut meal, soak 4 cups raw hazelnuts overnight in warm water. Drain, rinse, and place into your food dehydrator. Set the temperature to 110°F and dehydrate for 24 to 48 hours, or until dry and crisp. Place the nuts into your food processor and grind to a fine meal.

KITCHEN TIP

Make sure all ingredients are at room temperature when starting; the melted coconut oil or butter can clump up if added to cold whisked eggs.

lemon blueberry muffins

FREE OF

MAKES 1 DOZEN MUFFINS

Beautiful and light, these egg-free muffins are bursting with lemon and juicy, sweet berries. You can use either fresh or frozen blueberries, making it a perfect treat any time of the year.

DRY INGREDIENTS

2¼ cups brown rice flour

¼ cup tapioca flour or arrowroot powder

1 tablespoon baking powder

½ teaspoon baking soda

½ teaspoon sea salt

WET INGREDIENTS

¼ cup ground golden flax seed

2 tablespoons whole psyllium husks

1¼ cups hemp milk or coconut milk

2 tablespoons fresh lemon juice

½ cup pure maple syrup

½ cup melted coconut oil or extra-virgin olive oil

½ cup unsweetened applesauce

2 teaspoons vanilla extract

1 to 2 teaspoons grated lemon zest

1 to 1½ cups fresh or frozen blueberries

1. Preheat the oven to 350°F. Grease a 12-cup muffin pan or line with paper liners.

2. In a medium bowl, whisk together the dry ingredients and set aside. In another bowl, combine the ground flax and psyllium husks. Use your fingers to break apart any clumps in the ground flax. Whisk in the milk and lemon juice. Let the mixture rest for about 2 minutes to thicken, then whisk in the remaining wet ingredients.

3. Pour the wet mixture into the dry and combine using a large spoon. Since this batter is egg-free, it will be thicker than muffin batter made with eggs. Fold in the blueberries. Fill each muffin cup to the top. You may want to smooth the tops with wet fingers before baking. Bake for 30 minutes. Cool the muffins on a wire rack.

overnight oatmeal cinnamon muffins

FREE OF

MAKES 1 DOZEN MUFFINS

This recipe uses whole grains instead of flours. By soaking the whole grains overnight in kefir, an acidic medium, the minerals in the grains become more available and the starches become more digestible. This method for making muffins is actually much easier and faster than using a flour-based recipe.

1 cup gluten-free rolled oats

1 cup raw buckwheat groats

2 cups kefir (cow's, goat's, or coconut milk)

1 large organic egg, lightly beaten

⅓ cup honey

2 tablespoons ground chia seeds

1 tablespoon ground cinnamon

¾ teaspoon baking soda

½ teaspoon sea salt

2 teaspoons vanilla extract

1. Place the oats and buckwheat groats into a medium bowl. Pour the kefir over them and stir together. Cover the bowl with a plate and leave on your kitchen counter for 12 to 24 hours.

2. Preheat the oven to 350°F. Line a 12-cup muffin pan with paper liners.

3. Pour the kefir-grain mixture into a high-powered blender. Add the egg and honey; blend on high until pureed, then add the chia seeds, cinnamon, baking soda, sea salt, and vanilla; blend again until combined. Pour the batter into the muffin cups. Bake for 25 to 30 minutes. Cool on a wire rack. These muffins will be fragile when hot, but will change consistency once they have cooled.

vegan corn muffins

FREE OF

MAKES 1 DOZEN MUFFINS

Serve these perfectly tender and mildly sweet corn muffins with your favorite chili, such as Three-Bean Vegetable Chili (page 182).

DRY INGREDIENTS

1½ cups yellow cornmeal (see Tip)

1 cup sorghum flour

¼ cup tapioca flour

1 tablespoon baking powder

1 teaspoon sea salt

WET INGREDIENTS

¼ cup ground golden flax seeds

½ cup hot water

⅓ cup coconut sugar

⅓ cup melted coconut oil, butter, or extra-virgin olive oil

⅓ cup unsweetened applesauce

1½ cups hemp milk or coconut milk

1. Preheat the oven to 350°F. Oil a 12-cup muffin pan or line with paper liners.

2. In a large bowl, whisk together the dry ingredients. In a medium bowl, whisk together the ground flax seeds and hot water. Let them rest for about 4 to 5 minutes, or until thickened. Add the coconut sugar, coconut oil, and applesauce; whisk until incorporated. Add the milk and whisk again.

3. Pour the wet ingredients into the dry and whisk the batter for a minute or two. It should be a little stringy and on the thicker side. Spoon the batter into the muffin cups, filling each to the top. Bake for 25 to 30 minutes. Run a knife around each muffin to gently release it from the pan, then cool on a wire rack.

> **INGREDIENT TIP**
>
> I like to use Arrowhead Mills brand cornmeal in this recipe because it is both gluten-free and organic.

coconut almond bread

MAKES 1 LOAF

Serve a slice of this high-protein, grain-free bread with a fried egg for a quick, nutritious breakfast. I also like to spread it with homemade honey-sweetened jam or Vanilla Plum Butter (page 481) for a real treat!

WET INGREDIENTS

5 large organic eggs, lightly beaten

½ cup creamy roasted almond butter

¼ cup unsweetened applesauce

¼ cup melted coconut oil or butter

1 tablespoon pure maple syrup

DRY INGREDIENTS

½ cup coconut flour

¼ cup ground golden flax seeds

2 tablespoons arrowroot powder

1 teaspoon baking soda

½ teaspoon sea salt

1. Preheat the oven to 350°F. Grease an 8½ by 4½-inch loaf pan.

2. Place the wet ingredients into a food processor or high-powered blender and blend on medium speed until pureed. Add the dry ingredients and blend again until well combined.

3. Scoop the batter into the loaf pan and bake for about 45 minutes. Cool on a wire rack for about 10 minutes, then remove the loaf from the pan and continue to cool on a wire rack.

NUTRITION TIP

If you need to lower your carbohydrate intake, this bread is ideal. It is very low in carbs and high in protein—perfect for anyone with blood-sugar regulation issues.

---

chocolate chip zucchini-almond bread

MAKES 1 LOAF

This moist and delicious bread is a great way to use the abundance of zucchini in season! Serve with green tea, poached eggs, and cultured vegetables for breakfast.

DRY INGREDIENTS

2½ cups blanched almond flour

¾ cup arrowroot powder or tapioca flour

2 tablespoons coconut flour

2 teaspoons baking powder

½ teaspoon baking soda

½ teaspoon sea salt

¼ teaspoon grated nutmeg

WET INGREDIENTS

4 large organic eggs, lightly beaten

⅓ cup pure maple syrup

⅓ cup melted coconut oil

2 cups grated zucchini

½ cup organic dark chocolate chips

1. Preheat the oven to 350°F. Grease an 8½ by 4½-inch glass loaf pan or four mini loaf pans with coconut oil.

2. In a large bowl, whisk together the dry ingredients. In a small bowl, whisk together the wet ingredients. Pour the wet ingredients into the dry, and whisk until combined. Fold in the zucchini and chocolate chips. Pour the batter into the loaf pan and bake for 50 to 60 minutes for the loaf pan, or 35 to 40 minutes for the mini loaf pans, or until a knife inserted into the center comes out clean. Remove from the oven and let cool in the pan for about 20 minutes, then invert onto a wire rack to completely cool.

cranberry orange bread

FREE OF

MAKES 1 LOAF

Tart cranberries paired with sweet oranges creates a flavorful grain-free rendition of a traditional favorite. Try this bread during the holidays, when fresh cranberries are in season.

DRY INGREDIENTS
¾ cup coconut flour
½ cup arrowroot powder
2 teaspoons baking powder
½ teaspoon baking soda
½ teaspoon sea salt
1 tablespoon grated orange zest

WET INGREDIENTS
6 large organic eggs, lightly beaten
⅓ cup melted coconut oil

⅓ cup pure maple syrup
⅓ cup unsweetened applesauce
⅓ cup fresh orange juice

¾ to 1 cup fresh or frozen cranberries

1. Preheat the oven to 350°F. Grease an 8½ by 4½-inch glass loaf pan with coconut oil.

2. In a large bowl, whisk together the dry ingredients. In a small bowl, whisk together the wet ingredients. Pour the wet ingredients into the dry, and whisk together until combined. Fold in the cranberries.

3. Pour the batter into the loaf pan and bake for 50 to 60 minutes. Remove from the oven and let cool in the pan for about 20 minutes, then invert onto a wire rack to completely cool.

chocolate banana bread

FREE OF

MAKES 2 SMALL LOAVES

Chocolate lovers don't have to wait for dessert to enjoy chocolate! This bread is light, yet rich with chocolate flavor and chunks of sweet banana melting in your mouth with every bite. Have a slice with your breakfast smoothie or as a mid-afternoon snack. Our favorite is always to have it fresh from the oven! If you don't have teff flour on hand, replace it with brown rice flour for equally delicious results.

DRY INGREDIENTS

1¾ cups teff flour

¼ cup tapioca flour or arrowroot powder

6 tablespoons raw cacao powder

2 teaspoons baking powder

½ teaspoon baking soda

½ teaspoon sea salt

WET INGREDIENTS

2 tablespoons ground chia seeds

¼ cup warm water

1½ cups mashed banana (about 3 to 4 bananas)

¾ cup coconut sugar

½ cup melted coconut oil

2 large organic eggs, lightly beaten

2 teaspoons vanilla extract

OPTIONAL ADDITIONS

Chopped organic dark chocolate bar

Chopped walnuts

1. Preheat the oven to 350°F. Grease two 4½ by 8½-inch loaf pans with coconut oil.

2. In a large bowl, whisk together the dry ingredients. In a medium bowl, add the ground chia and warm water; whisk together immediately so the chia doesn't clump up. Then add the remaining wet ingredients and whisk together.

Pour the wet ingredients into the dry, and mix using a large wooden spoon. Fold in any optional additions.

3. Pour the batter into the two loaf pans and bake for 35 to 40 minutes. Cool for about 20 minutes, then remove the breads from pans and continue to cool on a wire rack.

pumpkin cornbread

FREE OF

MAKES 8 TO 10 SERVINGS

Both gluten-eating and gluten-free folks will enjoy this cornbread recipe. It is moist, slightly sweet, and full of that traditional cornbread flavor. If you don't have any sugar pumpkins on hand to make your own puree, you can use canned pumpkin or any type of winter squash puree, such as butternut, kabocha, or acorn. Sprouted brown rice flour also works well here in place of regular brown rice flour.

DRY INGREDIENTS

1½ cups organic cornmeal (see Tip on page 123)

1 cup brown rice flour

1 tablespoon baking powder

¾ teaspoon sea salt

WET INGREDIENTS

1 cup pumpkin puree

1 cup hemp milk

⅓ cup melted coconut oil or butter

⅓ cup honey

2 large organic eggs, lightly beaten

1. Preheat the oven to 350°F. Oil a 7 by 11-inch glass baking dish.

2. In a medium bowl, whisk together the dry ingredients. In a large bowl, whisk together the wet ingredients. Pour the dry into the wet, and whisk well. Scoop the batter into the baking dish and spread it out evenly with the back of a spoon. Bake for about 35 minutes, or until a knife inserted in the center comes out clean. Let cool slightly before serving.

VARIATION: Any type of dairy (raw goat's or cow's milk) or nondairy milk can work in this recipe in place of the hemp milk.

spiced butternut squash bread

FREE OF

MAKES 4 MINI LOAVES

This bread makes an excellent after-school snack for children. Serve it with sliced fresh apples and almond butter. It is also excellent as a quick breakfast, spread with almond or sunflower butter and paired with a green smoothie.

DRY INGREDIENTS

2½ cups raw buckwheat flour (see Tip on page 98)

¾ cup tapioca flour

2 teaspoons baking powder

1 teaspoon baking soda

½ teaspoon sea salt

1 tablespoon pumpkin pie spice

WET INGREDIENTS

2 cups cubed cooked butternut squash

¾ cup coconut sugar

½ cup melted coconut oil

¾ cup apple cider or apple juice

¼ cup ground chia seeds

2 teaspoons vanilla extract

1. Preheat the oven to 350°F. Grease 4 mini loaf pans; the pans I use are about 6 by 3½ by 2½ inches. In a large bowl, whisk together the dry ingredients. Place the squash, coconut sugar, coconut oil, apple cider, chia seeds, and vanilla into a blender and puree until smooth. Pour the wet mixture into the dry, and whisk well to achieve a smooth batter.

2. Pour the batter into the pans and bake for 35 to 40 minutes, or until a toothpick inserted in the center comes out clean. Cool on a wire rack. Let the breads cool completely before slicing. When this bread is hot out of the oven it can be a little gummy. Once cooled, the texture firms up.

amaranth and sun-dried tomato crackers

FREE OF

MAKES 15–25 CRACKERS

These crackers are beautiful, speckled with black chia seeds and little chunks of red tomato. Serve them with pesto or hummus for dipping, or with a good-quality raw organic cheese. When I make this recipe I double or triple it so I can have a jar of crackers on the counter ready for school lunches or an on-the-go snack. I use homemade Sun-Dried Tomatoes (page 482), but you can also use organic dehydrated tomatoes found at your local health food store.

¼ cup sun-dried tomatoes

2 tablespoons whole chia seeds

½ cup hot water

3 tablespoons extra-virgin olive oil

½ teaspoon Herbamare or sea salt

1 cup amaranth flour

1. Preheat the oven to 350°F. Set out a large baking sheet.

2. Use scissors to cut the dried tomatoes into tiny pieces, then place them in a medium bowl along with the chia seeds and hot water. Whisk together with a fork and let soak for 5 to 7 minutes. Add the olive oil and Herbamare, then whisk again and add the flour, stirring it into the mixture using a fork until the dough forms a ball.

3. Place the dough ball between two pieces of parchment paper and roll using a rolling pin until

you have a very thin sheet of dough. Place the rolled dough and parchment onto the baking sheet. Remove the top layer of parchment. Use a pizza cutter to cut the dough into square crackers.

4. Bake for 20 minutes, then remove from the oven and take out the crackers that are crisp. If there are some that still feel soft, put them back in the oven for a few more minutes, or until crisp.

soupsandstews

Orange Creamsicle Smoothie, p. 63

Baby Green Smoothie, p. 67

Green Chia Smoothie, p. 68

Kale and Egg Scramble, p. 87

Overnight Quinoa Hot Cakes, p. 100

Date-Glazed Banana Donuts, p. 92

Whole-Grain Waffles, p. 104

Sourdough Buckwheat Crepes, p. 98

Cranberry Orange Bread, p. 146

Hazlenut Banana Muffins, p. 140

Glorious Greens Soup, p. 159

Hot and Sour Soup, p. 158

Homemade Chicken Broth, p. 156

Super Immune-Boosting Chicken Soup, p. 185

Curried Lima Bean Soup, p. 177

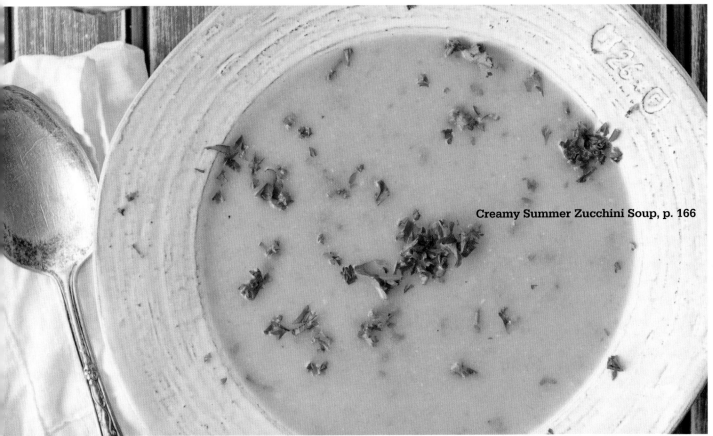

Creamy Summer Zucchini Soup, p. 166

Baby Arugula Salad with Zucchini Lime Dressing, p. 198

Cabbage Salad with Mandarins and Mung Bean Sprouts, p. 200

Kid-Friendly Salad with Apple Cider Vinaigrette, p. 210

Winter Salad with Blood Orange Vinaigrette, p. 226

Raw Kale Salad with Lemon Tahini Dressing, p. 220

Nasturtium and Kohlrabi Salad with Creamy Lemon-Dill Dressing, p. 213

Roasted Brussels Sprouts, p. 233

Quinoa Tabouli, p. 262

Thai Coconut Fish Sticks, p. 304

Tandoori Salmon, p. 301

Herb-Roasted Halibut, p. 303

Garlic Ginger Salmon, p. 298

Soup making is one of the oldest forms of cooking. Vegetables, meats, and beans simmered for hours in a stock made from animal bones has been an easily digestible source of nourishment throughout the ages, and a traditional remedy to treat the weak and sick.

Soups and stews are often a main dish in our house during the winter months. I find it easy to make a large pot of soup for dinner, and serve it with a cooked whole grain or slices of homemade bread. Just before serving, I add finely chopped kale, spinach, collard greens, or parsley. The bright green color lends a lovely contrast, as well as providing additional flavors and nutrients.

Adding beans or meat to a soup boosts its protein content, which helps quickly satisfy hunger. Since all of the vegetables, herbs, and meat are cooked directly in the liquid, their nutrients are released into the broth. This nutrient-rich broth signals the brain that you are full—meaning that by consuming such nutrient-dense foods, you end up eating less. Using homemade bone broths in your soups boosts nutrient and mineral content even more.

HOMEMADE BONE BROTHS

With our fast-paced lifestyles, not many people routinely make their own broths or stocks. That's a big loss because homemade broth is far more nutritious than store-bought, even the organic brands. Historically, broth has been used to treat disorders of the gastrointestinal tract, joints, lungs, blood, and skin. They add depth and richness to soups, vegetable purees, and cooked whole-grain dishes that couldn't be achieved with just water.

The Decline of Commercial Broths

Commercial broths—whether chicken, beef, or vegetable—use many different "natural" flavorings. These flavorings can be made of anything, but most often include man-made items containing MSG (monosodium glutamate, a free glutamic acid), an inexpensive additive classified by the FDA as "natural." By using other terms such as "natural flavoring" or "yeast extract," manufacturers can deceive label-reading consumers into buying these products.

We have receptors on our tongues for glutamate, the amino acid we recognize as the common "meat" flavor (otherwise known as *umami*) in foods, which MSG activates. Companies can cut corners and make a profit by using MSG in foods like chicken broth. Unfortunately, MSG is a neurotoxic substance that causes headaches and, in large amounts, can lead to brain damage (in vitamin B_6 and magnesium deficient people). Broths prepared with high-quality ingredients have so much flavor that nothing else needs to be added.

The Benefits of Homemade Broth

Homemade broth made from animal bones contains nutrients that strengthen digestion, heal the intestinal tract, and sooth the joints—specifically, gelatin and the amino acids proline, glycine, and glutamine. Homemade broth also contains many minerals in an easily absorbable form, including calcium, magnesium, and fluoride. Once you begin making your own broth and start noting the benefits in your health and the better flavors in your meals, it will be easier to add it to your weekly or monthly cooking routine.

10 Tips for Making Broths and Soups

1. When making homemade broth, add very little salt. This way, when you go to use it in a soup, you can salt the soup to your liking.

2. Add a tablespoon or two of vinegar to your simmering broth to help release minerals from the bones. I always use raw apple cider vinegar.

3. For large batches of soup, a high-quality stainless steel 8-quart stockpot is essential. Most of the recipes in this chapter use this size of pot.

4. Heat the soup pot first before adding the oil, then add the oil and let it heat for 20 to 30 seconds before adding the onions or other ingredients.

5. Start the soup by sautéing an onion to create a flavor base from which to work. If you are not using a homemade broth, sautéing the onion for at least 10 minutes will create a rich depth of flavor.

6. When using lentils for soup, sort through them and pick out any gluten grains. Lentils are often cross-contaminated with gluten grains during growing, harvesting, and processing. Rinse and drain the lentils well before using them.

7. When a recipe calls for diced tomatoes, use fresh or frozen, not canned. Canned tomatoes often contain high levels of BPA (see page 49 for more details).

8. To make a pureed soup, use a high-quality stainless steel immersion blender or pour the soup into a blender and puree in batches.

9. Add chopped fresh herbs to the soup after you turn off the heat.

10. Most soups freeze well. The exceptions are soups made with potatoes or noodles, as these can create a mushy soup when reheated.

I know the thought of making your own broth seems overwhelming, but it doesn't need to be. Broths can be simmered slowly for hours on the stove or in a crockpot with very little supervision. When you roast a whole chicken and have pulled all the meat from the bones, simply toss the bones in an 8-quart stockpot, add some vegetables, water, vinegar, and salt, and then cover and simmer for 6 hours or more. If you don't have time to make broth within a few days of roasting the chicken, put the carcass in the freezer and take it out when you are ready.

healing beef bone broth

FREE OF

MAKES 4 TO 5 QUARTS

A broth made from beef bones is rich in flavor and nutrients. Sip a mug of it when you are feeling under the weather, or use it as a base for soups and stews. If you don't have burgundy or red wine on hand, replace it with ¼ cup red wine vinegar. In the wintertime, I like to simmer my broth on the stove all day, and then place it in my cold garage overnight. The next morning, I return the pot to the stove and let it simmer again all day. I keep doing this for three or four days. Alternatively, you can use a large crockpot and cook the broth for a few days.

5 pounds organic beef soup bones (knuckle, marrow, and some meaty bones)

3 onions, chopped

3 or 4 carrots, chopped

4 or 5 celery stalks, chopped

2 garlic heads, chopped

5 or 6 sun-dried tomatoes

3 dried bay leaves

1 tablespoon whole black peppercorns

Handful of fresh thyme

1 cup burgundy cooking wine (I use Napa Valley Naturals brand) or red wine

5 quarts water

1 tablespoon sea salt

1. Preheat the oven to 375°F. Place the bones on a rimmed baking sheet and roast for 45 to 60 minutes.

2. Use tongs to transfer the bones to an 8- or 12-quart stockpot. Add the remaining ingredients. Bring to a gentle boil. Watch for any scum to rise to the top and skim it off. Cover and simmer over medium-low heat for 12 to 72 hours, adding more water as needed to keep the ingredients submerged.

3. Remove the bones and pick off any meat left on them. Save the meat and incorporate into another dish (salads, tacos, soup, etc.), if you would

like. Strain the broth into another pot or large bowl using a fine-mesh strainer, then transfer to containers for storage.

4. If you plan on using your broth within a week, refrigerate until ready to use. A layer of fat will form at the top of the container. Skim this off before using (you can save the fat in a small jar to sauté with, if you wish). If you want to freeze the broth, ladle it into quart jars using a wide-mouthed funnel, leaving 1 to 2 inches of space from the top. Let the broth completely cool, then freeze uncovered. Once frozen, you can screw the lids on. Doing it this way prevents the jars from cracking.

homemade chicken broth

FREE OF

MAKES 3 QUARTS

Every time we roast a chicken I make broth from the bones and cartilage. Then I pour it into glass mason jars and freeze the majority of it right away. This way my freezer is continually stocked with homemade organic broth. I use this broth to make soups and stews, or to replace the water used for cooking whole grains. It can also be added to mashed potatoes and sauces, or used basically anytime a liquid is needed for a savory dish. And if I am making soup and need some broth—and have not thought about thawing it in advance—I take a jar out of the freezer and put it into a pot of warm water. By the time my vegetables are chopped and I am ready to add the liquid, enough of it will be thawed to use in the soup. For this reason, I always use wide-mouthed glass pint or quart jars for freezing.

1 chicken carcass (from a 3- to 4-pound organic chicken)

4 to 8 organic chicken wings (optional)

1 large onion, chopped

1 garlic head, cut in half crosswise

1 or 2 leeks, rinsed well and chopped

4 celery stalks, chopped

2 carrots, chopped

½ bunch fresh parsley

Few sprigs fresh rosemary and thyme

1 strip kombu or wakame

1 teaspoon black peppercorns

2 to 3 teaspoons Herbamare or sea salt (optional)

1 to 2 tablespoons raw apple cider vinegar

12 to 14 cups water

1. Place all the ingredients in an 8-quart stockpot. Gently bring to a simmer over low or medium-low heat. Cook, covered, for 3 to 12 hours. The longer cooking times will extract more nutrients and produce a richer-flavored broth.

2. Strain the broth into another pot or large bowl using a fine-mesh strainer. Discard the solids.

3. If you plan on using your broth within a week, then refrigerate until ready to use. If freezing the broth, ladle into quart jars using a wide-mouthed funnel, leaving 1 to 2 inches of space from the top. Let the broth completely cool, then freeze uncovered. Once frozen, you can screw on the lids. Doing it this way prevents the jars from cracking.

VARIATION: In springtime, we harvest fresh nettles and add about 2 cups of the leaves and stems to the pot. This is a great way to add even more minerals to the broth.

> **NUTRITION TIP**
> The vinegar helps extract the minerals from the chicken bones. The broth won't have a vinegary taste as long as you don't add too much.

vegetable mushroom broth

FREE OF

MAKES 3 QUARTS

This nutrient-dense vegan broth obtains much of its flavor from slowly sautéing the onion and mushrooms before adding the water. Any type of mushroom, or a combination of mushrooms, can be used; try white button, cremini, portabello, shiitake, or oyster. The seaweed adds trace minerals, antioxidants, and algin—which is an important nutrient for gut health. If you want to add more nutrients, consider including some organic beef bones and a few tablespoons of raw apple cider vinegar.

1 tablespoon extra-virgin olive oil

1 large onion, chopped

1 leek, trimmed and chopped

1 pound fresh mushrooms, chopped

1 garlic head, cut in half crosswise

1 large carrot, chopped

2 or 3 celery stalks, chopped

2 large strips kombu

1 dried bay leaf

1 teaspoon black peppercorns

3 sprigs fresh thyme

Handful of fresh parsley

2 to 3 teaspoons sea salt

12 to 14 cups water

1. Heat an 8-quart stockpot over medium. Add the oil, then add the onion; sauté for 10 to 15 minutes, lowering the heat if needed so the onion doesn't brown too much. Then add the leek and mushrooms; sauté about 10 minutes more.

2. Add the remaining ingredients, cover the pot, and simmer for 3 to 4 hours. Place a large colander over another pot or large bowl, and pour the broth through it, discarding the solids. Pour the broth into quart jars, cover, and refrigerate. If you plan on freezing the broth, let the jars cool down first, then freeze them uncovered. Once frozen, you can screw on the lids.

hot and sour soup

FREE OF

MAKES 6 TO 8 SERVINGS

The key to this soup is a good homemade broth—using a store-bought one doesn't even compare in flavor and nutrition. I prefer to use chicken broth but the homemade Vegetable Mushroom Broth (page 157) works well, too. Serve with Thai rice noodles, zucchini noodles, or a scoop of cooked spaghetti squash for a light meal.

10 cups chicken or vegetable broth

8 ounces button mushrooms, thinly sliced

3 carrots, cut into matchsticks

3 garlic cloves, crushed

4 tablespoons brown rice vinegar or coconut vinegar

4 tablespoons coconut aminos or wheat-free tamari (see Tip)

1 to 3 tablespoons hot pepper sesame oil

3 cups thinly sliced napa cabbage

1 bunch green onions, trimmed and sliced into rounds

1 cup chopped fresh cilantro

Herbamare or sea salt

1. Pour the broth into a 4-quart pot. Add the mushrooms, carrots, and garlic. Cover the pot, bring to a boil, then reduce the heat and simmer for about 20 minutes, or until the carrots and mushrooms are tender.

2. Add the vinegar, coconut aminos, sesame oil, cabbage, green onions, and cilantro. Simmer another 2 to 3 minutes. Taste and add a little Herbamare, if necessary.

INGREDIENT TIP

If you are soy sensitive, use the coconut aminos in this recipe rather than the wheat-free tamari.

---

glorious greens soup

FREE OF

MAKES 6 TO 8 SERVINGS

This soup tastes best just after it's made. It's a great choice for days when you might be feeling a little under the weather. If I have fresh tomatoes in the house, I add one to this soup, but it is delicious just the way it is, too.

2 tablespoons extra-virgin olive oil

1 onion, halved and sliced into crescent moons

6 or 7 garlic cloves, crushed

1 to 2 teaspoons dried thyme

10 cups Homemade Chicken Broth (page 156)

8 cups chopped dark leafy greens (kale, chard, collard, spinach)

2 to 4 cups cooked cannellini beans

Juice of 1 lemon

Herbamare or sea salt

Freshly ground black pepper

1. Heat a 6-quart pot over medium. Add the oil, then add the onion and sauté for 5 to 10 minutes, until soft. Add the garlic and thyme and sauté a minute more. Add the broth and simmer for about 5 minutes so the onion softens a little more.

2. Add the greens and beans. Cover and simmer for 10 to 20 minutes, or until the greens are tender. Young, fresh greens will take only a few minutes, while large older greens may need the full 20 minutes. Add the lemon juice and season to taste with Herbamare and pepper.

healing ginger miso soup

FREE OF

MAKES 6 SERVINGS

We like to serve miso soup as a nourishing breakfast with leftover fish and cooked brown rice. This recipe also makes a light dinner when someone is feeling under the weather. (We use gluten-free miso from the South River Miso Company. In addition to making gluten-free miso, they have soy-free miso made from adzuki beans or chickpeas. Our favorite variety is the Garlic-Red Pepper Miso.) Serve this soup with a scoop of brown rice in each bowl, and top with leftover halibut or salmon, if desired.

6 cups water

3 tablespoons chopped fresh ginger

3 to 6 garlic cloves, chopped

1 strip wakame seaweed, broken into pieces

3 carrots, sliced

½ teaspoon red pepper flakes (optional)

1 to 2 cups thinly sliced savoy cabbage

4 green onions, trimmed and sliced into thin rounds

Handful of fresh cilantro, chopped

2 tablespoons coconut aminos or wheat-free tamari (see Tip on page 158)

4 to 5 tablespoons gluten-free miso

2 to 3 teaspoons coconut vinegar or brown rice vinegar

1. Place the water, ginger, garlic, seaweed, carrots, and red pepper flakes into a 3-quart pot. Cover and simmer for 10 to 12 minutes, until the carrots are tender. Add the cabbage, green onions, and cilantro; simmer for about 2 minutes more.

2. Turn off the heat and add the coconut aminos, miso, and vinegar. Stir the miso completely into the soup. Taste and adjust the seasonings, if necessary.

healing quinoa cabbage soup

FREE OF

MAKES 6 SERVINGS

The large sweet onion in this recipe is sautéed for a long time and then the garlic, ginger, and carrots are added. Once the water is added, a beautiful, flavorful clear broth forms. Then with the addition of Herbamare, the flavors deepen. Complexity is formed when the quinoa and cabbage are dropped in. With the final touch of cilantro, you have a bright, colorful, and flavorful soup just waiting to help your cells and liver detoxify!

2 to 3 tablespoons extra-virgin olive oil

1 very large sweet onion, halved and sliced into crescent moons

2 or 3 garlic cloves, crushed

1 to 2 teaspoons grated fresh ginger

4 large carrots, cut into matchsticks

6 cups Homemade Chicken Broth (page 156) or Vegetable Mushroom Broth (page 157)

2 to 3 teaspoons Herbamare or sea salt

2 cups cooked quinoa

2 to 3 cups sliced savoy cabbage

½ cup chopped fresh cilantro

Freshly ground black pepper

1. Heat a 6-quart pot over medium. Add the olive oil, then the onion and sauté for 10 to 15 minutes. Make sure your heat isn't too high, or your onion will brown too much and cause the broth to be off in flavor. Lower the temperature, if necessary.

2. Add the garlic, ginger, and carrots; sauté 5 minutes more. Add the broth, Herbamare, and quinoa and simmer for 10 to 15 minutes, or until the carrots reach desired tenderness. Add the cabbage and cook a few minutes more. Turn off the heat and add the cilantro and pepper. Taste and adjust the seasonings, if necessary.

> **KITCHEN TIP**
>
> To create carrot matchsticks, cut the carrots into ¼-inch-thick diagonal rounds and then cut them lengthwise into thin strips.

african peanut and red quinoa soup

FREE OF

MAKES 8 SERVINGS

This is a favorite spicy—but not too spicy—soup. It's full of vegetables, with the addition of red quinoa for extra protein and energy. Red quinoa holds its shape better than regular quinoa and has a lovely nutty flavor. But if you can't find red quinoa, simply use the regular variety. This soup makes a great light lunch!

1 to 2 tablespoons extra-virgin olive oil or coconut oil

1 onion, halved and sliced into crescent moons

4 or 5 garlic cloves, crushed

2 to 3 tablespoons grated fresh ginger

4 carrots, cut into 4-inch strips

2 small red bell peppers, cored, seeded, and chopped

8 cups water, vegetable broth, or chicken broth

6 to 7 tablespoons creamy peanut butter

½ teaspoon red pepper flakes, or more for serving

2 cups thinly sliced savoy cabbage

Large handful of fresh cilantro, chopped

3 to 4 cups cooked red quinoa

1 to 3 teaspoons Herbamare or sea salt

1. Heat an 8-quart stockpot over medium. Add the oil, then the onion and sauté for 5 to 10 minutes, or until softened. Add the garlic and ginger, and sauté a minute more. Then add the carrots and bell peppers; sauté for 3 to 5 minutes more.

2. Add the water, peanut butter, and red pepper flakes. Cover and simmer for 15 to 20 minutes, or

until the vegetables are tender. Stir in the cabbage, cilantro, and quinoa. Add Herbamare to taste. (If you are using a salted broth you may not need much salt at all.) Simmer for a few minutes more, or until the cabbage is tender. Serve each bowl with a sprinkling of additional red pepper flakes, if desired.

cream of broccoli soup

FREE OF

MAKES 6 TO 8 SERVINGS

This dairy-free soup gets its creaminess from a small amount of Yukon Gold potatoes and cashew butter. My children love this soup and pack it in a small thermos for their school lunches. I always use homemade chicken broth, which adds nutrients and a depth of flavor you can't get with just water. If you use water, though, you will need extra salt, garlic, and herbs to bring up the flavor.

2 to 3 tablespoons extra-virgin olive oil

1 large onion, chopped

3 garlic cloves, chopped

2 or 3 small Yukon Gold potatoes, peeled and chopped

2 pounds broccoli, chopped

6 to 7 cups Homemade Chicken Broth (page 156) or water

1 to 2 teaspoons dried tarragon (see Tip)

½ cup cashew butter

Sea salt and freshly ground black pepper

Chopped fresh parsley, for garnish

1. Heat an 8-quart stockpot over medium. Add the olive oil, then add the onion and sauté for 5 to 10 minutes, or until softened. Add the garlic, potatoes, and broccoli; sauté for about 1 minute, then add the broth and tarragon. Cover and simmer for 20 to 30 minutes, or until the broccoli is tender but still bright green.

2. Add the cashew butter and simmer for about 5 minutes more. Use an immersion blender to puree the soup in the pot, or blend it in batches in your blender. Pour the soup back into the pot and add salt and pepper to taste. Heat on low until ready to serve. Serve each bowl garnished with chopped fresh parsley, if desired.

> **INGREDIENT TIP**
>
> If you don't have dried tarragon on hand, substitute about ¼ cup fresh basil or a few teaspoons dried thyme or oregano.

cream of mushroom soup

MAKES 6 SERVINGS

The deep earthy flavor of the mushrooms mingles beautifully with the nutty cashews. Serve this soup with a vegetable salad for a light, nutritious lunch or dinner.

¼ cup extra-virgin olive oil, butter, or ghee (clarified butter)

1 onion, chopped

4 garlic cloves, chopped

3 large carrots, chopped

1 pound cremini mushrooms, chopped

5 cups water, vegetable broth, or chicken broth, or more as needed

Few sprigs fresh thyme (pull the leaves from the stems)

Few sprigs fresh rosemary

1 teaspoon freshly ground black pepper

2 to 3 teaspoons Herbamare

½ cup raw cashews

GARNISH

Sautéed mushrooms

Fresh parsley, chopped

Edible flowers

1. Heat a 6-quart pot over medium. Add the olive oil, then the onion and sauté for 5 to 10 minutes, or until soft. Add the garlic, carrots, and mushrooms; sauté for a few minutes more. Add the water, herbs, pepper, and the Herbamare to taste; cover and simmer for 25 to 30 minutes.

2. Remove the pot from the heat and ladle some of the soup into a blender. Add the cashews. Blend on high until smooth and creamy, then transfer to a clean pot. Puree the remaining soup in batches (blend for a short time for more texture or longer for a smoother consistency). Stir the soup to blend well, then taste and adjust the seasonings, if necessary. Or, add more water for a thinner consistency. Garnish each serving with sliced and sautéed mushrooms, chopped fresh parsley, and edible flowers.

NUTRITION TIP

Cremini mushrooms Just might be that elusive cure for the common cold. Antibodies are secreted in the gastrointestinal tract to combat harmful bacteria and viruses. The most common antibody is called Sectratory IgA (SIgA). Research has shown that higher levels of this important antibody lead to reduced incidences of colds and flus. A recent study found that eating 100 grams a day of blanched cremini mushrooms raised SIgA levels by 53 percent. Interestingly, those levels stayed elevated by 56 percent for an additional week after the mushroom consumption. The take-home message is that eating approximately 3 ounces of cremini mushrooms a day for a week may boost your immunity for two weeks.

creamy potato leek soup

FREE OF

MAKES 6 TO 8 SERVINGS

I like to use Yukon Gold potatoes in this recipe, though any variety will do. If you use russets (baking potatoes), you may want to peel them. For all other potato varieties, it is preferable to leave the peel on. Serve this delicious dairy-free soup with the Chia Dinner Rolls (page 124) and a fresh garden salad with Dairy-Free Ranch Dressing (page 326).

3 to 4 tablespoons extra-virgin olive oil

2 large leeks, trimmed and sliced into rounds

4 celery stalks, chopped

4 carrots, chopped

2 to 3 teaspoons Herbamare or sea salt

1 teaspoon freshly ground black pepper

1 to 2 teaspoons dried dill

1 teaspoon dried thyme

2 pounds potatoes, chopped

6 cups Homemade Chicken Broth (page 156) or water

Cooked or smoked salmon, for garnish

Chopped fresh parsley, for garnish

1. Heat a 6- to 8-quart pot over medium. Add the olive oil, then the leeks and sauté for 4 to 5 minutes to soften, being careful not to let them brown. Add the celery, carrots, Herbamare, pepper, and herbs; sauté for 5 to 10 minutes more to soften the vegetables and deepen the flavors. Add the potatoes and broth, cover the pot, and simmer for about 45 minutes.

2. Use an immersion blender to puree some of the soup in the pot or remove half the soup at a time and puree in a blender. Return the puree to the pot and stir together. Taste and add more seasoning, if necessary. Garnish each bowl with strips of cooked salmon and a sprinkle of chopped parsley.

creamy summer zucchini soup

MAKES 8 SERVINGS

This soup is a great way to make use of all that zucchini growing in your vegetable garden! You can use green zucchini, yellow summer squash, or pattypan in this recipe— I prefer the yellow and pattypan because they give the soup such a bright yellow hue. For the liquid, I use homemade chicken broth, which adds a nice depth of flavor and many important gut-healing nutrients. It is very rare that we consume white rice, but it works quite nicely in this soup to provide creaminess without the use of nuts or dairy. If you would like to replace it with something else, use either uncooked quinoa or 1 cup of cooked brown rice. Uncooked brown rice will not work, as it will not cook fully in the 15 to 20 minutes needed to simmer the soup. The soup will last in the fridge for up to five days or can be frozen for up to a year.

2 to 3 tablespoons extra-virgin olive oil

1 large onion, chopped

2 to 4 garlic cloves, chopped

1 teaspoon ground cumin

8 to 10 cups chopped zucchini (from 5 to 6 medium zucchini)

½ cup uncooked white rice

8 cups Homemade Chicken Broth (page 156) or vegetable broth

1 small bunch cilantro, coarsely chopped

2 tablespoons fresh lemon juice

Sea salt or Herbamare

1. Heat a 6- to 8-quart pot over medium. Add the olive oil, then add the onion and sauté for 8 to 10 minutes, or until the onion softens and is beginning to change color. Add the garlic and cumin; sauté a minute more. Add the zucchini, rice, and broth; cover and simmer for 15 to 20 minutes, or until the zucchini is tender and the rice is cooked. Then add the cilantro and lemon juice to the pot.

2. Remove the pot from the heat and puree the soup in batches. (I puree just enough so it is creamy but still has some texture.) Pour the soup into another clean pot or bowl, stir well, and taste. If it needs a flavor boost, add some salt to taste.

creamy tomato asparagus soup

FREE OF

MAKES 8 TO 10 SERVINGS

This fantastic recipe was inspired by a soup I tasted while in Kauai, Hawaii. The original version used all local produce, including mushrooms, sweet potatoes, summer squash, leeks, tomatoes, fennel, basil, carrots, celery, and asparagus. You can add different vegetables to this soup, of course. I have made it several ways, and it is always delicious! The kids love it, too. And the leftovers can be frozen in jars for future use.

2 to 3 tablespoons extra-virgin olive oil

1 heaping cup diced shallots

1 leek, trimmed and chopped

4 to 5 garlic cloves, chopped

1 teaspoon dried thyme

¼ teaspoon red pepper flakes (optional)

2 to 3 teaspoons Herbamare or sea salt

1 teaspoon freshly ground black pepper

1 large sweet potato (about 1 pound), peeled and diced

1 pound asparagus, trimmed and chopped

4 cups diced ripe tomatoes

2 cups cooked garbanzo or cannellini beans

6 cups water, vegetable broth, or chicken broth

1 large handful fresh basil leaves

Heat an 8-quart stockpot over medium. Add the olive oil, then add the shallots and leek; sauté for 5 to 10 minutes. Add the garlic, thyme, red pepper flakes (if using), Herbamare, and pepper; sauté a minute more. Add the sweet potato, asparagus, tomatoes, beans, water, and basil; cover and simmer for about 25 minutes. Puree the soup in batches, then taste and adjust the seasonings, if necessary.

> **INGREDIENT TIP**
>
> If you are avoiding plants in the nightshade family, then exclude the red pepper flakes.

spiced pumpkin soup

FREE OF

MAKES 8 TO 10 SERVINGS

My sister-in-law made a delicious soup while we were visiting for Christmas one year, and I didn't have her original recipe, so I improvised, based on memory. I think this one is just as good! Serve the soup with roasted chicken and a cabbage slaw for a balanced meal.

2 to 3 tablespoons extra-virgin olive oil

1 large onion, chopped

1 to 2 tablespoons finely chopped fresh ginger

4 or 5 large carrots, chopped

4 or 5 celery stalks, chopped

2 Granny Smith apples, cored and chopped

10 cups water, vegetable broth, or chicken broth

8 cups sugar pumpkin puree (see Tip)

2 to 3 cups cooked white beans

2 to 3 teaspoons pumpkin pie spice

3 to 4 teaspoons Herbamare or sea salt

½ to 1 teaspoon freshly ground black pepper

Coconut milk, to swirl

Chopped fresh cilantro, for garnish

Heat an 8-quart stockpot over medium. Add the olive oil, then add the onion and sauté for about 5 minutes. Add the ginger, carrots, celery, and apples; sauté for 5 to 10 minutes more. Add the water, pumpkin puree, beans, pumpkin pie spice, Herbamare, and pepper. Bring to a boil, then reduce the heat to a simmer and cook for about 20 minutes, covered. Puree the soup in batches. Taste and adjust the seasonings, if necessary. Garnish each serving with a swirl of coconut milk and a sprinkle of cilantro.

> **KITCHEN TIP**
>
> If you don't have any pumpkin puree on hand, you can bake two sugar pie pumpkins as directed on page 480 and skip pureeing the cooked pumpkin flesh— since your soup will already be pureed. Just scoop the cooked pumpkin flesh out of the skin and measure before adding it to the soup. If you don't have sugar pie pumpkins on hand, you can substitute another type of cooked winter squash, such as hubbard or butternut.

creamy carrot and lentil ginger soup

FREE OF

MAKES 6 TO 8 SERVINGS

Serve this warming, nourishing soup with a swirl of coconut milk in each bowl. Use South River Miso Company's Adzuki Bean Miso, which is gluten-free and soy-free. Remember to sort through your lentils and pick out any gluten grains, then rinse very well.

2 tablespoons extra-virgin olive oil or coconut oil

1 onion, chopped

3 garlic cloves, crushed

2 tablespoons chopped fresh ginger

8 large carrots, chopped

1 cup red lentils, sorted and rinsed

8 cups Homemade Chicken Broth (page 156) or water

2 teaspoons Herbamare or sea salt

¼ cup gluten-free miso (see Headnote), or to taste

Handful of fresh cilantro, chopped

1. Heat a 6-quart pot over medium. Add the olive oil, then add the onion and sauté for 5 minutes, or until softened. Add the garlic and ginger, and sauté a minute more. Then add the carrots, lentils, broth, and Herbamare. Cover and bring to a boil, then reduce the heat and simmer for about 40 minutes, or until the lentils are cooked and the carrots are soft.

2. Add the miso. Use an immersion blender to puree the soup or blend it in batches using your blender. Return the soup to the pot, and stir in the cilantro. Taste and adjust the seasonings, if desired.

red lentil dal

FREE OF

MAKES 6 TO 8 SERVINGS

This dal is easy to prepare and comes together quickly. Serve it over red quinoa or brown jasmine rice, along with the Raw Cilantro Lime Chutney (page 347) and Chile-Garlic Fermented Green Beans (page 474).

2 cups red lentils, sorted and rinsed

6 cups water

1 teaspoon ground turmeric

1 teaspoon ground cumin

¼ teaspoon cayenne pepper

4 tablespoons coconut oil

1 tablespoon finely chopped fresh ginger

1 tablespoon cumin seeds

1 tablespoon brown mustard seeds

1 large onion, cut in half and sliced into crescent moons

2 teaspoons sea salt

2 cups diced ripe tomatoes

1. Place the lentils in a 6-quart pot along with the water, turmeric, cumin, and cayenne. Cover and simmer over medium heat for about 30 minutes.

2. While the lentils are cooking, heat a large skillet over medium-high. Add the coconut oil, then the ginger, cumin seeds, and mustard seeds; sauté for 20 to 30 seconds. Add the onion and salt, and sauté

for 10 to 12 minutes, or until the onion is very soft and beginning to change color. Add the tomatoes and sauté for 2 minutes more.

3. Transfer the onion-tomato mixture, scraping the bottom of the pan to get all of the spices out, into the lentils; simmer for 10 to 15 minutes more.

soothing red lentil soup

FREE OF

MAKES 8 SERVINGS

Serve this nourishing tomato-free soup with a scoop of cooked quinoa or brown basmati rice. You can freeze portions of it before adding the greens. When you are ready to serve it, heat it in a small pot and add a handful of greens. This will keep the soup tasting fresh and the colors bright.

2 tablespoons extra-virgin olive oil

1 tablespoon cumin seeds

1 large onion, chopped

2 or 3 large carrots, diced

2 or 3 garlic cloves, crushed

1 to 2 teaspoons grated fresh ginger

1 tablespoon mild curry powder

1½ teaspoons freshly ground black pepper

2½ cups red lentils, rinsed and drained

10 cups water or Homemade Chicken Broth (page 156)

1 or 2 zucchini, diced

4 cups thinly sliced greens (kale, spinach, collards)

1 cup frozen peas

2 to 3 tablespoons fresh lemon juice

2 teaspoons Herbamare or sea salt

1. Heat a 6- to 8-quart pot over medium. Add the olive oil, then the cumin seeds and sauté for about 30 seconds. Add the onion and sauté for about 5 minutes. Add the carrots, garlic, ginger, curry powder, and pepper; sauté a minute or so more. Add the lentils and water, cover, and simmer for about 30 minutes.

2. Add the zucchini, greens, peas, lemon juice, and Herbamare. Stir well and simmer, uncovered, for about 10 minutes more, or until all the vegetables are tender. Taste and adjust the seasonings, if necessary.

curried lentil and sweet potato soup

MAKES 8 SERVINGS

This is one of our favorite quick and easy evening meals. Serve it with a scoop of cooked quinoa or basmati rice, and a dollop of Raw Cilantro Lime Chutney (page 347) for a balanced family meal.

2 to 3 tablespoons extra-virgin olive oil or coconut oil

1 onion, chopped

1 to 2 teaspoons grated fresh ginger

1 tablespoon ground cumin

2 teaspoons curry powder

1 teaspoon ground coriander

½ teaspoon ground turmeric

2 sweet potatoes, peeled and diced (4 to 5 cups)

2 cups French lentils, sorted and rinsed

8 cups water

2 to 3 teaspoons Herbamare or sea salt

1. Heat an 8-quart stockpot over medium. Add the olive oil, then add the onion and sauté for 5 to 10 minutes, or until the onion is soft and beginning to change color. Add the ginger, cumin, curry powder, coriander, turmeric, and sweet potatoes; sauté for a few minutes more.

2. Stir in the lentils and water, cover, and bring to a boil. Reduce the heat to a simmer and cook for 35 to 40 minutes, or until the lentils are cooked. Add the Herbamare and simmer a minute more. Taste and adjust the seasonings, if necessary.

moroccan lentil and cabbage soup

FREE OF

MAKES 8 SERVINGS

Our children love anything with curry, but they are especially fond of the flavors of Morocco. I think it's because I ate a lot of curried dishes while pregnant and breastfeeding and then offered them curried dishes by the time they were one year old. We like to make this recipe on a busy weeknight, and serve it over cooked quinoa for a simple, balanced meal.

2 to 3 tablespoons extra-virgin olive oil

1 onion, diced

4 carrots, diced

2 teaspoons curry powder

1 teaspoon ground cardamom

½ teaspoon garam masala

Pinch of cayenne pepper (optional)

2 cups French lentils, sorted and rinsed

10 cups water or chicken broth

4 to 6 tablespoons tomato paste

4 cups sliced savoy cabbage

2 teaspoons Herbamare or sea salt

Heat an 8-quart stockpot over medium. Add the olive oil, then add the onion and sauté for 5 to 10 minutes, until softened and beginning to change color. Add the carrots and spices, and sauté a minute more. Add the lentils, water, and tomato paste. Cover and simmer for 35 to 40 minutes, or until the lentils are cooked. Turn off the heat, stir in the cabbage and Herbamare, then taste and adjust the seasonings, if necessary.

KITCHEN TIP

Remember to sort through your lentils before you use them and pick out any gluten grains. Lentils are often cross-contaminated during harvest and storage. I have a helpful video on my blog, www.NourishingMeals.com.

lentil minestrone

FREE OF

MAKES 8 TO 10 SERVINGS

Serve this soup as a main dish with a loaf of crusty gluten-free bread. The soup freezes well as long as you don't add the noodles.

3 to 4 tablespoons extra-virgin olive oil

1 large onion, chopped

1 tablespoon Italian seasoning

2 teaspoons smoked paprika

2 cups sliced carrots

2 cups chopped celery

4 or 5 garlic cloves, crushed

2 cups French lentils, sorted and rinsed

10 to 12 cups water, chicken broth, or vegetable broth

2 cups chopped ripe tomatoes

8 ounces brown rice elbow noodles

1 cup chopped fresh Italian parsley

2 to 3 teaspoons Herbamare or sea salt

Freshly ground black pepper

1. Heat an 8-quart stockpot over medium. Add the olive oil, then add the onion and sauté for 5 to 10 minutes, or until softened and beginning to change color. Add the seasoning, paprika, carrots, celery, and garlic; sauté a minute more. Add the lentils, water, and tomatoes. Cover and simmer for about 45 minutes, or until the lentils are cooked.

2. While the soup is cooking, cook the pasta until al dente, according to the directions on the package.

3. Turn the heat off under the lentils and add the parsley, Herbamare, and pepper. Gently stir in the cooked rice noodles, adjust the seasonings, and serve.

gingered yellow split pea dal

FREE OF

MAKES 6 SERVINGS

This dal is a bit thicker than most dals we make. We like to serve a scoop of it alongside other Indian-inspired recipes, such as the Fresh Vegetable Curry (page 286) or the Red Quinoa Masala (page 266).

2 tablespoons extra-virgin olive oil or
   coconut oil

2 teaspoons cumin seeds

1 teaspoon brown or black mustard seeds

1 onion, finely diced

3 tablespoons grated fresh ginger

2 garlic cloves, crushed

2 teaspoons ground coriander

1 teaspoon ground turmeric

2 cups yellow split peas, rinsed and drained

6 cups water, or more as needed

Juice of 1 lemon

2 teaspoons Herbamare or sea salt

1. Heat a 3-quart pot over medium. Add the olive oil, then add the cumin and mustard seeds; sauté for 30 to 60 seconds, or until the seeds begin to pop and you smell a fragrant aroma. Immediately add the onion and sauté for 5 to 7 minutes. Add the ginger, garlic, coriander, and turmeric; sauté a minute more.

2. Add the split peas and water; cover and bring to a boil. Reduce the heat to a simmer and cook for 40 to 60 minutes, stirring occasionally, until the split peas have turned into a creamy, thick stew. Add more water if you prefer a thinner stew. Stir in the lemon juice and Herbamare. Taste and adjust the seasonings, if necessary.

chipotle black bean and yam stew

MAKES 6 TO 8 SERVINGS

Serve this spicy tomato-free stew with a large scoop of Cilantro Cabbage Slaw (page 202). Sometimes we also add a scoop of cooked brown rice. If you are using canned black beans, figure on about four cans; and use the canning liquid as well. I prefer to use bean cooking liquid rather than water in this recipe, as it gives a thicker stew. You can also replace the yams with a small butternut squash that has been peeled and diced.

2 tablespoons extra-virgin olive oil

1 onion, chopped

2 teaspoons ground cumin

½ teaspoon dried oregano

½ to 1 teaspoon chipotle chile powder

2 to 3 teaspoons Herbamare or sea salt

2 yams (sweet potatoes), peeled and diced (about 4 cups)

4 garlic cloves, crushed

6 cups cooked black beans

4 cups bean cooking liquid or water

1 red bell pepper, cored, seeded, and diced

Juice of 1 lime (2 to 3 tablespoons)

1. Heat a 6- to 8-quart pot over medium. Add the olive oil, then add the onion and sauté for 5 to 7 minutes. Add the spices, Herbamare, yams, and garlic and sauté a minute or two more.

2. Add the beans and bean cooking liquid, and simmer uncovered for 10 to 15 minutes, or until the yams are barely tender but not yet cooked. Add the bell pepper and simmer for 10 minutes more. Taste and adjust the seasonings, if necessary. Remove from the heat and stir in the lime juice.

NUTRITION TIP

More and more research is pointing to the importance of consuming foods that make your intestinal bacteria happy. Researchers in Mexico, for instance, have found that black beans do a great job at that. Black beans contain more fiber that is not digestible (indigestible fractions) by our own enzymes, but is digested by organisms in our intestines. This fiber feeds beneficial bacteria and allows them to produce a substance called butyric acid. It just happens that butyric acid is one of the preferred sources of energy for the cells lining the colon.

curried lima bean soup

MAKES 10 SERVINGS

Lima beans are often called butter beans because of their soft buttery texture. They can be found in bulk at your local food co-op or health food store. Soak them in warm water for at least 12 hours, preferably 24 hours, ahead to aid digestibility. Feel free to add any vegetables to the soup in place of the sweet potatoes and peas, such as carrots, potatoes, kale, or zucchini. Leftover soup can be frozen for up to six months.

3 cups dried lima beans, soaked for 12 to 24 hours

2 tablespoons coconut oil

1 large onion, chopped

1 tablespoon curry powder

1 teaspoon ground cumin

1 teaspoon ground coriander

12 to 14 cups water

2 sweet potatoes, peeled and cut into cubes

2 to 3 cups fresh or frozen peas

2 to 3 teaspoons Herbamare or sea salt

Freshly ground black pepper

Chopped fresh cilantro, for garnish

1. Drain and rinse the beans using a large colander. Set aside. Heat an 8-quart stockpot over medium. Add the coconut oil, then add the onion and sauté for 5 to 10 minutes, or until softened and beginning to change color. Add the spices and sauté a minute more. Stir in the beans and the water, then cover, bring to a boil, and reduce the heat to low; simmer for 45 to 60 minutes, or until the beans are tender and cooked through.

2. Add the sweet potatoes, peas, Herbamare, and pepper; simmer uncovered for 20 minutes more, or until all the vegetables are tender. Taste and adjust the seasonings, if necessary. Garnish each serving with a sprinkle of cilantro.

ginger-coconut mung bean soup

FREE OF

MAKES 6 TO 8 SERVINGS

We often serve this as a main meal with a scoop of brown basmati rice in each bowl. Since mung beans are one of the easiest legumes to digest, people with compromised digestive systems often tolerate them well. The fresh ginger and spices further aid digestion.

1 to 2 tablespoons coconut oil

1 onion, diced

2 tablespoons grated fresh ginger

3 or 4 garlic cloves, crushed

2 teaspoons garam masala

1 to 2 teaspoons red pepper flakes

½ teaspoon ground coriander

½ teaspoon ground turmeric

1¾ cups dried mung beans

8 cups chicken broth or water

2 large carrots, diced

1 sweet potato, peeled and cut into cubes

1 (14.5-ounce) can coconut milk

3 to 4 cups thinly sliced greens (kale, collards, or chard)

1 to 2 teaspoons sea salt

1. Heat an 8-quart stockpot over medium. Add the coconut oil, then add the onion and sauté for 5 to 10 minutes, or until softened and beginning to change color. Add the ginger and garlic; sauté a minute more. Then add the garam masala, red pepper flakes, coriander, and turmeric.

2. Rinse the mung beans in a fine-mesh strainer and add them to the pot. Add the broth, cover, and cook for about 25 minutes. Add the carrots, sweet potato, and coconut milk; cover and simmer for 25 to 30 minutes more, or until the vegetables are tender. Turn off the heat and add the sliced greens and salt. Taste and adjust the seasonings, if necessary.

italian white bean soup

FREE OF

MAKES ABOUT 12 SERVINGS

Our children beg me to make this soup; they love to heat it in the morning and pack it into their school lunchboxes. We serve it with a scoop of sticky brown rice. Of course, a good crusty loaf of bread pairs well with this soup, too. In the wintertime I use frozen whole tomatoes gently thawed in a bowl of warm water. Within ten minutes their skins easily peel off and they become soft enough to chop. Store any leftovers in the refrigerator for up to a week; this soup can also be frozen in jars and reheated when needed.

2 to 3 tablespoons extra-virgin olive oil

1 large onion, chopped

3 or 4 garlic cloves, crushed

1 teaspoon paprika

1 teaspoon freshly ground black pepper

2 tablespoons Italian seasoning

4 or 5 carrots, diced

3 or 4 celery stalks, chopped

½ pound green beans, trimmed and cut into 2-inch pieces

12 cups Homemade Chicken Broth (page 156)

4 cups diced ripe tomatoes

3 to 4 tablespoons tomato paste

6 cups cooked navy beans

2 to 3 cups thinly sliced kale

½ to 1 cup chopped fresh parsley

3 teaspoons Herbamare or sea salt

1. Heat an 8-quart pot over medium. Add the olive oil, then add the onion and sauté for 8 to 10 minutes, or until very soft and beginning to change color. Add the garlic and spices; sauté a minute more. Then add the carrots, celery, and green beans; sauté about 2 minutes. Then add the broth, tomatoes, and tomato paste. Cover and simmer for 20 to 25 minutes, or until the vegetables are tender.

2. Stir in the beans, kale, and parsley; simmer 5 minutes more. Add the Herbamare; taste and adjust the seasonings, if necessary.

harvest vegetable soup

MAKES ABOUT 12 SERVINGS

I love making this soup in autumn, when the weather cools and the fall harvest of root vegetables is in! You can replace the cooked beans with beef stew meat, if desired (see Tip). I like to use locally grown heirloom beans, such as Redhawk kidney beans and Mayacoba beans. Red beans or cannellini work quite well, too. If you don't have fresh herbs on hand, then use a few teaspoons dried poultry seasoning. Soup recipes are very forgiving, so if you do not have some of these ingredients, just use what you do have. You can store leftovers in the refrigerator for up to a week and reheat as needed.

2 to 3 tablespoons extra-virgin olive oil

1 onion, chopped

1 leek, trimmed and chopped

5 carrots, chopped

3 red potatoes, chopped

3 small rutabagas, peeled and chopped

2 celeriac (celery root), peeled and chopped

2 parsnips, peeled and chopped

8 cups water or homemade beef broth

4 to 5 cups crushed ripe tomatoes

4 to 5 cups cooked beans

½ head green cabbage, sliced

1 small bunch kale, chopped

1 cup chopped fresh parsley

1 to 2 tablespoons chopped fresh sage

1 tablespoon chopped fresh thyme

1 tablespoon chopped fresh marjoram

1 tablespoon chopped fresh rosemary

1 to 2 teaspoons freshly ground black pepper

2 to 3 teaspoons sea salt

1. Heat a large, heavy-bottomed soup pot (at least 9 quarts). Add the olive oil, then add the onion and leek, and sauté for a few minutes; add the carrots, potatoes, rutabagas, celeriac, parsnips, water, and tomatoes. Cover and simmer over medium-low heat for 30 minutes.

2. Add the beans, cabbage, kale, fresh herbs, pepper, and salt. Simmer for about 15 minutes more. Taste and adjust the seasoning, if desired. Serve.

INGREDIENT TIP

If you are using beef instead of beans, add 2 pounds organic, grass-fed stew meat just after sautéing the onion and leek so it has enough time to cook and tenderize.

spicy black-eyed pea soup

FREE OF

MAKES 8 TO 10 SERVINGS

We like to serve this soup with sautéed collard greens and Chipotle Yam Fries (page 236). It is also delicious served with a scoop of polenta. Sprinkle extra red pepper flakes on top of individual servings for added kick.

2 to 3 tablespoons extra-virgin olive oil

1 large onion, chopped

4 or 5 garlic cloves, crushed

2 tablespoons ground cumin

½ to 1 teaspoon red pepper flakes

½ teaspoon freshly ground black pepper

2 cups dried black-eyed peas

8 to 10 cups water

3 or 4 carrots, sliced

1 large red bell pepper, cored, seeded, and diced

3 cups broccoli florets

3 teaspoons sea salt or Herbamare

1. Heat an 8-quart pot over medium. Add the olive oil, then add the onion and sauté for 6 to 7 minutes, or until soft. Add the garlic and spices, and sauté a minute more. Add the peas and water, cover, and bring to a boil, then reduce the heat to a simmer and cook for 25 minutes.

2. Add the carrots and cook for 10 to 15 minutes more. Add the bell pepper and broccoli, and simmer until the vegetables are tender and the peas are cooked, 5 to 10 minutes more. Stir in the salt; taste and adjust the seasonings, if necessary.

three-bean vegetable chili

FREE OF

MAKES 8 TO 10 SERVINGS

Serve this colorful chili when the weather begins to get cold. It is great with Pumpkin Cornbread (page 148) or with a scoop of cooked short-grain brown rice with slices of avocado on top.

2 tablespoons extra-virgin olive oil

1 onion, chopped

4 garlic cloves, crushed

4 teaspoons chili powder

2 teaspoons ground cumin

2 to 3 teaspoons Herbamare or sea salt

3 or 4 carrots, diced

4 cups diced ripe tomatoes

2 cups cooked black beans

2 cups cooked kidney beans

2 cups cooked pinto beans

2 to 4 cups water

½ pound fresh or frozen corn kernels

½ bunch curly green kale, finely chopped

1 cup fresh cilantro, chopped

1. Heat an 8-quart stockpot over medium. Heat the olive oil, then add the onion and sauté for about 10 minutes. Add the garlic, spices, and Herbamare; sauté a minute more. Add the carrots, tomatoes, beans, water, and corn. Cover and simmer for about 60 minutes.

2. Add the chopped kale and cilantro, then simmer 5 minutes more. Serve hot!

NUTRITION TIP

Use diced fresh or frozen tomatoes to avoid canned tomatoes. Most cans of tomatoes have BPA in the lining, which easily migrates to the tomatoes because of their acidity. BPA is a hormone-disrupting chemical, its effects include birth defects, reproductive dysfunction, increased incidence of miscarriages, and potentially cancer. Testing has found that pregnant women and infants who eat even a single serving of some canned foods are exposed to unsafe doses of BPA.

chicken and chard chili

FREE OF

MAKES 6 TO 8 SERVINGS

We like to make this recipe on a very busy weeknight. It's ten minutes to toss the ingredients into the pan and then it simmers on the stove while I listen to my children practice their music or help them with reading or writing. You can accompany this stew with a batch of Vegan Corn Muffins (page 143) or a simple pot of short-grain brown rice.

2 to 3 tablespoons extra-virgin olive oil

1 onion, chopped

3 garlic cloves, crushed

1 to 2 jalapeño peppers, seeded and finely diced

2 boneless organic chicken breasts, chopped into small pieces

1 tablespoon ground cumin

1 tablespoon mild chili powder

1 teaspoon smoked paprika (optional)

2 cups tomato sauce (see Tip)

3 cups water

5 to 6 cups cooked pinto or red beans

2 teaspoons Herbamare or sea salt

2 cups chopped chard

Heat a 6-quart pot over medium. Add the olive oil, then add the onion and sauté for 5 to 10 minutes, or until it is soft and beginning to change color. Add the garlic, jalapeño, and chicken; sauté for 2 to 3 minutes more. Add the cumin, chili powder, and paprika (if using); sauté a minute more. Add the tomato sauce, water, beans, and Herbamare. Stir, cover, and simmer over medium-low heat for about 45 minutes. When the chicken is tender and the flavors have melded, add the chard and simmer for 5 minutes more. Turn off the heat, taste, and adjust the seasonings, if necessary.

INGREDIENT TIP

I use Bionaturae Strained Tomatoes in place of the tomato sauce in this recipe. It comes in a glass jar, not a can. I always use it in place of canned tomato sauce.

slow cooker chicken stew

FREE OF

MAKES 4 TO 6 SERVINGS

I don't have many slow cooker recipes because I usually get inspired to cook when I'm hungry—close to dinnertime. However, this recipe came to me early one day, and I knew I just had to pull out my old cooker. The flavors come together beautifully, and the chicken is so tender you'll hardly need to chew! Serve this stew over basmati rice alongside a salad of crispy romaine lettuce. It is also pairs well with the Farmhouse Seed Bread (page 122).

1 cup diced shallots

3 celery stalks, diced

4 carrots, diced

1½ pounds boneless organic chicken breasts, cut into chunks

2 cups diced ripe tomatoes

1 cup water

¼ to ½ cup dry white wine

¼ cup extra-virgin olive oil

1 tablespoon Italian seasoning

1 to 2 teaspoons Herbamare or sea salt

Freshly ground black pepper

Place all the ingredients in a slow cooker and cook on high for 4 to 5 hours or on low for 6 to 8 hours. (If you do not have a slow cooker, place all the ingredients in a covered casserole dish or Dutch oven, and bake at 300°F for about 2½ hours, or until the vegetables and meat are soft and tender.)

super immune-boosting chicken soup

FREE OF

MAKES ABOUT 12 SERVINGS

This is one of my favorite soups to make during cold and flu season. Feel free to add any other vegetables, such as diced sweet potatoes or winter squash, or finely chopped hot chiles. You can also use green or savoy cabbage. Astragalus is a medicinal root that stimulates the immune system making it more effective in fighting colds and flus. If you can't find astragalus then simply omit it.

BROTH

A 4- to 5-pound organic roasting chicken

4 quarts water

1 onion, chopped

3 celery stalks, chopped

2 carrots, chopped

4 or 5 shiitake mushrooms, chopped

1 garlic head, cut in half crosswise

2 to 3 inches fresh ginger, cut into thin slices

2 tablespoons dried astragalus (see Headnote)

1 teaspoon black peppercorns

1 lemongrass stalk, trimmed and chopped (optional)

SOUP

1 onion, chopped

3 carrots, sliced

4 celery stalks, chopped

2 cups shiitake mushrooms, thinly sliced

1 large red bell pepper, cored, seeded, and chopped

2 to 3 teaspoons grated fresh ginger

1 tablespoon sea salt

1 teaspoon red pepper flakes

4 to 5 cups sliced napa cabbage

1 cup chopped fresh cilantro

OPTIONAL ADDITIONS

Cooked rice noodles

Chopped fresh basil

Chopped fresh Thai green chiles

Lime wedges

KITCHEN TIP

If substituting a 3- to 4-pound chicken, use only 3 quarts water.

---

1. Put the broth ingredients in an 8-quart stockpot, cover, and simmer over low heat for 1½ to 2 hours. Place a large colander over another 8-quart pot or large stainless steel bowl and pour the broth through it to strain out the chicken and vegetables.

2. Place the pot of broth back on the stove. Transfer the chicken to a plate to cool. Bring the broth to a boil, then add all the soup ingredients except the cabbage and cilantro. Cover and simmer

for 15 to 20 minutes, or until the vegetables are tender.

3. While the vegetables are cooking, pull the meat from the bones of the chicken and cut into smaller pieces. Add the chicken meat to the soup. Turn off the heat and add the cabbage and cilantro. Taste and adjust the seasonings, if desired.

grass-fed beef chili

FREE OF

MAKES 6 SERVINGS

When purchasing beef, always choose grass-fed, organic meat, as it is the most sustainable and nutritious. Serve this chili with the Pumpkin Cornbread (page 148) and a spoonful of raw cultured vegetables to maximize digestion.

1 tablespoon extra-virgin olive oil or coconut oil

1 large onion, finely chopped

6 garlic cloves, crushed

1 tablespoon ground cumin

1 tablespoon chili powder

1 red bell pepper, cored, seeded, and diced

1 jalapeño pepper, finely diced (optional)

1 pound ground grass-fed beef

4 cups cooked red beans

2 cups tomato sauce

2 cups water

2 teaspoons Herbamare or sea salt

½ cup chopped fresh cilantro

1. Heat a 6-quart pot over medium. Add the olive oil, then add the onion and sauté for about 10 minutes, or until very soft and beginning to change color. Add the garlic, cumin, chili powder, bell pepper, jalapeño, and ground beef; sauté for a few minutes.

2. Add the beans, tomato sauce, water, and Herbamare; cover and simmer for about 35 minutes, stirring occasionally. Stir in the cilantro, then taste and adjust the seasonings, if necessary.

halibut and potato chowder

FREE OF

MAKES 6 SERVINGS

A bowl of hot chowder is welcoming to come home to after a long afternoon of skiing, sledding, or playing in the snow. This chowder is wonderful served with a slice of freshly baked Gluten-Free Sourdough Bread (page 114) and a large serving of sautéed dark leafy greens.

2 tablespoons extra-virgin olive oil

1 large onion, diced

2 slices organic bacon (optional)

4 garlic cloves, crushed

1 to 2 teaspoons dried thyme

1 to 2 teaspoons dried dill

2 or 3 large carrots, diced

3 celery stalks, diced

6 large red or yellow potatoes, peeled and diced

5 to 6 cups chicken or vegetable broth

1 to 2 pounds fresh halibut fillet, any skin removed, cut into 1-inch chunks

Large handful of fresh parsley, chopped

Herbamare or sea salt

Freshly ground black pepper

1. Heat a 6-quart pot over medium. Add the olive oil, then add the onion and sauté for 5 to 7 minutes, or until soft and starting to turn a little golden. Add the bacon (if using), garlic, and herbs; sauté a minute or so more. Add the carrots, celery, and potatoes and sauté a few minutes. Add the broth and simmer, covered, for about 30 minutes, or until the vegetables are very soft.

2. Take a large spoon and mash some of the potatoes against the side of the pot to make the chowder creamy. Add the fish and simmer for about 5 minutes more, until the fish is cooked through. Remove the bacon and discard. Add the parsley and stir, along with the Herbamare and pepper, to taste.

saladsandvegetables

We've always included a lot of fresh vegetables in our diet, so our children have grown up not knowing any different. It's the home environment that helps develop the taste buds to favor or not favor vegetables. The trick is to keep the junk food out of the house so the only alternatives for snacking are fresh vegetables, fruits, and nuts—the things that can be grabbed easily when needed.

Of course, our children all have their own likes and dislikes when it comes to foods, which is completely normal. A few don't like beets, one loves grapefruit, some love bitter greens while others don't, some love beef and some don't. Try not to get too caught up in what they *don't* eat and instead focus on all the good things that they *do* enjoy. We introduced chopped green salads with homemade dressing to our children at around one year. If your child is not quite ready for a big plate of greens, then keep it simple—cut up raw vegetables such as carrots, cucumbers, and celery for a side dish and serve that instead of the vegetable dish you made with more complex flavors.

Having vegetables as the centerpiece of your meals is one of the healthiest choices you can make for your family. Vegetables are vital to all aspects of human health and contain literally thousands of phytochemicals that offer innumerable health benefits, including decreased risk of cancer, hypertension, type 2 diabetes, age-related macular degeneration, obesity, and early-stage cognitive decline. The fibers in vegetables also feed the beneficial microbes in the developing gut microbiome of a child, which is incredibly crucial for lifelong health and wellness.

VITAL PHYTOCHEMICALS

Plant phytochemicals signal our cells to produce antioxidant and detoxification proteins after we eat. Why would this be important? We hear from the media on a daily basis about all the harmful chemicals in our environment—the BPA in plastics and the linings of food cans, pesticides sprayed on our produce, and heavy metals like arsenic in our drinking water or mercury in the air from nearby coal plants. Every one of these substances needs to be filtered from our body by the liver, and we need extra antioxidants to protect our cells from the damaging effects of these chemicals.

In particular, you'll want to make sure you get a lot of sulforaphane, which is found in broccoli, cauliflower, brussels sprouts, collards, cabbage, kale, and kohlrabi. It initiates the reading of an incredible portion of our genes called the *antioxidant response element,* which leads to the production of antioxidant and detoxification proteins for more than 72 hours! As a result, our body's overall ability to survive in an increasingly toxic world gets a big boost.

HOW MUCH SHOULD I EAT?

Incorporating vegetables into breakfast, lunch, and dinner is necessary if you want to continuously bathe your cells with disease-fighting nutrients. Go a step further: drink green smoothies and eat chopped raw vegetables as snacks throughout the day.

The daily minimum is this: consume 2 to 3 cups each of the following daily:

- Leafy greens such as lettuce, arugula, and spinach
- Cruciferous vegetables such as broccoli, kale, and cabbage

- Brightly colored vegetables such as carrots, beets, and peas
- Fresh or frozen fruit

It is best to start a meal with a salad or plate of vegetables, before the starchy or meat-based parts of the meal are served. Our taste buds are hardwired to seek out salt, starch, and fat for survival. Oftentimes we need to retrain the taste buds to accept new and interesting flavors. Starting out the meal with raw vegetables can help in both training the taste buds and stimulating digestion.

GETTING KIDS TO EAT MORE VEGGIES

Fresh fruits and vegetables are some of the easiest foods to snack on, but if your home is stocked with snack foods filled with empty calories, your children will most likely seek those first. We have found that our children will reach into the refrigerator and snack on carrots, radishes, celery, cucumbers, and snap peas, or into the freezer for frozen blueberries, cherries, and peaches, when there is nothing else available in the house to eat that doesn't require some sort of preparation. If I have made cookies, muffins, or bread, they usually go for those first. I make it a habit to bake treats only on occasion, so fresh fruits and vegetables can easily make up the bulk of their diet.

Gardening with Children

Gardening with children provides a way for them to connect with how food grows while also having easy access to fresh vegetables. I once lived next door to two young boys who loved eating sweets and junk food. Their mom often asked me how to get the boys to eat vegetables. I promptly went into my garden with the boys and marked off rectangular areas for them to plant their own mini-vegetable patches. I then handed them a box of vegetable seeds and had them dig the soil and plant the vegetables they wanted. Over the next few months, they came by often to check on their vegetable plants and admire how quickly they grew. When they were ready to harvest, we found both boys eating raw kale, collards, broccoli, and peas! From then on, they had a completely different relationship with vegetables.

Cooking with Children

Cooking with your children provides a nonthreatening way to be introduced to vegetables. Imagine sitting at a table and being told you can't leave until you have finished eating your cauliflower and peas. But what if your children helped in chopping and prepping them for dinner? They might be more inclined to taste one of those brightly colored, fresh, raw vegetables! Our first daughter cut the cauliflower florets with us when she was a toddler; she sampled the raw cauliflower we were chopping and ended up eating about a cup or more during the preparation.

10 Tips for Adding More Vegetables to Your Child's Diet

1. Make sure your children are hungry and have not been snacking all afternoon or evening. Hungry children are more likely to try new foods, including vegetables.

2. Serve the new vegetable or salad first. This is especially true for young children between two and four years of age.

3. Sit down as a family and talk about everything but the meal. Focusing on the food can lead to food battles.

4. Suggest a "try-it bite" for a child who seems really uncomfortable about sampling something new. The child may spit it out, and that is okay. Sometimes it can take ten "try-it bites" over a series of weeks for a child to accept a new food.

5. Start early! As soon as a child is old enough to chew, he or she begins munching on raw or cooked greens. A one-year-old won't digest much of it, but will gain so much in the way of programming the taste buds to accept these types of foods.

6. Model eating vegetables. Young children learn how to eat and what to eat by watching the adults and caregivers around them. This starts from infancy on.

7. Cook and garden with your children. When given the opportunity, young children are naturally curious to try new things, including vegetables like brussels sprouts! Cooking with your children and planting a small backyard vegetable patch provide nonthreatening ways to be introduced to new foods.

8. When grocery shopping with your children, have them pick out one vegetable that they get to try and possibly help incorporate into a meal. This can't be the usual carrots or celery. This "vegetable treat" can be exciting to have as part of your grocery shopping routine.

9. Only have snacks and foods around your house that you are comfortable with your children eating at any time. When they are hungry they will learn to reach for what is easily available. Fresh vegetables and fruits are the easiest and most nutritious snacks!

10. Give your children green smoothies! We can't think of a better way to pack a lot of vegetables into one snack. Adding carrots, beets, cucumbers, leafy greens, and fruit to a blender along with a little water creates a delicious, refreshing drink! See our "Smoothies" chapter for recipes.

10 Tips for Storing Fresh Vegetables and Fruits

1. Store potatoes and sweet potatoes in a dark, cool place such as a pantry or root cellar. Light causes them to turn green and begin to sprout. When potatoes turn green, it is an indicator that solanine—a toxic compound—has increased. If this happens, it is best to not eat them.

2. Cut the leafy green parts off root vegetables before storage. Otherwise, the nutrients and water will continue to flow into the leafy parts, causing the root to go limp. This includes carrots, beets, radishes, parsnips, celery root, and turnips. For best storage, wrap the root vegetables in damp kitchen towels and place them in your refrigerator's crisper drawer.

3. Onions and garlic do best stored away from other vegetables and fruits. I store mine in a large open box in my pantry and keep a few out on my counter in a separate basket.

4. Place bunched fresh herbs in small glasses of water and cover loosely with a produce bag. This includes parsley, cilantro, mint, dill, thyme, and oregano.

5. Store apples in the refrigerator to keep them fresh and crisp. Some varieties of apples can be stored like this for three months or more. We dedicate one whole drawer in our refrigerator just to apples!

6. Citrus fruits and tomatoes need to be stored in a place with airflow, such as an open basket on your counter.

7. Berries like to be kept dry and cool. Never wash your berries before refrigerating. A paper bag can be used for strawberries. Other berries can be stored in shallow layers in open rectangular glass containers.

8. Kale, collards, napa cabbage, and lettuce liked to be wrapped in a damp kitchen towel and stored in a plastic bag or loosely covered glass container in the refrigerator.

9. Freshly picked zucchini can be left on the counter for a few days. For longer storage, place them in your refrigerator's crisper drawer. We do the same with cucumbers, peppers, and eggplant.

10. Winter squash like to be stored in a cool, dark well-ventilated area. After harvesting squash from our garden, we set them inside our house at room temperature to cure for about two weeks. Then we put them in shallow cardboard boxes in our garage. Winter squash store best at 50 to 55°F, where they should keep until March.

apple walnut salad with fig-balsamic vinaigrette

FREE OF

MAKES 6 SERVINGS

Heirloom apples are available in early autumn at your local farmers' market or health food store. Each variety has its unique flavors. This dressing was inspired by a dish at the lovely Café Gratitude in California. The blended figs work as a natural emulsifier, meaning that the oil and vinegar won't separate. They also add a seedy texture and a touch of sweetness. Any variety of fresh figs works in this recipe. Transfer any remaining dressing to a glass jar; it will keep in the refrigerator for seven to ten days.

SALAD

8 to 10 cups mixed organic baby greens

1 cup Candied Walnuts (page 374)

2 organic heirloom apples, cored and thinly sliced

5 or 6 fresh figs, quartered

Crumbled feta cheese (optional)

DRESSING

5 fresh figs, stems removed

6 tablespoons balsamic vinegar

1 to 2 tablespoons maple syrup

½ teaspoon sea salt or Herbamare

½ cup extra-virgin olive oil

Freshly ground black pepper (optional)

1. Place all the salad ingredients in a large bowl. Add the feta cheese, if desired.

2. Place the figs, vinegar, maple syrup, and salt in a blender and blend on medium until lightly pureed.

With the motor running on low, slowly pour in the olive oil. Add the pepper, if desired, and blend a bit more on low speed to incorporate. Pour the desired amount of dressing over the salad.

asian chicken salad

FREE OF

MAKES 4 SERVINGS

This high-protein, low-carbohydrate salad is the perfect thing to serve for lunch—it will keep you energized for hours afterward! You could use sliced almonds in place of the slivered. Try adding daikon radish, chopped cilantro, and sliced green onions to this salad as well. Any leftover dressing will keep in the fridge for up to a week.

SALAD

6 to 8 cups thinly sliced greens (kale, collards, savoy cabbage, bok choy; see Tip)

2 to 3 cups shredded cooked organic chicken

2 large carrots, julienned

1 cup slivered almonds, lightly toasted

Sesame seeds, for garnish

DRESSING

4 tablespoons extra-virgin olive oil

1 tablespoon toasted sesame oil

3 tablespoons coconut vinegar or brown rice vinegar

3 tablespoons coconut aminos or wheat-free tamari (see Tip on page 158)

2 to 3 teaspoons honey

1 garlic clove

A 1-inch piece of fresh ginger, peeled

Toss the salad ingredients into a large bowl if serving immediately. (If you want to stretch the salad over a few days, place the ingredients in separate containers and store in the fridge. Use what you would like for each serving.) Place the dressing ingredients into a blender and blend on high until combined. Pour the dressing over the salad, toss, and serve. Garnish with sesame seeds, if desired.

> **KITCHEN TIP**
>
> To thinly slice the greens, stack them on top of each other, then roll them; use a sharp knife to cut into thin slices—this is called *chiffonade*.

arugula salad with shaved fennel

MAKES 6 TO 8 SERVINGS

This simple salad is perfect as part of a Sunday brunch or weeknight dinner. Serve it with poached eggs and roasted vegetables for brunch; for dinner, pair it with the Mushroom Millet Risotto (page 259) and Poached Salmon with Green Onions and White Wine (page 300). I like to add Twice-Roasted Golden Beets (page 235) to the salad for more color, flavor, and nutrients.

SALAD

2 bunches arugula, rinsed and spun dry

1 large fennel bulb, trimmed

¼ cup snipped fresh chives

DRESSING

3 tablespoons extra-virgin olive oil

3 tablespoons Champagne vinegar

1 teaspoon Dijon mustard

Sea salt and freshly ground black pepper

Tear the arugula into pieces and place it in a large salad bowl. Using a sharp knife, thinly slice the fennel bulb. Place the shaved fennel in the bowl with the arugula. Add the chives and toss. In a small bowl, whisk together the dressing ingredients. Just before serving, pour the dressing over the salad and toss. Serve immediately.

NUTRITION TIP

Besides being an excellent source of vitamin C, fennel has the important compound anethole, which can block the response of a potent inflammatory chemical called the *tumor necrosis factor*. Researchers are examining the role that anethole may play in reducing the incidence of cancer.

avocado and sweet potato salad with lime

FREE OF

MAKES 4 TO 6 SERVINGS

This simple salad can dress up a plate of plain brown rice and black beans for a tasty, nutritious meal. It is also great served at potlucks or as part of a large family taco dinner!

2 sweet potatoes, peeled and cut into ½-inch cubes

3 small ripe avocados, cubed

¼ cup finely chopped fresh cilantro

Juice of 2 small limes

2 to 3 tablespoons extra-virgin olive oil

1 garlic clove, crushed

¼ teaspoon sea salt or Herbamare

Pinch of red pepper flakes (optional)

1. Place the sweet potatoes into a steamer basket fitted over about 1 inch of water. Cover and steam until fork-tender, about 10 minutes. Be careful not to overcook or the sweet potatoes will be too mushy. Let cool completely in the basket.

2. Place the sweet potatoes in a medium bowl and add the avocados, cilantro, lime juice, olive oil, garlic, salt, and red pepper flakes, if using. Gently toss, then taste and adjust the seasonings, if desired. Serve immediately.

> **NUTRITION TIP**
>
> The area closest to the skin of the avocado has concentrated amounts of the carotenoids zeaxanthin, beta-carotene, lutein, and beta-cryptoxanthin. Use the nick-and-peel method to keep this part in your salad instead of putting it in your compost.

> **INGREDIENT TIP**
>
> If you are avoiding foods in the nightshade family, omit the red pepper flakes.

baby arugula salad with zucchini lime dressing

Baby arugula is slightly spicy and pungent, but milder and sweeter than fully mature arugula. The zucchini adds a luscious creaminess to this dressing. Serve the salad along with the Roasted Squash and Corn Frittata (page 89) for a festive Sunday brunch. It is also delicious served with cooked black beans and quinoa for an easy, nutritious weekday meal. If you have leftover dressing, store it in a small glass jar in the fridge for up to a week.

SALAD

8 cups baby arugula

½ small onion, sliced into very thin rounds

1 ear of corn, kernels cut from cob

1 small red bell pepper, cored, seeded, and diced

1 small avocado, diced

½ cup pumpkin seeds, toasted (see Tip)

DRESSING

½ cup finely diced zucchini

½ cup fresh lime juice

½ cup extra-virgin olive oil

⅛ to ¼ teaspoon ground cumin

¼ teaspoon Herbamare

Place the arugula, onion, corn, bell pepper, and avocado in a large salad bowl and toss. Sprinkle the pumpkin seeds atop the salad. Place the dressing ingredients into a blender and blend until smooth. Taste and adjust the seasonings, if necessary. Pour the desired amount of dressing over the salad, and serve.

INGREDIENT TIP

To toast the pumpkin seeds, heat a 10-inch skillet over medium heat. Add the seeds and keep them moving in the pan until they begin to pop and turn slightly golden, about 5 minutes. Set aside on a plate to cool.

blanched kale salad with green apple dressing

FREE OF

MAKES 4 SERVINGS

Blanching the kale begins to break down its tough fibers while retaining its nutrient content; also, it turns the kale a beautiful bright green that is attractive in a salad. I usually use any type of cold leftover cooked salmon I have in the fridge; if you don't have any, simply omit it. This salad pairs well with a side of baked winter squash. Store any leftover dressing in a sealed glass jar in the fridge for up to a week. Store any remaining blanched kale in the fridge in a sealed glass container; use it in other salads or toss into an egg scramble, burritos, or soup.

SALAD

2 bunches curly kale, trimmed and chopped

1 cup flaked cooked salmon fillet

1 pomegranate, arils removed

½ cup sunflower seeds, toasted

DRESSING

1 Granny Smith apple, cored and chopped

½ cup water

⅓ cup extra-virgin olive oil

1 or 2 garlic cloves

A 1-inch piece of fresh ginger, peeled

Herbamare or sea salt to taste

1. Fill an 8-quart stockpot with filtered water until about three-fourths full and bring to a rapid boil. Quickly add all the kale, pushing it down with a large spoon. Blanch for about 60 seconds, or until bright green and tender. Pour the kale and boiling water through a colander set into your sink and immediately run icy-cold water over the kale to stop it from cooking any longer. Gently squeeze the water out of the kale. Place the desired amount of kale on each plate, top with some salmon, the pomegranate arils, and sunflower seeds.

2. Place the dressing ingredients into a blender and blend for about 60 seconds, until smooth and creamy. Taste, adjusting the seasonings if needed, and blend again. Drizzle some dressing over each salad.

cabbage salad with mandarins and mung bean sprouts

MAKES 4 TO 6 SERVINGS

This easy and nutritious salad is best paired with the Garlic Ginger Salmon (page 298) along with a side of mashed sweet potatoes or cooked quinoa. If you don't have slivered almonds or have a nut allergy, use sunflower seeds instead.

SALAD

5 cups thinly sliced napa cabbage (about ½ head)

1 cup thinly sliced red cabbage

2 mandarin oranges, sectioned

3 or 4 green onions, trimmed and sliced into thin rounds

1 cup mung bean sprouts

DRESSING

¼ cup extra-virgin olive oil

2 tablespoons toasted sesame oil

3 tablespoons coconut vinegar or brown rice vinegar

1 to 2 tablespoons creamy peanut butter or cashew butter

2 to 3 teaspoons honey

½ teaspoon Herbamare or sea salt

½ cup slivered almonds, toasted (see Tip)

Place the cabbages, mandarin sections, green onions, and sprouts in a large bowl and set aside. Whisk together the dressing ingredients in a separate bowl. Pour the dressing over the salad and sprinkle with the toasted almonds. Serve immediately.

INGREDIENT TIP

To toast the almonds, heat a large skillet over medium heat. Add the slivered almonds and keep them moving in the pan. Once they are lightly golden in color and are very fragrant, remove them from the pan and place onto a plate to cool. It should take only a few minutes to do this.

cherry pecan salad with cherry balsamic vinaigrette

MAKES 6 SERVINGS

We like to make this salad a few times a week when sweet cherries are in season. To keep the dressing an appealing dark color, we use a dark red cherry variety, such as Lapin or Bing. We usually serve the salad with the dressing on the side—that way each person can add as much as desired. I usually pour the dressing into a tall jam jar to serve it and then store any leftovers in the fridge for up to ten days.

SALAD

1 head red leaf lettuce, rinsed and spun dry

1 cup pecans, toasted (see Tip)

1 cup fresh cherries, pitted and cut in half

DRESSING

½ cup fresh or frozen pitted cherries

½ cup extra-virgin olive oil

5 to 6 tablespoons balsamic vinegar

1 tablespoon maple syrup

¼ teaspoon sea salt

Tear the lettuce into bite-size pieces and place in a salad bowl. Chop the pecans and sprinkle them on top of the lettuce. Add the cherries. Place the dressing ingredients into a blender and blend until smooth and creamy. Pour into a glass jar for serving. Pour the dressing over the salad or serve alongside the salad. Serve immediately.

INGREDIENT TIP

To toast the pecans, place them in a small glass baking dish or pie plate. Roast in a preheated 350°F oven for 10 to 15 minutes. Cool on a plate before chopping.

cilantro cabbage slaw

FREE OF

MAKES 4 TO 6 SERVINGS

One of our children's favorite vegetables is napa cabbage, so this dish makes a frequent appearance on our dinner table! Serve this fresh-tasting slaw atop the Chipotle Black Bean and Yam Stew (page 176) or with a piece of grilled chicken.

5 cups thinly sliced napa cabbage

2 cups chopped fresh cilantro

2 or 3 green onions, trimmed and sliced into thin rounds

Juice of 1 lime

1 to 2 tablespoons extra-virgin olive oil

½ teaspoon Herbamare or sea salt

Place the cabbage, cilantro, green onions, lime juice, olive oil, and Herbamare in a medium mixing bowl and toss. Dress only what you will eat with your meal; otherwise, the salad will be soggy and unappealing the next day.

NUTRITION TIP

Cilantro can assist with heavy-metal detoxification in the body. Heavy metals enter the body via amalgam tooth fillings, vaccines, pesticides and herbicides in conventional foods, paint chips from old buildings, the water supply, and flame retardants found in children's pajamas, crib mattresses, and furniture. Most people have varying levels of heavy metals in their systems that can be chelated with regular consumption of cilantro.

cucumber arame salad

MAKES 6 SERVINGS

Incorporating sea vegetables into your weekly diet is one of the healthiest things you can do. Seaweed is a rich source of iodine—a mineral needed to make thyroid hormones. Serve this refreshing salad with adzuki beans and rice, or grilled fish. This salad will keep in a covered glass container in your refrigerator for up to three days.

¼ cup arame kelp

2 cucumbers

3 green onions, trimmed and sliced into thin rounds

½ chopped fresh cilantro

3 tablespoons brown rice vinegar or coconut vinegar

2 tablespoons extra-virgin olive oil

1 to 2 teaspoons grated fresh ginger

¾ teaspoon sea salt

1. Place the arame in a small pot and cover with about 2 cups water. Bring to a boil, then reduce the heat to low and simmer for 5 to 7 minutes. Remove from the heat and drain through a fine-mesh strainer. Let cool.

2. Cut the cucumbers in half lengthwise, then slice into thin half-moons; place in a medium bowl and add the arame, green onions, cilantro, vinegar, olive oil, ginger, and salt; toss together. Taste and adjust the seasonings if necessary. Serve.

> **NUTRITION TIP**
>
> The thyroid hormones triiodothyronine (T3) and thyroxine (T4) are primarily composed of iodine. T3 is one tyrosine amino acid molecule attached to three iodine molecules, while T4 is four iodine molecules attached to tyrosine. Out of all the foods found in nature, sea vegetables are the best source of iodine. Arame is also a particularly rich source of the carotenoid fucoxanthin. This powerful antioxidant compound has been researched for its effects on increasing the burning of body fat leading to weight loss. Fucoxanthin appears to have anticancer and antidiabetic effects as well.

fresh cauliflower salad

FREE OF

MAKES 4 TO 6 SERVINGS

The displays of organic cauliflower at the farmers' market or grocery store always inspire me to create new recipes using this beautiful vegetable. Often we cut it into florets for dipping into a bean or nut spread. Serve this refreshing salad with grilled fish or cooked quinoa and beans for a simple, nutritious meal.

1 head cauliflower, cored and chopped

3 or 4 green onions, trimmed and sliced into thin rounds

Large handful of fresh parsley, finely chopped

3 to 4 tablespoons extra-virgin olive oil

3 to 4 tablespoons fresh lemon juice

Herbamare or sea salt

OPTIONAL ADDITIONS

Sliced Kalamata olives

Halved cherry tomatoes

Grated carrots

Thinly sliced fresh basil

1. Add the cauliflower to a large bowl along with the green onions, parsley, olive oil, and lemon juice. Toss, then add the Herbamare to taste and any additions of choice. Toss again.

2. Serve immediately or store in the refrigerator for a few hours. Bring to room temperature before serving.

garden salad with creamy herb dressing

FREE OF

MAKES 4 TO 6 SERVINGS

This dressing is so nutritious and flavorful that it might become your family's favorite. Walnuts are an excellent source of healthy fats; recent research shows that eating walnuts can improve brain function and memory. Soaking the walnuts overnight makes them more digestible and also creates a creamy white salad dressing! Store any leftover dressing in a small glass jar in the refrigerator for up to five days.

SALAD

1 head green leaf lettuce, rinsed, spun dry, and torn

1 cucumber, sliced

2 or 3 carrots, sliced

1 pint cherry tomatoes, halved

Handful of fresh parsley, chopped

DRESSING

½ cup raw walnuts, soaked for 6 to 8 hours

½ cup water

¼ cup extra-virgin olive oil

Juice of 1 large lemon

1 garlic clove

½ teaspoon sea salt or Herbamare

2 to 3 tablespoons chopped fresh chives

1 to 2 tablespoons fresh oregano leaves

1 tablespoon fresh rosemary leaves

1 tablespoon fresh thyme leaves

Place the salad ingredients in a large bowl and toss. Rinse and drain the walnuts. Add them to a blender with the water, olive oil, lemon juice, garlic, and salt. Blend until smooth and creamy. Add the herbs and blend on low speed until just combined. Serve the dressing with the salad.

KITCHEN TIP

If you blend everything in the dressing at once you will create a greenish dressing, so add the herbs at the end to create a white dressing with little flecks of green.

---

grapefruit, radish, and cabbage salad

FREE OF

MAKES 4 TO 6 SERVINGS

This salad is quick to prepare. It has a light dressing that doesn't overpower the flavors of the grapefruit or vegetables. Serve it with grilled chicken breasts or baked salmon and cooked quinoa.

SALAD

6 cups thinly sliced napa cabbage

2 pink grapefruit

5 or 6 small radishes, thinly sliced

DRESSING

2 tablespoons extra-virgin olive oil

2 tablespoons Champagne vinegar

Freshly ground black pepper

Few pinches of sea salt

1 to 2 tablespoons snipped chives, for garnish

1. Place the cabbage in a medium bowl, set aside. Trim the top and bottom off the grapefruit. Place the grapefruit on one of the cut ends and begin taking the peel and pith off with a sharp paring knife. Slice the grapefruit into rounds and cut each round into quarters. Add the grapefruit to the salad along with the radishes.

2. In a separate bowl, whisk together the dressing ingredients. Pour over the salad and toss well, then sprinkle the chives over and serve immediately.

greek salad with chickpeas

FREE OF

MAKES 6 SERVINGS

This salad is a complete meal. Serve it in the summertime when your garden is overflowing with fresh tomatoes, cucumbers, and lettuce. It pairs well with the Rosemary Sea Salt Breadsticks (page 121). Store any extra salad in the refrigerator for up to two days. The dressing will last about ten days in the fridge.

SALAD

1 head romaine lettuce, rinsed and spun dry

2 cups cherry tomatoes, halved

2 cups cooked chickpeas, rinsed and drained

1 cup pitted Kalamata olives, sliced

½ small red onion, diced

1 large cucumber, sliced

Chopped fresh mint leaves (optional)

Crumbled feta cheese (optional)

GREEK DRESSING

½ cup extra-virgin olive oil

6 tablespoons fresh lemon juice

1 or 2 garlic cloves

2 tablespoons fresh oregano leaves

½ teaspoon sea salt

½ teaspoon freshly ground black pepper

Chop the lettuce and place it in a large salad bowl. Top with the remaining salad ingredients. Add the mint leaves and feta cheese, if desired. Place the dressing ingredients into a blender and blend until smooth. Pour the dressing over the salad and toss (or pour the dressing into a small glass jar and let each person dress his or her own salad).

VARIATION: To make this dressing citrus-free, replace the lemon juice with organic red or white wine vinegar.

jalapeño-lime kale slaw

FREE OF

MAKES 4 TO 6 SERVINGS

Eating raw vegetables and bitter greens with your meals can help stimulate digestion, including gastric acid secretion and gut motility. Serve this salad with cooked black beans and quinoa for a simple, nutritious meal.

SALAD
5 to 6 cups thinly sliced lacinato kale
½ to 1 cup diced red bell pepper

DRESSING
¼ cup packed fresh cilantro
1 jalapeño pepper, seeded

1 garlic clove
4 tablespoons extra-virgin olive oil
3 tablespoons fresh lime juice
¼ teaspoon sea salt or Herbamare

Place the kale and bell pepper in a large bowl; set aside. Place the dressing ingredients into a blender and blend on medium until smooth. Pour the dressing over the salad and toss. Taste and add more salt, if needed. Let the dressing mingle with the kale for 2 to 24 hours; the kale will tenderize and become softer the longer it sits.

> **NUTRITION TIP**
> Kale is high in lutein, a carotenoid that helps prevent age-related macular degeneration. It has been shown that increased consumption of green leafy vegetables can lead to a 35 percent reduction in overall neurologic decline. Kale is also high in fiber, which helps keep cholesterol levels in check.

kale apple-walnut salad

FREE OF

MAKES 4 TO 6 SERVINGS

Serve this crisp salad in autumn, when kale and green apples are at their peak. I use one Granny Smith apple when making this recipe; half goes into the salad and the other half into the dressing. Use the candied walnut recipe or simply roast a cup of walnuts in the oven for about 10 minutes—either way works well. This salad pairs well with a bean soup and a whole-grain salad or it can be served with the Roasted Whole Chicken with Root Vegetables (page 308).

SALAD
1 bunch kale
½ apple, diced
1 cup Candied Walnuts (page 374)

DRESSING
½ apple
6 tablespoons extra-virgin olive oil

4 tablespoons raw apple cider vinegar
1 garlic clove
½ teaspoon sea salt

1. Remove the thick stem from the middle of each kale leaf. (If your kale is young and tender, you don't need to do this step.) Then chop or tear the kale into bite-size pieces. Toss the kale in a medium bowl with the diced apple half. If you are serving this salad immediately, then toss in the candied walnuts; if not, wait until ready to serve to add the walnuts.

2. Place the dressing ingredients into a blender and blend until smooth. Pour the dressing over the salad and toss.

kid-friendly salad with apple cider vinaigrette

Our children adore a salad made with fresh carrots, cucumbers, and garbanzo beans! The vinaigrette is one of their favorite dressings. They also like the salad with thinly sliced napa cabbage and peeled mandarins—another easy side dish for a family meal. We also use this dressing for making impromptu grain and bean salads. For example, combining cooked quinoa, white beans, parsley, and green onions with this dressing creates a delicious, nutritious quick lunch! Store any extra dressing in the refrigerator for up to three weeks. Place the jar under hot running water to "thin" the olive oil when you're ready to use it again, and then shake well.

SALAD

1 to 2 heads red or green leaf lettuce, rinsed, spun dry, and torn

1 or 2 cucumbers, sliced

3 or 4 carrots, cut into ¼-inch-thick rounds

1 to 2 cups cooked garbanzo beans

Handful of fresh microgreens or broccoli sprouts

DRESSING

½ cup extra-virgin olive oil

⅓ cup raw apple cider vinegar

1 to 2 tablespoons honey

2 teaspoons Dijon mustard

¾ teaspoon sea salt or Herbamare

1 teaspoon dried dill

Place the salad ingredients in a large bowl and toss well. Put the dressing ingredients into a pint-size glass jar, cover, and shake. Serve alongside the salad.

kohlrabi apple slaw

FREE OF

MAKES 6 SERVINGS

I was introduced to kohlrabi when I worked at a local state park during the summer following my first year in college. A fellow coworker, 65-year-old Ben, grew much of his own produce and used to bring me sliced kohlrabi packed in cold water. It's so refreshing and crisp, a little like radish but less spicy! Ever since then I've been enjoying it and finding new ways to prepare it. If you don't have any dairy-free yogurt on hand, substitute the Egg-Free Mayonnaise (page 334), but thin it with some water.

SLAW

3 kohlrabi, peeled, sliced, and cut into matchsticks

3 carrots, cut into matchsticks

2 small apples, cut into matchsticks

3 or 4 green onions, trimmed and thinly sliced

DRESSING

¾ cup plain yogurt (cow's, goat's, nut, or coconut milk)

1 tablespoon honey

1 tablespoon raw apple cider vinegar

½ teaspoon Herbamare or sea salt

Place the kohlrabi, carrots, apples, and green onions in a large bowl. In a separate bowl, whisk together the dressing ingredients, then pour over the slaw. Toss well, then let sit for about 20 minutes. Toss again, and serve.

NUTRITION TIP

Being part of the Brassica genus, kohlrabi is high in isothiocyanates. These amazing phytochemicals help protect against cancer by not allowing carcinogens that have entered your body to activate, and also by counteracting the carcinogens that have already been activated. Isothiocyanates also help with the speedy removal of carcinogens from your body, making kohlrabi an awesome cancer-fighting food!

lemon-walnut green bean salad

FREE OF

MAKES 4 TO 6 SERVINGS

This salad is quick to prepare and addictive. Blanching the green beans for a few minutes cooks them perfectly so they still have a bit of crispness. I always drain them in a colander, then run them under cold water to stop the cooking process. This salad can be made ahead of time, though I suggest leaving the walnuts out until you are ready to serve, or they will get quite soggy.

1½ pounds fresh green beans, ends trimmed

1 cup walnuts

2 to 4 tablespoons snipped fresh chives

2 tablespoons extra-virgin olive oil

2 tablespoons fresh lemon juice

½ teaspoon grated lemon zest

½ teaspoon Herbamare or sea salt

Freshly ground black pepper

1. Preheat the oven to 400°F. Bring a medium pot of water to a boil. Add the green beans and blanch for 4 to 5 minutes, or until desired doneness. Drain using a colander and run under cold water to stop the cooking process. Place in a large bowl.

2. Put the walnuts in an 8-inch square baking dish and roast for about 10 minutes. Place on a plate to cool, then chop. Add to the green beans. Add the remaining salad ingredients and toss well. Serve and enjoy!

nasturtium and kohlrabi salad with creamy lemon-dill dressing

FREE OF

MAKES 4 TO 6 SERVINGS

Use this dressing to drizzle over your favorite salad, or my suggestion here for a simple salad with lovely flavors—it's definitely a kid's favorite! I usually make a double batch of this dressing because my children enjoy it so much. Store any extra dressing in a glass jar in your refrigerator for up to ten days.

DRESSING

6 tablespoons extra-virgin olive oil

4 tablespoons fresh lemon juice

2 tablespoons water

2 tablespoons tahini or raw cashew butter

1 garlic clove

½ teaspoon sea salt

Small handful fresh dill, or 2 teaspoons dried

SALAD

1 large head green or red leaf lettuce, rinsed and spun dry

2 or 3 kohlrabi, peeled, sliced, and cut into strips

1 large cucumber, sliced

A few handfuls of nasturtium flowers

1. Put all the dressing ingredients except the dill into a blender and blend until smooth and creamy. Add the dill and blend on low speed until combined. You don't want to overblend the herbs; otherwise your dressing will be green instead of white with green flecks.

2. Place the salad ingredients in a large bowl and toss together. Serve the salad with the dressing.

pan-fried steak salad with sesame ginger dressing

FREE OF

MAKES 4 SERVINGS

Always purchase organic grass-fed beef for the best health benefits. Use either filet mignon or sirloin steak. The filet is more tender but also more expensive. Plan for 3 to 4 ounces per person. Serve this delicious, nourishing salad as a main dish with a side of Coconut-Lime Cauliflower "Rice" (page 227) or baked sweet potatoes.

STEAK

1 pound organic grass-fed beef filet or sirloin steak

Toasted sesame oil

Coconut aminos or wheat-free tamari (see Tip on page 158)

Ground white pepper

Coconut oil, for cooking

SALAD

1 head romaine lettuce, rinsed and thinly sliced

3 or 4 green onions, trimmed and sliced into thin rounds

2 or 3 carrots, shredded

½ cup slivered almonds or sprouted sunflower seeds

Handful of fresh cilantro, chopped

DRESSING

¼ cup sesame seeds, lightly toasted

¼ cup extra-virgin olive oil

3 tablespoons brown rice vinegar or coconut vinegar

1 tablespoon toasted sesame oil

1 to 2 tablespoons coconut aminos or wheat-free tamari (see Tip on page 158)

2 tablespoons chopped celery

A 1-inch piece of fresh ginger, peeled

1 or 2 garlic cloves

1. Heat a skillet over medium-high for a few minutes until very hot. While it is heating, rub the steak with a little sesame oil and coconut aminos on both sides, then sprinkle with a small amount of white pepper. Pour a few teaspoons of coconut oil into the pan. Add the steak and cook on each side for 3 to 5 minutes, or until desired doneness—3 minutes for rare and 5 minutes for medium to medium-well, depending on the thickness. Use tongs to turn the steak. Remove from the pan and place on a plate to rest for 5 minutes, retaining the juices. Then slice into thin strips with a sharp knife.

2. Toss the salad ingredients in a large bowl. Place the dressing ingredients into a blender and blend on high until smooth and creamy. Just before serving the salad, place the steak slices on top of the salad and pour the dressing over. Serve immediately.

INGREDIENT TIP

If you have a nut allergy, use the sunflower seeds instead of the almonds, or just omit altogether.

---

pear pomegranate salad
with orange vinaigrette

This salad makes a beautiful addition to your holiday table. To prep it ahead of time, make the dressing and store it in a tightly sealed glass jar in the fridge. Prep the pomegranate by removing the arils (beautiful juicy red seeds) and store them in a covered container in the fridge. Toast the pecans, cool them, and store in a sealed container on the counter. Then just before serving, slice the pear and toss all the ingredients together in a large salad bowl.

SALAD

8 to 10 cups mixed organic greens

1 pomegranate

1 ripe, firm pear, cored and thinly sliced

1 cup pecans, toasted (see Tip)

DRESSING

¼ cup extra-virgin olive oil

2 tablespoons fresh orange juice

2 tablespoons raw apple cider vinegar

½ teaspoon Herbamare or sea salt

¼ teaspoon grated orange zest

Pinch of ground cinnamon

Place the greens in a large bowl. Cut the pomegranate in half and gently remove the arils; add them to the greens. Add the pear and pecans. Place the dressing ingredients in a glass jar and shake well. Pour the dressing over the salad and toss again. Serve immediately.

INGREDIENT TIP

To toast the pecans, place them in a small glass baking dish or pie plate. Roast in a preheated 350°F oven for 10 to 15 minutes. Cool on a plate before chopping.

KITCHEN TIP

If you keep your olive oil–based dressing in the refrigerator, it will need to be warmed up before it can be used to dress the salad. Some of the fats in olive oil naturally harden at refrigerated temperatures. We usually place the jar into a large mug half-full of hot water for a few minutes and then shake.

pecan-crusted chicken and apple salad

FREE OF

MAKES 4 SERVINGS

This nourishing salad can be a main dish. Use a head of lettuce or a bag of mixed organic greens. Serve with roasted winter squash and the Rosemary Sea Salt Breadsticks (page 121) for a complete meal. Our children like to have the chicken on the side with their salad, so I keep it all separate and assemble each plate individually.

CHICKEN

1½ pounds organic chicken breasts, pounded thin

1½ cups pecans, finely ground

¼ teaspoon sea salt

¼ teaspoon freshly ground black pepper

6 tablespoons arrowroot powder

¼ cup water

Olive oil, for cooking

SALAD

1 head red leaf lettuce, rinsed and spun dry

1 tart apple, cored and thinly sliced

½ small red onion, thinly sliced

½ cup dried cranberries

DRESSING

¼ cup extra-virgin olive oil

3 tablespoons balsamic vinegar

1 tablespoon pure maple syrup

1 teaspoon Dijon mustard

¼ teaspoon sea salt

1. Preheat the oven to 400°F. Rinse the chicken breasts, pat dry, and set aside. Place the pecans, salt, and pepper into a food processor and process until finely ground, stopping before it turns into nut butter. Pour into a shallow, wide bowl. In another shallow bowl, whisk together the arrowroot powder and water. Dip each chicken breast in the arrowroot mixture so it is well coated. Then dip each breast into the ground pecans, coating completely. Set the chicken on a plate.

2. Heat a large, heavy-bottomed skillet over medium heat. Pour in about 3 tablespoons olive oil,

then add the chicken. Cook for 2 minutes on each side; any longer and the pecans will begin to burn. Transfer the chicken to an 8-inch square baking dish and bake for 15 to 20 minutes, or until cooked through. Cool for at least 5 minutes, then slice into strips.

3. Place the salad ingredients in a large bowl. Put the dressing ingredients in a small jar, cover, and shake. Arrange the chicken strips over the salad and drizzle with the dressing. Serve immediately.

picnic coleslaw

FREE OF

MAKES 6 SERVINGS

Crunchy cabbage coleslaw is always needed in the summertime to serve with barbecued chicken or fish, corn on the cob, roasted potatoes, and raw fruit pies! For this recipe I've made my mock vegan mayo, with quite satisfying results. If you have red cabbage, use a mix of red and green for a more colorful salad.

SALAD
8 cups shredded green cabbage
2 large carrots, shredded
¼ cup chopped chives

DRESSING
½ cup raw cashews
½ cup water

¼ cup extra-virgin olive oil
2 tablespoons raw apple cider vinegar
½ teaspoon Herbamare or sea salt
Small handful of fresh parsley

Place the cabbage, carrots, and chives in a large bowl. Put the cashews and water into a high-powered blender; blend until smooth. Then add the olive oil, vinegar, Herbamare, and parsley; blend until the ingredients are just incorporated. (If you blend it too long, the parsley will completely break down, creating a green dressing.) Pour the dressing over the cabbage and toss. Taste and add more Herbamare, if necessary. Refrigerate until ready to serve.

KITCHEN TIP

If you don't own a high-powdered blender, place the cashews and water into your regular blender and let soak for at least 3 hours, then add the remaining ingredients and blend.

NUTRITION TIP

Cashews are lower in overall fat content than other nuts and are high in monounsaturated fats, specifically oleic acid—the same fat as found in olive oil.

purple potato salad with radishes and chives

This potato salad has a creamy dairy-free dressing made from shelled hemp seeds and raw cashews. It is incredibly nutritious, as it's full of omega-3 fatty acids and magnesium. The dressing, if chilled in the fridge for a few hours, also makes a great dip for raw vegetables. If you cannot find purple potatoes, use red or yellow potatoes instead.

SALAD
2½ pounds purple potatoes
1 or 2 bunches radishes, thinly sliced
1 cup chopped fresh parsley
½ cup snipped chives
Freshly ground black pepper

DRESSING
¾ cup raw cashews
6 tablespoons raw hemp seeds

¾ cup water
3 tablespoons extra-virgin olive oil
3 tablespoons raw apple cider vinegar
1 or 2 garlic cloves
½ to 1 teaspoon Herbamare or sea salt
1 to 2 teaspoons dried dill

1. Place the potatoes in a pot of water, bring to a boil, and cook for about 15 minutes, or until tender. Watch carefully, you don't want to overcook potatoes or they will be mushy for the salad. Drain and place the potatoes on a plate to cool in the refrigerator. Cut the potatoes into chunks and place in a large bowl. Add the remaining salad ingredients.

2. Put the dressing ingredients, except the dill, in a high-powered blender and blend until ultra-smooth and creamy. Taste and add more Herbamare, if necessary. Add the dill, and blend on low speed for a few seconds to incorporate it. Pour the dressing over the salad and gently toss. Cover and refrigerate until ready to serve; this salad is best served at room temperature.

raw kale–avocado salad

FREE OF

MAKES 4 TO 6 SERVINGS

Serve this salad alone as a superfood meal, or over cooked quinoa with a bean soup. If you plan to keep the salad for a few days in your refrigerator, wait to add the avocado until serving. Feel free to add other seasonal vegetables to the salad—grated carrots, grated beets, diced heirloom tomatoes, or chopped parsley are all delicious. Note that the sunflower seeds need to be soaked at least 6 hours in advance.

1 large bunch curly kale

DRESSING
3 to 4 tablespoons fresh lemon juice
3 to 4 tablespoons extra-virgin olive oil
1 or 2 garlic cloves, crushed

½ teaspoon Herbamare or sea salt
Freshly ground black pepper

2 avocados, diced
1 cup sunflower seeds, soaked for 6 to
 8 hours

1. Remove the tough stems from the kale leaves, then chop the leaves into small pieces. Place in a colander and rinse well. Drain and pat dry with a towel, then place in a large bowl.

2. In a small bowl, whisk together the dressing ingredients. Add the dressing to the salad and gently massage it into the kale with your hands. This will soften the kale almost immediately. Add the diced avocado. Drain and rinse the sunflower seeds, and add them to the salad as well. Gently toss together. Serve.

NUTRITION TIP

Kale's nutrient density is unparalleled. It is packed full of vitamin K, vitamin C, carotenoids, and antioxidants. The nutrients in kale provide immense protection against oxidative stress and chronic inflammation.

---

raw kale salad with lemon tahini dressing

FREE OF

MAKES 4 TO 6 SERVINGS

Kale that is tender and young is best eaten raw. You'll find it is slightly sweet, rather than bitter. This salad pairs well with just about any meal. Serve it with a bean soup and dinner rolls, or as part of a summer picnic. Our children think this salad is one of the best and will eat platefuls of it! The salad will keep in the fridge for up to three days. Serve it at room temperature.

1 large bunch curly kale

DRESSING
¼ cup tahini
¼ cup extra-virgin olive oil
¼ cup fresh lemon juice
1 or 2 garlic cloves, crushed
1 teaspoon Herbamare or sea salt
Freshly ground black pepper

OPTIONAL ADDITIONS
Shredded carrots
Chopped fresh parsley
Snipped fresh chives
Toasted sunflower seeds

1. Remove the tough stems from the kale leaves, then chop the leaves into small pieces. Place in a colander and rinse well, then drain and pat dry with a towel. Place the kale in a large bowl.

2. In a small bowl, whisk together the dressing ingredients. It will taste very lemony, but when mixed with the kale, the flavors will balance out. Pour the dressing over the kale and toss. Use your hands to massage the dressing into the kale to soften it. Add any optional ingredients and serve.

roasted beet salad with orange vinaigrette

MAKES 6 SERVINGS

This salad is delicious as is and also is great over mixed baby greens. I like to serve this with Herb-Roasted Halibut (page 303) and cooked quinoa for a balanced family meal. The salad also makes a great potluck dish, as it can easily be made ahead of time. Just wait to add the walnuts until you're ready to serve.

SALAD
6 beets
1 cup walnuts
½ cup chopped fresh parsley

DRESSING
¼ cup fresh orange juice
¼ cup extra-virgin olive oil

2 tablespoons Champagne vinegar
½ teaspoon grated orange zest
Sea salt and freshly ground black pepper
  to taste

Crumbled feta cheese (optional)

1. Preheat the oven to 350°F. Trim the greens from the beets and any roots but don't peel them, and place in a casserole dish with a lid. Roast for 1 to 2 hours, or until soft.

2. Place the walnuts in a pie plate and toast for 10 to 12 minutes, until toasted. Coarsely chop and set aside. Remove the skins from the beets; they should just slip off. Trim the ends, then slice in half top to bottom. Slice each half into ¼-inch-thick half-moons. Place the beets, walnuts, and parsley in a large bowl and toss.

3. In a small bowl, whisk together the dressing ingredients. Pour the dressing over the beets and toss. Sprinkle with feta, if using.

smoked salmon salad with honey mustard dressing

FREE OF

MAKES 4 TO 6 SERVINGS

This salad and dressing were inspired by a salad served at a local organic pizzeria called Seven Loaves. They served their salad with shredded organic buffalo mozzarella on top, which is delicious. If you can tolerate dairy, try sprinkling some shredded cheese over this salad. Store any remaining dressing in the refrigerator for up to three weeks.

SALAD

1 head red leaf lettuce, rinsed and spun dry

1 cup chopped smoked salmon

1 small raw beet, peeled and very thinly sliced

½ small red onion, very thinly sliced

Large handful of alfalfa sprouts

½ to 1 cup sunflower seeds, toasted

DRESSING

¼ cup raw honey

¼ cup brown mustard

¼ cup extra-virgin olive oil

1 to 2 tablespoons raw apple cider vinegar

¼ teaspoon sea salt

1. Place the lettuce in a large bowl, tear into pieces, and top with the salmon, beets, onion, sprouts, and sunflower seeds.

2. In a small jar, add the dressing ingredients, screw on the lid, and shake well, until combined. If you are going to eat the entire salad in one sitting, then dress it just before serving. If not, have each person serve him- or herself.

spicy green salad with blueberry vinaigrette

MAKES 4 TO 6 SERVINGS

We love to make this blueberry vinaigrette any time of year with the blueberries we harvested and froze during late summer. The flavors mingle well with a spicy green salad mix and toasted hazelnuts. If you don't have access to a spicy salad mix, then use whatever lettuce varieties are available. Store any unused dressing in a sealed glass jar in the refrigerator for up to a week.

SALAD

8 cups spicy mixed greens, rinsed and spun dry

2 or 3 carrots, sliced into rounds

1 or 2 green onions, trimmed and thinly sliced

1 cup hazelnuts, toasted and chopped (see Tip)

DRESSING

½ cup fresh or frozen blueberries

½ cup Champagne vinegar

½ cup extra-virgin olive oil

1 tablespoon honey

½ teaspoon Herbamare or sea salt

Place the salad ingredients in a large bowl and toss. Place the dressing ingredients into a blender and puree for about 30 seconds, until smooth. Serve the salad with the dressing on the side.

INGREDIENT TIP

To toast hazelnuts, preheat the oven to 350°F. Place the hazelnuts in a pie plate and toast for 15 to 20 minutes or until lightly browned.

spicy summer black bean salad

FREE OF

MAKES 6 SERVINGS

Nearly all these ingredients can be purchased at a local farmers' market in the summer. This fresh salad is full of antioxidants, vitamins (especially vitamin C), and live enzymes from the raw vegetables. It is low in fat and high in fiber—a perfect cholesterol-lowering meal. Serve it for a party or bring it to a potluck. It can also be served in lettuce leaves as a wrap.

SALAD

6 cups cooked black beans

4 cups chopped ripe heirloom tomatoes

3 ears raw corn, kernels cut off the cob (see Tip)

3 spicy chiles, such as jalapeño or banana, finely diced (see Tip)

1 red bell pepper, cored, seeded, and diced

2 cups sliced green onions or chopped sweet onions

1 cup chopped fresh cilantro

DRESSING

¼ cup extra-virgin olive oil

Juice of 2 limes

2 teaspoons Herbamare or sea salt

1 to 2 teaspoons ground cumin

Place the salad ingredients in a large glass bowl. Whisk together the dressing ingredients, then pour over the salad and gently toss. Serve immediately or store in the fridge for later.

> **KITCHEN TIP**
>
> To cut the corn kernels from the cob, hold the ear upright over a plate. Use a serrated knife and a gentle sawing action to cut the kernels free of the cob.
>
> To easily remove the seeds from chiles, hold the chile upright on a cutting board and cut away the sides into fourths, leaving the "core." Rinse the pieces under running water to remove the seeds.

raw super green salad

FREE OF

MAKES 4 TO 6 SERVINGS

This salad is delicious anytime you want it. Serve it with beans and rice or baked fish. Use it as part of the filling for the Collard Wraps with Raw Sunflower Pâté (page 364).

8 cups thinly sliced dark greens (kale, collards, chard)

¼ cup extra-virgin olive oil

Juice of 1 lemon

2 or 3 garlic cloves, crushed

1 teaspoon sea salt

Grated carrots (optional)

Toasted sunflower seeds (optional)

Place all the ingredients in a large bowl and mix well. Let rest for about 30 minutes before serving. Toss again and serve.

thai cucumber salad

FREE OF

MAKES 4 TO 6 SERVINGS

We grow both Thai basil and cucumbers in our garden, which our children like to snack on all summer long. This salad has a little zing from the coconut vinegar and a little spice from the red pepper flakes. Serve it with the Thai Fish Curry with Garden Veggies (page 305) for a nutritious summer meal. Leftovers can be stored in the refrigerator for up to four days.

2 cucumbers, cut into thin slices

½ cup thinly sliced Thai basil

2 or 3 garlic cloves, chopped

½ to 1 teaspoon red pepper flakes

3 tablespoons coconut vinegar

1 tablespoon coconut nectar

Sea salt

In a medium bowl, toss together the cucumbers, basil, garlic, and red pepper flakes. In a small bowl, whisk together the coconut vinegar and coconut nectar. Pour over the cucumbers, then season to taste with sea salt. Allow the cucumbers to marinate for about an hour, then serve.

winter salad with a blood orange vinaigrette

MAKES ABOUT 8 SERVINGS

Serve this salad with baked wild-caught salmon and roasted winter squash, or a bean and root vegetable stew. If you can't find blood oranges, use navel oranges. You will need about 4 oranges for the salad and dressing. Leftovers can be stored in a glass container in your refrigerator for about three days.

SALAD

½ large head red cabbage, thinly sliced (about 8 cups)

1 large fennel bulb, trimmed and thinly sliced

½ small red onion, thinly sliced

2 or 3 blood oranges, peeled and segmented (or chopped)

½ to 1 cup chopped fresh parsley

½ to 1 cup almonds, toasted and chopped (see Tip)

DRESSING

6 tablespoons fresh blood orange juice

3 tablespoons extra-virgin olive oil

1 to 2 tablespoons raw apple cider vinegar or Champagne vinegar

1 to 2 teaspoons finely chopped fresh thyme

½ teaspoon sea salt

Place the cabbage, fennel, red onion, blood oranges, and parsley in a large bowl. If you are planning on serving the salad right away, add the almonds; if you would like to extend the salad over a few days, sprinkle the almonds over what you plan on serving now (or they will get soft and lose their crunch if sitting in the dressing too long). In a small bowl, whisk together the dressing ingredients. Pour over the salad and toss, then serve.

KITCHEN TIP

To toast almonds, preheat your oven to 375°F. Place the raw almonds in a glass pie plate or baking dish. Toast for about 15 minutes, or until lightly browned. Remove from oven and let cool before chopping.

INGREDIENT TIP

When purchasing almonds, be sure to buy organic. All almonds now sold in the United States (unless you are buying direct from a farmer) need to be pasteurized. Nonorganic almonds are typically chemically treated while organic almonds are heat-treated (so they actually are not raw anymore).

coconut-lime cauliflower "rice"

FREE OF

MAKES 4 TO 6 SERVINGS

Cauliflower is a fantastic grain-free alternative to rice. By grinding it in a food processor, you get the look and consistency of white rice but many more nutrients and cancer-fighting compounds, like sulforaphane. Serve this "rice" dish along with baked fish or roasted chicken and a green salad.

1 head cauliflower

1 cup coconut milk

½ cup water or chicken broth

1 to 2 tablespoons fresh lime juice

2 garlic cloves, crushed

1 to 2 teaspoons grated fresh ginger

½ to 1 teaspoon red pepper flakes

½ teaspoon Herbamare or sea salt

GARNISHES

Sliced green onions

Chopped fresh cilantro

Lime zest

1. Break or cut the cauliflower into smaller pieces and place into a food processor fitted with the "s" blade. Pulse until the cauliflower is coarsely ground, about 2 minutes. Be careful not to overprocess and turn the cauliflower into mush.

2. In an 11- or 12-inch skillet or wide pot, heat the coconut milk, water, lime juice, garlic, ginger, red pepper flakes, and Herbamare over medium heat. When the mixture is simmering, add the cauliflower. Stir and simmer, uncovered, over low heat for 10 to 15 minutes, or until cooked to your liking. Garnish with the green onions, cilantro, and lime zest. Serve hot.

creamed kale

FREE OF

MAKES 4 TO 6 SERVINGS

Serve this simple dairy-free dish with cooked quinoa and black-eyed peas or grilled chicken. You might think that 10 to 12 cups of chopped kale is a lot, but remember that it cooks down considerably. We don't have any leftovers in our house when I make this recipe!

10 to 12 cups finely chopped kale (1½ to 2 bunches)

2 to 3 tablespoons extra-virgin olive oil

1 small onion, chopped (about 1 heaping cup)

2 garlic cloves, chopped

½ cup raw cashews

2 cups water

½ jalapeño pepper, seeded

1 tablespoon fresh lemon juice

2 tablespoons nutritional yeast

1 to 2 teaspoons Herbamare or sea salt

1. Heat an 11- or 12-inch skillet over medium. Add the olive oil, then the onion and garlic and sauté for about 5 minutes, or until softened and beginning to change color. Transfer to a high-powered blender and add the cashews, water, jalapeño, lemon juice, nutritional yeast, and Herbamare. Blend until smooth and creamy.

2. Place the sauce and chopped kale in the skillet and simmer for 10 to 15 minutes, or until the kale has softened and the sauce has thickened. Taste and adjust the seasonings, if necessary.

VARIATION: In the summer, when fresh organic sweet corn is in season, I like to cut the kernels off of 2 or 3 ears and add them to the kale. It provides a nice color contrast and a slight crunch.

curried root vegetables

FREE OF

MAKES 8 SERVINGS

This savory root vegetable dish can be adjusted to the number of people you are serving. I have a large family and we like leftovers, so I cook larger batches. If you are cooking only for one, two, or three, I suggest you cut this recipe in half. Also, cut all your vegetables so they are about the same size; otherwise, some will turn to mush while others may still be underdone at the end of cooking time. Serve this over quinoa and garnish with chopped cilantro, if desired. Store any leftovers in a tightly sealed container in the refrigerator for up to a week.

2 to 4 tablespoons extra-virgin olive oil or coconut oil

1 teaspoon cumin seeds

1 large onion, chopped

2 garlic cloves, crushed

4 teaspoons mild curry powder

1 teaspoon ground cumin

½ teaspoon ground turmeric

Pinch or two of cayenne pepper

2 to 3 teaspoons sea salt

3 parsnips, peeled and cut into chunks

3 large carrots, cut into chunks

2 sweet potatoes, peeled and cut into chunks

6 small yellow or red potatoes, cut into chunks

4 cups chopped ripe tomatoes

2 cups water

1. Heat a Dutch oven or 6-quart pot over medium. Add the olive oil, then the cumin seeds and cook for 30 to 60 seconds, or until fragrant. Add the onion and sauté for about 10 minutes, until softened and beginning to change color.

2. Add the spices and sauté for another 60 seconds. Add the root vegetables and sauté for a few minutes to coat with the spices and oil, then add the tomatoes and water. Partly cover the pot with a lid, and simmer over medium heat, stirring occasionally, for 25 to 30 minutes, or until the vegetables are tender.

sautéed winter greens
with caramelized onions

FREE OF

MAKES 4 TO 6 SERVINGS

With just a few ingredients, this recipe can be ready in a snap. Kale and collards are great for breakfast, lunch, or dinner. For breakfast, I like to serve sautéed greens over cooked quinoa, with two fried pastured eggs. For dinner, I serve this dish with beans and rice or roasted chicken.

1 to 2 tablespoons extra-virgin olive oil or coconut oil

1 large red onion, halved and sliced

Herbamare or sea salt

1 large bunch of kale, thinly sliced

1 large bunch of collard greens, thinly sliced

Water, as needed

1. Heat a large skillet over medium-low. Add the olive oil and onion, and add a few dashes of Herbamare to draw out the moisture from the onion. Sauté for 15 to 20 minutes, or until caramelized and very fragrant.

2. Add the kale and collards, and sauté for 5 to 10 minutes, depending on the tenderness of the kale and the desired doneness. Add a few tablespoons of water to quickly finish the steaming, if desired. Season to taste with Herbamare and serve warm.

sautéed snow peas
and pattypan squash

FREE OF

MAKES 4 TO 6 SERVINGS

This is a great recipe to make in summer, when the warm-weather vegetables are in abundance! By doing a quick sauté the vegetables stay crisp and bright, with all of their vibrant flavors intact. Serve with barbecued chicken or Herb-Roasted Halibut (page 303).

1 tablespoon extra-virgin olive oil

3 small pattypan squash, quartered and cut into ¼-inch slices

½ pound fresh snow peas

¼ teaspoon sea salt

1 to 2 teaspoons fresh thyme leaves

1. Heat a large skillet over medium-high. Add the olive oil, then the squash and snow peas and sauté for 5 to 7 minutes, stirring frequently. Turn the heat down if they start to brown; you will want to quickly cook but not brown or burn the vegetables.

2. Sprinkle with the salt and thyme and then serve immediately.

sautéed brussels sprouts with shallots and cranberries

FREE OF

MAKES 6 SERVINGS

This recipe is quick to prepare—about 12 minutes from start to finish. If you are planning on making it for your Thanksgiving meal, have all the ingredients prepared ahead of time. About 20 minutes before you are ready to sit down to eat, sauté the shallots. If you don't have slivered almonds, use chopped pecans instead.

2 tablespoons extra-virgin olive oil

4 shallots, thinly sliced

½ cup slivered almonds

2 pounds brussels sprouts, trimmed and halved

1 teaspoon Herbamare or sea salt

½ cup dried cranberries

½ cup water

Freshly ground black pepper

Heat an 11- or 12-inch skillet over medium. Add the olive oil, then the shallots and sauté for about 2 minutes. Stir in the almonds, brussels sprouts, and Herbamare and sauté for about 5 minutes. Add the cranberries and water, cover the pan, and cook, stirring occasionally, for 5 to 10 minutes, or until the sprouts are tender. Season with pepper to taste.

INGREDIENT TIP

When shopping for dried cranberries, look for organic cranberries that have been sweetened with fruit juice. These can usually be found in the bulk bins at your local food co-op or health food store.

---

roasted brussels sprouts

FREE OF

MAKES 4 SERVINGS

This recipe is so easy and simple. Once you try it, I am sure you will make it again and again, as we do! When brussels sprouts are in season, in late autumn and winter, we make this at least three times a week.

1 to 1½ pounds brussels sprouts, ends trimmed and sliced in half

1 to 2 tablespoons extra-virgin olive oil

Sea salt or Herbamare

Freshly ground black pepper

Preheat the oven to 425°F. Place the sprouts in a 9 by 13-inch glass baking dish and toss with the olive oil, salt, and pepper. Roast for 10 to 20 minutes, or until tender.

> **NUTRITION TIP**
>
> Sulfur compounds in brussels sprouts have been shown to benefit the liver by altering the function of liver enzymes. These enzymes allow for the metabolism of hormones and other fat-soluble substances that the liver might otherwise perceive as toxic. Sulfur compounds also up-regulate the gene expression of antioxidants in our bodies. Cancer researchers have determined these substances to be so important that they recommend at least two servings of cruciferous vegetables per week, and some suggest as many as two servings per day.

roasted cauliflower

FREE OF

MAKES 4 SERVINGS

Even those who aren't fans of cauliflower will probably love it prepared this way. When our twin boys were young toddlers they would fight over the roasted cauliflower on the dinner table. Sometimes I garnish the roasted cauliflower with a little freshly grated lemon zest, which adds a nice touch. We like to serve a bowlful of roasted cauliflower and brussels sprouts on movie night, in lieu of popcorn!

1 head cauliflower, cored and cut into florets

2 tablespoons extra-virgin olive oil

¼ teaspoon Herbamare or sea salt

Freshly ground black pepper

Preheat the oven to 425°F. Place the cauliflower in a 9 by 13-inch baking dish or on a large rimmed baking sheet. Toss with the olive oil, Herbamare, and pepper. Roast for 20 to 25 minutes, or until tender; it is helpful to turn the cauliflower once during baking, though it isn't necessary.

twice-roasted golden beets

FREE OF

MAKES 4 SERVINGS

This is one of my favorite ways to prepare beets. The first roasting slowly cooks the beets to perfection, and then the second roasting brings out their flavor while slightly caramelizing them. Roasted beets can be used to top any salad or can be eaten as a simple side dish. Use any variety of beets you have on hand, though here we use golden. Top a plate of baby arugula with these and toss with Champagne vinegar.

4 golden beets, ends trimmed

2 tablespoons coconut oil or extra-virgin olive oil

¼ teaspoon sea salt

Freshly ground black pepper

1. Preheat the oven to 350°F. Place the beets in a small baking dish with a lid. Cover and bake for 2 hours, or until tender. When cool enough to handle, slip off the skins.

2. Turn the oven temperature up to 400°F. Cut the beets into 1-inch cubes. Place in a glass baking dish and toss with the coconut oil, salt, and pepper. Roast for another 40 to 45 minutes, turning once. Be careful not to overcook the beets, as they can burn easily.

chipotle yam fries

MAKES 4 TO 6 SERVINGS

Yam fries are completely addictive, especially with the chipotle spice! I've made these using russet (baking) potatoes with equally delicious results. Serve them with the Spicy Black-Eyed Pea Soup (page 181) or the Chipotle-Lime Roasted Chicken (page 310).

2 yams (sweet potatoes), peeled

1 tablespoon sea salt

2 to 3 tablespoons extra-virgin olive oil, ghee (clarified butter), or coconut oil

¼ to ½ teaspoon chipotle chile powder

2 teaspoons smoked paprika

¼ to ½ teaspoon Herbamare or sea salt

1. Cut the yams lengthwise into ¼-inch-thick slices, then cut each slice into ¼-inch fries. Place the yam fries in a square baking pan and cover with water. Sprinkle with 1 tablespoon sea salt. Soak for about 30 minutes. This helps remove excess moisture and starch so the fries cook properly. Rinse the fries, and thoroughly pat dry using a towel.

2. Preheat the oven to 400°F. Place the fries on a large baking sheet and toss with the olive oil, chipotle chile powder, paprika, and Herbamare. Spread out evenly on the sheet. Bake for 20 minutes. Use a spatula to carefully turn the fries over, and bake for 20 minutes more, or until cooked through and crisp. Continue baking a few minutes more if not quite done yet. Let cool slightly, then serve!

rutabaga fries

FREE OF

MAKES 4 SERVINGS

Practically any starchy vegetable can be used to make fries. I've used parsnips, carrots, and celery root, but my favorite is the humble rutabaga. You can keep it simple and season the fries with sea salt, or for more flavor try adding freshly ground black pepper, curry powder, or dried thyme.

2 rutabagas, peeled

2 tablespoons extra-virgin olive oil, ghee (clarified butter), or coconut oil

Herbamare or sea salt

1. Preheat the oven to 400°F. Slice the rutabagas into ¼-inch rounds, then cut into strips about ¼ inch wide so they look like french fries. Place the fries on a large baking sheet. Add the olive oil and a few dashes of Herbamare and toss. Make sure the fries are not too close together or they will steam instead of crisp up. Use two baking sheets, if necessary.

2. Bake for 20 to 25 minutes, then use a spatula to flip them over, and bake for 10 minutes or so, until cooked through and lightly golden.

mashed cauliflower with chives

FREE OF

MAKES 6 SERVINGS

This is a low-glycemic alternative to mashed potatoes. While I love potatoes, sometimes I feel a little weighted down after eating them. This is diabetic-friendly, so go ahead and enjoy them with roast chicken and gravy! I've also made this dish into a "cheesy" casserole by adding a few tablespoons of nutritional yeast to the food processor along with the cauliflower.

2 small heads cauliflower, or 1 large one

3 to 4 tablespoons butter or extra-virgin olive oil

2 tablespoons snipped fresh chives

Herbamare and freshly ground black pepper

1. Core the cauliflowers and chop into florets. Place in a pot fitted with a steamer basket. Add a few inches of water, cover, and steam for 7 to 10 minutes, or until tender. Drain the cauliflower completely.

2. Place the cauliflower into a food processor fitted with the "s" blade. Add the butter and process until creamy and smooth. Add the

chives, Herbamare, and black pepper; pulse until combined. Taste and adjust the seasonings, if necessary. Either serve this as is, or put it into a buttered casserole dish and bake at 450°F until lightly browned on top.

> **INGREDIENT TIP**
>
> If you are dairy-sensitive, then use the olive oil instead of the butter in this recipe.

olive oil garlic mashed potatoes

MAKES 4 TO 6 SERVINGS

This dairy-free recipe is just as creamy and flavorful as the traditional one made with milk and butter. Although you might think that using six cloves of garlic could be overpowering, the garlic flavor is actually quite subtle. Using the cooking liquid to mash the potatoes is a great alternative to any type of milk.

6 russet (baking) potatoes, cut into chunks

6 garlic cloves

6 tablespoons extra-virgin olive oil

½ to ¾ teaspoon Herbamare or sea salt

1. Scrub the potatoes and cut them into 1- to 2-inch chunks. (I like to leave the peels on, which keeps valuable nutrients in your meal.) Place the potatoes and whole garlic in a 6-quart pot and cover with an inch or two of water. Boil at medium-high heat for 15 to 20 minutes, or until the potatoes are tender.

2. Drain the potatoes and reserve ½ cup cooking liquid. Pour the cooking liquid back into the pot with the potatoes, then add the olive oil and Herbamare. Use a hand-held electric mixer to whip the potatoes, beating for 1 to 2 minutes, or until light and fluffy. Taste and add more Herbamare, if necessary.

whipped sweet potatoes with cardamom

MAKES 6 TO 8 SERVINGS

Serve this with roasted chicken, gravy, and sautéed kale for a balanced meal. You can use any milk of your choice, but I prefer the Raw Almond Milk (page 451). I normally use dark orange sweet potatoes, but white sweet potatoes work just as well.

2 to 3 pounds sweet potatoes (4 to 5 medium)

½ cup almond milk

¼ to ½ teaspoon ground cardamom

1. Peel the sweet potatoes and cut them into chunks. Place in a 3-quart pot and add an inch or two of water. Cover, and cook over medium heat until tender, about 10 minutes.

2. Drain off the cooking water and add the milk and cardamom. Beat with an electric mixer until light and fluffy. Serve warm.

zucchini almond bake

FREE OF

MAKES 6 SERVINGS

My children call this recipe "Cheesy Zucchini Bake" because the flavors are reminiscent of cheese! Greek seasoning can be made by combining sea salt, dried oregano, garlic, dried lemon peel, ground black pepper, and dried marjoram in a small jar. Serve with roasted chicken or a fresh bean and vegetable salad.

2 to 3 tablespoons extra-virgin olive oil

2 or 3 zucchini, sliced

1 large sweet onion, halved and sliced

1 tablespoon Greek seasoning or Italian seasoning

½ teaspoon Herbamare or sea salt

½ cup blanched almond flour

1. Preheat the oven to 375°F. Add about 1 tablespoon of the olive oil to the bottom of a 10-inch deep-dish pie plate. Add a layer of zucchini, then a few onion slices, then sprinkle with a little Greek seasoning and Herbamare. Add about 3 tablespoons of the blanched almond flour.

2. Repeat the layers, ending with a drizzle of the remaining olive oil. Bake uncovered for 40 to 45 minutes, or until the zucchini is tender.

winter vegetable gratin

FREE OF

MAKES 6 TO 8 SERVINGS

This nourishing gratin dish contains winter vegetables and a sauce made from raw dairy. Research has shown that raw milk from cows that graze on grasses, and dairy products made with that raw milk, contain higher levels of essential fatty acids, such as conjugated linoleic acid (CLA). Pasteurization decreases the minerals and vitamin C in milk and makes the vitamin A much harder to absorb because the protein that assists with its absorption in the intestines is destroyed during pasteurization. Serve this gratin with sautéed winter greens or a raw kale salad, and baked chicken or fish.

VEGETABLES

1 tablespoon extra-virgin olive oil or ghee (clarified butter)

1 small onion, halved and sliced into half-moons

1 small celery root, peeled and thinly sliced

½ small butternut squash, peeled and thinly sliced

2 to 3 small yellow potatoes, thinly sliced

1 large rutabaga, peeled and thinly sliced

SAUCE

1 cup raw cream

2 tablespoons arrowroot powder

⅓ cup plain organic yogurt

1⅓ cups grated raw cheddar cheese

½ teaspoon Herbamare or sea salt

Freshly ground black pepper

1. Preheat the oven to 400°F. Coat an 8 by 12-inch casserole dish with a little olive oil. Heat a 10-inch skillet over medium-low. Add the olive oil, then the onion and sauté for 5 to 10 minutes, or until soft, being careful not to let it brown. Layer the remaining vegetables in the casserole dish, with the cooked onion between the layers.

2. In a small saucepan, whisk together the cream and arrowroot powder. Then whisk in the yogurt. Turn the heat to medium-low and cook until hot but not really simmering. Add 1 cup of the cheese, the Herbamare, and pepper, whisking until the cheese has melted into the sauce.

3. Pour the cream sauce over the vegetables, evenly coating the top layer. Cover the casserole dish and bake for about 1 hour. Remove the lid and sprinkle with the remaining ⅓ cup cheese. Return the dish to the oven and bake for about 15 minutes more, or until bubbly.

> **KITCHEN TIP**
>
> Use only the neck of the butternut squash. Save the rest and use it for mashed baked squash or to make pumpkin pie!

wholegrainsandnoodles

As you walk down a supermarket aisle these days, notice all the labels that claim, "made with whole grains" or "whole grain goodness." Labels like these can be misleading. "Made with whole grains" doesn't make it a nourishing food. These products may contain some whole-grain flour, but they are also filled with many refined ingredients that are not beneficial for health.

WHAT IS A WHOLE GRAIN?

So, what exactly is a whole grain? Whole grains are the entire seeds of a plant. If you soak them in water for a period of time, they could germinate because they contain the bran, endosperm, and germ intact. The bran is a protective sheath around the grain; it holds all the nutrients inside until the seed is ready to grow into a plant. The endosperm is the starchy part, the energy storehouse that is used for growing the plant. The germ is the embryo of the grain—the part that can form a new plant—where most of the healthy fats, vitamin E, B vitamins, and antioxidants reside. It's important to understand that processing whole grains removes the germ and bran, leaving only the starchy endosperm.

White rice and white flour are examples of refined grains or grain products. Refining the rice and wheat grains removes about 25 percent of their protein and over 17 nutrients that the body needs to properly assimilate the starchy part of the grain.

Gluten-Free Whole Grains

The seeds of grasses, including brown rice, millet, teff, and sorghum, are gluten-free whole grains. Pseudo-grains, which behave much like other whole grains but are actually the seeds of broad-leafed plants, include quinoa, amaranth, and buckwheat. Wild rice is not a grain nor the seed of a broad-leafed plant, but actually is the seed of an aquatic grass that is native to North America. Wild rice contains more protein, zinc, and potassium than brown rice; it is also significantly higher in folates and most of the other B vitamins.

THE HEALTH BENEFITS OF GRAINS

Whole grains are an excellent source of a wide variety of phenolic compounds, such as ferulic acid, vanillic acid, p-coumaric acid, anthocyanidins, quinines, and flavones. These compounds act in the body as antioxidants by donating hydrogen atoms to free radicals. In fact, certain whole grains, such as corn, oats, and brown rice, have an antioxidant capacity similar to those of berries and plums! Whole grains are also an excellent source of plant lignans, which have been shown to have strong antioxidant and phytoestrogenic effects.

Whole grains may provide protection against chronic diseases such as hormone-related cancers, diabetes, and heart disease. Actually, a plant-based diet rich in vegetables, whole grains, fish, and olive oil—such as the Mediterranean diet—has been found to significantly lower the risk of cardiovascular disease. Additionally, certain antinutrients present in whole grains, such as phytic acid, lectins, protease inhibitors, amylase inhibitors, and saponins, have been shown to lower plasma glucose, insulin, and cholesterol levels, and also to lower the risk of certain cancers, such as colon cancer and breast cancer.

Whole Grains Promote Gut Health

Whole grains contain some starches that are indigestible in the small intestine. They are then broken down—or fermented—by bacteria in the colon. These resistant starches and oligosaccharides actually promote GI health by acting as prebiotics, feeding beneficial bacteria in the colon and thereby decreasing the amount of pathogens and increasing short-chain fatty acid production, especially of butyrate. Did you know that butyrate is the primary fuel for the cells that line the colon? Butyrate lowers inflammation and oxidative stress, while increasing mineral absorption and detoxifying enzymes!

THE PHYTIC ACID STORY

A hot topic concerning whole grains is phytic acid, so let's delve into this subject to gain a better understanding of it. For a grain to sprout, it must be moistened. In a garden, you sow your seeds in the springtime so the frequent rains can help them germinate. There is a compound in whole grains, legumes, nuts, seeds, and some tubers called phytic acid, otherwise known as inositol hexaphosphate, or IP-6. This very important compound stores phosphorus and other nutrients until exposed to moisture. Soaking the grain signals an enzyme, called phytase, to wake up. The phytase partially breaks down the phytic acid, which frees the nutrients that allow the grains to sprout and grow into plants.

By soaking your whole grains overnight in filtered water, you can partially break down the phytic acid and increase the mineral availability, as well as the digestibility of the proteins and carbohydrates in the grains. This is especially important for those who have mineral deficiencies and suffer the symptoms associated with them, such as osteoporosis, iron-deficiency anemia, lowered immune function, learning disabilities, lack of taste/picky eating, muscle cramping, infertility, and dental cavities.

The minerals that have the most affinity for phytic acid are iron, calcium, magnesium, manganese, zinc, and copper—zinc and iron being the most influenced. Phytic acid can depress the bioavailability of dietary zinc, meaning that eating zinc-rich foods with phytate-rich foods at the same time can cause the two to bind together into an insoluble complex.

Phytic acid can also substantially reduce the reabsorption of intestinal endogenous zinc.

Phytic Acid in Grains

Interestingly, phytic acid is found in higher amounts in oats, corn, and gluten grains such as wheat, barley, and rye. Soaking rolled oats doesn't break down much of the phytic acid because oats do not contain enough phytase to break it down. (Phytase is the enzyme responsible for breaking down phytic acid.) The phytic acid in corn, though, can be broken down through a traditional preparation called nixtamalization, a process by which the corn is soaked and cooked in limewater, an alkaline solution. If you eat corn chips, corn tortillas, tamales, or anything else made from masa harina, it has undergone this process.

Teff, buckwheat, amaranth, and sorghum grains contain the lowest amounts of phytic acid. Additionally, buckwheat contains a high amount of phytase. That's why soaking rolled oats with raw buckwheat groats overnight in water, with the addition of a few tablespoons of cultured coconut water, yogurt, kefir, or apple cider vinegar, can help break down the phytic acid in the rolled oats; afterward, both grains can be cooked into a porridge.

Mineral Deficiencies in Developing Countries

People in developing countries where grains make up most of the diet often have major mineral deficiencies, notably iron-deficiency anemia, zinc deficiency, and iodine deficiency. This is because the people are not absorbing most of the minerals in the grains they eat, owing to the presence of phytic acid and a low fruit intake (vitamin C is needed to absorb iron). They also do not eat other foods like meat, seafood, and vegetables in a great enough quantity to obtain enough available minerals.

Higher intakes of phytic acid from whole grains are not always associated with mineral deficiencies and poor health, however. Those who eat a balanced diet and who have excellent digestive health may have no problems consuming unsoaked grains.

Their adequate stomach acid begins to break apart the phytic acid, and certain strains of beneficial bacteria in the gut produce the phytase that helps further break it down.

The Benefits of Phytic Acid

While phytic acid, or IP-6, can cause some problems with mineral absorption, it has also been found to be a potent chelator of heavy metals and can reduce the risk for numerous forms of cancer, type 2 diabetes, and formation of kidney stones. The research on phytic acid's reducing cancer cell growth is widespread. It seems that phytic acid stimulates the immune system by increasing the activity of natural killer cells. Directly, IP-6 from rice bran reduces cell proliferation and increases the differentiation of cancer cells. Phytic acid can also suppress the oxidant damage associated with the oxygen radicals that are produced by the colonic bacteria, thereby protecting the intestinal epithelium.

It's All About Balance

In nature, there are always two sides to every story. For some people, whole grains may be partly to blame for certain health problems and nutrient deficiencies, while for others these grains can be a miraculous healing food. It's important to be aware of phytic acid, but know that it is nearly impossible to remove completely from the diet. The most important times to keep dietary phytic acid to a minimum are during pregnancy and early childhood, when bone formation and growth are at their highest and neuro-cognitive development is at its peak.

Remember that unfermented soy products (fake meats, soy flour, and soy milk) are very high in phytic acid; so are nuts, seeds, and beans. See the "Getting Started" chapter for information on preparing these foods. We soak most of our grains before cooking them, but we still use unsoaked whole-grain flours on occasion for cookies, muffins, and pancakes. Most of the homemade bread we make is from our Gluten-Free Sourdough Starter (page 112). We also like to use sprouted gluten-free flours in place of regular stone-ground gluten-free flours for some of our recipes. We make sure that some of our meals are grain-free and contain mineral-rich meat or poultry, combined with nonstarchy green vegetables for optimal mineral absorption.

If your gut is in good shape, you are eating a diet full of fresh vegetables and fruits, and you don't rely on grain-based products at every meal and snack, you will most likely have a good mineral status. And let's not forget about stress. Chronic stress can cause more mineral depletion in the body than phytic acid! As with anything, you need to find a balance that works best for you.

HOW TO COOK WHOLE GRAINS

Following these basic steps for cooking whole grains, you can prepare highly nourishing, plant-rich meals for your family. We cook a few pots of whole grains every week to use in salads, soups, and as part of our main meals.

Sort

Sort through your grains for tiny rocks and other foreign particles. Dry quinoa often contains small stones. Millet and buckwheat can be cross-contaminated with gluten grains if not certified gluten-free. Remove these foreign elements from the grains before cooking. You can do this by pouring ⅓ cup of the grain at a time onto a plate. Simply sort through the grains with your fingers and pick out any foreign material. Young kids actually love to help out with this!

Rinse

Some grains need to be rinsed prior to cooking to remove chaff, dust, or other debris. These grains include millet, quinoa, amaranth, and sometimes brown rice. Quinoa also has a bitter saponin coating that repels insects and birds, and if it is not rinsed off, may cause digestive upset when consumed. To rinse grains, place them in a fine-mesh strainer and run warm water through them until the water runs clear. You can also place the grains in a pot with water and swirl them around using your hand, then pour off the water through a fine-mesh strainer.

Soak

To soak your grains, measure the desired amount and place in a bowl. Cover with at least 1 inch of warm water and add 1 to 2 tablespoons raw apple cider vinegar or raw coconut vinegar for each cup of grain. Let soak, uncovered, on your kitchen counter for 12 to 24 hours, then drain and rinse through a fine-mesh strainer. Follow the guidelines in the chart below for water requirements and cooking times.

Add Salt

Adding sea salt when cooking your grains brings out their sweetness and helps them open up. Grains cooked without salt taste flat. We generally use ⅛ to ¼ teaspoon sea salt per 1 cup of grain.

COOKING CHART FOR SOAKED WHOLE GRAINS

GRAINS (1 CUP DRY)	WATER (CUPS)	COOKING (MIN)	YIELD (CUPS)
Short-Grain Brown Rice	1½	50	3½
Long-Grain Brown Rice	1¼ to 1½	45	3
Sweet Brown Rice	1½	50	2½
Wild Rice	1¾	75	4
Buckwheat	1	15	2
Millet	1½	25 to 30	3½
Quinoa	1¼ to 1½	12 to 15	3
Teff	-	-	-
Amaranth	-	-	-

COOKING CHART FOR UNSOAKED WHOLE GRAINS

GRAINS (1 CUP DRY)	WATER (CUPS)	COOKING (MIN)	YIELD (CUPS)
Short-Grain Brown Rice	2	55 to 60	3½
Long-Grain Brown Rice	1¾	50	3
Sweet Brown Rice	2	55 to 60	2½
Wild Rice	2½	75	4
Buckwheat	1½	15 to 20	2
Millet	2 to 2½	30 to 35	3½
Quinoa	1¾	15 to 20	3
Teff	3	15 to 20	2½
Amaranth	2½	20 to 25	2

10 Steps to Creating Great Whole-Grain Dishes

1. Follow the cooking charts on page 247. Grains cooked with too much water will be mushy and unsuitable for grain salads.

2. Use part homemade chicken broth and part water to cook your whole grains. This adds more nutrients and flavor!

3. Make sure the cooked grains have cooled to room temperature before using in a preparation. Hot grains can become mushy when stirred together.

4. Add olive oil to grain salads to not only increase flavor and nutrients but also to help keep the grains from sticking together.

5. Add an acid such as lemon juice or vinegar to cold whole-grain salads to make the flavors pop! I typically use ⅓ to ½ cup vinegar per 6 cups cooked grain.

6. Add cold or room-temperature legumes to whole-grain salads. Hot, freshly cooked legumes can break apart when you mix the salad ingredients.

7. Just before serving, add toasted nuts or seeds to your whole-grain salad. Crispy toasted nuts or seeds become soft and soggy as they sit in the salad.

8. Use completely cooled grains for stir-fries. Stir-frying hot grains causes them to lump together.

9. Allow refrigerated whole-grain salads to warm to room temperature before serving. Both olive oil and whole grains become hard in cold temperatures.

10. To reheat a grain casserole, add it to a small pot with a few tablespoons of water, cover, and warm over low heat. Grain dishes become harder when cold.

Cook

To cook whole grains, you need to first bring the pot of grain and water to a boil over high heat. Once it is boiling, you immediately lower the heat to a simmer and start timing. Grains that have been boiled for too long can be tough and chewy. If the grains are mushy or clumped together, you may have added too much water or not brought the water rapidly to a full boil.

It is also important to use the proper cookware. A stainless steel pot with a thick bottom that contains an aluminum core will distribute the heat evenly and prevent the bottom layer of grains from getting burned. Use a 1-quart pot for cooking 1 cup of grain, a 2-quart pot for cooking 2 cups of grain, and a 3-quart pot for cooking 3 cups of grain.

No Stirring!

Never stir a pot of cooking grains. Whole grains create steam holes in the cooking grain, so the top layer of grains cooks as evenly as the bottom layer. When you stir a pot of cooking whole grains, you destroy the steam holes, which causes some of the grain to not cook fully.

lean, mean, and green rice salad

FREE OF

MAKES 8 SERVINGS

I've been making this salad for years without a recipe. It's our go-to salad when we have too much produce in our refrigerator that needs to be used up. Try adding fresh corn off the cob, cherry tomatoes, sliced baby zucchini, fresh peas, cooked beans, chopped mustard greens, and any chopped fresh herbs. The dressing is bright green, which turns the rice a beautiful green hue once everything is tossed together. The salad will last in the refrigerator for up to five days.

SALAD

6 cups cooked brown basmati rice

4 cups thinly sliced fresh kale

2 large carrots, grated

DRESSING

⅓ cup fresh lemon juice or raw apple cider
   vinegar

⅓ cup extra-virgin olive oil

Large handful of fresh parsley

Small handful of fresh basil

2 to 4 garlic cloves

1 teaspoon sea salt

Place the rice, kale, and carrots in a large bowl and toss well. Place the dressing ingredients into a blender and blend on high for about 60 seconds, or until smooth and creamy. Pour over the salad and toss.

brown rice, black bean, and avocado salad

FREE OF

MAKES 8 SERVINGS

Black beans, avocado, spicy chiles, and lime juice are one of our family's favorite combinations. In fact, our children devour this salad. If you plan on storing this salad in the fridge for a while, then leave out the avocado; simply place a little chopped avocado on top of each bowl at serving time. Serve this salad with the Chipotle Yam Fries (page 236) and the Cilantro Cabbage Slaw (page 202) for a balanced meal.

6 to 7 cups cold cooked short-grain brown rice, preferably a day old

4 cups cooked black beans

4 green onions, trimmed and sliced into thin rounds

1 cup chopped fresh cilantro

2 jalapeño peppers, seeded and finely diced

½ cup fresh lime juice

6 tablespoons extra-virgin olive oil

1 teaspoon ground cumin

1 to 2 teaspoons Herbamare or sea salt

2 avocados, diced

Lime wedges (optional)

Place the rice in a large bowl and add the beans, green onions, cilantro, and jalapeños. Add the lime juice, olive oil, cumin, and Herbamare and toss well. Taste and adjust the seasonings, if necessary. Top with the diced avocado and serve. Garnish with lime wedges, if desired.

coconut rice

MAKES 8 SERVINGS

Coconut milk jazzes up plain brown rice to complement cooked beans, fish, or chicken. Serve this plain or with lime wedges, mint, cilantro, chopped chiles, minced fresh ginger, and chopped roasted peanuts for a Thai-style meal!

2 cups short-grain brown rice

3 to 3½ cups water (see Tip)

1 cup coconut milk

¼ teaspoon sea salt

Place the rice, water, coconut milk, and salt in a 2-quart heavy-bottomed pot. Bring to a boil over high heat, cover, then reduce the heat to low and cook for about 50 minutes, or until the rice is done. Remove the pot from the heat and let stand for at least 15 minutes before serving.

KITCHEN TIP

If you are using unsoaked brown rice, use 3½ cups water; if using soaked brown rice, use 3 cups water.

NUTRITION TIP

Rice has a high affinity for arsenic and is more likely than most other grains to have elevated levels of it. The arsenic may come from the soil or water that the rice is grown in, and is likely to be higher in rice from areas where arsenic-laden herbicides are used or where there are oil refineries or chemical plants. Jasmine and basmati rice may come from India or Thailand, where chemical use is not as regulated as in the United States. In general, California-grown rice has a lower risk of arsenic contamination. When rice is concentrated into either rice syrup or rice syrup solids, the potential for elevated arsenic levels increases tremendously. A recent study found that baby formulas with Organic Brown Rice Syrup (OBRS) had 20 times the amount of arsenic than formulas not sweetened with OBRS. Similar elevations were found in energy bars and athletic energy "shots" that contained OBRS.

everyday rice salad

FREE OF

MAKES 4 TO 6 SERVINGS

This simple salad can be used as a base recipe to create many variations according to what you have on hand. In the springtime, try replacing the tofu with chopped hard-boiled egg, diced radishes, and fresh dill. Use sea salt in place of the tamari. In the summer, add diced red bell peppers, blanched green beans, chopped kale, and chopped sugar snap peas. If you are sensitive to soy, replace the tofu with one or two cubed and sautéed chicken breasts. If you have a citrus sensitivity, replace the lemon juice with one to two tablespoons brown rice vinegar. Sometimes I like to sprinkle the salad with toasted sunflower seeds just before serving.

TOFU

1 pound organic firm tofu, cut into 1-inch cubes

2 tablespoons wheat-free tamari

2 to 3 teaspoons extra-virgin olive oil or coconut oil

SALAD

5 cups warm cooked short-grain brown rice

1 cup fresh or frozen peas

2 large carrots, diced

2 to 3 green onions, trimmed and sliced into thin rounds

½ to 1 cup chopped fresh parsley

2 tablespoons fresh lemon juice

2 tablespoons extra-virgin olive oil

2 tablespoons wheat-free tamari or coconut aminos (see Tip on page 158)

1. In a medium bowl, toss the tofu with the tamari and let it marinate for 20 minutes. Heat a large skillet over medium-high and add the olive oil. Add the tofu and sauté for about 5 minutes, then set aside on a plate.

2. Place the rice in a large bowl and add the remaining salad ingredients. Stir in the warm tofu.

If the tofu and rice are sufficiently still warm, the frozen peas will gently cook. (If not, you can blanch the peas in hot water for a minute or two, then drain and add to the salad.) Toss everything well and serve.

VARIATION: If you have chives growing in your garden, use a handful of them, snipped, to replace the green onions.

rice and garbanzo bean salad with kale

FREE OF

MAKES 4 SERVINGS

This super-nutritious salad is even better on the second day, after the kale has been softened from the olive oil and lemon juice! This salad makes an excellent quick lunch and can also be packed into your child's lunchbox.

SALAD

4 cups cooked long-grain brown rice

1 to 2 cups cooked garbanzo beans

2 cups chopped raw kale

2 large carrots, diced

3 green onions, trimmed and thinly sliced

Handful of fresh basil leaves, thinly sliced

DRESSING

¼ cup extra-virgin olive oil

Juice of 1 lemon

½ teaspoon Herbamare or sea salt

Freshly ground black pepper

Place the salad ingredients into a large bowl and toss. Add the dressing ingredients and toss again. Taste and adjust the seasonings, if needed.

vegetable fried rice

FREE OF

MAKES 6 TO 8 SERVINGS

This dish can easily be a meal by itself, but with the addition of sautéed tofu, tempeh, chicken, or fish, you'll boost the protein content even more. You can vary the vegetables according to what is in season. We like to add a lot of green vegetables to the mix, such as bok choy, kale, mustard greens, and spinach. Garnish with toasted sesame seeds for a beautiful presentation.

2 to 3 tablespoons coconut oil or toasted sesame oil

½ cup raw cashews

5 green onions, trimmed and cut diagonally into 2-inch pieces

1 cup broccoli florets

1 cup cauliflower florets

1 large carrot, sliced on the diagonal

2 celery stalks, sliced on the diagonal

4 garlic cloves, crushed

1 to 2 teaspoons grated fresh ginger

6 cups cold cooked brown basmati rice (see Tip)

2 to 3 cups chopped spinach, chard, cabbage, or bok choy

3 tablespoons coconut aminos or wheat-free tamari (see Tip on page 158)

1 tablespoon brown rice vinegar or coconut vinegar

1. Heat a deep 11- or 12-inch skillet over medium-high. Add 2 tablespoons of the coconut oil and then the cashews; sauté for about 30 seconds, or until golden. Quickly add the green onions, broccoli, cauliflower, carrot, and celery. Sauté for 5 to 7 minutes, or until the vegetables are crisp-tender. Add the garlic and ginger, and sauté for 30 seconds more.

2. Stir in the rice, adding the remaining tablespoon oil, if necessary. Keep everything moving in the pan. Add the spinach and sauté for a minute, then stir in the aminos and vinegar. Taste and adjust the seasonings, if necessary. Serve immediately.

> **INGREDIENT TIP**
> You will need to cook 2 cups of long-grain, jasmine, or brown basmati rice for this recipe. Make sure the rice is completely cool before adding it to the vegetables. It is best to use rice that is at least a day old and straight from the refrigerator. Warm, fresh rice will clump together and become mushy when fried.

wild rice stuffing

FREE OF

MAKES 8 SERVINGS

This recipe is a delicious, savory addition to your holiday table or it can be enjoyed any other time! It makes enough to stuff one twenty-pound turkey and fill one medium casserole dish. I have also successfully made this using all wild rice instead of half wild and half brown rice.

1 cup wild rice

1 cup long-grain brown rice

4 cups vegetable or chicken broth

¼ cup extra-virgin olive oil

3 cups chopped red onions

1 tablespoon dried thyme

1 to 2 teaspoons dried sage

1 teaspoon freshly ground black pepper

3 to 4 cups chopped fresh mushrooms

2 to 3 cups chopped celery

1 cup pecans

½ to 1 cup unsweetened dried cranberries

1 apple, cored and diced

1 cup chopped fresh parsley

Herbamare or sea salt

1. In a medium pot with a tight-fitting lid, combine the wild rice, brown rice, and broth. Cover, bring to a boil over high heat, then reduce the heat to low and simmer for 45 minutes, or until the rice is cooked. Let stand in the pot for at least 15 minutes.

2. In a large skillet, heat the olive oil over medium. Add the onions and sauté for 5 to 6 minutes, until softened. Add the herbs, mushrooms, and celery and sauté for 5 minutes more. Turn off the heat and add the pecans, cranberries, apple, and parsley. Stir in the cooked rice and season to taste with Herbamare.

3. Place some of the stuffing in the cavity of a turkey and roast in accordance with the turkey's weight. Place the remaining stuffing in a covered casserole dish. Bake in a 350°F oven for 35 to 40 minutes, or until heated through.

wild rice, kale, and apple salad

FREE OF

MAKES 6 TO 8 SERVINGS

This festive autumn salad pairs well with roasted turkey breast, roast chicken, or a hearty vegetable bean soup. You will need to cook 1½ cups of wild rice to yield the 6 cups cooked. Store any extra rice salad in a glass container in the refrigerator for up to five days.

SALAD

6 cups cooked wild rice

½ small red onion, finely diced

1 tart apple, cored and diced

4 to 5 large kale leaves, rinsed and thinly sliced

1 to 1½ cups almonds, toasted and chopped (see Tip)

½ cup dried currants (optional)

DRESSING

½ cup balsamic vinegar

½ cup extra-virgin olive oil

1 tablespoon pure maple syrup

1 to 1½ teaspoons Herbamare or sea salt

Freshly ground black pepper

Place the salad ingredients in a large bowl and toss. In a small bowl, whisk together the dressing ingredients. Pour the dressing over the salad and toss well. Taste and add more Herbamare and pepper, if needed. Serve.

KITCHEN TIP

To toast the almonds, place them in a shallow baking dish and toast in the oven at 350°F for 15 to 20 minutes, or until golden. Cool on a plate, then chop on a cutting board.

chicken and wild rice salad

MAKES 6 TO 8 SERVINGS

Serve this scrumptious salad over mixed organic greens for a balanced meal. It is best served at room temperature. You will need to cook 1½ cups of wild rice to yield the 6 cups cooked. Store extra rice salad in a glass container in the refrigerator for up to five days.

SALAD

6 cups cooked wild rice

2 cups diced cooked chicken

1 cup hazelnuts, toasted and chopped (see Tip)

4 mandarin oranges, peeled and segmented

4 green onions, trimmed and sliced into rounds

¼ to ½ cup dried currants

Large handful of fresh parsley, chopped

DRESSING

½ cup fresh orange juice

½ cup extra-virgin olive oil

2 tablespoons white wine vinegar

1 to 1½ teaspoons Herbamare or sea salt

Freshly ground black pepper

Place the rice, chicken, hazelnuts, mandarin sections, green onions, currants, and parsley in a large bowl. In a small bowl, whisk together the dressing ingredients. Pour the dressing over the salad and toss well. Taste and adjust the seasonings, if needed. Serve.

> **KITCHEN TIP**
>
> To toast the hazelnuts, place them in a shallow baking dish and toast in the oven at 350°F for 15 to 20 minutes, or until golden. Cool on a plate, then chop on a cutting board.

millet salad with roasted pistachios and dried cranberries

FREE OF

MAKES ABOUT 8 SERVINGS

This nutritious whole-grain salad is perfect as part of a big Thanksgiving or Christmas dinner with family and friends. It also makes a nice light lunch any other time of year. If you are cooking for one or two, make just half of this recipe.

SALAD
1 cup shelled raw pistachios
6 to 7 cups cooked millet
1 cup dried cranberries
1 cup chopped flat-leaf parsley

DRESSING
½ cup fresh orange juice
½ cup extra-virgin olive oil

2 to 3 tablespoons Champagne vinegar
1 teaspoon Herbamare or sea salt
1 teaspoon ground coriander

1. Preheat the oven to 350°F. Place the pistachios in a small baking dish or glass pie plate and toast for about 10 minutes, or until lightly browned.

2. Place the millet in a large bowl and fluff with a fork. Add the toasted pistachios, the cranberries, and parsley. In a small bowl, whisk together the dressing ingredients. Pour the dressing over the salad and toss well. The millet will absorb some of the dressing as it sits for a little while. Taste and adjust the seasonings, if necessary.

> **INGREDIENT TIP**
> Millet can be cross-contaminated with gluten grains, so be sure to purchase certified gluten-free millet.

mushroom millet risotto

FREE OF

MAKES ABOUT 6 SERVINGS

I usually use half homemade chicken broth and half water for this recipe. If using a salted broth, you may want to omit the Herbamare so the risotto isn't overly salted. Serve this savory whole-grain dish with the Poached Salmon with Green Onions and White Wine (page 300) and the Arugula Salad with Shaved Fennel (page 196) for a balanced, nutritious meal.

3 tablespoons extra-virgin olive oil

1 large leek, trimmed, cut in half lengthwise, and thinly sliced

½ pound button mushrooms, sliced

3 garlic cloves, crushed

½ teaspoon Herbamare or sea salt

1½ cups millet, rinsed and drained

6 cups Homemade Chicken Broth (page 156) or water

¼ cup dry white wine

Freshly ground black pepper

1. Heat a wide pot or deep 11-inch skillet over medium. Add the olive oil and leek, and sauté for a few minutes, or until soft. Add the mushrooms and sauté for 5 to 10 minutes more. Add the garlic and Herbamare, and sauté an additional minute. Stir in the millet and 2 cups of the broth, plus the wine. Cover, bring to a boil, then reduce the heat to a simmer and cook for 15 to 20 minutes.

2. Remove the lid and add 2 more cups of the broth; stir for a minute, then cover and cook for 10 minutes more. Add the remaining 2 cups broth, stir, cover, and cook for 15 to 20 minutes more. By this time, the millet should be well cooked. Stir and add more liquid if you desire a thinner consistency. Taste and adjust the seasonings, adding the black pepper.

dilled quinoa with peas and parsley

FREE OF

MAKES 6 TO 8 SERVINGS

Fresh herbs, peas, and greens are abundant during the spring months. Serve this lively quinoa salad with poached salmon, hard-boiled eggs, or baked chicken for a light springtime meal. You will need to cook 2 cups of quinoa to yield the 6 cups cooked. Store any leftovers in a covered container in the refrigerator for up to five days.

SALAD

6 cups cooked quinoa

2 cups blanched fresh or frozen peas

1 bunch radishes, thinly sliced

½ cup chopped fresh dill

½ cup chopped fresh parsley

DRESSING

½ cup fresh lemon juice

⅓ cup extra-virgin olive oil

1 or 2 garlic cloves, crushed

1½ teaspoons sea salt or Herbamare

Scoop the quinoa into a large bowl. Add the peas, radishes, dill, and parsley. In a small bowl, whisk together the dressing ingredients. Pour the dressing over the quinoa and vegetables and toss well.

INGREDIENT TIP

Higher lysine, methionine, and cysteine levels assist quinoa in having one of the best amino acid profiles compared to other grains. Lysine is an amino acid that assists with tissue repair—helpful for repairing a damaged gut.

quinoa salad with arame and daikon

MAKES 6 TO 8 SERVINGS

Although this ingredient list looks long, the recipe is quick to prepare. Arame is a sea vegetable that is high in trace minerals. Daikon radishes are long, white root vegetables that look somewhat like large carrots. You can find both of these at your local health food store. The quinoa salad will last up to five days in the refrigerator.

SALAD

¼ cup arame

2 cups water

6 cups cooled cooked quinoa

2 daikon radishes, peeled and sliced

2 large carrots, sliced

3 or 4 green onions, trimmed and sliced into thin rounds

1 to 2 cups thinly sliced red cabbage

3 to 4 cups thinly sliced kale

1 cup sunflower seeds, toasted (see Tip)

DRESSING

½ cup fresh lemon juice

⅓ cup coconut aminos or wheat-free tamari (see Tip on page 158)

⅓ cup extra-virgin olive oil

1 garlic clove, crushed

Rinse the arame, then place in a small saucepan with the water and simmer for 10 to 15 minutes. Drain through a fine-mesh strainer. Place the quinoa in a large bowl, and add the arame, daikon, carrots, green onions, cabbage, kale, and sunflower seeds. In a small bowl, whisk together the dressing ingredients and pour over the salad. Toss well and serve.

KITCHEN TIP

To toast sunflower seeds, place them in a 10-inch skillet over medium heat and stir for 5 to 6 minutes, until light golden brown and fragrant.

NUTRITION TIP

Sea vegetables are an excellent source of iodine—a mineral needed to make thyroid hormones. Those without sufficient thyroid hormone production can experience weight-loss resistance, hair loss, constipation, chronic fatigue, cold hands and feet, and may have difficulty becoming pregnant.

quinoa tabouli

FREE OF

MAKES 6 TO 8 SERVINGS

We make this recipe quite often during mid to late summer, when cucumbers, tomatoes, and mint are at their peak. Combined with some homemade energy bars, this salad makes a great picnic lunch for a day hike. We pack it in small stainless steel lunch containers for each child. Store any leftovers in a covered container in the refrigerator for up to five days.

SALAD
6 cups cooled cooked quinoa
1 large cucumber, diced (2 to 3 cups)
2 cups diced ripe tomatoes
½ cup finely chopped fresh mint
½ cup finely chopped fresh parsley

DRESSING
½ cup fresh lemon juice
⅓ cup extra-virgin olive oil
2 garlic cloves, crushed
1 teaspoon Herbamare or sea salt

Scoop the quinoa into a large bowl. Add the cucumber, tomatoes, mint, and parsley. In a small bowl, whisk together the dressing ingredients. Pour the dressing over the salad and toss well.

quinoa and lentil salad
with caramelized onions

MAKES 6 TO 8 SERVINGS

This salad is a favorite for summertime picnic potlucks. People who are new to quinoa usually enjoy this dish very much. Black beluga lentils are very small and hold their shape well in salads like this. You can find them at your local health food store or order them online. I often cook a large pot of them and store some in the freezer to use later.

4 tablespoons extra-virgin olive oil

2 to 3 red onions, halved and sliced into crescent moons

1 teaspoon Herbamare or sea salt

6 cups cooked quinoa

2 cups cooked black beluga lentils (see Tip)

2 or 3 Roma (plum) tomatoes, chopped

Large handful of fresh basil, thinly sliced

3 tablespoons balsamic vinegar

Freshly ground black pepper

Crumbled feta cheese (optional)

Chopped flat-leaf parsley (optional)

1. Heat an 11- or 12-inch skillet over medium. Add 2 tablespoons of the olive oil, then add the onions and Herbamare; sauté for a few minutes, or until the onions begin to release some of their moisture. Reduce the heat to low and cook for 25 to 30 minutes, or until the onions are caramelized.

2. Place the quinoa in a large bowl. Add the onions, lentils, tomatoes, basil, vinegar, the remaining 2 tablespoons olive oil, some Herbamare, and pepper to taste; toss together. Taste and adjust the seasonings, if necessary. Sprinkle with the feta and parsley, if desired.

KITCHEN TIP

To cook the black beluga lentils, rinse and drain approximately 2 cups of lentils, then add them to a medium saucepan and cover with water. Bring to a gentle simmer, cover the pot, and cook for about 20 minutes, or until tender. Drain and set aside to cool.

mexican quinoa

FREE OF

MAKES 6 TO 8 SERVINGS

This is a great way to jazz up plain quinoa. I like to serve it with cooked black beans, roasted sweet potatoes, and sautéed collard greens for a quick, balanced weeknight meal. You can also add salsa and top with diced avocado. Sometimes I also serve this with the Cumin-Spiced Pinto Beans (page 283) and a shredded napa cabbage salad dressed with fresh lime juice and sea salt.

2 tablespoons extra-virgin olive oil or coconut oil

1 small onion, finely diced

1 small green or red bell pepper, cored, seeded, and finely diced

1 jalapeño pepper, seeded and finely diced

2 or 3 garlic cloves, crushed

1 to 2 teaspoons ground cumin

1 teaspoon paprika

¼ teaspoon chipotle chile powder

1 teaspoon Herbamare or sea salt

2 cups quinoa, rinsed

3½ cups water

4 to 5 tablespoons tomato paste

1. Heat a 3-quart heavy-bottomed pot over medium. Add the olive oil, then the onion, bell pepper, and garlic; sauté for a few minutes, until softened. Add the spices and Herbamare; sauté a minute more.

2. Stir in the quinoa, water, and tomato paste. Stir, cover, and bring to a boil. Reduce the heat to low and simmer for about 25 minutes, or until the quinoa is cooked. Let rest for about 10 minutes, then fluff with a fork and serve.

moroccan quinoa pilaf

This recipe can be made ahead of time and then reheated. To reheat, add a few tablespoons of water to a pan, then add the pilaf and sauté until warmed. You will need to cook 2 cups of quinoa for this recipe. It works best if your quinoa is completely cooled before using it in the recipe. Serve this with roasted chicken and sautéed kale for a balanced meal.

2 to 4 tablespoons extra-virgin olive oil

1 onion, diced

4 carrots, sliced into rounds

1 cup raw almonds, chopped

½ cup dried currants

1½ to 2 teaspoons mild curry powder

½ teaspoon ground turmeric

½ teaspoon ground cardamom

1 teaspoon Herbamare or sea salt

4 cups chopped kale

4 to 5 cups cooled cooked quinoa

Juice of 1 small lemon

Freshly ground black pepper

1. Heat an 11- or 12-inch deep skillet or wide pot over medium. Add 2 tablespoons of the olive oil, then the onion and sauté for 4 to 5 minutes, until softened. Add the carrots and sauté about 10 minutes more, until the onion is soft but not browned.

2. Add the almonds, currants, spices, and Herbamare and sauté for 5 minutes more. Add the kale and sauté for 5 additional minutes, or until the kale is tender. Stir in the quinoa and heat over low. Add the remaining 2 tablespoons olive oil, if necessary, to keep the mixture from sticking to the pan; add a few tablespoons of water if the pilaf seems dry. Remove the pan from the heat and add the lemon juice and pepper. Stir well, taste, and adjust the seasonings, if needed.

VARIATION: Replace the currants with chopped dried apricots, and the quinoa with cooked brown basmati rice.

INGREDIENT TIP

It is best if your kale is still dripping wet from the rinsing when adding it to the pot; the moisture helps it to cook thoroughly.

---

red quinoa masala

MAKES 6 TO 8 SERVINGS

Using red quinoa creates a beautiful presentation and a nutrient-rich dish. We like to serve this with the Red Lentil Dal (page 170) along with a yogurt-cucumber sauce or the Raw Cilantro Lime Chutney (page 347).

2 cups red quinoa

3½ cups water

Pinch of sea salt

3 to 4 tablespoons extra-virgin olive oil or coconut oil

1 teaspoon cumin seeds

1 teaspoon brown or black mustard seeds

2 tablespoons finely chopped fresh ginger

1 large onion, halved and sliced into crescent moons

½ teaspoon ground turmeric

2 or 3 plum tomatoes, chopped

1 to 1½ teaspoons Herbamare or sea salt

½ to 1 cup chopped fresh cilantro

1. Rinse the quinoa in a fine-mesh strainer under running water, then drain well. Place in a 2-quart pot, add the water and salt, cover, and bring to a boil. Reduce the heat to low and simmer for 15 to 20 minutes, or until the quinoa is cooked. Let cool for at least 30 minutes. (You can also cook the quinoa up to a day before and then let it cool in the refrigerator overnight before using it.)

2. Heat a 6-quart stainless steel pot or 12-inch cast-iron skillet, add the oil, let it heat for 10 to 20 seconds, then add the cumin and mustard seeds and sauté for 30 to 60 seconds, until they begin to pop. Immediately add the ginger and onion, and sauté for about 10 minutes, or until the onion is very soft and beginning to change color. Add the turmeric, tomatoes, and Herbamare. Sauté a minute more, then gently stir in the quinoa. Cover the pot and cook for 5 to 10 minutes over medium-low heat. Turn off the heat, add the cilantro, and fluff with a fork.

spicy coconut quinoa amaranth casserole

This recipe is great on its own or serve it with baked fish and steamed broccoli for a heartier meal. It also pairs well with sautéed tempeh and greens. Leftovers can be frozen in serving-size containers and then reheated in a small covered pot on the stove.

2 tablespoons coconut oil

1 large onion, chopped

2 or 3 jalapeño peppers, seeded and diced

3 garlic cloves, crushed

1 teaspoon red pepper flakes (optional)

1½ cups quinoa, rinsed and drained

½ cup amaranth, rinsed and drained

6 cups water

1 (14.5-ounce) can coconut milk

1 to 2 teaspoons sea salt or Herbamare

1 large red bell pepper, cored, seeded, and diced

2 or 3 green onions, trimmed and sliced

Large handful of fresh cilantro, chopped

1. Heat a 6-quart pot over medium. Add the coconut oil, then the onion and sauté for 5 to 10 minutes, or until soft. Add the jalapeños, garlic, and red pepper flakes, if using. Sauté a few minutes more, then stir in the quinoa and amaranth. Cover with the water, stir, then cover the pot and bring to a boil. Reduce the heat to a simmer and cook for 30 minutes, or until the quinoa is done.

2. Preheat the oven to 350°F. Coat a 9 by 13-inch glass baking dish with a little coconut oil. Add the coconut milk, salt, bell pepper, and green onions. Stir, then scoop the mixture into the baking pan, spread evenly with the back of a spoon, and bake for about 30 minutes, or until bubbly. Sprinkle with the cilantro and serve.

cold spaghetti salad

MAKES 6 TO 8 SERVINGS

Serve this noodle salad at a summer picnic or as a main meal paired with a large garden salad and our Everyday Salad Dressing (page 325).

2 (12-ounce) packages brown rice spaghetti noodles

1 to 2 tablespoons extra-virgin olive oil

1 large onion, chopped

2 tablespoons minced garlic

4 ripe tomatoes, chopped

1 cup chopped fresh parsley

½ cup pine nuts, lightly toasted (see Tip)

1 cup pitted Kalamata olives

4 tablespoons red wine vinegar

Sea salt or Herbamare

Freshly ground black pepper

1. Cook the noodles until al dente, according to the package directions. Rinse with cold water in a colander to stop the cooking.

2. Heat a large stainless steel skillet over medium. Add 1 to 2 tablespoons of the olive oil and the onion; sauté for 10 to 15 minutes, or until soft but not browned. Add the garlic and cook for a minute more. Place the noodles in a large bowl. Add the cooked onion and garlic along with the tomatoes, parsley, pine nuts, olives, and vinegar. Toss well, then season to taste with the Herbamare and pepper.

> **KITCHEN TIP**
>
> To toast the pine nuts, place them in a dry skillet over medium heat. Stir to keep them moving in the pan for a few minutes, until lightly browned. Watch them closely, as they can burn easily!

> **INGREDIENT TIP**
>
> Pine nuts are not true nuts; they are the edible seed of a pinecone from various species of pine trees.

dairy-free macaroni and cheese

FREE OF

MAKES 4 TO 6 SERVINGS

This "cheese" sauce has a lovely yellow color that's similar to traditional mac and cheese. It gets its color from the turmeric and red bell pepper, while the nutritional yeast gives this a cheesy flavor and the cashews make a creamy sauce.

A 16-ounce package brown rice elbow macaroni

1 cup raw cashews

2 cups water, or more as needed

1 very small red bell pepper, cored, seeded, and chopped

¼ cup sweet rice flour

¼ cup nutritional yeast

2 tablespoons minced onion

1 garlic clove

2 tablespoons fresh lemon juice

1 teaspoon Dijon mustard

1½ teaspoons Herbamare or sea salt

½ teaspoon ground turmeric

1. Cook the pasta according to the package directions. Drain and set aside. Place the cashews and water into a high-powered blender. Blend until very smooth and creamy. Add the remaining ingredients and blend again until smooth.

2. Pour the sauce in a large pot and simmer over low heat until thickened and warm. If the sauce seems too thick, add a little water. Taste and adjust the seasonings, if necessary. Add the noodles and stir to coat, heating until warmed. Serve.

dairy-free fettuccini alfredo

MAKES 4 TO 6 SERVINGS

We like to boost the nutrition of this meal by adding sautéed zucchini, carrots, cauliflower, peas, and a sprinkling of fresh garden herbs. Try the grain-free variation using zucchini noodles, and serve it with roasted chicken.

A 16-ounce package brown rice fettuccini noodles
½ cup raw cashews
1 cup water
½ cup dry white wine
¼ cup extra-virgin olive oil
1 small shallot, chopped
2 garlic cloves

2 tablespoons nutritional yeast
1 tablespoon sweet rice flour
1 teaspoon Herbamare or sea salt
Pinch of grated nutmeg
Freshly ground black pepper
Finely chopped flat-leaf parsley, for garnish

1. Cook the noodles according to the package directions. Rinse and drain in a colander.

2. Place the cashews, water, wine, olive oil, shallot, garlic, yeast, flour, Herbamare, and nutmeg into a high-powered blender and blend until ultra-smooth and creamy. Pour the sauce into a 2-quart saucepan and simmer for 10 minutes, until thickened. Toss the warm sauce and noodles together in a large bowl, sprinkle with the pepper, and garnish with the parsley. Serve immediately.

VARIATION: For a grain-free version, replace the rice noodles with zucchini noodles and replace the sweet rice flour in the sauce with 2 tablespoons of arrowroot powder. To make zucchini noodles, trim the ends from 2 or 3 zucchini and use a spiralizer fitted with the "wide" noodle blade to cut long noodles. Cook the noodles in the sauce for 2 to 3 minutes, just to soften; don't overcook them!

mainmeals

Balsamic Roasted Chicken with Figs and Sweet Onion, p. 307

Chicken Pot Pie, p. 311

Apricot Glazed Chicken, p. 306

Nourishing Meat Loaf, p. 317

oppy Joes, p. 318, with Grain-Free Burger Buns, p. 117

Ginger Plum Sauce, p. 332

Cashew Roasted Red Pepper Dip, p. 337

Pumpkin Seed Pesto, p. 339

Spicy Peach Chutney, p. 348

Thai Cucumber Salad,
p. 225

Blueberry-Orange-Coconut Swirl Pops, p. 381

Ginger-Macadamia Nut Energy Bars, p. 377

Dark Chocolate Coconut Custard, p. 392

Cashew Orange Date Balls, p. 376

Watermelon Sorbet, p. 402

Lime Avocado Tart with a
Macadamia Nut Crust, p. 404

Healthy Lactation Oatmeal
Raisin Cookies, p. 417

Blueberry Peach Crisp, p. 414

Pumpkin Cupcakes, p. 431, with
Dairy-Free Cream Cheese Frosting, p. 441

Vanilla Coconut Cake, p. 435, with
Chocolate Avocado Frosting, p. 439

Chocolate Chip Cookie Bars, p. 424

Whipped Coconut Cream, p. 443

Beet Sauerkraut, p. 473

Pickled Carrots and Cauliflower, p. 476

Fresh Tomato-Basil Marinara Sauce, p. 478

Nettle Mint Tea, p. 456

Rooibos Rose Iced Tea, p. 458

At our house, the main meal is what brings us all together. Little hands help with the chopping, peeling, stirring, and sautéing. The table gets set with colorful napkins and sometimes even a vase of freshly picked flowers. Our kids say things like, "Mmm, this is good" and "Yummy, thanks for the meal, Mommy." Mostly it's a time to relax and be thankful for such nourishing food, though like most families, mealtimes can also be very busy.

CREATING BALANCED FAMILY MEALS

How do I create a balanced meal for my family, and how do I feed my family nourishing meals every day? Like most of you, I'm juggling work, school, and after-school activities for the whole family. Life can be harried and crazy, and sometimes it's easier just to go out to eat. But with eating out we run the risk of eating unintentional gluten, potential food allergens, and genetically engineered food, not to mention the drain on our bank account. With a little thought and a well-stocked kitchen, though, you can make simple meals for your family every day.

Whole and Unprocessed

When putting together meals for your family, use whole, unprocessed foods—both raw and cooked, with more raw in the summer and fewer in the winter. Centering your meals on whole foods that are naturally gluten-free makes those meals simpler and easier to implement. Consider incorporating a lot of color, as well. The beautiful colors of fresh fruits, vegetables, nuts, beans, and whole grains are also signs of disease-protective phytochemicals that can change the way in which our genes are read!

Carbohydrates for Energy

Does the meal contain some form of unprocessed carbohydrates for fuel? As the energy of the sun falls to the earth, it is captured in the leaves of plants and combined with air (CO_2) and water (H_2O) to become carbohydrates like glucose ($CH_{12}O_6$). It is no wonder that our cells are designed to use glucose as their primary source of energy. "Time-released" glucose can be found in foods that are rich in complex carbohydrates. These are often chains of glucose molecules that need to be broken down over time in the body. Examples of unrefined complex carbohydrates include cooked starchy vegetables, such as root vegetables and winter squash, and cooked whole grains and beans. Non-starchy vegetables also contain smaller amounts of sugars. These include lettuce, kale, green beans, broccoli, radishes, and mushrooms.

Healthy Fats

Does the meal have some type of healthy fat? Fats are essential for all cell membranes in our bodies, especially the brain cells of a growing baby and child. They help our cells communicate properly, contributing to a healthy, functioning nervous system. Avoiding trans fats and focusing on healthy fats also contribute to increased fertility in women. Fat is needed to absorb the fat-soluble vitamins A, D, E, and K. Healthy fats, like conjugated linoleic acid and omega-3 fatty acids, can be found in the fats of animals raised on a natural diet of grasses and other foliage. You may, however, consider limiting the amount of animal fat in your family's diet because persistent organic pollutants (POPs) bio-accumulate in animals and are stored in their fatty tissues. Sources of healthy fats include extra-virgin olive oil, virgin coconut oil, nuts, seeds, avocados, wild-caught fish, and pastured eggs.

Enough Protein?

Is there an adequate amount of protein in the meals? Proteins are the building blocks for all cells and are needed for tissue repair. Sedentary people require less protein, while athletes and pregnant women require more. We often think of protein and meat as synonymous; however, proteins are also found in dark leafy greens, beans, whole grains, seeds, and nuts. We would need to eat a lot of greens to match the protein content in a small piece of fish, but it is possible. Three ounces of steak has about 24 grams of protein. Two cups of cooked quinoa has about 16 grams. A quarter cup of almonds has about 6 grams of protein, and 1 cup of cooked beans has about 20 grams. Daily protein requirements easily add up when we are consuming a whole foods diet.

Vitamins and Minerals

What about vitamins and minerals? Using vegetables as the basis for at least one meal a day while also incorporating vegetables into other meals and snacks will greatly contribute to meeting your family's overall nutrient requirements. Vitamin C, potassium, folate, vitamins B_2 and B_6, magnesium, beta-carotene, polyphenols, and flavonoids are all found abundantly in fruits and vegetables. Incorporate both raw and fermented foods daily in your family's meals, as cooking may destroy certain vitamins—but not minerals—present in vegetables and fruits. Whole carbohydrate and protein foods also contain a vast amount of the necessary vitamins and minerals required. To incorporate enough iodine and trace minerals, use sea vegetables several times a week, kelp granules as a condiment, and unrefined sea salt daily.

SAMPLE BALANCED DINNER MENU PLANS

DAY 1

Moroccan Roasted Chicken (page 309)

Baked sweet potatoes

Sautéed Winter Greens with Caramelized Onions (page 230)

DAY 2

Apple Cider Baked Beans (page 277)

Roasted Delicata squash

Kohlrabi Apple Slaw (page 211)

DAY 3

Garlic Ginger Salmon (page 298)

Whipped Sweet Potatoes with Cardamom (page 239)

Lemon-Walnut Green Bean Salad (page 212)

DAY 4

Zucchini Lasagna with Pine Nut Ricotta (page 292)

Arugula Salad with Shaved Fennel (page 196)

DAY 5

Black Bean and Yam Casserole (page 278)

Cooked basmati rice (see page 247)

Jalapeño-Lime Kale Slaw (page 208)

DAY 6

Red Lentil Dal (page 170)

Red Quinoa Masala (page 266)

Cilantro Cabbage Slaw (page 202)

DAY 7

Halibut and Potato Chowder (page 187)

Gluten-Free Sourdough Bread (page 114)

Dilly Radishes (page 475)

10 Steps to Creating Balanced Meals

1. What is in season right now? We have a number of garden beds on our lot. In the summer and fall, we can make a lot of meals that revolve around food harvested from our yard. In the winter, we eat a lot of stored root vegetables, cabbage, and preserved or fermented foods. Shopping at your local farmers' market can provide inspiration for seasonal dishes as well.

2. Use what you have before buying more. Are there any grains or beans in the pantry that need be used before buying anything new? Grains and beans don't last that long, so it is important to use them up within six to nine months of purchasing them. What about meat in the freezer? Meat should be used within a year of freezing. I like to check and see if there is any available that needs to be thawed out before shopping for anything new.

3. In the morning make a plan for the day. When I wake up, I think about what I will make for dinner and I calculate if anything needs to be done earlier in the afternoon or if I can simply toss it all together at 5 P.M.

4. How do the meals fit into the bigger nutrition picture? What was the composition of the other meals we had that day? I like to recall what we ate for breakfast or lunch before prepping dinner. For example, if we had homemade gluten-free bread for breakfast, I don't want to serve bread or a starchy meal for dinner. By that same token, if we had eggs and kale for breakfast and a green salad topped with salmon for lunch, I will serve something starchy for dinner, such as roasted sweet potatoes with rice and beans.

5. Plan meals ahead. Before I go grocery shopping, I plan at least three main meals and buy what I need. The remainder of our meals I create from what is left in the refrigerator or pantry, as well as leftovers.

6. Use the weekends to prep food for the week. On Saturday mornings we head off to the farmers' market to load up on seasonal organic produce. We also like to fit in a grocery shopping day on the weekend. With a plan of action in hand, I use Sunday afternoon to prep a few things for the week, such as cooking one pot of beans and two pots of grains, so I have them on hand to quickly make soup or grain-bean salads for dinner later in the week. Cutting celery and carrot sticks and placing them in a container filled with a small amount of water makes a handy snack for school lunches. We also like to make raw energy bars, wrap them individually in waxed paper, and store them in the refrigerator for quick snacks.

7. Make large batches of certain recipes. If you make more than you'll need at one sitting, you can have nutritious home-cooked meals on evenings when you are too busy to cook. Or, you can cook a double batch of soup to make packing lunches for kids a breeze. Just make sure you have a few small stainless steel thermoses on hand. Big pots of rice or quinoa can be divided into individual Pyrex dishes and topped with chopped veggies, beans, or soup for a grab-and-go meal.

8. What meals do other members of the household, including the children, enjoy eating? Have your children requested anything for the week? If not, then how about involving them in a quick brainstorming session before heading to the market? Even better, have them help you pick out the items at the market in anticipation of the meal. With our children, we never cease to be surprised about what they will eat when they have been involved in the preparation.

9. Include the children in meal preparation. At least one night a week, plan to have your children make a meal. You'll be amazed at how much cutting a three-year-old can do, or even that an eight- or nine-year-old can cook a whole meal. Plus, they learn so much in the process. Reading skills are enhanced by following printed recipes; math skills are built up by doubling or halving the amounts in a recipe. Communication skills are improved when they need to work together.

10. Bring baby into the kitchen. If you have a baby, use a wrap or sling to have it nearby while you get things done. As soon as my babies were about five months old, we could put them on our backs in either a backpack or an Ergo carrier. Newborns can ride snug up against your chest in a Moby wrap while you prepare dinner. Just think of the brain stimulation as the baby smells the food cooking and hears all the chopping and cooking noises!

apple cider baked beans

FREE OF

MAKES 8 TO 10 SERVINGS

Baked beans have always been part of our summer family picnics. We like to serve them with a cabbage slaw such as the Picnic Coleslaw (page 217) and a potato salad such as the Purple Potato Salad with Radishes and Chives (page 218). Baked beans freeze well, so if you have leftovers you cannot finish within a few days, you can freeze the remainder in portion-size containers. Just reheat in a small covered saucepan on the stove.

5 to 6 cups cooked cannellini beans, drained and rinsed

2 to 3 tablespoons extra-virgin olive oil

1 onion, chopped

4 to 6 garlic cloves, crushed

1½ cups organic apple cider or apple juice

1 cup tomato sauce

½ cup coconut sugar

¼ cup raw apple cider vinegar

2 tablespoons blackstrap molasses

1 to 2 teaspoons dry mustard powder

1 tablespoon smoked paprika

2 teaspoons Herbamare or sea salt

Preheat the oven to 375°F. Place the beans in a large casserole dish. Heat a 10-inch skillet over medium and add the olive oil and onion; sauté for 5 to 10 minutes, until very soft and beginning to change color. Add the garlic and sauté a minute more. Scrape the onion, garlic, and oil into the casserole dish. Add the apple cider, tomato sauce, coconut sugar, vinegar, molasses, mustard powder, paprika, and Herbamare. Gently stir together, then cover and bake for about 1 hour. Remove the lid, stir, and bake uncovered for another 30 to 45 minutes, or until bubbly. Taste and adjust the seasonings, if necessary. Serve warm.

black bean and yam casserole

FREE OF

MAKES 6 SERVINGS

Casseroles are oh-so comforting on a cold winter evening. I like to serve this over cooked quinoa with sautéed dark leafy greens in the wintertime, or with an arugula salad in early autumn.

2 tablespoons extra-virgin olive oil

1 large onion, chopped

2 teaspoons Herbamare or sea salt

1 to 3 small jalapeño peppers, seeded and diced

3 or 4 garlic cloves, crushed

2 teaspoons ground cumin

2 teaspoons smoked paprika

1 teaspoon dried oregano

½ teaspoon chipotle chile powder

2 large yams (sweet potatoes), peeled and diced

1 large red bell pepper, cored, seeded, and chopped

4 cups cooked black beans

1 cup water

1 cup tomato sauce (see Tip on page 183)

1 tablespoon honey, agave nectar, or coconut nectar

3 tablespoons arrowroot powder

1. Preheat the oven to 350°F. Heat a 10-inch skillet over medium and add the olive oil, onion, and Herbamare; sauté for 5 to 10 minutes, or until the onion is tender. Transfer the onion to a large casserole dish and add the jalapeños, garlic, and spices. Stir together. Then add the yams, bell pepper, and black beans. Stir to combine.

2. In a medium bowl, whisk together the water, tomato sauce, honey, and arrowroot powder. Pour over the beans mixture and stir. Cover the casserole dish and bake for 30 minutes, then remove the lid and bake uncovered for about 30 minutes more, until bubbly.

> **INGREDIENT TIP**
> Any type of hot chile is suitable for this recipe.

butternut squash and pinto bean enchiladas

FREE OF

MAKES 6 SERVINGS

This is a great child-friendly recipe. The sauce isn't too spicy, so even the youngest of children can enjoy it. Our children like to help with preparation. Once, I made this using steamed sweet potatoes instead of butternut squash and asked my son, who was only three, to remove the potato peels and mash the sweet potatoes. He took those peels off so fast that mashing was already in full swing before I knew it. All I saw was sweet potato oozing through little fingers and a huge smile! Then comes the fun part of filling and rolling the tortillas. You can use just about any filling you would like. Be sure to heat the tortillas so they won't crack.

SAUCE

2 tablespoons extra-virgin olive oil

1 small onion, chopped

3 or 4 garlic cloves, chopped

1 tablespoon ground cumin

1½ to 2 teaspoons Herbamare or sea salt

2 dried ancho chiles, seeded

1½ to 2 cups water

2 cups tomato sauce

¼ cup arrowroot powder

ENCHILADAS

12 to 16 sprouted corn tortillas or collard greens

2 cups mashed cooked butternut squash

3 cups cooked pinto beans

2 cups baby spinach leaves

Grated raw organic jack cheese (optional)

1. Preheat the oven to 400°F. Lightly oil a 9 by 13-inch glass baking dish.

2. Heat a 3-quart saucepan over medium and add the olive oil and onion; sauté for 5 to 10 minutes, or until softened. Add the garlic, cumin, and Herbamare and sauté a few minutes more. Stir in the ancho chiles, water, and tomato sauce. Cover and simmer for about 20 minutes. Pour the sauce into a blender, add the arrowroot powder, and blend until smooth. (Makes 4 cups sauce.)

3. Warm the tortillas or, if you are using collard greens, cut off the bottom part of the stems and blanch before using. Lay a tortilla on a cutting board and add a few small spoonfuls of mashed squash, then some beans, and a small handful of spinach leaves. Roll tightly and place seam side down in the baking dish. Repeat with the remaining tortillas and filling, pushing them close together in the dish. Top with the sauce, and sprinkle cheese on top, if using. Cover and bake for 30 to 35 minutes, or until bubbly.

KITCHEN TIP

The easiest way to warm the tortillas is to add a little oil to a hot skillet and heat each one in the oil for about 10 seconds on each side. You can fill each tortilla while the next one is heating in the pan.

cajun red beans and quinoa

FREE OF

MAKES 4 TO 6 SERVINGS

This is a spin on the classic southern red beans and rice. Here, I use cooked quinoa and cooked beans for a meal than can be made in about 15 minutes. If desired, add one or two chopped organic andouille sausages to the mix. Serve this with braised collard greens or steamed broccoli for a balanced meal. You'll need to cook 1 cup of quinoa to yield the 3 cups for this recipe. (See page 247 for directions on cooking quinoa.)

2 to 3 tablespoons extra-virgin olive oil

1 onion, diced

1 large red bell pepper, cored, seeded, and diced

1 teaspoon Herbamare or sea salt

1 teaspoon smoked paprika

½ teaspoon freshly ground black pepper

Pinch of cayenne pepper

2 cups cooked red beans

3 cups cooked quinoa

Chopped fresh parsley, for garnish

Thinly sliced green onions, for garnish

1. Heat an 11-inch skillet or a 3-quart pot over medium and add the olive oil and onion; sauté for 10 to 15 minutes, or until beginning to caramelize. Add the bell pepper and cook for about 5 minutes more, or until softened. Add the Herbamare and spices, and sauté a minute more.

2. Stir in the red beans and quinoa, and simmer for 3 to 5 minutes more. Remove from the heat, then taste and adjust the seasonings, if necessary. Garnish with the parsley and green onions.

chana masala

FREE OF

MAKES 4 TO 6 SERVINGS

Chana Masala is a common North Indian dish typically served over basmati rice and topped with a yogurt-cucumber sauce. My version might not be authentic, but it is still lip-smackin' good! Sometimes we add two or three chopped red potatoes and some spinach to this, too. We serve it over brown basmati rice, with a slew of other Indian dishes.

3 tablespoons extra-virgin olive oil or coconut oil

3 cups minced onions (about 2 onions)

3 jalapeño peppers (or another spicy chile), seeded

A 1-inch piece of fresh ginger, peeled

4 garlic cloves

1 tablespoon ground cumin

1 tablespoon ground coriander

1 teaspoon ground turmeric

1 teaspoon garam masala

3 cups fresh tomato puree (see Tip)

3 to 4 cups cooked garbanzo beans

2 teaspoons Herbamare or sea salt

1 to 2 tablespoons fresh lemon or lime juice

1. Heat an 11-inch deep skillet over medium (or use a wide pot). Add the olive oil and onions, and sauté for about 10 minutes, until soft.

2. While the onions are sautéing, place the jalapeños, ginger, and garlic into a food processor fitted with the "s" blade and process until minced. Add to the onions in the pan and sauté for a few minutes more. Add the cumin, coriander, turmeric, and garam masala. Stir in the tomato puree, garbanzo beans, Herbamare, and lemon juice. (If

you would like to add diced potatoes, do so now, along with ½ to 1 cup of water.) Simmer for 25 to 30 minutes, or until the flavors are well blended. Taste and adjust the seasonings, if necessary.

INGREDIENT TIP

To make fresh tomato puree, place 1½ to 2 pounds of ripe tomatoes into a food processor fitted with the "s" blade and process until you get a slightly chunky, but mainly smooth, puree.

---

coconut cashew curry

MAKES 4 SERVINGS

Curry is a staple in our house. Our children will eat anything flavored with curry spices. For this dish, use any vegetables you have on hand—just keep in mind the total amounts. You may need to add extra coconut milk, water, and/or spices to compensate for the additional ingredients. We like to serve this over quinoa with a generous amount of fresh cilantro sprinkled on top. This recipe doesn't freeze very well, so I have kept it on the smaller size. In fact, I double this recipe to feed our large family.

1 tablespoon coconut oil or extra-virgin olive oil

1 teaspoon brown or black mustard seeds

1 teaspoon cumin seeds

1 tablespoon curry powder

Pinch of red pepper flakes

1 (14.5-ounce) can coconut milk

1 cup water

2 to 3 tablespoons cashew butter

A 1-inch piece of fresh ginger, peeled

3 large carrots, sliced on the diagonal

3 small red potatoes, or 1 sweet potato, peeled and cut into cubes

¼ pound fresh green beans, trimmed and cut in half

1 to 2 cups cauliflower florets

1 to 2 cups chopped savoy or napa cabbage

1 tablespoon fresh lemon juice

1 teaspoon Herbamare or sea salt

Chopped fresh cilantro, for garnish

1 cup raw cashews, toasted and chopped, for garnish (see Tip)

1. Heat a large pot or 11-inch skillet over medium, and add the coconut oil and mustard and cumin seeds; sauté for about 30 seconds, or until the seeds begin to pop. Stir in the curry powder and red pepper flakes, then immediately (so the spices don't burn) pour in the coconut milk and water. Blend in the cashew butter. Grate the ginger, using a microplane, right into the pot. Add the carrots and potatoes. Cover and simmer for 5 to 10 minutes, or until the vegetables are tender.

2. Add the green beans and simmer for 5 minutes more. Add the cauliflower and simmer another 5 minutes. Add the cabbage, lemon juice, and Herbamare; cover and simmer for a few minutes more, or until all the vegetables are tender but not overcooked. The total cooking time should be 25 to 30 minutes. Serve the curry in individual bowls over cooked quinoa. Garnish each bowl with the chopped cilantro and roasted cashews.

> **KITCHEN TIP**
>
> To toast the cashews, place them in a small glass baking dish and toast in a preheated 350°F oven for about 12 minutes, or until just slightly golden.

cumin-spiced pinto beans

FREE OF

MAKES 8 TO 10 SERVINGS

This is one of our family's favorite weekday meals. We serve the beans over cooked brown basmati rice and then offer a variety of toppings, such as Salsa Fresca (page 350), sliced avocados, thinly sliced romaine lettuce, sliced black olives, and fresh lime wedges. Allow time overnight to soak the beans.

3 cups dried pinto beans

2 tablespoons extra-virgin olive oil

1 large onion, chopped

6 garlic cloves, crushed

1 to 2 jalapeño peppers, seeded and finely diced

2 tablespoons ground cumin

8 to 10 cups water

3 teaspoons Herbamare or sea salt

1. Rinse the beans and sort through them to pick out any old, shriveled beans or clumps of dirt. Rinse again and place in a large bowl. Cover with a few inches of water and soak overnight. When ready to cook, drain the beans.

2. Heat an 8-quart pot over medium and add the olive oil and onion; sauté for about 10 minutes, or until very soft and beginning to change color. Add the garlic, jalapeños, and cumin. Sauté a few minutes more, then add the beans. Cover with the water, bring to a boil, reduce the heat to a simmer, partially cover, and cook for about 1 hour, or

until the beans are tender. Remove the lid, add the Herbamare, and continue cooking, uncovered, until most of the water has evaporated, another 30 to 40 minutes. Serve the beans hot or puree in a food processor to make "refried beans."

> **NUTRITION TIP**
>
> Pinto beans contain certain phytochemicals—such as cinnamic acid, secoisolariciresinol diglucoside, and coumestrol—that have been shown to be beneficial in the prevention of stomach cancer.

curried lentil and rice casserole

FREE OF

MAKES 4 TO 6 SERVINGS

Lentils have been consumed since prehistoric times and are one of the first foods to have ever been cultivated. They have been found at archeological dig sites dating back 8,000 years! This dish has a long baking time and is not suitable for a quick weeknight meal. If you work during the week, try making this recipe on the weekend to have the lentils available for the week. I use a stoneware casserole dish for this recipe, though a 9 by 13-inch glass baking dish also works well. Portions can be frozen into small containers for future use.

2 tablespoons extra-virgin olive oil or coconut oil

1 onion, chopped

2 tablespoons finely chopped fresh ginger

1 tablespoon finely chopped fresh turmeric, or 1 teaspoon ground

2 teaspoons curry powder

1 teaspoon ground cumin

1 teaspoon ground coriander

½ teaspoon ground cinnamon

2 teaspoons sea salt

4 carrots, chopped

1½ cups French lentils or black beluga lentils, sorted and rinsed

1 cup long-grain brown rice

5 cups water

1 (14.5-ounce) can coconut milk

1. Preheat the oven to 350°F. Heat a 10-inch skillet over medium and add the olive oil and onion; sauté for 5 to 6 minutes. Add the ginger, turmeric, spices, and salt. Continue to sauté for 2 minutes more, until fragrant.

2. Place the onion-spice mixture in a large casserole dish. Add the carrots, lentils, rice, water, and coconut milk. Mix well, cover, and bake for 2 hours. After 2 hours, turn the temperature up to 425°F. Remove the cover and cook for 20 to 30 minutes more to let excess liquid cook off. Stir and serve.

> **NUTRITION TIP**
>
> Lentils are high in both soluble and insoluble fibers, which readily bind to toxins so they can easily be excreted from the body.

eggplant and white bean ragout

MAKES ABOUT 8 SERVINGS

This stew is more like a thick, nutritious sauce that can be served over quinoa, polenta, brown rice noodles, or spaghetti squash. You can also omit the white beans and serve it over grilled fish or chicken. I usually use navy beans, but great northern or cannellini also work well. I prefer to cut the onions and vegetables into larger chunks so everything doesn't turn to mush. Any extra sauce can be frozen for six months.

2 to 4 tablespoons extra-virgin olive oil

1 red onion, chopped

4 or 5 garlic cloves, crushed

1 eggplant, cut into cubes

2 zucchini, chopped

8 to 10 cremini mushrooms

3 cups cooked white beans

2 to 3 cups tomato sauce or pureed tomatoes

1 tablespoon Italian seasoning

1 teaspoon sea salt

½ teaspoon red pepper flakes (optional)

1. Heat an 11- or 12-inch skillet over medium, then add 2 tablespoons of the olive oil and the onion; sauté for about 5 minutes, or until soft. Add the garlic, eggplant, zucchini, and mushrooms; sauté for 5 to 10 minutes more, or until the vegetables have softened, adding more olive oil if necessary. The timing will depend on the size of your vegetables.

2. Stir in the beans, tomato sauce, Italian seasoning, salt, and red pepper flakes, if using. Simmer for 8 to 10 minutes more, or until the sauce has thickened slightly. Taste and adjust the seasonings, if necessary.

> **NUTRITION TIP**
>
> The beautiful purple hue you see on the skin of eggplants comes from the potent antioxidant anthocyanin. This amazing phytochemical has been found to be protective against cardiovascular disease, diabetes, and age-related macular degeneration.

fresh vegetable curry

FREE OF

MAKES 4 TO 6 SERVINGS

This delectable vegan curry recipe uses cooked chickpeas for added protein. It can also be made with chunks of salmon, halibut, or chicken breast. Try adding any vegetable you have on hand. I often make this with diced sweet potatoes or squash in autumn. Chopped fresh spinach is another fantastic addition. Since spinach cooks so quickly, you'll want to toss it in when you take the pan off the stove. Serve the curry over cooked long-grain brown rice or quinoa.

2 to 3 tablespoons coconut oil

1 teaspoon black mustard seeds

2 to 3 teaspoons finely chopped fresh ginger

4 red potatoes, cut into cubes

3 carrots, sliced

2 teaspoons curry powder

1 teaspoon ground cumin

1 teaspoon ground coriander

½ teaspoon ground turmeric

Dash of cayenne pepper

1½ to 2 teaspoons Herbamare or sea salt

6 Roma (plum) tomatoes, diced

1 cup water

1 tablespoon arrowroot powder

½ pound green beans, trimmed and cut into pieces

¾ pound cauliflower, cored and cut into florets

½ pound button mushrooms, cut in half

3 garlic cloves, crushed

2 cups cooked chickpeas

Chopped fresh cilantro, for garnish

1. Heat a deep 11-inch skillet over medium to medium-high for a few minutes. Add the coconut oil, mustard seeds, and ginger; sauté for about 30 seconds, until the seeds begin to pop. Add the potatoes and carrots, and sauté for 10 to 15 minutes, or until tender but not browned. Add the spices and Herbamare; stir well and sauté for about 1 minute more. Sautéing the spices in oil is the key to a good curry!

2. Stir in the tomatoes and sauté for about 2 minutes. Mix the water with the arrowroot in a small bowl, whisking with a fork. Add to the cooking veggies and stir. Then add the green beans, cauliflower, mushrooms, garlic, and chickpeas. Stir gently, cover, and cook for about 15 minutes, stirring occasionally, or until the vegetables are fork-tender. Sprinkle with the cilantro and serve.

lentil and kale dal

I add kale to everything because we grow it in our backyard garden and because we love the flavor and nutrition it imparts. Of course, you can add spinach, chard, broccoli leaves, or any other green you have on hand. You can also add whatever other vegetables you like to this dish. I keep it simple so it takes 10 minutes or less to prepare, then I walk away while it simmers on the stove. Serve this dal over brown basmati rice with a dollop of Spicy Peach Chutney (page 348).

2 tablespoons extra-virgin olive oil or coconut oil

1 small onion, finely diced

2 tablespoons finely chopped fresh ginger

2 teaspoons ground cumin

2 teaspoons ground turmeric

1½ teaspoons garam masala

⅛ to ¼ teaspoon cayenne pepper

2½ cups French lentils or black beluga lentils, sorted and rinsed

6 cups water

4 cups chopped kale

1½ teaspoons sea salt

Handful of fresh cilantro, chopped

1. Heat a 6-quart pot over medium and add the olive oil and onion; sauté for 6 to 7 minutes. Add the ginger and spices, and sauté for 1 minute more. Add the lentils and water, cover, and simmer for 40 minutes.

2. Stir in the kale and salt; simmer uncovered for about 10 minutes, or until the kale is cooked and the liquid is reduced somewhat. Continue cooking if you like your dal thicker. Turn off the heat and add the cilantro. Serve over rice or quinoa.

> **INGREDIENT TIP**
>
> Sort through your lentils and pick out any gluten grains, then rinse very well before proceeding with this recipe.

quick curried chickpeas and potatoes

MAKES 6 SERVINGS

This is one of our children's favorite meals. It is quick to put together if you have the chickpeas on hand. About once a month I cook a large pot of chickpeas. Some of them go into hummus, some into bean soups and stews such as this one, and the rest I freeze in 2-cup containers to have on hand for busy weeknight meals. Feel free to add about 4 cups of chopped greens near the end of cooking; spinach, kale, and chard are our favorites.

2 tablespoons extra-virgin olive oil or coconut oil

1 small onion or 1 large shallot, finely diced

1 small jalapeño pepper, seeded and finely diced

2 teaspoons Herbamare or sea salt

2 teaspoons curry powder

½ teaspoon ground cumin

½ teaspoon ground coriander

⅛ teaspoon ground cinnamon

3 yellow or red potatoes, diced (about 4 cups)

3 to 4 cups cooked chickpeas

2 cups tomato sauce

1 cup water

Handful of fresh cilantro, chopped

Heat a 4-quart pot or a deep 11-inch skillet over medium, then add the olive oil and onion; sauté for 5 to 10 minutes, until very soft and beginning to change color. Add the jalapeño and sauté a minute more, then add the Herbamare and spices; sauté about 30 seconds more, being careful not to burn the spices. Immediately add the potatoes and stir to coat with the oil and spices. Stir in the chickpeas, tomato sauce, and water. Cover and simmer over medium or medium-low heat for 25 to 30 minutes, or until the potatoes are fork-tender. Sprinkle with the chopped cilantro and serve over cooked brown rice or quinoa.

summer vegetable kitcheree

MAKES ABOUT 8 SERVINGS

Kitcheree is a highly nourishing, easy-to-digest, hypoallergenic Indian stew made with mung beans and brown rice; spices and vegetables make up the remaining ingredients, which can vary widely. The spices and summer vegetables create a luscious stew that can be made in just minutes using a pressure cooker, though you don't need one to make this.

2 tablespoons coconut oil or extra-virgin olive oil

2 tablespoons finely chopped fresh ginger

1 tablespoon black mustard seeds

1 tablespoon cumin seeds

Pinch of red pepper flakes

2 cups dry mung beans, rinsed

2 cups brown jasmine or basmati rice, rinsed

3 or 4 large carrots, cut into large chunks

1½ teaspoons ground turmeric

½ teaspoon ground coriander

8 to 10 cups water

4 cups finely chopped kale or spinach

1 to 2 cups fresh or frozen peas

3 ripe tomatoes, chopped

½ cup chopped fresh cilantro

2 to 3 teaspoons sea salt or Herbamare

Chilled coconut milk

1. Heat an 8-quart pot or pressure cooker over medium and add the coconut oil, ginger, mustard seeds, cumin seeds, and red pepper flakes; sauté for about 60 seconds, or until the seeds begin to pop. Add the mung beans, rice, carrots, turmeric, and coriander; stir together a bit so the spices evenly coat the rice and beans, then add 8 cups of the water.

2. If you're using a pressure cooker, lock the lid into place, bring to high pressure, and cook for about 10 minutes. Use the quick release method to bring the pressure down. If the stew needs more time, bring the cooker to high pressure again and cook for 1 to 2 minutes more. Add some of the remaining 2 cups water, if necessary.

3. If you are cooking this on the stove, bring the stew to a boil, cover, and simmer over low heat for about 45 minutes, adding some of the remaining 2 cups water, if necessary, to keep the ingredients covered.

4. To either pot, add the kale, peas, tomatoes, cilantro, and salt. Stir until just mixed. Turn off the heat, cover, and let stand for about 5 minutes. The vegetables will quickly become tender in the hot stew. Adjust the seasonings, if necessary. Top the servings with a dollop of coconut milk.

spicy lentils and rice in cabbage leaves

This is one of our family's favorite meals. Our children adore cabbage, especially with a spicy lentil filling! In fact, they prefer raw cabbage to nearly any other vegetable. Napa cabbage is quite mild and slightly sweet, so start with this variety if your children are not accustomed to eating cabbage. Elevate this recipe to the next level with Spicy Pepper Coconut Cream (page 341) or Raw Cilantro Lime Chutney (page 347).

3 cups French lentils or black beluga lentils, sorted and rinsed

8 cups water

1 bunch chard

2 large shallots

1 jalapeño pepper, seeded

3 garlic cloves

A 1-inch piece of fresh ginger, peeled

1 tablespoon coconut oil

2 teaspoons black mustard seeds

2 teaspoons curry powder

1 teaspoon garam masala

Sea salt

Cooked long-grain brown rice

Napa cabbage leaves

1. Put the lentils and water in a large pot and bring to a boil over high heat. Reduce the heat to low, cover, and simmer for 40 to 45 minutes, or until the lentils are cooked. Drain through a fine-mesh strainer.

2. Place the chard, shallots, jalapeño, garlic, and ginger into a food processor fitted with the "s" blade. Process until minced. Heat an 11-inch deep skillet over medium and add the coconut oil and mustard seeds; sauté for 20 to 30 seconds, or until the seeds begin to pop. Add the curry powder and garam masala; sauté for 10 seconds or so. Quickly add the chard mixture to the skillet and sauté for a few minutes, stirring frequently. Add the lentils and gently stir. Add salt to taste. To serve, place a small scoop of brown rice and the lentil-chard mixture on each cabbage leaf. Accompany with your favorite sauces and chutneys.

collard burritos with a spicy raw mole sauce

FREE OF

MAKES 6 SERVINGS

Blanching large collard leaves for 60 seconds creates a beautiful, bright green, pliable wrap. The filling for these burritos is made from raw nuts, vegetables, and spices. You'll need to soak the walnuts ahead of time. And you can store any leftover burritos in a glass container in the refrigerator for up to three days.

BURRITOS

6 large collard greens

3 cups raw walnuts, soaked for 6 hours

1 cup fresh cilantro

3 or 4 green onions, trimmed and coarsely chopped

1 or 2 garlic cloves, crushed

2 teaspoons ground cumin

2 teaspoons smoked paprika

1 teaspoon Herbamare or sea salt

¼ cup fresh lime juice

SAUCE

2 dried ancho chiles, seeded

3 medjool dates, pitted

1 cup warm water

1 ripe tomato, chopped

¼ cup raw pumpkin seeds

2 tablespoons raw cacao powder

1 teaspoon ground cumin

¾ teaspoon Herbamare or sea salt

OPTIONAL FILLING EXTRAS

Fresh salsa

Guacamole

Sliced avocado

Thinly sliced napa cabbage

1. Fill an 8-quart pot three-fourths full with water and bring to a boil. Trim the ends of the collard greens, then place the leaves in the pot all at once and blanch for 60 seconds. Remove immediately and place onto a towel to drain and cool. Place the remaining burrito ingredients into a food processor fitted with the "s" blade and process until finely ground and sticky.

2. Place the chiles and dates in a small bowl and cover with the warm water. Let soak for 15 to 30 minutes, or until softened. Drain and reserve the soaking water. Place the chiles and dates, the tomato, pumpkin seeds, cacao, cumin, and Herbamare into a blender and blend into a smooth sauce. Add the reserved soaking water as needed to thin the sauce enough to blend properly.

3. Lay one collard leaf on a plate, place a scoop or two of the burrito filling in the middle near the bottom of the leaf. Add any other filling ingredients, such as the salsa, avocado slices, or cabbage, then fold the left and right side edges in. Roll up the burrito from the bottom to the top, encasing the filling. Repeat with the remaining leaves and filling. Arrange the burritos on a platter and either drizzle the mole sauce over or serve in a bowl for dipping.

zucchini lasagna with pine nut ricotta

MAKES 8 TO 10 SERVINGS

Cut long, flat, thin strips from medium zucchini to create simple, nutritious gluten-free lasagna noodles. You can sauté about a pound of ground grass-fed beef and add it to the pasta sauce for a heartier meal, if desired. Just remember to soak the pine nuts ahead of time. The pine nut spread is also great dolloped atop the Almond Herb Pizza Crust (page 125) and spread with freshly made pesto.

PINE NUT RICOTTA

1 cup pine nuts, soaked for 4 to 6 hours

1 cup blanched almond flour

2 to 3 tablespoons fresh lemon juice

1 to 2 tablespoons water

½ teaspoon Herbamare or sea salt

LASAGNA

2 or 3 medium zucchini

3 to 4 cups pasta sauce, as needed

Sautéed sliced mushrooms (optional)

Fresh baby spinach (optional)

Fresh basil leaves (optional)

2 tablespoons extra-virgin olive oil

1 to 2 teaspoons Italian seasoning

2 to 3 tablespoons blanched almond flour

1. Preheat the oven to 350°F. Lightly oil a 9 by 13-inch baking dish with a little olive oil. Drain the pine nuts and place them into a food processor fitted with the "s" blade. Add the flour, lemon juice, water, and Herbamare. Process until thick, smooth, and pasty. Using a microplane, cut the zucchini into long, thin, flat strips, about ⅛ to ¼ inch thick.

2. Pour about 1 cup of the pasta sauce into the bottom of the baking dish and spread out evenly.

Place a layer of zucchini noodles over the sauce. Spread half the ricotta mixture over the noodles. Add the mushrooms, spinach, or fresh basil, as desired. Add another cup of pasta sauce and repeat with more zucchini noodles. Then add the remaining sauce and a final layer of noodles. Drizzle olive oil over the noodles and sprinkle with the Italian seasoning and almond flour. Bake, uncovered, for 40 to 45 minutes, or until bubbly. Let the lasagna rest for about 10 minutes, then slice and serve.

walnut rice loaf

FREE OF

MAKES ABOUT 6 SERVINGS

We like to serve this delicious vegan alternative to meat loaf with baked potatoes or baked sweet potatoes and a large green salad. Make sure your rice is completely cooled; in fact, day-old rice is better than freshly cooked.

2 cups raw walnuts

½ small red onion

1 or 2 small carrots

2 teaspoons poultry seasoning

1 teaspoon sea salt

½ teaspoon black pepper

¼ cup ground golden flax seeds

4 cups cooled cooked brown basmati rice

¼ cup ketchup

1. Preheat the oven to 350°F. Oil a 9 by 5-inch glass loaf pan. Place the walnuts into a food processor fitted with the "s" blade. Process until finely ground. Add the onion and carrots, and process again until ground. Add the poultry seasoning, salt, pepper, and ground flax; pulse a few times to combine. Add the brown rice and process until the rice breaks down and the mixture begins to form into a ball.

2. Press the rice mixture evenly into the loaf pan, and spread with a thin layer of the ketchup.

3. Bake for approximately 1½ hours, or until the interior is darkened slightly. The loaf is done when it slices easily without falling apart; if you cut into it and it crumbles, it is not done. Place it back into the oven and cook for an additional 10 minutes. Let cool for about 10 minutes before slicing.

sweet potato falafels

FREE OF

MAKES 4 TO 6 SERVINGS

I like to serve these easy falafels on a weeknight when my cooking time is limited. As long as I have cooked sweet potatoes in the fridge, the recipe can be made in about 10 minutes. Serve these over a bed of lettuce and cooked quinoa with the Mint Tahini Sauce (page 327). To mince the green onions and parsley, just process them in a food processor for about 30 seconds.

1½ cups mashed cooked sweet potatoes (from 1 large or 2 small potatoes) (see Tip)

1½ cups sprouted garbanzo bean flour

3 or 4 green onions, trimmed and minced

Large handful of fresh parsley or cilantro, minced

1 teaspoon grated lemon zest

½ to ¾ teaspoon Herbamare or sea salt

¼ teaspoon baking soda

2 to 4 tablespoons coconut oil or extra-virgin olive oil, for cooking

1. Place all the ingredients, except the coconut oil, in a medium bowl and use a fork to mash together. Use wet hands to roll the mixture into 1- to 2-inch balls, then place them on a plate. Flatten the balls into thin burgers. (This allows them to cook properly since we are not deep-frying them.)

2. Heat a large cast-iron skillet over medium and add 2 tablespoons of the coconut oil. Place half the falafels in the skillet and cook for 1 to 2 minutes on each side, or until lightly browned. Transfer them to a plate and add the remaining coconut oil to cook the second batch. Serve hot or at room temperature.

KITCHEN TIP

To cook the sweet potatoes, slice them with the skins on into 1- to 2-inch slices. Place in a steamer basket, cover, and steam until soft, about 15 minutes. You can also bake whole sweet potatoes in a 350°F oven for about 1 hour. Let them cool completely before mashing.

garbanzo bean burgers

FREE OF

MAKES 5 TO 6 BURGERS

If you have brown rice and garbanzo beans already cooked, these burgers can be made in a snap—you just need a food processor. We like to use either a romaine lettuce leaf or a napa cabbage leaf for a "bun." Add a dollop of dairy or nondairy plain yogurt and a few fresh mint leaves; or add mustard and ketchup on your burger. We like to serve these with a side of Rutabaga Fries (page 237) or Chipotle Yam Fries (page 236).

2 small carrots, chopped

2 to 3 green onions, trimmed and chopped

Handful of fresh parsley

1 teaspoon Herbamare or sea salt

2 cups cooled cooked short-grain brown rice

1 heaping cup cooled cooked garbanzo beans, drained well

1 to 2 tablespoons ground golden flax seeds

Olive oil, for cooking

1. Place the carrots, green onions, parsley, and Herbamare into a food processor fitted with the "s" blade; process until finely minced. Add the rice, garbanzo beans, and ground flax; pulse until the ingredients are combined and begin to form a doughy ball. Using either wet or lightly oiled hands, form the mixture into 5 or 6 patties, and set onto a plate.

2. Heat an 11- or 12-inch skillet over medium to medium-high. Add 1 to 2 tablespoons olive oil, then place the burgers in the skillet and cook for a few minutes on each side, or until light golden brown.

> **KITCHEN TIP**
>
> Make sure both the beans and rice are completely cooled, or better yet, straight out of the refrigerator. It is best to cook the brown rice with a little less water than usual—moist rice creates very moist burgers.

spicy thai mung bean burgers

FREE OF

MAKES 6 BURGERS

Mung beans take 45 to 60 minutes to cook on the stovetop and about 10 minutes to cook in a pressure cooker. Drain them well before using in this recipe, as the burgers won't stick together if there is too much liquid. To help the burgers hold together, use less water to cook the quinoa: 1 cup quinoa to 1½ cups of water. Lastly, be sure all your ingredients are either cool or at room temperature before making this recipe. Serve these burgers in a napa cabbage leaf with sliced avocado and a dollop of Spicy Pepper Coconut Cream (page 341).

Small handful of fresh cilantro

4 green onions, trimmed

2 fresh hot chiles, seeded

3 garlic cloves

A 1-inch piece of fresh ginger, peeled

2 teaspoons grated lime zest

1 teaspoon sea salt

2 cups cooled cooked mung beans, drained well

2 cups cooled cooked quinoa

Coconut oil or extra-virgin olive oil, for cooking

6 napa cabbage leaves

1. Place the cilantro, green onions, chiles, garlic, ginger, zest, and salt into a food processor fitted with the "s" blade and process until finely minced. Add the mung beans and quinoa, and process again, until the mixture comes together and forms a ball. With slightly oiled hands, shape into 6 patties.

2. Heat a heavy-bottomed skillet over medium to medium-high and add a tablespoon of coconut oil. Cook the patties for 3 to 5 minutes on each side, or until nicely browned. Serve each burger inside a napa cabbage leaf and top with your favorite condiments.

quinoa salmon burgers

FREE OF

MAKES 6 BURGERS

This is one of the most popular recipes on my blog! I serve these burgers with a raw green salad and homemade parsnip fries. Use your hands or tweezers to pull out any remaining bones. I have found that the bones are easiest to remove from wild-caught King salmon instead of Sockeye. If you don't want to bother removing the skin, have it done when you purchase the fish. When the patties are formed, you can refrigerate them between pieces of waxed paper for a few days or freeze them the same way for up to six months.

3 or 4 green onions, trimmed

Large handful of fresh cilantro

1 to 2 teaspoons grated lemon zest (optional)

1 teaspoon Herbamare or sea salt

Freshly ground black pepper

1 to 1½ pounds wild-caught salmon fillet, skin removed

1 cup cooked quinoa

Extra-virgin olive oil or coconut oil, for cooking

1. Place the green onions, cilantro, lemon zest, Herbamare, and pepper into a food processor fitted with the "s" blade. Process until finely minced. Add the salmon and quinoa, and process again until desired consistency. I like to have a few little chunks of salmon in the patties. Form into 6 patties and place on a plate.

2. Heat a large skillet over medium to medium-high and add a tablespoon or so of oil. Place a few patties in the skillet. (I cook 3 at a time in a 10-inch skillet.) Cook for 2 to 3 minutes per side, or until lightly browned. (If your pan is not hot enough, the patties may stick a little.) Set the patties on a plate; they will continue to cook once off the stove, so be sure not to overcook them. Continue cooking the remaining burgers, then serve.

garlic ginger salmon

FREE OF

MAKES 4 TO 6 SERVINGS

Serve this salmon over mashed sweet potatoes, along with sautéed mustard greens and oyster mushrooms that have been seasoned with coconut aminos and brown rice vinegar. Note: allow at least three hours for the fish to marinate.

1½ to 2 pounds wild-caught salmon fillet

¼ cup coconut aminos or wheat-free tamari (see Tip on page 158)

1 to 2 tablespoons brown rice vinegar or coconut vinegar

1 tablespoon pure maple syrup

1 tablespoon toasted sesame oil

2 garlic cloves

A 1-inch piece of fresh ginger, peeled

1. Rinse the salmon, pat dry, and place skin side up in a glass baking dish. Place all the remaining ingredients into a blender and blend until smooth. Pour the marinade over the fish, cover, and refrigerate for 3 hours or until ready to use.

2. Preheat the oven to 400°F. Pour off the marinade and flip the salmon over so the skin is on the underside. Bake for approximately 10 minutes per inch of thickness; most fillets are about 1 inch in thickness, so this is about 10 minutes. The fish will continue to cook after it comes out of the oven, so it is best to take it out when still a little undercooked.

orange pepper salmon

MAKES 6 SERVINGS

Since we live in the Pacific Northwest, we have easy access to fresh, wild-caught salmon. In autumn, we take our children to nearby rivers and watch the salmon run while the bald eagles fly above us. But even if local salmon isn't available in your region, use another variety of local fish. Remember to always avoid farmed salmon or Atlantic salmon, both of which are high in accumulated toxic chemicals. Serve this salmon with cranberry sauce in place of turkey at your Thanksgiving table.

2 pounds wild-caught salmon fillet
  (Sockeye, Coho, King)

1 orange

½ teaspoon Herbamare or sea salt

Freshly ground black pepper

Extra-virgin olive oil or coconut oil, for
  drizzling

1. Preheat the oven to 400°F. Rinse the salmon and pat dry with a paper towel. Cut into 6 pieces. Arrange the pieces on a baking sheet or in a large glass baking dish. Grate the orange for its zest, then juice it—you should have ¼ cup juice.

2. Drizzle the orange juice over the salmon and sprinkle with the zest, the Herbamare, and plenty of pepper. Drizzle with a little olive oil. Bake for about 8 minutes for Sockeye, 10 minutes for Coho, and 20 minutes for King, depending on the thickness; it is usually 10 minutes per 1 inch thickness.

KITCHEN TIP

It is best to zest an orange before you juice it. I use my microplane fine grater to do this.

NUTRITION TIP

The positive effects of eating salmon start at 4 ounces per week. Research has demonstrated that consumption of omega-3 fatty acids can provide protection from cardiovascular disease, improve mood, decrease joint pain, increase eye health, and decrease ADD/ADHD symptoms. Consuming 12 ounces of salmon per week has been shown to raise anti-inflammatory omega-3 fatty acid levels in red blood cells from 4 to 6 percent in just four months.

poached salmon with
green onions and white wine

FREE OF

MAKES 4 TO 6 SERVINGS

I use a stainless steel fish poacher pan for this recipe, which helps to create a gorgeous presentation. You could also use a 10-inch skillet, though you would need to cut the fillet in half crosswise to make it fit correctly. I prefer using Coho salmon fillets for all poached recipes because the fish is thin and cooks evenly in the liquid. Serve this recipe with the Mushroom Millet Risotto (page 259) and the Arugula Salad with Shaved Fennel (page 196).

2 pounds wild-caught salmon fillet

2 green onions

3 or 4 sprigs fresh thyme

3 tablespoons extra-virgin olive oil

½ cup dry white wine

Sea salt or Herbamare

Freshly ground black pepper

1. Rinse the salmon and pat dry. Place skin side down in a fish poacher or skillet. Trim the ends of the green onions and cut in half lengthwise; run under cool water to remove any dirt or sand. Place the green onions and thyme sprigs on top of the salmon, then drizzle with the olive oil. Add the wine and season with sea salt and black pepper.

2. Cover and poach at a low simmer over medium-low heat for 10 to 12 minutes, or until the salmon is cooked through. Serve immediately.

tandoori salmon

FREE OF

MAKES 4 TO 6 SERVINGS

Tandoori food is traditionally cooked in an extremely hot clay oven. Here, I use the traditional Indian tandoori seasonings, but I bake the salmon in a regular oven. The seasoning is ground coriander, cumin, sweet paprika, garlic, ginger, cardamom, and saffron. Combined with a little coconut milk and lemon juice, the taste is fresh and flavorful! Serve this salmon with whipped sweet potatoes and a crunchy romaine, cucumber, and tomato salad for a balanced meal.

Coconut oil, for the pan

1½ to 2 pounds wild-caught salmon fillet
(Sockeye, Coho, King)

¼ teaspoon sea salt

Juice of 1 small lemon

1 to 2 teaspoons tandoori seasoning

½ cup coconut milk

1. Preheat the oven to 400°F. Place a little coconut oil on the bottom of a baking dish small enough to just fit the salmon. You want the coconut milk to surround the fillet. Rinse the salmon, pat dry, and place it skin side down in the dish. Sprinkle the salt and lemon juice on the salmon, and then evenly scatter the tandoori seasoning over it. Pour the coconut milk over the salmon.

2. Bake the fish for about 10 minutes per inch of thickness: sockeye needs about 8 minutes, coho 12 to 15 minutes, and king usually 20 to 25 minutes. The fish will continue to cook when it comes out of the oven.

fish tacos

FREE OF

MAKES 4 TO 6 SERVINGS

Use a fish here that is on the firmer side, such as salmon or halibut. Also, note that the fish marinates for 1 hour before use. We like to serve fish tacos with Homemade Corn Tortillas (page 358) or Plantain Tortillas (page 357), along with fresh salsa, sprouts, thinly sliced napa cabbage, and homemade guacamole. If you don't want to use a tortilla to hold your fillings, use a napa cabbage leaf!

1½ to 2 pounds firm white fish fillets, any skin removed
Juice of 2 large limes
2 or 3 garlic cloves

1 or 2 jalapeño peppers, seeded
1 to 2 teaspoons ground cumin
1 to 2 teaspoons Herbamare or sea salt
Coconut oil, for cooking

1. Rinse the fish and pat dry. Cut the fish with a sharp knife into 1- to 2-inch cubes. Place in a shallow small baking dish. Place the lime juice, garlic, jalapeños, cumin, and Herbamare in a blender and blend for 30 to 60 seconds. Pour the marinade over the fish cubes and marinate for about 1 hour.

2. Heat a large, heavy-bottomed, stainless steel skillet over medium-high heat until hot. Pour in about 2 tablespoons coconut oil, then add gradually the fish, starting with a third to half of the cubes. If you add too much fish at once, it will not sear and will give off its liquid. Sauté for 3 to 4 minutes, or until cooked through. Remove from the skillet, add a little more coconut oil, then add the remaining fish cubes and cook until done. Serve the fish with tortillas, salsa, guacamole, sprouts, and thinly sliced napa cabbage or your favorite taco fixings.

> **NUTRITION TIP**
>
> Mercury, a heavy metal commonly found in large fish, has the potential to damage tissues of the body. The rapidly growing brain tissue of developing fetuses, infants, and young children is particularly susceptible to mercury's adverse effects. Mercury is also capable of damaging adults, particularly the heart tissue, male reproductive organs, and sperm. Two-thirds of the mercury in our environment comes from coal-burning power plants, and a significant amount comes from medical and municipal waste. Microorganisms convert elemental mercury to methylmercury, a toxic form of mercury that our bodies cannot get rid of. It accumulates in organisms at the bottom of the food chain and moves up the food chain, ultimately reaching the highest levels in predatory fish. For more information on "safe" fish, and to download regional Seafood Watch pocket guides, visit www.MontereyBayAquarium.org.

herb-roasted halibut

FREE OF

MAKES 4 TO 6 SERVINGS

This is one of our favorite ways of preparing fish in spring and summer, when halibut is in season. At this time, our garden is flourishing with fresh herbs, and this is a perfect way to use them. Serve this fish with a variety of sautéed summer vegetables, such as the Sautéed Snow Peas and Pattypan Squash (page 231), and a large garden salad.

FISH

1½ to 2 pounds halibut fillet

¼ teaspoon sea salt

Freshly ground black pepper

2 tablespoons extra-virgin olive oil

HERB TOPPING

½ cup packed fresh basil

½ cup packed snipped fresh chives

2 to 3 tablespoons fresh oregano leaves

1 tablespoon thyme leaves

3 garlic cloves

Grated zest of ½ lemon

1. Preheat the oven to 400°F. Rinse and pat dry the fish. Place in a baking dish skin side down, if it still has the skin. Sprinkle with the salt and pepper, and drizzle with the olive oil.

2. Place the topping ingredients into a mini food processor and process until minced. (You can also place them on a wooden cutting board and mince using a large, sharp knife.) Using your fingers, rub the herb topping evenly over the top of the fish. Place in the oven and roast the fish for 10 minutes per inch of thickness. Halibut fillets usually don't take long to cook, about 15 minutes. The fish will continue to cook after it comes out of the oven, so take it out when it's still a little undercooked.

thai coconut fish sticks

FREE OF

MAKES 4 TO 6 SERVINGS

Fish cooks rapidly and dries out if overcooked, so watch these carefully. If your fish still has the skin, use a very sharp knife to cut just beneath the layer. Serve this with the Garlic Ginger Peanut Sauce (page 331) or the Ginger Plum Sauce (page 332).

1½ to 2 pounds halibut fillet, any skin removed

½ cup arrowroot powder

4 to 6 tablespoons water

1 to 2 teaspoons red curry paste

1 teaspoon Herbamare or sea salt

2 cups unsweetened shredded coconut

3 to 4 tablespoons coconut oil

1. Rinse and pat dry the halibut, then cut into "sticks" about ½ inch wide and 3 inches long. In a small bowl, whisk together the arrowroot powder, water, curry paste, and Herbamare. Place the coconut in another bowl.

2. Begin heating an 11- or 12-inch skillet over medium-high; the skillet needs to be hot. Dip the fish sticks into the arrowroot mixture and coat evenly, then dip into the shredded coconut, using your hands to press the coconut into the fish.

3. Pour half the coconut oil into the skillet, and make sure the oil spreads out quickly—this means your pan is hot enough. Add the fish sticks in batches so they don't steam in the pan. Cook for 2 to 3 minutes on each side, using tongs to flip them. Check for doneness by breaking apart the thickest one with a fork. Remember that the fish sticks will continue to cook after you remove them from the pan. Add the remaining coconut oil to the skillet and cook the remaining fish sticks.

thai fish curry with garden veggies

FREE OF

MAKES 4 TO 6 SERVINGS

Any variety of garden vegetables will work in this simple curry; try Walla Walla sweet onions, cauliflower, cabbage, green beans, or mushrooms. Kaffir lime leaves, which give curried dishes an authentic Thai flavor, can be found at your local Asian market; I keep a few small bags in my freezer and take them out as I need them. Remember that fish takes only a few minutes to cook, so be sure to add it last! Serve this curry over cooked brown jasmine rice for a satisfying meal.

1 tablespoon coconut oil or extra-virgin olive oil

1 onion, halved and sliced into crescent moons

4 carrots, sliced diagonally

4 or 5 garlic cloves, crushed

1 teaspoon ground turmeric

1 (14.5-ounce) can coconut milk

1 cup water, chicken broth, or fish stock

4 kaffir lime leaves

4 teaspoons red curry paste

2 tablespoons Thai fish sauce or coconut aminos

½ to 1 teaspoon Herbamare or sea salt

2 zucchini, sliced in half lengthwise and cut into half-moons

2 small red bell peppers, cored, seeded, and cut into 1-inch pieces

2 ripe tomatoes, diced

1½ to 2 pounds halibut fillet, any skin removed, cut into cubes

Handful of fresh Thai or Holy basil leaves, thinly sliced

1. In an 11-inch skillet or other large pan, heat the coconut oil over medium-high, then add the onion and sauté for about 5 minutes. Add the carrots and garlic, and sauté a few minutes more. Stir in the turmeric, coconut milk, water, lime leaves, curry paste, fish sauce, and Herbamare. Simmer for 5 to 7 minutes, or until the carrots are partway cooked.

2. Add the zucchini and bell peppers; simmer until all the veggies are crisp-tender, about 5 to 7 minutes more. Add the tomatoes and fish, and simmer for an additional 3 minutes, or until the fish is cooked through. Be careful not to stir too much, or the fish will fall apart. Sprinkle with the basil and serve.

apricot glazed chicken

MAKES 4 TO 6 SERVINGS

This chicken can made ahead and set in the fridge, covered, to marinate while you are at work. When you get home, drain off the marinade and pop the chicken in the oven. Serve with the Cabbage Salad with Mandarins and Mung Bean Sprouts (page 200) and cooked brown rice.

4 bone-in, skin-on organic chicken thighs

¼ cup fruit-sweetened apricot jam

¼ cup coconut aminos or wheat-free tamari (see Tip on page 158)

2 tablespoons extra-virgin olive oil or toasted sesame oil

1 to 2 teaspoons grated fresh ginger

1. Rinse the chicken, pat it dry, and place it in an 8-inch square or 7 by 11-inch baking dish. In a small bowl, whisk together the jam, coconut aminos, olive oil, and ginger, then pour over the chicken. Marinate for 30 minutes at room temperature, or cover the pan and place it in the refrigerator to marinate for up to 8 hours.

2. Preheat the oven to 400°F. Pour off any excess marinade from pan, and place it in the oven and bake the chicken for 25 to 30 minutes, or until the juices run clear.

INGREDIENT TIP

I use Bionaturae's sugar-free organic apricot jam in this recipe, or my own honey-sweetened homemade apricot jam.

NUTRITION TIP

Always purchase organic chicken. Nonorganic chicken, including "free-range" and "naturally raised," often contains high levels of arsenic. This heavy metal can easily get absorbed into the body, where it can cause certain nutrient deficiencies, such as of zinc and thiamin.

balsamic roasted chicken with figs and sweet onion

FREE OF

MAKES 6 TO 8 SERVINGS

This recipe is simple and kid-friendly, and the chicken is delicious even as leftovers! Serve the chicken with a large, raw green salad, which helps stimulate gastric acid secretion and proper digestion.

1 organic chicken, 3½ to 4 pounds
Herbamare or sea salt
Freshly ground black pepper
1 large sweet onion, chopped
8 to 10 fresh figs

¼ cup balsamic vinegar
¼ cup extra-virgin olive oil
1 tablespoon pure maple syrup
Sprigs of fresh rosemary

1. Preheat the oven to 450°F. Rinse the chicken under cold running water, pat it dry, then place it in a 9 by 13-inch baking dish or other roasting pan. Generously sprinkle with the Herbamare and pepper. Put some of the chopped onion in the cavity of the chicken and some on the bottom of the pan. Place the figs around the chicken.

2. Whisk together the vinegar, olive oil, and maple syrup in a small bowl or cup, then pour over the chicken. Place the rosemary sprigs on and around the chicken. Add about ½ cup water to the bottom of the pan. Roast the chicken for about 20 minutes to seal in the juices, then reduce the temperature to 325°F and roast for another 1½ hours, or until the juices run clear.

3. Remove the chicken from the pan and place it on a platter. Wait 10 minutes, then carve as desired. Place the cooked figs and sweet onions on the platter with the sliced chicken. Drizzle the pan juices over and serve.

roasted whole chicken with root vegetables

FREE OF

MAKES 6 TO 8 SERVINGS

In autumn, when root vegetables are in abundance, I add them to just about everything I cook. We usually serve a simple blanched kale salad with this meal, and possibly some Chia Dinner Rolls (page 124).

CHICKEN
1 organic chicken, 3½ to 4 pounds
½ cup Madeira wine
½ cup water
½ cup chopped celery
½ cup finely chopped shallots or red onion
Extra-virgin olive oil, for roasting
Sea salt and freshly ground black pepper

VEGETABLES
1 sweet potato, peeled and cut into chunks
2 Yukon Gold potatoes, cut into chunks

2 large carrots, cut into ½-inch rounds
2 parsnips, peeled and cut into ½-inch rounds
1 red onion, cut into chunks
¼ cup extra-virgin olive oil
½ teaspoon sea salt

HERBS
5 sprigs fresh thyme
1 tablespoon chopped fresh sage
1 tablespoon chopped fresh rosemary
2 tablespoons fresh marjoram leaves

1. Preheat the oven to 450°F. Rinse the chicken under cold running water, pat it dry, then place it in a 9 by 13-inch baking dish or other roasting pan. Pour the wine and water over the chicken. Place the celery and shallots in the cavity. Drizzle a little olive oil over the chicken and generously sprinkle with salt and pepper.

2. Place the prepared vegetables, olive oil, and salt in a large bowl and toss well. Place in the pan around the chicken. Sprinkle the chicken and vegetables with the herbs. Roast the chicken for about 20 minutes to seal in the juices, then reduce the heat to 325°F and continue to roast for another 1½ hours, or until the juices run clear. Remove the chicken from the pan and place on a platter. Wait 10 minutes, then carve the meat. Place the roasted

vegetables in a serving bowl. Pour the pan juices into a gravy boat and serve alongside the chicken and vegetables.

INGREDIENT TIP

In autumn, the herbs used in this recipe are all right there at my fingertips in my front garden. However, feel free to use whatever you have on hand or use a few tablespoons of poultry seasoning in place of the fresh herbs.

KITCHEN TIP

Cut the root vegetables into largish chunks. If they are too small, they will get quite mushy during the long roasting time.

moroccan roasted chicken

FREE OF

MAKES 6 TO 8 SERVINGS

This is an easy weeknight meal that can be prepared in 10 minutes. Some days we are so busy with after-school activities and other events that I need to put together a balanced meal quickly. I serve this over cooked millet with a green salad, sautéed kale, or steamed green beans.

3 or 4 bone-in, skin-on organic chicken breasts, split in half

1 small red onion, cut into large chunks

1 Meyer lemon, cut into wedges

½ to 1 cup dried apricots

1 teaspoon Herbamare or sea salt

1 teaspoon ground cumin

1 teaspoon ground coriander

1 teaspoon ground cardamom

1 teaspoon freshly ground black pepper

½ teaspoon ground turmeric

Pinch of cayenne pepper

2 to 3 tablespoons butter or coconut oil

Chopped fresh cilantro, for garnish

Green onion slices, for garnish

1. Preheat the oven to 425°F. Rinse the chicken under cold running water, pat it dry, and place in one layer in a casserole dish or 9 by 13-inch baking pan. Arrange the onion chunks, lemon wedges, and apricots around the chicken.

2. In a small bowl, mix the Herbamare and spices. Sprinkle the spice mixture over the chicken, then dot with the butter. Roast for 30 to 40 minutes, or until the juices run clear. Slice the meat from the bone and serve with the roasted apricots and red onion, as well as the juices from the bottom of the roasting pan. Garnish with the cilantro and green onions.

INGREDIENT TIP

If you are on a nightshade-free diet, then simply omit the cayenne pepper to make this recipe. If you are dairy-free, use coconut oil instead of butter.

NUTRITION TIP

Purchase organic, sulfite-free apricots. Sulfite is a preservative that reduces discoloration and oxidation—you'll notice that organic apricots are a dark brownish-orange because they don't have sulfites added. The FDA estimates that 1 out of 100 people have a reaction to sulfites; a sensitivity to sulfites may lead to difficulty with breathing, hives, excessive sneezing, or swelling of the throat. And this may be exacerbated by a deficiency in molybdenum, a mineral commonly found in legumes. When "contains sulfites" is listed on a food label, that could include sulfur dioxide, sodium sulfite, sodium bisulfite, potassium bisulfite, sodium metabisulfite, or potassium metabisulfite.

chipotle-lime roasted chicken

FREE OF

MAKES 6 TO 8 SERVINGS

This is another of those easy meals, one that can be prepared in minutes. I use any leftover chicken to make chicken salads, such as wild rice and chicken or the Chicken Salad Lettuce Wraps (page 366). When I put the chicken in the oven, I also put in four or five small sweet potatoes to bake. Serve this chicken with baked sweet potatoes, quinoa, and a green salad.

3 or 4 bone-in, skin-on organic chicken
 breasts, split in half
1 teaspoon Herbamare or sea salt
1 to 2 teaspoons chipotle chile powder

2 to 3 tablespoons butter or coconut oil
1 lime, cut into wedges
Chopped fresh cilantro, for garnish
Green onion slices, for garnish

Preheat the oven to 425°F. Rinse the chicken under cold running water, pat it dry, and place it in a single layer in a casserole dish or 9 by 13-inch baking pan. Sprinkle with the Herbamare and chile powder, then dot each breast piece with the butter. Gently squeeze the lime wedges over the chicken, then add them to the pan. Roast for 30 to 40 minutes, or until the juices run clear. Garnish with the cilantro and green onions.

VARIATION: If you have more time, you can slow-cook the chicken at 325°F for 60 to 75 minutes, which makes it more flavorful and tender.

chicken pot pie

FREE OF

MAKES 6 SERVINGS

Chicken pot pie is a timeless classic that never gets boring. Our children love this meal and always ask for seconds—in fact, I double the recipe and bake it in a 10 by 14-inch glass baking dish! This is delicious served on a cold winter's evening alongside the Sautéed Winter Greens with Caramelized Onions (page 230) or a fresh green salad.

1 to 2 tablespoons extra-virgin olive oil

1 onion, diced

1½ cups diced carrots

1½ cups chopped green beans

1½ cups diced red potatoes

2 cups Homemade Chicken Broth (page 156)

2 to 3 tablespoons sweet rice flour or arrowroot powder

2 cups chopped cooked chicken

1 teaspoon dried thyme

1 teaspoon dried marjoram

1 cup frozen peas

½ cup chopped fresh parsley

Herbamare or sea salt

Freshly ground black pepper

Dough for single Flaky Grain-Free Pie Crust (page 407) or Gluten-Free Pie Crust (page 408)

1. Preheat the oven to 350°F. Heat a large skillet over medium and add the olive oil and onion; sauté for 5 to 6 minutes, until golden. Add the carrots, green beans, and potatoes; sauté for about 10 minutes more, being careful not to let the vegetables brown.

2. In a medium bowl, whisk together the broth and flour, then pour into the skillet with the vegetables. Add the chicken and dried herbs; simmer, uncovered, for 5 to 10 minutes, or until thickened. Turn off the heat and add the peas and parsley. Season to taste with Herbamare and pepper. Pour the filling into a 9½-inch deep-dish pie plate.

3. Roll out the ball of dough between two pieces of waxed paper. Carefully remove the top piece of waxed paper, then pick up the crust and flip it over onto the pie filling. Peel off the other piece of waxed paper. Tuck in the crust edges or trim them off with a knife. Set the pie on a baking sheet to catch any overflow and bake for 45 to 60 minutes, or until the filling is bubbling up and the crust is cooked.

KITCHEN TIP

I always make some chicken broth from a leftover roasted whole chicken. I pull the remaining meat from the bones and store it in a container for uses such as this pot pie. Then I simmer the skin and bones with onions, carrots, celery, herbs, Herbamare, and a dash of raw apple cider vinegar to create a rich, healing chicken broth. After it is strained, I store the broth in quart jars in my freezer. See page 156 for more details.

grain-free chicken nuggets

FREE OF

MAKES 4 TO 6 SERVINGS

This is the healthiest take on a chicken nugget that I've been able to create. The low-glycemic almond flour, organic chicken breasts, and heat-stable coconut oil make them so nutritious. Serve these nuggets with the Honey Mustard Dressing (page 222) for dipping, along with a green salad. For optimal digestion, serve the meal with a few spoonfuls of raw sauerkraut or cultured vegetables.

2 to 3 teaspoons poultry seasoning

½ to 1 teaspoon Herbamare or sea salt

4 tablespoons arrowroot powder

4 tablespoons water

1½ cups almond flour

1½ pounds boneless, skinless organic chicken breasts

6 tablespoons coconut oil, for cooking

1. Set out two shallow, wide bowls. In one, mix the poultry seasoning, Herbamare, arrowroot powder, and water. In the other, place the almond flour. Rinse the chicken breasts under cold running water, pat dry, and cut them into small chunks of equal size. Dip the chunks into the arrowroot slurry and mix around to coat evenly. Then toss a few of the chunks at a time in the almond flour. The almond flour will feel moist; you can press some of it into each nugget to help with the coating.

2. Heat a deep 11- or 12-inch skillet over medium and add 3 tablespoons of the coconut oil. When the oil is hot, add half the chicken nuggets and cook for about 3 minutes on each side. Transfer to a plate. Add the remaining 3 tablespoons coconut oil to the skillet and cook the rest of the chicken nuggets.

minty chicken-zucchini kebabs

FREE OF

MAKES 6 TO 8 SERVINGS

We have a little herb garden outside our front door. I planted spearmint the year we bought the house. A month later, I began pulling it all out because it began to take over the garden. I thought I had eradicated it, but it began to creep back the next year. Mint is impossible to get rid of. I learned later that it should be planted in a bottomless bucket to contain the roots. Now I have mint every summer that can be made into tasty recipes like this one. You can add more vegetables to the kebabs to make the meat go further. For instance, try adding mushrooms, peppers, onions, or tomatoes. Serve these kebabs with a large garden salad and quinoa for a balanced meal. Just be sure to allow sufficient time for the marinating before you grill.

1½ to 2 pounds boneless, skinless organic chicken breasts, cut into 1-inch cubes

4 or 5 small zucchini, cut into thick rounds

1 recipe Pepper-Mint Dressing and Marinade (page 327)

1. Alternately thread the chunks of chicken and zucchini on bamboo skewers, then arrange in a 9 by 13-inch or 10 by 14-inch glass baking dish. Pour the dressing over the kebabs and turn them a few times to coat evenly. Cover, refrigerate, and let marinate for 30 minutes to 4 hours.

2. Heat your grill to medium-high. Arrange the kebabs on the grill and grill for 10 to 15 minutes, turning two or three times during cooking, until the chicken is cooked through and the juices run clear.

> **NUTRITION TIP**
>
> Chicken is an excellent source of B vitamins, particularly niacin. A deficiency of niacin in the diet has been linked to DNA damage. In the 1950s, Linus Pauling and others found that a niacin deficiency may be associated with neuropsychiatric disorders. Tryptophan is the precursor to the neurotransmitters serotonin and melatonin. When your body is deficient in niacin, it uses 60 tryptophan molecules to make one niacin molecule, leading to a decrease in available tryptophan for making these vital neurotransmitters that are so responsible for regulating mood and sleep.

slow-cooked chicken tacos

MAKES 8 TO 10 SERVINGS

This recipe can be made ahead of time, refrigerated or frozen, and then reheated when needed. It also works well made in a slow cooker. The taco filling can be used to fill corn or gluten-free flour tortillas, lettuce or cabbage leaves, or even collard greens. Add brown rice, avocado, a squeeze of lime juice, and cherry tomato halves for a complete, balanced meal. Store any leftover filling in the refrigerator for up to five days or freeze in portion sizes for up to six months.

1 dried ancho chile, seeded

1 cup boiling water

4 garlic cloves

½ teaspoon chipotle chile powder, or more to taste

1 to 2 tablespoons ground cumin

3 teaspoons sea salt or Herbamare

3 pounds boneless, skinless organic chicken breasts or thigh meat

1 onion, diced

3 cups tomato puree

2 to 3 tablespoons extra-virgin olive oil

1. Preheat the oven to 325°F. Place the ancho chile in a small bowl and pour the boiling water over it; let it soak for 5 to 10 minutes. Add the chile and its soaking water to a blender along with the garlic, chile powder, cumin, and salt. Blend on high until pureed.

2. Place the spice puree in a large casserole dish and add the chicken, onion, tomato puree, and olive oil. Cover and bake for 1 hour. Remove the cover, stir, and bake uncovered for an additional hour, or until the chicken is very tender and shreds easily.

3. Use the back of a large spoon to mash the chicken until it falls apart. Taste and adjust the seasonings, then use as a filling for tacos or serve over quinoa.

INGREDIENT TIP

I use Bionaturae Strained Tomatoes when I need tomato puree. Ancho chiles are dried poblano peppers; I buy mine in the bulk spice section at my local co-op.

---

herb-roasted turkey breast

If you have ever felt intimidated by the idea of roasting a whole turkey, try a turkey breast instead. You can make the marinade ahead and let the turkey breast marinate for 3 to 24 hours in the refrigerator. Then just pop it into the oven and walk away. Serve this with baked potatoes, roasted winter squash, or the Mushroom Millet Risotto (page 259) and a green salad.

A 3½- to 4-pound bone-in turkey breast
½ cup dry white wine
¼ cup extra-virgin olive oil
¼ cup fresh sage leaves
¼ cup fresh rosemary leaves

¼ cup fresh thyme leaves
¼ cup fresh oregano leaves
2 small shallots
2 teaspoons Herbamare or sea salt
1 teaspoon black peppercorns

1. Rinse the turkey breast, pat it dry, and place it in the smallest roasting pan that will hold it. I use a stoneware roasting dish with a lid, which works perfectly. Place the remaining ingredients into a blender and blend until smooth and creamy. Pour the marinade over the turkey, cover the pan, and let marinate in the refrigerator for at least 3 hours or up to 24 hours. (For longer marinating you may want to place the turkey breast and marinade into a large zippered bag.)

2. Preheat the oven to 325°F. Place the pan with the turkey and marinade in the oven with the lid on. Bake for about 1 hour, then remove the lid, baste the turkey with some of the liquid at the bottom of the pan, and return it to the oven to roast, uncovered, for 1 to 1½ hours more, or until a meat thermometer inserted in the thickest part reads 170°F.

turkey quinoa meatballs

FREE OF

MAKES 8 SERVINGS

The food processor helps bind these together without eggs. I use a 14-cup processor, but an 11-cup will work as well. If you don't have any homemade marinara sauce on hand, then use your favorite organic store-bought Italian-type pasta sauce. Serve these meatballs and sauce over brown rice noodles, quinoa, or baked spaghetti squash with a large green salad. Additionally, these meatballs freeze amazingly well. I like to freeze them in serving-size containers to have a quick lunch ready to go when needed.

MEATBALLS
2 to 3 tablespoons extra-virgin olive oil
1 onion, diced
3 or 4 garlic cloves, crushed
2 pounds ground organic turkey
2 cups cooked quinoa
1 tablespoon Italian seasoning
1 teaspoon paprika
1 to 2 teaspoons Herbamare or sea salt
½ to 1 teaspoon freshly ground black pepper
Large handful of fresh parsley

SAUCE
2 cups chicken or turkey broth
2 tablespoons arrowroot powder
½ to 1 cup Fresh Tomato–Basil Marinara Sauce (page 478)

1. Heat a 10-inch skillet over medium-high and add 1 tablespoon of the olive oil and the onion; sauté for 5 to 10 minutes, or until softened and beginning to change color. Add the garlic and sauté for another minute or so.

2. Place the turkey, quinoa, Italian seasoning, paprika, Herbamare, pepper, and parsley into a food processor fitted with the "s" blade. Add the onion and garlic, then process until well combined and the ingredients are broken down (such as the parsley and cooked onions). You may need to pulse the mixture a few times and scrape down the sides. Scoop portions of the mixture and roll into meatballs. Set on a plate.

3. Preheat the oven to 325 °F. Heat a large skillet over medium to medium-high, then add another tablespoon of the olive oil. Place only enough meatballs in the pan so as to cook them without steaming. Sauté for about 5 minutes, moving them around a little so they cook on all sides. (They won't be cooked completely at this point so don't sample one.) Add more oil in between batches. Reserve the pan.

4. Place the sautéed meatballs in a 9 by 13-inch baking pan to cool briefly. Meanwhile, combine the broth, arrowroot powder, and marinara sauce in a bowl and whisk to dissolve the arrowroot. Pour the sauce into the reserved pan, and simmer for about 2 minutes, scraping up any browned bits on the bottom. Then pour the sauce over the meatballs in the baking dish. Cover and bake for about 45 minutes. Remove the cover and bake for 15 to 20 minutes more.

nourishing meat loaf

MAKES ABOUT 6 TO 8 SERVINGS

This nightshade-free meat loaf is infused with the flavors of bacon and honey mustard. Serve it with baked winter squash and either sautéed kale or a large green salad for a hearty dinner. The egg in this recipe helps hold the mixture together, but the loaf can be made without it, with good results.

MEAT LOAF

1 tablespoon extra-virgin olive oil

1 small red onion, cut into quarters

1 large carrot, coarsely chopped

2 celery stalks, coarsely chopped

2 pounds ground grass-fed beef

1 large organic egg, lightly beaten (optional)

½ cup chestnut flour (see Tip)

1½ teaspoons dried thyme

1½ teaspoons Herbamare or sea salt

½ teaspoon freshly ground black pepper

½ teaspoon garlic powder

Small handful of fresh parsley, chopped

TOPPING

2 tablespoons organic yellow mustard

2 tablespoons raw honey

4 strips organic bacon

1. Preheat the oven to 350°F. Coat a 9 by 5-inch loaf pan with a little olive oil. Place the tablespoon of olive oil in a large skillet over medium heat. Place the onion, carrot, and celery into a food processor fitted with the "s" blade; pulse until finely chopped, then add to the skillet and sauté for 5 to 10 minutes, until soft.

2. Combine the beef, egg, chestnut flour, thyme, Herbamare, pepper, garlic powder, and parsley in a large bowl. Add the onion mixture. Use your hands or a large spoon to blend well. Evenly press the loaf mixture into the loaf pan.

3. In a small bowl, combine the mustard and honey. Spread evenly over the top of the loaf. Lay the bacon strips on top. Bake, uncovered, for about 60 minutes. Let cool for 10 to 20 minutes before slicing and serving.

INGREDIENT TIP

Chestnut flour is a delicious grain-free flour made from ground chestnuts. It's lower in fat and higher in carbohydrates than other nut-based flours. Use it in cookies, crepes, or a gluten-free flour mix for baking breads and muffins. You can find it online at www.Nuts.com.

---

sloppy joes

MAKES 4 TO 5 SERVINGS

Try serving this with the Sourdough Buckwheat Burger Buns (page 115) or the Grain-Free Burger Buns (page 117) and a side of Beet Sauerkraut (page 473) for a balanced, nourishing meal. Cultured vegetables, like sauerkraut, help stimulate gastric acid secretion in the stomach, which is essential for properly digesting meat proteins.

1 tablespoon extra-virgin olive oil or butter

1 small onion, finely diced

1 small green bell pepper, cored, seeded, and finely chopped

1 or 2 garlic cloves, crushed

½ to 1 teaspoon Herbamare or sea salt

½ teaspoon paprika

¼ teaspoon celery salt

¼ teaspoon dry mustard powder

Pinch of ground cloves

Freshly ground black pepper

1 pound ground grass-fed beef

A 7-ounce jar tomato paste (about ½ cup)

½ cup water, or more as needed

2 tablespoons coconut sugar

1 tablespoon coconut vinegar

1. Heat a 10-inch skillet over medium and add the olive oil, onion, and bell pepper; sauté about 5 minutes, until softened. Add the garlic, Herbamare, paprika, celery salt, dry mustard, cloves, and pepper; sauté a minute more. Stir in the beef and cook, breaking it up with a spatula as it cooks, until it is no longer pink.

2. Reduce the heat to medium-low and add the tomato paste, water, coconut sugar, and vinegar; cover and simmer for 7 to 10 minutes, adding more water if necessary. Taste and adjust the seasonings, if needed. Serve.

slow-cooked beef stew

FREE OF

MAKES 4 SERVINGS

During the deepest, coldest part of winter, I crave warming, hearty stews such as this one. Using a slow cooker can make getting dinner on the table an easy task, especially on busy days. This stew can be started in the morning before you go to work or just after lunchtime if you are home. I like to serve it over mashed potatoes with a raw cabbage slaw. Sometimes I sauté the onion before adding it to the cooker to give the stew more flavor.

1 onion, diced

3 or 4 large carrots, cut into ¼-inch rounds

½ pound button mushrooms, quartered

1 pound boneless grass-fed beef for stew, cubed

½ cup water

¼ cup dry red wine

¼ cup tomato puree or sauce

2 tablespoons arrowroot powder or sweet rice flour

1½ teaspoons sea salt or Herbamare

½ teaspoon freshly ground black pepper

Place the onion, carrots, mushrooms, and beef in a 3-quart slow cooker. In a small bowl, whisk together the water, wine, tomato puree, and arrowroot powder. Pour into the slow cooker and add the salt and pepper. Mix well. There won't be enough liquid to cover the ingredients; this is correct, so don't be tempted to add more liquid. Cook on high for 4 hours or on low for 8 hours. Sometimes I crack the lid for the last 45 minutes or so to cook off some of the liquid and thicken the stew.

> **NUTRITION TIP**
>
> Why grass-fed beef? Grass-fed or "pasture finished" beef is higher in essential omega-3 fatty acids, lower in antibiotic and pesticide residues, and has no growth hormones. This safer type of cattle husbandry simultaneously reduces the use of tractor fuel, pesticides, herbicides, fertilizers, and GMO feed crops. Cattle farming is responsible for 28 percent of global methane emissions, which contribute to global warming. When cows are exclusively fed grasses, their production of these greenhouse gases decreases.

slow-cooked mexican beef roast

FREE OF

MAKES 8 SERVINGS

This easy, flavorful roast can be shredded for beef tacos or quesadillas, or simply served with mashed yams and sautéed dark leafy greens. I like to store whole tomatoes from the summer harvest in my freezer and thaw a few on my counter before adding them to this recipe—that's a great alternative to canned tomatoes! If fresh chiles are unavailable, use 2 to 3 teaspoons pure chile powder.

A 2- to 3-pound boneless grass-fed beef roast
1 small onion
2 to 4 garlic cloves
2 to 3 cups diced ripe tomatoes

2 to 3 jalapeño peppers or serrano chiles
1 tablespoon ground cumin
2 teaspoons sea salt
1 cup water

1. Preheat the oven to 325°F. Place the roast in a small roasting pan that has a lid—the smaller and taller the pan, the better, so as to keep the liquid up around the roast, ensuring it stays moist.

2. Place the onion, garlic, tomatoes, chiles, cumin, salt, and water into a blender and blend on high until smooth and pureed. Pour over the roast,

cover, and cook for about 4 hours, or until the meat is very tender and can shred easily. (For tacos, shred and serve with corn tortillas, shredded cabbage, and salsa.)

VARIATION: You can also make this recipe using a slow cooker. For best results, cook on low for about 8 hours.

dressings, dips, and sauces

Store-bought condiments often have many ingredients that are unnecessary for our bodies, but by preparing your own you know exactly what is in your food. Plus, having a variety of homemade dressings, dips, salsas, and sauces on hand means you can make fun meals without much effort. Use them to dress greens, dip vegetables or crackers, as a sauce over meat and grains, or in sandwiches or wraps. Steamed greens over cooked quinoa with grilled salmon is rather plain, but a drizzle of peanut-ginger sauce, fresh plum sauce, or mango chutney elevates your meal to the next level!

SALAD DRESSINGS

Have you ever looked at the labels on commercial salad dressings, including natural and organic brands? Most have gums and stabilizers, sugars, highly processed vegetable oils, and a long list of other ingredients. Since a homemade dressing can be whipped up in two minutes or less, there really isn't any need to rely on commercial salad dressings.

It's our habit to have at least two different homemade salad dressings in our refrigerator every week. We like to reuse small jam jars for salad dressings. Just add all your ingredients and shake! Store any unused dressing in a glass jar in the refrigerator. Olive oil will harden in the refrigerator, so when you are ready to use your dressing again, simply place the jar under hot running water or put it in a bowl of hot water to "thin" out the oil, then shake well and serve. See the "Salads and Vegetables" chapter for additional dressing recipes.

DIPS AND SPREADS

You'll find a variety of dips and spreads in this chapter and learn how to make from scratch all your comfort favorites, like sour cream and red pepper dip. From homemade egg-free mayonnaise to herbed hummus and raw vegetable-seed dips, there is something for everyone.

We like to make large batches of bean dips and then freeze them in small containers. This way we can take out a small amount when we need it for school lunches or a healthy snack when nothing else is readily available. Generally, recipes using nuts and seeds don't freeze well; instead, store them in covered glass containers in your refrigerator for up to a week.

Spread bean or raw vegetable-seed dips on tortillas, then add shredded carrots, strips of cucumbers, sprouts, and lettuce to create nutritious wraps. Or set out the dip in a small bowl surrounded by a variety of raw vegetables. Carrots and celery are old faithfuls, but consider trying thinly sliced kohlrabi or homemade kale chips.

FRESH SALSAS AND CHUTNEYS

In the summertime, fresh tomatoes and peppers are in abundance, and it is our favorite time to serve a simple meal of cooked beans, quinoa or rice, chopped salad greens from our garden, and a fresh salsa. Chutneys complement Indian flavors quite nicely, such as in the spicy curries and main-dish recipes in this book. Cooked chutneys freeze well, but fresh, raw salsas and chutneys do not and should be kept in the refrigerator for only a few days. Store them in small glass jars or glass containers.

10 Tips for Dressings, Dips, Salsas, and Sauces

1. Store salad dressings in small glass jars in your refrigerator.

2. Bring the dressing to room temperature before serving, as olive oil partially solidifies in the refrigerator. You can place your jar of dressing in a bowl of hot water or put it under running hot water to quickly warm before serving.

3. Salad dressings made with an acid—vinegar or citrus—can also be used as a marinade for meat, fish, or vegetables.

4. Leftover salad tossed in dressing won't keep, so unless you are serving a salad to a large crowd it is best to let each person dress his or her own salad. You can easily store the undressed leftover salad greens in the refrigerator for days and take a serving out when needed.

5. Most sauces, especially those thickened with a starch, will firm up once chilled in the refrigerator. To reheat and serve, simply place the sauce in a small pot, add 1 to 2 table-spoons water, and gently reheat over low heat, whisking occasionally.

6. Sauces made with tomatoes freeze well, such as pizza sauce or barbecue sauce.

7. Bean dips freeze very well. When ready to use, remove them from the freezer and let them thaw in the refrigerator.

8. Use dips to add extra flavor and protein to sandwiches and wraps.

9. Salsas and chutneys actually taste better the day after they are made. The more time the ingredients have to mingle, the better the flavors.

10. Store freshly made salsa in the refrigerator for three to four days.

SAUCES

Sauces have been around for centuries. During Roman times, sauces made from a variety of seasonings were used to disguise the taste of meat that wasn't very fresh. Now, they continue to be used to marinate meat, fish, or vegetables and can be drizzled over the finished meal. Sauces are made with a liquid base such as vegetable juice, broth, milk, nut butters mixed with water, or blended tomatoes. They are generally thickened with heat or sometimes a starch such as arrowroot powder, though I've also created some very thick raw sauces in the blender using soaked nuts, garlic, spices, and soft dates. Sauces can literally be made in a matter of minutes, though those that require cooking need constant attention and whisking so they don't burn. Many of the sauces in this chapter freeze well; check the headnote of each recipe for storage tips.

everyday salad dressing

FREE OF

MAKES 1½ CUPS

I like to store this dressing in the refrigerator to have on hand for all the fabulous greens my children pick from our garden during the spring and summer. It can also be a marinade for grilled chicken or fish. You can use your favorite combination of fresh herbs in this recipe—ours is oregano and basil. Store this in a sealed glass jar in the refrigerator for up to two weeks.

¾ cup extra-virgin olive oil

¼ cup red wine vinegar

2 tablespoons balsamic vinegar

2 tablespoons raw honey

Juice of 1 small lemon

6 garlic cloves, crushed

2 to 3 tablespoons minced red bell pepper

2 to 3 tablespoons minced fresh herbs

¾ to 1 teaspoon sea salt or Herbamare

½ teaspoon freshly ground black pepper

Place all the ingredients in a glass jar, cover, and shake. Taste and adjust the seasonings, if necessary.

dairy-free ranch dressing

FREE OF

MAKES ABOUT 2 CUPS

This dressing is better after the flavors have had time to meld. Give it about a day and the tartness from the lemon juice will lessen. Use this as a salad dressing over crispy greens or as a dip for carrot and celery sticks. Plan three hours ahead for the nuts to soak, plus the overnight to refrigerate. You can store the dressing in the refrigerator for up to ten days.

1 cup raw cashews, soaked for 3 hours

1 cup water

2 garlic cloves

½ cup extra-virgin olive oil

¼ cup fresh lemon juice

2 tablespoons raw apple cider vinegar

1 to 1½ teaspoons Herbamare or sea salt

1 tablespoon dried dill

1 teaspoon dried thyme

1 teaspoon dried basil

1 to 2 teaspoons cracked black peppercorns

1. Rinse and drain the cashews. Place them along with the water and garlic into a high-powered blender fitted with a sharp blade. Blend until very smooth and creamy, then add the remaining ingredients and blend until just combined.

2. Pour into a glass jar and refrigerate overnight. The dressing will thicken up in the refrigerator.

Shake and pour over your favorite salad or use as a dip for raw vegetable sticks.

VARIATION: Replace the dried herbs with fresh. I like to add a handful of fresh parsley and dill.

pepper-mint dressing and marinade

FREE OF

MAKES ABOUT 1¼ CUPS

This lemony, peppery, garlicky, minty salad dressing is fantastic over a crisp romaine lettuce salad topped with toasted pine nuts, green onions, and shredded carrots. It also works as a marinade for grilled meat or vegetables. I only use the shallot if it's going to be a marinade for fish or chicken. You can store the dressing in the refrigerator for up to ten days.

½ cup packed fresh spearmint leaves

½ cup fresh lemon juice

4 or 5 garlic cloves

1 small shallot (optional)

1 teaspoon whole black peppercorns

1 teaspoon sea salt

¾ cup extra-virgin olive oil

Place all the ingredients except the olive oil into a blender. Blend on high until very smooth, 1 to 2 minutes. Add the olive oil, blending on low speed until just incorporated.

mint tahini sauce

FREE OF

MAKES ABOUT 1½ CUPS

Tahini is made from ground sesame seeds and is very high in calcium. You can reduce the water called for in this recipe to make it into a sauce; if so, serve the sauce over the Sweet Potato Falafels (page 294). Store the dressing in the refrigerator for up to ten days.

½ cup sesame tahini

½ cup fresh lemon juice

¼ cup extra-virgin olive oil

4 to 6 tablespoons water

Handful of fresh mint leaves

2 garlic cloves, crushed

½ to 1 teaspoon sea salt

Place all the ingredients into a blender and blend until smooth. Taste and adjust the seasonings, if necessary.

chipotle barbecue sauce

MAKES ABOUT 4 CUPS

Use this sauce to marinate chicken for the grill or to simmer with cooked beans. It is also a great dipping sauce for the Grain-Free Chicken Nuggets (page 312). Store any unused sauce in a glass jar in the refrigerator for up to ten days or freeze for longer storage.

¼ cup extra-virgin olive oil

½ cup diced onion

6 to 8 garlic cloves, coarsely chopped

A 24-ounce jar strained tomatoes or tomato sauce (see Tip on page 314)

½ cup pure maple syrup

½ cup raw apple cider vinegar

1 tablespoon blackstrap molasses

2 teaspoons Herbamare or sea salt

1 to 2 teaspoons chipotle chile powder

1 to 2 teaspoons smoked paprika

½ to 1 teaspoon freshly ground black pepper

Water, if needed

1. Heat a 3-quart saucepan over medium and add the olive oil. Let the oil heat up for a minute, then add the onion and sauté for about 10 minutes, or until very soft and golden brown. Add the garlic and sauté a minute more. Add the remaining ingredients except the water, stir, reduce the heat to medium-low, cover, and simmer for 15 to 20 minutes, stirring occasionally.

2. Transfer the sauce to a blender and blend until smooth. If you would like a thinner sauce, add a little water. Taste and adjust the seasonings, if necessary.

easy homemade pizza sauce

FREE OF

MAKES ABOUT ¾ CUP

I use one batch of this sauce for a 12-inch pizza, baking the pizza on a 12 by 15-inch stoneware baking sheet. I also use Bionaturae's tomato paste because it is packed in glass (found at most food co-ops and health food stores). When the jars are empty, I soak them in hot water to remove the labels, wash them, and use them to store dried herbs. They also make great travel cups for smoothies. You can store any unused sauce in the refrigerator for up to ten days.

A 7-ounce jar tomato paste

2 tablespoons extra-virgin olive oil

2 teaspoons honey or coconut sugar

2 teaspoons dried Italian herbs

1 teaspoon onion powder

½ teaspoon garlic powder

½ teaspoon Herbamare or sea salt

2 to 3 tablespoons water

Place all the ingredients except the water in a medium bowl and mix well. Add enough water to reach your desired consistency.

oven-roasted pizza sauce

FREE OF

MAKES ABOUT 2 CUPS

Use this fabulous sauce to top your favorite pizza or as a dip for the Rosemary Sea Salt Breadsticks (page 121). If you have an abundance of tomatoes in your garden, make a few batches of this sauce and freeze in glass jars for up to a year.

2 to 3 pounds Roma (plum) tomatoes, chopped

½ cup diced shallots or onion

4 to 6 garlic cloves, coarsely chopped

½ cup chopped fresh basil

1 teaspoon honey or coconut sugar

1 teaspoon sea salt

¼ to ½ teaspoon red pepper flakes

4 to 6 tablespoons extra-virgin olive oil

Preheat the oven to 450°F. Place all the ingredients in a 9 by 13-inch or 10 by 14-inch baking pan and toss well. Roast for 60 to 70 minutes, stirring the sauce occasionally. Lightly mash with the back of a spoon.

fresh thai green curry sauce

FREE OF

MAKES ABOUT 2½ CUPS

This delicious Thai-style sauce can be made in about 20 minutes. My favorite way to use this is to sauté some fresh vegetables in a little coconut oil until crisp-tender, then add the sauce to the pan and simmer for a minute or two. I then serve this over basmati rice. I also poach salmon and halibut in this sauce, and I serve the fish over a bed of steamed spinach and basmati rice, garnished with Thai basil leaves. In the summer, when the cilantro is taking over our garden and fresh chiles are available at the market, I freeze the blended sauce in glass jars to use during the winter months. This sauce will keep in the fridge for up to a week.

1 (14.5-ounce) can coconut milk

2 handfuls of fresh cilantro (leaves and stems)

2 small shallots

4 garlic cloves

1 to 2 jalapeño peppers, seeded

A 1-inch piece of fresh ginger, peeled

2 teaspoons coconut sugar

1 teaspoon sea salt

½ teaspoon grated lime zest

¼ to ½ cup water

Place all the ingredients except the water into a blender; add ¼ cup water and blend until smooth, adding the remaining ¼ cup to reach desired consistency. Pour into a small pot and simmer for 10 to 15 minutes, uncovered, until thickened. Or pour over some sautéed vegetables in a skillet pan and simmer for a few minutes.

VARIATION: For a spicier sauce, use 2 to 4 whole Thai chiles (with the seeds) in place of the jalapeños.

garlic ginger peanut sauce

FREE OF

MAKES ABOUT 1 CUP

We love to use this sauce to top sautéed dark leafy greens and quinoa, or as a dip for the Thai Salad Wraps (page 363). You can also thin it with a small amount of water and use it as a salad dressing. If you are allergic to peanuts, replace the peanut butter with sunflower seed butter. Store in a covered glass container for up to five days in the refrigerator.

½ cup creamy organic peanut butter

½ cup water

2 tablespoons toasted sesame oil

1½ tablespoons wheat-free tamari or coconut aminos (see Tip on page 158)

1 tablespoon brown rice vinegar or coconut vinegar

1 or 2 garlic cloves

A 1-inch piece of ginger, peeled

Pinch of red pepper flakes

Place all the ingredients into a blender and blend until smooth. Pour into small serving dishes to use as a dip or add a little more water and use as a salad dressing.

ginger plum sauce

FREE OF

MAKES 2 CUPS

This recipe creates a beautiful purple-hued sauce, reminiscent of sweet-and-sour sauce. In the summertime here in the Pacific Northwest, we go around town and pick boxes full of fresh Italian prune plums straight from the trees. I pit and freeze many of them to use for sauces like this one throughout the year. Dip nori rolls into this sauce or drizzle it over sautéed vegetables and rice. Use it as a dip for chicken. We love it over grilled salmon, too! Store any unused sauce in a covered glass container in the refrigerator for up to a week. The sauce may also be frozen in small jars for later use.

1 pound fresh Italian prune plums, pitted

½ cup organic apple juice

1 tablespoon arrowroot powder

2 or 3 garlic cloves, crushed

2 to 3 teaspoons grated fresh ginger

3 to 4 tablespoons finely chopped shallots

2 tablespoons brown rice vinegar

1 tablespoon raw honey

½ to 1 teaspoon sea salt

Place all the ingredients in a 2-quart stainless steel saucepan and whisk to dissolve the arrowroot powder in the juice. Simmer over medium-low heat for about 25 minutes, covered, or until it is thickened and transluscent. Use an immersion blender to puree the sauce in the pot until smooth, or transfer to a blender and blend until smooth. Simmer for 5 to 10 minutes more, or until thickened and clear.

VARIATION: If you can tolerate soy products, then replace the sea salt with about 2 tablespoons wheat-free tamari.

cranberry-pear sauce

FREE OF

MAKES ABOUT 2½ CUPS

This flavorful cranberry sauce can be served over turkey, roasted salmon, and even on top of oatmeal for breakfast! The pears sweeten the tart and tangy cranberries, thereby reducing the need for a ton of sugar. I always use ¼ cup of coconut sugar, which is just enough to sweeten it a little but still keep it tart. You could add more if you like it sweeter.

2½ cups fresh or frozen cranberries (about 10 ounces)

2 small ripe pears, peeled, cored, and diced

½ cup fresh orange juice or apple cider

¼ cup coconut sugar

¼ teaspoon ground allspice

1 cinnamon stick

1. Place all the ingredients in a 2-quart saucepan and bring to a boil; reduce the heat to medium-low, and simmer for about 7 minutes. Use a large spoon to mash the pears and cranberries until the sauce begins to thicken, and continue cooking until thickened and translucent. The sauce will thicken more as it cools.

2. Remove the cinnamon stick, cover, and refrigerate until ready to use. Serve cold or heat on low to warm it slightly.

egg-free mayonnaise

MAKES ABOUT 1½ CUPS

You will need a high-powered blender to make this mayonnaise. I store it in a wide-mouthed mason jar; it keeps in your refrigerator for two to three weeks. Use this mayo for chicken salad and cabbage slaws, or spread it on bread for a turkey sandwich. Advance preparation includes the three hours to soak the nuts.

1 cup raw cashews, soaked for about
  3 hours

¼ cup water

2 tablespoons raw apple cider vinegar

2 tablespoons fresh lemon juice

½ teaspoon dry mustard powder

¾ to 1 teaspoon sea salt

6 tablespoons extra–virgin olive oil

1. Rinse and drain the cashews. Add them along with the water, vinegar, lemon juice, mustard powder, and salt to a high-powered blender. Blend until thick and creamy, then slowly add the olive oil and blend until ultra-smooth. You may need to stop the blender, stir, and then blend again.

2. Use a small spatula or spoon to scoop the mayo into a jar. Place into your refrigerator to chill and thicken.

avocado mayonnaise

MAKES ABOUT 1¼ CUPS

When making this, I usually add ingredients just until the mayonnaise reaches the right consistency and flavor. Use this mayo for your favorite sandwich or to make salmon, tuna, or chicken salads. Leftovers can be stored for up to three days in the refrigerator.

2 small avocados, pitted

2 to 3 tablespoons fresh lemon juice

2 to 3 tablespoons extra-virgin olive oil

2 to 3 tablespoons water

Sea salt or Herbamare

Place all the ingredients in a bowl or large mug, starting with the 2 tablespoons for the lemon juice, olive oil, and water. Blend with an immersion blender, adding the remaining tablespoon if needed to reach desired consistency. You can also use a blender or food processor, but given the small quantity of mayo here, it is much easier and more efficient to use a hand blender.

> **NUTRITION TIP**
>
> Avocados are a rich source of monounsaturated fats, specifically oleic acid, which helps to lower LDL cholesterol while increasing the good HDL cholesterol. Some research has indicated that oleic acid may provide protection against breast cancer. Avocados are also a rich source of the carotenoid lutein and vitamins E and K, all of which are lipid soluble, meaning you need to eat these nutrients with fat for them to be absorbed. That is why eating the "whole food"—the avocado—works, as nature intended, of course.

cashew sour cream

FREE OF

MAKES ABOUT 2 CUPS

It is so easy to make your own cultured dairy-free sour cream once you get the hang of the different times required for soaking and culturing. Use your sour cream to create a fabulous dip for vegetables, serve it with beans and rice, or put it into an egg and salsa burrito. In fact, use it anytime you would use regular cow's milk sour cream. We use a high-quality dairy-free probiotic powder from Klaire Labs, called Ther-Biotic Complete Powder, for this recipe, which is the same powder we feed our children daily. Bear in mind you need to soak the nuts for eight hours in advance, in addition to the 24 hours of curing.

2 cups raw cashews or macadamia nuts, soaked for 8 hours

1 cup water or more as needed

½ to 1 teaspoon probiotic powder

Pinch of sea salt (optional)

Raw apple cider vinegar (optional)

1. Drain and rinse the nuts. Place them into a high-powered blender and add the 1 cup water. Puree until ultra-smooth, stopping the machine to scrape down the sides, if necessary; it will take a few minutes to do this. Add a little more water if necessary to get the right consistency. Then add the probiotic powder and blend again until well incorporated. Place a fine-mesh strainer over a bowl and line it with a large piece of cheesecloth or thin clean dishtowel that overhangs the strainer. Pour the sour cream into the strainer, then fold over the edges of the cheesecloth and let sit on your kitchen counter for about 24 hours, or until thickened and it has reached desired sourness.

2. Stir in a little salt and some vinegar to balance the flavors, if desired. Store in your refrigerator in a sealed glass container for up to 10 days.

cashew roasted red pepper dip

FREE OF

MAKES ABOUT 1½ CUPS

Serve this cheese-like dip with a platter of crackers and vegetables such as cauliflower florets, raw green beans, celery sticks, cucumber slices, and kohlrabi slices. Place into a bowl and sprinkle with chopped chives, if desired. If you don't have a high-powered blender, then you'll have to soak the cashews for three hours before making this dip.

1 cup raw cashews

½ cup water

2 large roasted red bell peppers, or 4 small ones, cored and seeded

¼ cup extra-virgin olive oil

2 tablespoons fresh lemon juice

2 tablespoons nutritional yeast

1 garlic clove

1 teaspoon Herbamare or sea salt

1. If using a regular blender, place the cashews in water to cover and soak for about 3 hours. Drain and then proceed with the recipe. If you are using a high-powered blender, place all the ingredients into the blender and blend until smooth and creamy.

2. Put in a container and place in the refrigerator to chill before serving. The dip will thicken slightly as it chills. Store in a covered glass container in the refrigerator for up to a week.

macadamia nut cheese

FREE OF

MAKES ABOUT 1¼ CUPS

You'll need a high-powered blender to get this spreadable "cheese" ultra-creamy. When purchasing the macadamia nuts, buy the raw, unsalted variety. This vegan nut cheese is perfect for topping homemade gluten-free pizza or for spreading between layers of noodles, vegetables, and sauce for a tasty lasagna. I find the flavors of this cheese are best balanced with the acidity of tomatoes, such as the Easy Homemade Pizza Sauce (page 329).

1 cup raw macadamia nuts

½ cup hot water

1 small roasted red bell pepper, cored and seeded (optional)

2 tablespoons extra-virgin olive oil

1 to 2 tablespoons nutritional yeast

½ teaspoon onion powder

¼ teaspoon garlic powder

½ to 1 teaspoon Herbamare or sea salt

Place all the ingredients into a high-powered blender and blend for 1 to 2 minutes, or until smooth and creamy. Store in a covered glass container in the refrigerator for up to a week.

> **KITCHEN TIP**
>
> To roast red bell peppers, set the oven to broil, then place the peppers on a baking sheet and broil on the center rack of the oven for 8 to 10 minutes, turning occasionally, until the skins are charred. Place the peppers into a paper bag or a covered glass bowl and let stand at room temperature for about 10 minutes. Then peel off the charred skins and remove the seeds. You can store extra roasted red peppers in your freezer.

pumpkin seed pesto

FREE OF

MAKES ABOUT 1½ CUPS

Use this delicious nut-free pesto tossed with raw cucumber noodles or cooked brown rice pasta, or spread it atop your favorite gluten-free pizza crust. It's also delicious spread over baked salmon fillets. You'll need to soak the pumpkin seeds for six hours before preparing this pesto.

1 cup raw pumpkin seeds, soaked for
  6 hours

½ cup fresh lemon juice

2 or 3 garlic cloves

1 teaspoon sea salt

4 cups packed fresh basil

½ cup extra-virgin olive oil

Drain and rinse the pumpkin seeds. Place the seeds, lemon juice, garlic, and salt into a food processor fitted with the "s" blade and process until finely ground. Then add the basil and process again until smooth. Lastly, add the olive oil and process until combined. Taste and add more salt, if necessary.

sunny raw zucchini dip

FREE OF

MAKES 2 CUPS

This dip is perfect to make during the summer, when there is an abundance of fresh garden zucchini! You can use this recipe as a spread in a veggie wrap, thinned out with a little water as a salad dressing, or as a dip for vegetables. Try serving the dip with more unusual vegetables, such as kohlrabi, cauliflower, bok choy stems, or radishes. A high-powered blender will create the luscious, creamy dip that we prefer, though a food processor works well, too. The sunflower seeds will have to be soaked for at least six hours before you make this dip.

1 cup raw sunflower seeds, soaked for 6 to 8 hours

1 zucchini, chopped (about 1 heaping cup)

¼ to ½ cup fresh parsley

1 or 2 garlic cloves

¼ cup fresh lemon juice

¼ cup extra-virgin olive oil

¼ cup water

1 teaspoon Herbamare or sea salt

Few pinches of red pepper flakes (optional)

1. Rinse and drain the sunflower seeds. Place them into a high-powered blender or food processor fitted with the "s" blade and add the zucchini, parsley, garlic, lemon juice, olive oil, water, Herbamare, and red pepper flakes, if using.

2. Blend or process until you reach a creamy consistency. Store in a covered glass container until ready to serve.

spicy pepper coconut cream

FREE OF

MAKES ½ CUP

The trick to making this coconut cream is to chill the can of coconut milk overnight. When you open the can, the cream will have hardened and separated at the top, and the watery part will be on the bottom of the can. We then use this thick, luscious cream to dollop on top of the Spicy Thai Mung Bean Burgers (page 296) or over the Spicy Lentils and Rice in Cabbage Leaves (page 290). It is also delicious over quinoa and beans with chopped avocado and cilantro on top. This will keep in the fridge for up to ten days.

½ cup coconut cream from a chilled
  14.5-ounce can full-fat coconut milk

2 cherry peppers, seeded

1 or 2 garlic cloves

½ to 1 teaspoon grated lime zest

Sea salt or Herbamare

Juice of 1 lime (optional)

Place the coconut cream in a blender or mini food processor along with the cherry peppers, garlic, lime zest, and salt to taste. Blend until a smooth puree forms. Taste and adjust the seasonings, if necessary. Add a squeeze of lime juice, if desired. Place the pepper-cream in a small, covered container in the refrigerator until ready to serve.

> **INGREDIENT TIP**
>
> Be sure to use a can of full-fat coconut milk. Light coconut milk does not contain enough fat to provide the "cream" layer.

garlic and rosemary white bean dip

FREE OF

MAKES ABOUT 3½ CUPS

This dip can be prepared in just minutes if you have cooked beans. I use cannellini beans, but great northern or navy would also work. My kids love to dip carrots and celery into this dip. It also makes a delicious wrap when used as a filling for tortillas, lettuce leaves, or collard greens.

3 cups cooked white beans, with some
    cooking liquid reserved
¼ cup extra-virgin olive oil
Juice of 1 large lemon (about ¼ cup)

1 or 2 garlic cloves, coarsely chopped
1 tablespoon chopped fresh rosemary
1 teaspoon Herbamare or sea salt

1. Place all the ingredients except the bean-cooking liquid into a food processor fitted with the "s" blade. Process until very smooth and creamy, adding the cooking liquid as necessary to reach desired consistency (start by adding a tablespoon or so at a time).

2. Chill until ready to serve. The flavors become deeper and more pronounced as the bean dip sits in the refrigerator.

herb and olive oil hummus

MAKES 4 CUPS

Hummus is a traditional Middle Eastern dish made from chickpeas and tahini. I've added fresh herbs and a drizzle of olive oil for a more sophisticated dip. Use it to spread onto the Amaranth and Sun-Dried Tomato Crackers (page 150) or as a filling for wraps using either tortillas or blanched collard greens. It will store in a covered glass container in the refrigerator for up to a week.

3 cups cooked garbanzo beans, some cooking liquid reserved

½ cup sesame tahini

½ cup fresh lemon juice

¼ cup extra-virgin olive oil, plus a bit more for serving

2 or 3 garlic cloves, crushed

1 teaspoon ground cumin

1 to 2 teaspoons sea salt or Herbamare

Small handful of fresh parsley

2 to 3 tablespoons fresh oregano leaves

1 to 2 tablespoon fresh marjoram leaves

1. Place the beans and all remaining ingredients except the fresh herbs into a food processor fitted with the "s" blade and process until smooth and creamy. Add up to ¼ cup reserved cooking liquid or water for a thinner consistency. Taste and adjust the seasonings. Add the parsley, 2 tablespoons of the oregano, and 1 tablespoon of the marjoram and pulse until combined but not completely pureed.

2. Place the hummus in small serving dishes and drizzle on more olive oil, if desired. Sprinkle with the additional oregano and marjoram.

> **NUTRITION TIP**
>
> We have all heard that the Mediterranean diet offers protective effects for the heart. Some researchers are now attributing that benefit to the beneficial phenolic compounds found in the fruits and vegetables, and the high-quality olive oil used. One study found that when people used olive oil exclusively, they could reduce their likelihood of developing coronary heart disease by 47 percent. If just their saturated fats were replaced with olive oil, their total cholesterol would drop by 13.4 percent and their LDL by 18 percent.

red pepper chickpea spread

FREE OF

MAKES ABOUT 2½ CUPS

Roasting your own red bell peppers is very easy; it only takes about 10 minutes. This spread is used in the Roasted Cauliflower and Arugla Wraps (page 360) and is also quite good spread on a piece of Dark Teff Sandwich Bread (page 119). This will store in the refrigerator for up to a week.

1 or 2 small red bell peppers

2 cups cooked chickpeas

4 tablespoons creamy almond butter

3 tablespoons extra-virgin olive oil

2 garlic cloves, crushed

1 to 2 teaspoons Herbamare or sea salt

1. Preheat the oven to broil. Place the peppers on a baking sheet and broil on the center rack of the oven for 8 to 10 minutes, turning occasionally, until the skins are charred. Place the peppers in a paper bag or covered glass bowl, and let stand at room temperature for about 10 minutes. Peel off the charred skins, then trim and remove the seeds.

2. Place the peppers and the remaining ingredients into a food processor and process until smooth and creamy. Taste and adjust the seasonings, if needed.

mexican bean dip

FREE OF

MAKES ABOUT 2½ CUPS

This flavorful bean dip can be served with crackers or corn chips—our children prefer to dip carrot sticks in it. I also like to double this recipe and make a layered bean dip with shredded lettuce, chopped tomatoes, olives, guacamole, and Cashew Sour Cream (page 336). Store this in a covered glass container in the refrigerator for up to a week.

1 to 2 tablespoons extra-virgin olive oil

1 shallot, diced

1 carrot, diced

1 celery stalk, diced

2 teaspoons ground cumin

½ teaspoon chili powder

½ teaspoon smoked paprika (optional)

2 cups cooked kidney or pinto beans, drained

Squeeze of lime or dash of raw apple cider vinegar

Sea salt

1. Heat a small skillet over medium-low and add the olive oil, then the shallot, carrot, and celery; sauté for 5 to 10 minutes, or until the vegetables are tender. Add the spices and sauté for 30 seconds more.

2. Place the sautéed vegetables, the beans, lime juice, and salt into a food processor fitted with the "s" blade. Process until smooth and combined.

raw caramel dip

MAKES ABOUT 2 CUPS

Every autumn, when apple season comes around and the grocery store shelves are lined with glistening apples dipped in caramel, we make this healthier version of caramel and serve it as a dip with crisp apple slices. It's great served as an after-school snack for your children! The dip is very easy to make; you just need a few hours for the dates and cashews to soak. You can also thin the dip with some water and drizzle it over your favorite dessert. To make this dip, figure on soaking the nuts and dates for two to three hours.

1 cup raw cashews
1 cup medjool dates, pitted (8 to 10 dates)
¼ cup pure maple syrup

2 teaspoons vanilla extract
Pinch of sea salt

1. Place the cashews in a small bowl and cover with water. Let soak at room temp for 2 to 3 hours. Place the pitted dates in another small bowl and cover with water. Let soak for 2 to 3 hours.

2. Drain and rinse the cashews. Drain the dates and save the soaking water. Place the cashews into a blender. Add the dates, the maple syrup, vanilla, and salt. Add 6 to 8 tablespoons of the date soaking water and blend until ultra-smooth, scraping down the sides if needed. Scoop into small bowls and serve with sliced fresh apples.

raw cilantro lime chutney

Serve this chutney with a spicy lentil dal or curried vegetable dish. Use these measurements or just toss the ingredients into a food processor with wild abandon and see what comes of it. Most likely it will be delicious! This will store in a small covered glass container in your refrigerator for up to a week.

2 large jalapeño peppers, seeded

A 2-inch piece peeled ginger

4 large garlic cloves

Grated zest of 1 large lime

½ teaspoon sea salt

2 large bunches fresh cilantro (stems and leaves)

Juice of 1 large lime

½ cup unsweetened shredded coconut

Place the jalapeños, ginger, garlic, lime zest, and salt into a food processor fitted with the "s" blade and process until minced. Add the cilantro, lime juice, and coconut and pulse until combined.

spicy peach chutney

MAKES ABOUT 2 CUPS

Serve this flavorful, fresh chutney over dal and rice or your favorite curry. We like to make extra churtney during peach season and then freeze small jars of it to enjoy during the winter. If you would like a milder chutney, omit the habanero chiles. If you don't have coconut sugar on hand, use another granulated sugar such as raw cane sugar or Sucanat. Store this in small glass jars in the refrigerator for up to three weeks. The chutney can also be frozen for up to six months for longer storage.

8 ripe peaches, peeled and diced

Juice of 2 limes

1 to 3 habanero chiles, seeded and finely diced

2 to 3 jalapeño peppers, seeded and finely diced

1 tablespoon grated fresh ginger

4 garlic cloves, crushed

½ cup coconut sugar

Few dashes of sea salt or Herbamare

1. Place all the ingredients in a medium saucepan over medium heat. Simmer, covered, for about 20 minutes. Remove the cover and simmer for 10 minutes more to let some of the liquid evaporate. The chutney should be thickened and translucent.

2. Serve warm or chill and serve the next day. The flavors will definitely improve with age.

fresh apple salsa

FREE OF

MAKES ABOUT 3 CUPS

I like making this salsa in autumn, when apple season is in full swing. The best apples to use are crisp, firm ones like Honeycrisp. Soft, sweet apples are better for sauce and baking. Use whatever chiles you have on hand—serrano, jalapeño, or cherry peppers are good choices. Use this to top grilled fish, fish tacos, or a bowl of quinoa. This salsa will keep in the refrigerator for about three days.

2 large apples

½ cup chopped fresh cilantro

¼ cup finely diced red onion

1 to 4 hot fresh chiles, seeded and finely diced

1 tablespoon extra-virgin olive oil

1 tablespoon raw apple cider vinegar

Sea salt or Herbamare

Place all the ingredients in a medium bowl and mix well. Cover and place in the refrigerator for up to an hour to allow the flavors to meld.

INGREDIENT TIP

One to two jalapeños creates a mild salsa. Four jalapeños creates a very spicy salsa. We like to use one to two so our children will eat it, though we prefer the flavor and heat of four!

salsa fresca

FREE OF

MAKES ABOUT 5 CUPS

Serve this quick and easy salsa with tacos or to top homemade enchiladas. It's especially good with the Raw Breakfast Tacos (page 82). If you don't own a food processor, you can finely chop all the ingredients, though using a food processor cuts preparation time in half. I like to dice the tomatoes—if they are processed along with the rest of the ingredients, the salsa gets very watery. This salsa will keep in the refrigerator for about three days.

4 cups finely diced plum tomatoes

1 small orange or yellow bell pepper, cored and seeded

½ small red onion, ends trimmed

Large handful of fresh cilantro

2 to 4 jalapeño peppers, seeded

2 or 3 garlic cloves

½ teaspoon ground cumin

1 tablespoon raw apple cider vinegar

1 teaspoon sea salt or Herbamare

1. Place the tomatoes in a large bowl. Put the remaining ingredients into a food processor fitted with the "s" blade. Process until coarsely ground or a bit smaller than they would be if you had diced them.

2. Add the processor mix to the tomatoes. Gently stir, then chill for at least 1 hour before serving. The chilling gives the flavors a chance to meld.

wrapsandrolls

Wraps and rolls are simple to assemble and make a nutritious snack or meal. This is the easiest first swap you can make—trade up your sandwich bread for homemade tortillas, collard greens, cabbage leaves, or sheets of nori to wrap up your lunch. Fill with any combination of marinated vegetables, spicy greens, leftover fish or meat, cooked beans, raw nut and seed pâtés, or cooked whole grains.

CREATING A QUICK LUNCH

Although we have a number of recipes in this chapter for homemade tortillas, we've found that the best wraps come from nature—plants! If you are like most people and have little time in the morning to prepare breakfast, let alone lunch, consider using plants as wraps or rolls for quick lunch options.

Nori rolls can easily be made the night before and stored in a glass container ready to take to school or work. Napa cabbage or romaine lettuce leaves can be used as "tacos" and filled with scoops of leftover grain and bean salad, cooked fish or chicken, fermented vegetables, or fresh garden herbs. Collard greens make the best replacement for tortillas—just blanch, drain, and use!

A Few Ideas for Plant-Based Wraps

- Nori sheets
- Lettuce leaves
- Napa cabbage leaves
- Collard greens
- Lacinato kale leaves
- Grape leaves
- Long thin strips of raw zucchini

10 Tips for Using Wraps and Rolls

1. Use a tortilla press to make homemade tortillas. We have an 8-inch cast-iron press that comes in handy for making both corn and almond tortillas, though having one is not necessary to make the recipes in this book.

2. Store homemade gluten-free tortillas between pieces of waxed paper in a sealed plastic bag or glass container. If stored properly, the gluten-free tortillas will remain soft enough for wraps.

3. Save the bag and papers from store-bought gluten-free tortillas to use for storing your homemade wraps.

4. Steam gluten-free tortillas one at a time on a wire rack placed over a pot of simmering water.

5. Heat corn tortillas in a little olive or coconut oil in a hot skillet for 30 seconds on each side.

6. Blanch collard greens for 30 to 60 seconds in boiling water and then drain. When our garden is overflowing with collard greens, we use them in place of any other type of tortilla. For example, collard greens can be used in place of corn tortillas in enchiladas, they can be used for bean and rice burritos, and they also can serve as wrappers for pâté and vegetables.

7. Soak cabbage leaves in a pot of boiled water for 5 to 10 minutes. Use them to replace corn tortillas in enchiladas or for cabbage roll casseroles.

8. When using nori, be sure that some of your ingredients are moist. This will naturally moisten the nori sheet, making it easy to slice. Sticky brown rice or a moist pâté will do the trick.

9. When using Asian rice or tapioca wrappers, place them in a 10-inch skillet filled with hot water for 1 to 2 minutes to soften.

10. For a packed lunch, lay a wet paper towel or cloth napkin over an assembled gluten-free tortilla wrap and place in a tightly sealed container.

brown rice tortillas

FREE OF

MAKES 6 TO 8 TORTILLAS

Use these tortillas to make your favorite wrap, taco, or grilled quesadilla! You can also serve them alongside your favorite soup or stew, for dipping. They are soft and pliable when warm, but straight out of the fridge, like most gluten-free tortillas, they will crack. All you need do to make them pliable again is to place them one at a time on a wire rack over a pot of simmering water and steam for 30 seconds on each side. I use an 8-inch cast-iron tortilla press to get them super-thin and then cook them in a cast-iron pan.

1¼ cups brown rice flour, or more as needed

¾ cup arrowroot powder or tapioca flour

½ teaspoon sea salt

1 cup boiling water, or more as needed

Coconut oil, for cooking

1. In a small bowl, whisk together the flour, arrowroot powder, and salt. Add the boiling water and quickly mix with a fork. Knead the dough a few times to form into a ball. It should feel like playdough; if it is too wet and sticky, add more flour. If it is too dry, add a little more boiling water.

2. Heat a 10-inch cast-iron skillet over medium. Divide the dough into 6 to 8 balls. Place a piece of parchment paper on the bottom of a tortilla press, then place one of the balls in the center, and cover with a second sheet of parchment. Press to form a thin, round tortilla.

3. Add about 1 teaspoon coconut oil to the hot skillet. Gently remove the parchment papers and place the tortilla into the hot skillet. Cook for 2 minutes on each side. Remove to a plate and repeat with the remaining dough. Stack the cooked tortillas on the plate with another plate flipped over on top to keep them warm and soft. Let them sit for about 20 minutes between the plates; this way they will be nice and pliable for serving.

> **INGREDIENT TIP**
> Use organic sprouted brown rice flour in this recipe, which is the most nutritious and least contaminated brown rice flour available. I use the sprouted variety from Planet Rice in all recipes calling for brown rice flour.

buckwheat chia tortillas

FREE OF

MAKES 4 TO 6 TORTILLAS

These tortillas are soft, pliable, and full of flavor. I grind my own buckwheat flour from *raw* buckwheat groats in my high-powered blender. Use these gluten-free wraps to make quick turkey and lettuce roll-ups, or spread them with hummus and add steamed kale and shredded carrots for a vegetarian wrap! Store these tortillas between pieces of waxed paper in a plastic bag or sealed glass container for up to five days in the refrigerator.

½ cup ground chia seeds

2 cups warm water

2 tablespoons extra-virgin olive oil

1¾ cups raw buckwheat flour (see Tip on page 98)

¾ teaspoon sea salt

1. Preheat the oven to 350°F. Tear parchment paper into four large squares. Get out two baking sheets.

2. Place the chia seeds in a large bowl. Slowly whisk in the warm water. Let rest for 3 to 4 minutes so the chia can form its gel, then whisk in the olive oil. Add the buckwheat flour and salt, and stir with a wooden spoon until combined and thickened. The dough will be sticky.

3. Place a square of parchment on a baking sheet. Drop the dough by ½ cupfuls into the center of the parchment square. Cover with another parchment square. Using your hands, gently spread the batter into a large circle, about 8 to 10 inches in diameter. Try to get it fairly thin and the batter evenly distributed. After a few tries, you'll get the hang of it. Leave the tortilla between the parchment squares and continue making the remaining tortillas until you've used up all the dough. You may be able to bake two tortillas at once on the same sheet, depending on size. Bake for 6 to 7 minutes, then flip the tortillas, parchment and all, and bake for 3 to 4 minutes more. Watch carefully as overcooking will lead to a dry tortilla that can crack easily. Remove from the oven and discard the parchment; it should easily peel off. Stack the tortillas on a plate to cool.

plantain tortillas

FREE OF

MAKES ABOUT 8 TORTILLAS

Try these grain-free, vegan tortillas as your new wrap for any kind of filling. For a quick lunch on the go, fill them with sliced organic turkey, avocado, and lettuce. They work really well with the Fish Tacos (page 302) or the Slow-Cooked Chicken Tacos (page 314). Store any leftover tortillas in a covered container in your refrigerator. To reheat (and make pliable again), place a wire rack over a pot of simmering water or soup, and set each tortilla on it until it is heated through.

2 pounds green plantains (about 4 medium; see Tip)

½ teaspoon sea salt

½ to 1 cup arrowroot powder

Coconut oil, for cooking

1. Peel the plantains. To cut open, first cut off the top, run a knife down one of the ridges on the peel. Remove the peel and chop the plantain. If the plantain is very green, you will need to remove the peels as you would a potato—with a paring knife, peeling from top to bottom.

2. Place the chopped plantains and salt into a food processor fitted with the "s" blade. Process until very finely ground (this can take a few minutes). Add ½ cup arrowroot powder and process again until the mixture forms a ball. If the mixture seems too moist, gradually add the remaining ½ cup arrowroot powder and process again.

3. Heat a cast-iron skillet over medium. Form the dough into 8 balls. Place a piece of parchment paper down on the bottom of a tortilla press and add a ball of dough. Place another piece on top of the ball and press the dough into a flat round. Remove and continue to make rounds with the remaining dough balls.

4. Add 1 to 2 teaspoons of coconut oil to the skillet. Peel off the parchment paper and place one tortilla in the pan. Cook for about 2 minutes per side. You will see tiny bubbles form and parts of the tortilla will poof up. Set the cooked tortilla on a plate and repeat with the remaining tortillas.

INGREDIENT TIP

Use green plantains. If you use semi-ripe (yellow) or ripe (yellow-brown) plantains, there will be too much moisture in the dough and you will end up adding too much arrowroot powder, which in turn will cause the tortillas to become tough and gummy.

---

homemade corn tortillas

FREE OF

MAKES 10 TORTILLAS

Making our own corn tortillas is a fun family activity. Our twin boys like to mix the masa and water while our girls like to press the dough into tortillas and cook them. Use homemade tortillas for chicken fajitas, black bean tacos, or Fish Tacos (page 302). Be sure to purchase *organic* masa harina to avoid consuming genetically engineered food.

4 cups white, blue, or yellow masa harina, or more as needed
1 teaspoon sea salt

3 to 4 cups boiling water
Coconut oil, for cooking

1. Place the 4 cups masa harina and the salt in a large glass bowl; whisk well. Slowly pour in 3 cups of the boiling water, stirring with a large spoon, until it reaches playdough consistency, adding the remaining 1 cup boiling water as needed. The dough should not be too dry or too wet; if it is too moist, add more masa. Knead the dough a few times with your hands (it will be hot, so work fast). Form the dough into 10 balls. Place a piece of parchment paper down on the bottom of a tortilla press and add a ball of dough. Place another piece on top of the ball and press the dough into a flat round. Remove and continue to make rounds with the remaining dough balls.

2. Heat a cast-iron skillet over medium, then add about 1 tablespoon of coconut oil. Add a tortilla and cook for about 2 minutes on each side, or until slightly golden. Place on a plate to cool. Repeat with remaining tortillas, adding a little coconut oil for each.

> **KITCHEN TIP**
> We use an 8-inch cast-iron tortilla press. You can easily purchase these online.

grain-free wraps

MAKES ABOUT 6 WRAPS

This simple recipe can be made quickly—no tortilla press required! The wraps are cooked on the stove in a skillet similar to pancakes. They are also pliable and work well with a number of fillings—try turkey, mayo, cheese, and lettuce; chicken salad; Fish Tacos (page 302); or Herb and Olive Oil Hummus (page 343) and leftover raw kale salad! Once cooked, you can transfer these to a covered container for longer storage. Sometimes I make them at night and leave them on the counter, covered with another plate. They keep fine like this overnight, and are ready for school lunches in the morning!

1 cup blanched almond flour

1 cup arrowroot powder or tapioca flour

¼ teaspoon sea salt

4 large organic eggs

½ cup raw cream or full-fat coconut milk

Butter or coconut oil, for cooking

1. Preheat an 8- or 10-inch cast-iron skillet over medium-low. In a medium bowl, whisk together the almond flour, arrowroot powder, and salt. Add the eggs and cream, then whisk vigorously until smooth.

2. Add about ½ teaspoon butter to the skillet. Pour in the batter by ¼ or ½ cup measures, depending on how large you would like your wraps. Cook for 60 seconds on the first side, then flip and cook for about 30 seconds on the second side. Transfer to a plate to cool.

roasted cauliflower and arugula wraps with red pepper chickpea spread

FREE OF

MAKES 6 WRAPS

Once you have the ingredients for this recipe prepped, you will have tasty meals or snacks for days to come—just store finished items separately in the fridge for up to five days. When ready to assemble another wrap, steam a tortilla and fill it with the premade fillings. Our favorite gluten-free tortillas to use in this recipe are the Buckwheat Chia Tortillas (page 356) and the Grain-Free Wraps (page 359).

1 small red onion, cut into chunks

1 small head cauliflower, cored and cut into florets

2 tablespoons extra-virgin olive oil

⅛ teaspoon sea salt

6 gluten-free tortillas

Red Pepper Chickpea Spread (page 344)

Fresh arugula

1. Preheat the oven to 425°F. Place the onion and cauliflower on a baking sheet and toss with the olive oil. Sprinkle with the salt, and roast for about 20 minutes.

2. Steam and warm the tortillas. Spread the tortillas with a thin layer of the red pepper spread, add the roasted veggies and the arugula on one side, then tightly roll from the veggie side. Cut in half and serve immediately.

nori rolls with pumpkin seed–parsley pâté

MAKES 4 NORI ROLLS

This nutrient-dense lunch or snack will keep you energized all day. Soaked pumpkin seeds are more digestible and also easy to blend into a paste, so be sure to allow the 8 hours of soaking before you make these rolls. Add your favorite veggies along with the pâté. For instance, try sliced cucumbers, red bell peppers, shredded carrots, or spinach leaves.

PÂTÉ

1 cup raw pumpkin seeds, soaked for 8 hours

Juice of 1 lemon

1 tablespoon extra-virgin olive oil

1 garlic clove, crushed

¾ teaspoon Herbamare or sea salt

Large handful of fresh parsley

Water, as needed

OTHER INGREDIENTS

4 nori sheets

Sliced avocado

Microgreens

1. Rinse and drain the pumpkin seeds. Place into a food processor fitted with the "s" blade. Add the lemon juice, olive oil, garlic, and Herbamare. Process until smooth, scraping down the sides if necessary. Add the parsley and process again. Add a little water, a tablespoon at a time, until you get the desired consistency.

2. Spread the pâté on the nori. Add the avocado and microgreens to one end of the nori sheet, then roll up. Let rest for a few minutes before slicing.

NUTRITION TIP

Pumpkin seeds are high in minerals such as manganese, magnesium, phosphorus, copper, and zinc. Soaking the seeds enables these minerals to become more available. Manganese, for example, is needed to help maintain normal blood sugar levels, keep the thyroid functioning properly, and help build strong bones. Just ¼ cup of pumpkin seeds provides about 1.5 mg of manganese. Considering we need anywhere from 1.2 mg (if you are a toddler) to 2.3 mg (if you are a man), pumpkin seeds are a great source of this mineral!

nori rolls with salmon and mustard greens

FREE OF

MAKES 6 TO 8 ROLLS

One of our favorite on-the-go meals is a nori roll filled with delicious vegetables. This one combines spicy mustard greens, creamy avocado, and cooked salmon for a flavorful, nutritious meal or snack. If you pack these into your lunch, remember to bring a small bottle of coconut aminos or wheat-free tamari for dipping!

STICKY BROWN RICE

2 cups sweet brown rice, soaked overnight if desired

1 cup short-grain brown rice, soaked overnight if desired

6 cups water

¼ teaspoon sea salt

ROLLS

6 to 8 toasted nori sheets

1 avocado, sliced

2 green onions, trimmed and cut into thirds, then sliced into thin strips

2 large mustard greens, cut into strips

½ pound cooked salmon, cut into strips

Wasabi (optional)

Wheat-free tamari or coconut aminos (optional)

Toasted black sesame seeds (optional)

1. Place the rice, water, and salt in a 3-quart pot. Cover and bring to a boil over high heat. Immediately turn the heat to low or medium-low and simmer for about 45 minutes, or until the rice is cooked. Let stand for about 30 minutes before using.

2. Place one sheet of nori, shiny side down, on a large plate or wooden cutting board. Spread a thin layer of the rice on the nori, leaving 1 to 2 inches free of rice at the top of the sheet—this is so the nori can adhere to itself and hold together after rolling. On the bottom of the nori, place a thin strip of avocado slices, green onions, mustard greens, and salmon. Begin to tightly roll from the bottom. To seal the nori, dip your finger in water and place a little water along the seam and gently press. Repeat for the remaining nori sheets and filling. Use a clean serrated knife to slice the rolls into rounds. Dip the rolls in wasabi and tamari, then in black mustard seeds, if desired.

> **INGREDIENT TIP**
>
> If you have soaked the rice overnight, drain and rinse it, and use 4½ to 5 cups fresh water for cooking.

thai salad wraps

FREE OF

MAKES 6 SERVINGS

If you are craving a lot of vegetables but don't want a traditional salad, try these wraps! They are delicious dipped in the Garlic Ginger Peanut Sauce (page 331). These are not very filling but they are highly nutritious, so go ahead and eat five or more at a time! The tapioca flour paper wrappers can be found at your local Asian market or health food store; they are paper-thin and translucent when softened in warm water. To store leftovers, place them in a container, layered between wet paper towels. Cover the top layer with a wet paper towel.

15 to 20 tapioca or rice paper wrappers

1 small head leaf lettuce, rinsed and spun dry

2 cups thinly sliced red cabbage

1 large red bell pepper, cored, seeded, and sliced very thin

1 cucumber, sliced into very thin strips

2 or 3 carrots, shredded

Large handful of fresh basil leaves

Large handful of fresh cilantro, chopped

Large handful of sprouts of any kind (alfalfa, mung bean, broccoli)

Small handful of fresh spearmint leaves

1. Fill a 10-inch skillet with hot water, and place each wrap individually in the hot water to soften, 30 to 60 seconds. (If you leave them in the water for too long they will begin to break apart.) You will need to change the water about three times during this process to keep it fresh and hot.

2. Tear the lettuce into small pieces and place in a large bowl. Add the remaining ingredients and toss well. Place a softened wrapper on a plate. Add a handful of the filling to the bottom. Facing the wrapper (think north, south, east, west), your vegetables would be on the south. Fold the west and east ends in, then tightly roll up toward the north. Repeat this process with the remaining filling and wrappers.

collard wraps with raw sunflower pâté

MAKES ABOUT 8 WRAPS

The first few times I made this I used red pepper flakes in place of the black pepper. Go ahead and get creative by using whatever ingredients you like. These wraps can be stored in a glass container in your refrigerator for up to three days for a grab-and-go meal. Note, though, that you need to allow at least six hours to soak the sunflower seeds before proceeding with this recipe.

1 bunch large collard greens

SUNFLOWER PÂTÉ
2 cups raw sunflower seeds, soaked for 6 to 8 hours
1 cup chopped celery
¼ cup finely diced shallots
2 to 3 tablespoons fresh lemon juice
1 teaspoon dried thyme

½ to 1 teaspoon Herbamare or sea salt
½ teaspoon freshly ground black pepper

FILLING
1 recipe Raw Super Green Salad (page 225)
Grated carrots
Sprouts
Sliced avocados

1. Cut the stems off the bottoms of the collard greens. Bring a large pot of water to a boil, then blanch the collard greens for approximately 60 seconds. Gently remove with tongs and set on a plate to cool.

2. Drain and rinse the sunflower seeds in a fine-mesh strainer. Place all the remaining pâté ingredients into a food processor fitted with the "s" blade and pulse until desired consistency. I like mine processed until the pâté is fairly smooth.

3. Place a collard green on a large plate or cutting board. Put a few spoonfuls of the pâté on the bottom (stem end), then add the fillings. Fold the long ends of the leaves in slightly (about an inch on each side) and then tightly roll up. Refrigerate right away or cut in half and serve.

turkey and avocado wraps
with honey mustard

MAKES 3 WRAPS

Use this recipe for a simple lunch on the run. You can blanch a bunch of collard greens and then store them in your refrigerator in a covered glass container for a few days. This recipe also works with any gluten-free tortilla, of course. You can use the Honey Mustard Dressing (page 222) or use your favorite store-bought organic variety.

3 large collard greens

6 slices organic turkey breast

1 small avocado, sliced

Honey mustard

Grated carrot

Grated apple

Baby greens

1. Bring a pot of water to a boil. Trim the stems off the collards and then place them in the boiling water for 60 seconds. Carefully remove from the pot and place on a towel or plate to cool.

2. Lay one collard green on a plate or cutting board. Roll up 2 turkey slices and place them on the bottom, or stem end, of the collard green. Top with some of the sliced avocado, and drizzle with honey mustard. Add the carrot, apple, and greens, if desired.

3. Fold in the long sides of the collard green, then begin to roll up from the stem end, where the turkey is. Place seam side down on a plate or into a container and repeat with the remaining ingredients. Store leftover wraps in a covered container in the refrigerator for up to a day.

chicken salad lettuce wraps

MAKES 2 SERVINGS

This lunch is loaded with vegetables and some lean protein. I find I have plenty of energy for the rest of the day when I eat this. Use the Egg-Free Mayonnaise (page 334) or your favorite brand of store-bought healthy mayonnaise. For the chicken, I like to use leftover breast meat from a whole organic chicken I have roasted. Store any leftover salad in the refrigerator for up to three days.

1 cup chopped cooked chicken breast

½ cup diced celery

¼ cup diced carrots

¼ cup finely chopped fresh parsley

1 or 2 green onions, trimmed and sliced into thin rounds

1 tablespoon drained capers

2 to 4 tablespoons mayonnaise

Herbamare or sea salt

Freshly ground black pepper

Lettuce leaves, rinsed and patted dry

Place the chicken, celery, carrots, parsley, green onions, capers, mayonnaise, Herbamare, and pepper in a medium bowl and mix well. Adjust the seasonings, if necessary. Place a few scoops of the chicken salad onto each large lettuce leaf. Or, top a bed of mixed greens with the chicken salad.

snacksandtreats

The healthiest, freshest, and easiest foods for snacking are—you guessed it—plants! Fresh fruits, vegetables, nuts, and seeds are ready-made snacks that require little preparation. The billion-dollar snack industry has perpetuated the idea that children need and want processed snack foods on a daily basis. These highly processed foods have created many health problems in our population. Packaged "healthy" snacks from the health food store may not be much better, either.

HEALTHY SNACKING

Imagine if we did not have a food industry and every food we consumed was one we grew, hunted, or bought from a local farmer. We would probably stick to consuming foods that required the least amount of energy to prepare. If we approach food this way, fresh fruits and vegetables become the cornerstone of our diet.

When you are hungry and need something to snack on, look to plants to fill the need. Carrots and apples instead of chips, fruits and greens blended into a green smoothie, nuts and seeds for a traveling food, a bunch of kale turned into addictive chips, and fresh fruit made into popsicles.

10 Quick Snack Ideas

1. Celery sticks dipped in sunflower butter or almond butter.

2. Carrot sticks dipped in hummus.

3. Raw cauliflower dipped in pesto.

4. Sliced kohlrabi dipped in your favorite creamy salad dressing.

5. Sliced hard-boiled egg wrapped in a lettuce leaf and drizzled with honey mustard.

6. Green smoothies!

7. Nut and fruit smoothie made from soaked nuts and frozen fruit.

8. Handful of raw almonds and dried apricots.

9. Bowl of frozen blueberries, cherries, and raspberries.

10. Banana dipped in almond butter and shredded coconut.

lemon tahini kale chips

FREE OF

MAKES 4 SMALL SERVINGS

Kale chips are a nutritious way to satisfy the need for something crunchy and salty without sacrificing your health. They can either be baked at a very low temperature in the oven or dehydrated using a food dehydrator. If you are using a dehydrator, set the temp to 115°F and dehydrate for about 8 hours or until crisp. The oven method is obviously the fastest, but you need to watch them closely as the kale can begin to burn. Fresh lemon juice and sesame tahini is one of our favorite ingredient combinations. Extra kale chips can be stored in an airtight container on the counter for a few days.

2 bunches curly kale

¼ cup tahini

2 to 4 tablespoons water

2 tablespoons nutritional yeast

2 tablespoons extra-virgin olive oil

2 tablespoons fresh lemon juice

2 garlic cloves, crushed

¼ teaspoon sea salt

1. Preheat the oven to 250°F. Rinse the kale and pat dry. Remove the tough inner stem that runs lengthwise through the center of each kale leaf, then tear or chop into large pieces. In a small bowl, combine the remaining ingredients.

2. Place the kale pieces on a large baking sheet and toss with the tahini-lemon mixture. Gently massage the mixture into the kale so it is evenly coated. Spread the leaves out on the baking sheet. Bake for 30 to 35 minutes, turning once, until dry and crispy. Remove from the oven, let cool a little, and enjoy!

NUTRITION TIP

Isothiocyanates from kale have been found to regulate the body's detoxification mechanisms at a genetic level, and have been found to lower the risk of developing certain forms of cancer, including breast, bladder, colon, prostate, and ovarian.

---

sweet and spicy kale chips

FREE OF

MAKES 4 SMALL SERVINGS

When these kale chips come out of the oven, they disappear fast in our house! I like to use the full teaspoon of red pepper flakes to create a medium spiciness; use ½ teaspoon for a milder effect. Baking the kale chips at a temperature over 250°F causes them to burn—it may take longer at a lower temp, but the flavor and crispness are worth the extra time. Leftover kale chips can be stored in an airtight container for a few days on the counter.

2 large bunches kale

Juice of 1 small lime

2 tablespoons extra-virgin olive oil

2 tablespoons creamy almond butter

1 tablespoon pure maple syrup or honey

½ to 1 teaspoon red pepper flakes

½ teaspoon Herbamare or sea salt

1. Preheat the oven to 250°F. Rinse the kale and pat dry. Use a knife to cut out the tough inner stem that runs lengthwise through the center of each kale leaf, then tear or cut into large pieces. In a small bowl, whisk together the remaining ingredients.

2. Place the kale in a large bowl and add the sweet-spice mixture. Use your hands to gently massage the mixture in, coating each leaf. Spread the leaves in one layer on one very large baking sheet or two smaller sheets. Bake for about 40 minutes, or until crisp and dry, stirring and flipping the leaves over two or three times. Let cool on the baking sheet, then transfer to a bowl to serve.

VARIATION: For a nut-free version, replace the almond butter with sesame tahini or sunflower seed butter.

chipotle lime kale chips

FREE OF

MAKES 4 SMALL SERVINGS

I prefer to use black kale, also called lacinato kale, for this recipe, though regular kale will work fine, too. When the kale chips have cooled, you can tuck some away in a small stainless steel container for your child's lunchbox. Extra kale chips can be stored in an airtight container on the counter for a few days.

2 bunches kale

2 tablespoons extra-virgin olive oil

1 to 2 tablespoons fresh lime juice

¼ teaspoon chipotle chile powder

¼ teaspoon sea salt

1. Preheat the oven to 250°F. Rinse the kale and pat dry. Remove the tough inner stem from the middle of each kale leaf, then tear or chop into large pieces.

2. Place the kale pieces on a large baking sheet and toss with the olive oil, lime juice, chile powder, and salt. Gently massage the oil mixture into the kale so it is evenly coated. Spread the leaves out on the sheet. Bake for 25 to 30 minutes, turning once, until dry and crisp. Let cool a little and enjoy!

INGREDIENT TIP

The kale needs to be completely dry after rinsing or it won't crisp up into chips in the oven.

---

toasted sunflower seeds
with coconut aminos

FREE OF

MAKES 1 CUP

Coconut aminos can replace tamari in any recipe. This delectably delicious soy-free sauce, containing 17 amino acids, is dark, rich, and salty. I am amazed at its resemblance to soy sauce. It is made simply from raw coconut tree sap and sun-dried sea salt, which is then aged. We've used it in salad dressings, marinades, and as a seasoning for toasted nuts and seeds. It is also great used as a dipping sauce for nori rolls! Coconut aminos have a salty flavor with a slightly sweet aftertaste. When I use coconut aminos, I sometimes add a pinch or two of sea salt, as it isn't as salty as tamari. This recipe is so easy, it takes only about 5 minutes to prepare, and it's one of our children's favorite snacks! They are also delicious sprinkled on a green salad.

1 cup raw sunflower seeds

1 tablespoon coconut aminos

Pinch of sea salt

Heat an 11-inch skillet over medium for a few minutes or until the pan is hot. Add the sunflower seeds; use a spatula to keep them moving in the pan, and toast for 1½ to 2 minutes, or until fragrant and slightly golden. Turn off the heat and add the coconut aminos and sea salt. Immediately stir the mixture to coat the seeds evenly. Let cool on a plate, then transfer to a glass jar for storage.

> **NUTRITION TIP**
>
> Sunflower seeds are a good source of magnesium. Magnesium is nature's nerve calmer; it helps to relax tight muscles, prevent migraines, and lower high blood pressure. Only ¼ cup of sunflower seeds provides about 200 calories and 115 mg magnesium.

candied walnuts

MAKES 2 CUPS

These nuts make a fantastic appetizer, especially during the holidays. I like to use wide-mouth pint-size jars to package them. This preparation also works with other nuts such as pecans. Each year we like to make a few batches of candied nuts to give as holiday gifts.

2 cups walnut halves

3 tablespoons pure maple syrup

1 tablespoon coconut oil or extra-virgin olive oil

1 teaspoon ground cinnamon

Pinch or two of sea salt

1. Preheat the oven to 375°F. Place all the ingredients in a 7 by 11-inch baking dish. Stir well, then bake for 12 to 15 minutes, or until the syrup is bubbly and the nuts are golden, watching carefully so they don't burn.

2. As soon as they come out of the oven, stir the nuts so the syrup sticks to them and not the pan. Immediately transfer to a plate to cool.

cinnamon sunflower truffles

FREE OF

MAKES 1 DOZEN BALLS

You'll need a food processor to make these and other date-based snack balls. And try substituting different nuts or seeds for a different take on this. For example, use pecans, almonds, or cashews in place of the sunflower seeds. I have found that these truffles are even better on the second day, if they last that long! Store them in the fridge for up to two weeks.

2 cups raw sunflower seeds

2 tablespoons ground cinnamon

⅛ teaspoon sea salt

1 cup pitted medjool dates

2 tablespoons extra-virgin olive oil

2 tablespoons pure maple syrup (if needed)

Unsweetened shredded coconut

Place the sunflower seeds, cinnamon, and sea salt into a food processor fitted with the "s" blade. Process until the seeds are very finely ground, about 1 minute. Add the dates and olive oil, then process again until combined and sticky, another minute. Add the maple syrup, if needed; your dates may be moist enough and not require extra sweetener. Form a truffle by rolling some of the mixture in your hands; if it falls apart, add the sweetener and process again. Scoop out the sunflower mixture by large spoonfuls and roll into balls. Then roll in the shredded coconut.

> **NUTRITION TIP**
>
> Sunflower seeds are an excellent source of vitamin E. Each ¼ cup contains about 12 mg of vitamin E. The body uses this fat-soluble vitamin as an antioxidant, preventing cholesterol buildup and protecting the fat found in cell membranes and brain tissue from free-radical damage. Inflammation from free-radical damage is a root cause of conditions such as arthritis and asthma. Vitamin E has shown significant anti-inflammatory effects with these diseases.

cashew orange date balls

FREE OF

MAKES 1 DOZEN BALLS

If you are in the mood for a sweet snack, these can be whipped up in 10 minutes! I like to have a container of some sort of nut-date ball in the refrigerator for my children to pack into their school lunches. One ball serves as a sweet treat and also provides a good dose of protein and healthy fat. These keep in the refrigerator for up to two weeks.

1½ cups raw cashews
1 cup medjool dates, pitted
2 tablespoons coconut oil, softened

1 teaspoon grated orange zest
Pinch of sea salt
Unsweetened shredded coconut

1. Place the cashews into a food processor fitted with the "s" blade. Process until very finely ground, then add the dates, coconut oil, orange zest, and salt. Process again until the dates are finely ground and the mixture begins to form a ball.

2. Take small handfuls of the cashew-date mixture and form small balls. Roll each ball in the shredded coconut. Transfer to a glass storage container.

ginger–macadamia nut energy bars

FREE OF

MAKES 12 BARS

Having nut-date energy bars in our refrigerator is indispensable for our family. I can serve them for breakfast with a green smoothie or bring them along on hikes and other outings with my children. I prefer to make a double batch, which yields thicker bars. If you don't have macadamia nuts, try pecans.

1½ cups raw macadamia nuts

1 cup pitted medjool dates (about 10)

1 teaspoon ground cinnamon

½ teaspoon ground ginger

¼ teaspoon ground cardamom

Pinch of sea salt

Place the nuts into a food processor fitted with the "s" blade and process for 60 to 90 seconds, or until finely ground. Add the dates, spices, and salt. Process again for another 60 to 90 seconds, or until the dates are completely ground and the mixture is starting to form a ball. Press the mixture into an 8-inch square pan and refrigerate for 4 to 5 hours. Cut into bar shapes and individually wrap in waxed paper.

VARIATION: You can also roll the mixture into balls and then roll in shredded coconut. For chocolate energy bars, omit the spices and add 4 tablespoons raw cacao powder along with 2 tablespoons melted coconut oil.

herbed popcorn

FREE OF

MAKES ABOUT 5 QUARTS

Popcorn wins over sweet treats any day in our house. The children adore this and can polish off a large bowl in a matter of minutes. Popcorn makes a great snack for outings and can be used as part of a healthy school lunch. For more flavor, try adding ¼ teaspoon each garlic powder and onion powder to the topping mixture.

POPCORN

4 tablespoons coconut oil

½ teaspoon sea salt

1 cup organic popcorn kernels

TOPPING

1 tablespoon dried thyme

1 tablespoon dried rosemary

2 to 3 tablespoons dried nettles

2 to 3 tablespoons nutritional yeast

½ teaspoon Herbamare or sea salt

2 to 4 tablespoons coconut oil or butter, melted

1. Heat a 6- to 8-quart heavy-bottomed stainless steel pan over high. (It is really important that you use a high-quality pot with a thick bottom, or the popcorn will burn.) Add the coconut oil and salt. When the oil has melted, add the popcorn kernels. Cover and cook for a few minutes, moving the pot vigorously, until the popping has subsided. Immediately pour the popcorn into a large bowl.

2. Place the thyme, rosemary, nettles, yeast, and Herbamare in a coffee grinder or blender and grind until you have a somewhat coarse powder. Drizzle the popcorn with the melted coconut oil, then toss with the herb mixture.

maple caramel corn

MAKES ABOUT 4 QUARTS

Serve a large bowl of this tasty popcorn at your holiday party. It also makes a great gift for a teacher. If you want to double the recipe, make it in batches—popping 1 cup of popcorn will nearly fill an 8-quart stockpot!

POPCORN
2 to 3 tablespoons coconut oil
¼ teaspoon sea salt
1 cup organic popcorn kernels

CARAMEL
½ cup coconut oil or butter
1 cup pure maple syrup
Few dashes of sea salt

1. Preheat the oven to 325°F. Heat an 8-quart stockpot over high. Add the coconut oil and salt, then the popcorn kernels. Cover and cook for a few minutes, moving the pot vigorously, until the popping has subsided. Immediately pour the popcorn into two large bowls.

2. In a medium saucepan over medium heat, warm the coconut oil, maple syrup, and salt. When small bubbles form, cook for 4 to 5 minutes, whisking occasionally, until thickened and foamy. Quickly pour half the caramel over each bowl of popcorn and toss using two large spoons. Spread into two shallow baking pans or sheets and place in the oven. Bake for 10 minutes, stirring halfway through. Let cool completely. The caramel corn will crisp as it cools. Once completely cooled, store in a tightly sealed container to keep crisp.

honeydew-cucumber-mint pops

FREE OF

MAKES 8 TO 12 POPSICLES

I like to use a very ripe honeydew melon for this recipe. You could also add the juice from one or two limes to gain a refreshing tart flavor. If you don't have many popsicle molds, use either a small melon or half a melon and a medium cucumber. You can also add ice cubes to any leftovers that won't fit into the molds and make a smoothie.

1 medium to large honeydew melon, halved and seeded

1 large cucumber, chopped

Large handful of fresh spearmint leaves

Scoop the melon flesh into a bowl to catch the juices. Add both to a blender, then add the cucumber and mint. Blend until smooth, then pour into popsicle molds and freeze overnight.

NUTRITION TIP

Cucumbers contain lignans, or polyphenols found in plants, which can help reduce the risk of developing breast, uterine, ovarian, and prostate cancer, as well as cardiovascular disease.

blueberry-orange-coconut swirl pops

FREE OF

MAKES 4 TO 8 POPSICLES

I like to make a few batches of these just after we go blueberry picking. Making popsicles with freshly picked fruit is an effective way to preserve the harvest! Sometimes I use apple juice in place of the orange and other times I simply blend the blueberries with a little water or coconut water and a few fresh stevia leaves.

1 cup fresh or frozen blueberries

1 cup fresh orange juice

¼ to ½ cup full-fat coconut milk

Place the blueberries and orange juice into a blender and blend until smooth. Pour into popsicle molds, leaving a little room at the top of each. Top with a tablespoon or so of the coconut milk, then use a chopstick to lightly swirl it into the blueberry mix. Freeze overnight.

desserts

Maple Sunflower Seed Butter Candy
387

Almond Goji Berry Truffles
388

Raw Vanilla White Chocolates
389

Fresh Strawberries with Lemon Avocado Custard
390

Berry Parfaits with Orange Cashew Cream
391

Dark Chocolate Coconut Custard
392

Sweet Potato Custard
393

Mango Coconut Pudding
394

Vanilla Chia Pudding
395

Avocado Fudge Pops
396

Dark Chocolate Ice Cream
397

Mint Chocolate Chip Ice Cream
398

Strawberry Coconut Ice Cream
399

White Nectarine Ice Cream
400

Peach Blackberry Sorbet
401

Watermelon Sorbet
402

Frozen Banana Coconut Cream Pie
403

Lime Avocado Tart with a Macadamia Nut Crust
404

Raw Blueberry Cheesecake
405

Raw Chocolate Pie
406

Flaky Grain-Free Pie Crust
407

Gluten-Free Pie Crust
408

Deep-Dish Apple Pie
409

Classic Pumpkin Pie
410

Maple Pecan Pie
411

Fig-Pear Tart with a Hazelnut Crust
412

Apple Plum Crisp
413

Blueberry Peach Crisp
414

Banana Coconut Cookies
415

Cashew Ginger Cookies
416

Healthy Lactation Oatmeal Raisin Cookies
417

Chocolate Chip Almond Butter Cookies
418

Chocolate Sunflower Seed Butter Cookies
419

Gingerbread Hazelnut Cutout Cookies
420

Orange Hazelnut Thumbprint Cookies
421

Peanut Butter Monster Cookies
422

Sunflower Seed Cookies
423

Chocolate Chip Cookie Bars
424

Chocolate Chip Teff Brownies
425

Chocolate Walnut Brownies
426

Gingerbread
427

Carrot Orange Spice Cupcakes
428

Chocolate Brownie Cupcakes
429

Molasses Spice Cupcakes
430

Pumpkin Cupcakes
431

Almond Apricot Snack Cake
432

Apricot-Almond Skillet Cake
433

Blackberry Buckwheat Cake
434

Vanilla Coconut Cake
435

Warm Chocolate Cake
436

Cashew Date Frosting
437

Chocolate Ganache Frosting
438

Chocolate Avocado Frosting
439

Coconut Orange Buttercream Frosting
440

Dairy-Free Cream Cheese Frosting
441

Simple Lemon Icing
442

Whipped Coconut Cream
443

Our take on dessert is to keep them as simple and wholesome as possible. Natural sweeteners are used in place of refined sugars. Whole-grain gluten-free flours and grain-free flours are used instead of refined flours. Organic fruits and nuts are the base for many desserts, and avocados are added for healthy fats in some recipes. You'll find that when your diet consists of real, whole foods, with plenty of vegetables and enough fat and protein, you may not even crave sugar! Dessert will naturally become something to be savored and eaten in moderation.

When we consume dessert in our home, it is usually a scoop of homemade ice cream topped with frozen organic berries. Cookies are baked occasionally—only about twice a month. Baked pies are enjoyed a few times a year on special occasions, and fruit crisps are made when there is too much fruit to process in the summertime. By consuming dessert on occasion, instead of every day, your children will learn to develop a healthy relationship with the sweet flavor.

ALTERNATIVES TO REFINED SUGAR

Eliminating refined sugars from your family's diet can help improve everyone's health. When consuming white sugar, the body needs to tap into its stores of B vitamins and minerals, such as calcium and magnesium, to properly digest it. A child who is a picky eater and is consuming an unbalanced diet high in refined foods—or who has a damaged upper intestine and is therefore not absorbing sufficient magnesium and calcium—will suffer the most from sugar consumption. Over time, consuming sugar can lead to nutrient deficiencies, yeast overgrowth, inflammation, weight gain, dental cavities, insulin resistance, hypoglycemia, lowered immunity, erratic behavior, poor concentration, learning disabilities, and cancer cell growth. Sugar is a main ingredient in many processed foods, so working to eliminate those will drastically cut down on total daily intake.

Natural sweeteners contain all the vitamins, minerals, and phytochemicals found in the plant they came from. They often digest slower than refined white sugar, and they actually have some nutritional value. But remember, natural sweeteners are still sugar, so use them wisely and sparingly!

Most of the sugar in processed food these days does not even come from cane sugar anymore. When you see the word *sugar* on a food label, the product is typically made from sugar beets. Beet sugar is often genetically modified and carries a great amount of neo-nicotinoid pesticides—systemic pesticides that cannot be washed off. Neonic pesticides are also responsible for something that has been termed colony collapse disorder affecting our bee populations. Avoiding processed foods and sugars also means that you are helping to create a healthier planet!

10 Tips for Using Natural Sweeteners

1. Coconut Nectar is the sap from the coconut palm tree. It is very thick and rich with a low glycemic index of about 35, meaning it won't spike blood sugar as quickly as other sweeteners. It contains very little glucose and fructose, a small percentage of sucrose, and a high percentage of fructooligosaccharides (FOS). These indigestible sugars, or prebiotics, feed beneficial bacteria in the gut! Use coconut nectar anytime a liquid sweetener is called for.

2. Local Honey is a simple sugar of mostly glucose and fructose. It is easily digested and can be used anytime a liquid sweetener is called for. Raw honey has a much lower glycemic index than pasteurized honey, so always read labels or talk to your local beekeepers to find a source of raw honey. When combined with eggs in a baked good, honey can cause a lot of browning, which is why I prefer to use as little as possible in my recipes. You can replace part of the honey called for in a recipe with unsweetened applesauce and add liquid stevia to boost sweetness if desired.

3. Maple Syrup is mostly sucrose. Because of this it doesn't cause a lot of browning when baked, but it offers a distinct maple flavor. Use it anywhere a liquid sweetener is called for. Remember to always purchase *pure* maple syrup made entirely from the sap of the sugar maple tree. We prefer to use grade B, which is cheaper and richer in flavor than grade A. Imitation maple syrup is full of nonfood chemicals like caramel color, flavorings, and high fructose corn syrup.

4. Coconut Sugar is basically dried and granulated coconut nectar, and it comes with the same low-glycemic properties. It is light brown in color and the flavor is rich and caramel-like. Use it anytime a granulated sugar is called for.

5. Maple Sugar is simply dried and granulated pure maple syrup. It is quite expensive but very tasty. It will give your desserts a distinct maple flavor. Use it anytime a granulated sugar is called for.

6. Whole Cane Sugar is the dried juice of the sugar cane plant. It is dark brown in color and rich in flavor. It has a much higher glycemic index compared to coconut sugar, but is less expensive and easier to come by. You can use it in place of coconut sugar, if desired.

7. Medjool Dates can be soaked in hot water and pureed into a paste to be used in cakes, muffins, or cookies. You can use dates as a primary sweetener in many recipes, but you will need to lessen other liquids in the recipe.

8. Mashed Ripe Bananas are such a perfect natural sweetener! The riper your bananas, the sweeter they will be. You can puree bananas in a blender and use the puree to replace any liquid sweetener.

9. Prunes work in a similar fashion to dates, but are less sweet and higher in fiber. They can be used to thicken, bind, and sweeten most baked treats. To make prune puree, place 1 cup of prunes in a bowl and cover with 1 cup of boiling water. Soak for 20 minutes, then pour the soaked prunes and water into a blender and puree. You can use this in place of applesauce or other liquid sweeteners in most recipes.

10. Stevia has zero calories and a glycemic index of zero. It can be used to sweeten treats without adding sugar. Stevia is a green plant that grows in warm climates. We've been able to successfully grow it in our garden in the Northwest, but it doesn't survive our cool winters. We prefer to use the powdered whole dried leaf (it should be green) because it is less processed than other types of stevias. If you are using ingredients in a recipe that are naturally sweet, such as applesauce, mashed banana, or coconut flour, then add about ½ teaspoon powdered whole leaf stevia to boost the sweetness, if desired.

maple sunflower seed candy

FREE OF

MAKES ABOUT 3 DOZEN CANDIES

I use organic Sunbutter, a butter made from roasted sunflower seeds (the nonorganic versions have sugar and other stuff added). I also prefer to use grade B maple syrup over grade A because it has a richer flavor. This candy easily burns if it is not tended to or if the heat is too high, so watch it carefully. Add one of these candies to your child's lunchbox as a sweet treat. They are also fun to make for Halloween or as a Christmas stocking stuffer.

1 cup pure maple syrup
½ cup organic sunflower seed butter

⅛ teaspoon sea salt

1. Place the maple syrup, sunflower butter, and salt in a 2-quart stainless steel pot with a thick, heavy bottom. Whisk well, then turn the heat to high and bring to a boil, whisking constantly. Immediately reduce the heat to medium or medium-high to maintain a steady, low boil. Whisk continuously for about 8 minutes, or until the candy thickens and begins to stick to the bottom of the pan. Remove from the heat and remove the whisk (otherwise the candy will get stuck inside of the wires as it cools). Let cool until the temperature is low enough to handle, 5 to 10 minutes; any longer and the candy will get too hard to work with.

2. Place a piece of parchment paper on a clean work surface. Roll the warm candy into five thin, long logs, then slice each into 1- to 2-inch pieces. Wrap each piece in unbleached parchment or waxed paper. Let cool completely before serving.

VARIATION: This candy can be made with nut butters, if you desire. Almond butter is particularly delicious! You can also add a few dashes of vanilla extract or a little cocoa powder to make it extra special.

almond goji berry truffles

FREE OF

MAKES ABOUT 1 DOZEN TRUFFLES

These beautiful truffles contain a flavorful red filling and a rich chocolate exterior, making them a special treat for Valentine's Day.

FILLING
1 cup dried goji berries
½ cup creamy almond butter
¼ cup coconut nectar or pure maple syrup
1 teaspoon almond extract

CHOCOLATE COATING
1 cup organic dark chocolate chips
1 tablespoon coconut oil
1 teaspoon vanilla extract

1. Place the filling ingredients in a food processor fitted with the "s" blade; process. Pulse for a few minutes, until ground and sticky. Roll the filling into small balls and set on a plate.

2. Cover a large plate with a piece of parchment paper.

3. In a double boiler, combine the ingredients for the chocolate coating. (You can also use a stainless steel bowl over a pot filled with a few inches of water; just don't let the bowl touch the water.) Melt the chocolate over low heat, stirring, until completely melted.

4. Remove the pan from the heat and immediately drop the first truffle into the chocolate, gently swirling the chocolate over it using a spoon. Lift up and place onto the prepared plate. Repeat with the remaining truffles.

5. Place the plate of truffles in the freezer for about 30 minutes to set the chocolate. Then put the truffles in a sealed glass container and store in your refrigerator for up to a week.

NUTRITION TIP

Goji berries are a truly remarkable superfood. Ounce for ounce, goji berries contain more vitamin C than oranges, more beta-carotene than carrots, and more iron than spinach. They also contain over 20 trace minerals and 18 amino acids!

raw vanilla white chocolates

FREE OF

MAKES ABOUT 60 BITE-SIZE WHITE CHOCOLATES

I think these are one of my children's most loved treats. And I love serving these to them as well—they are packed with healthy fats! You'll need a few silicone candy molds, which can easily be found online or at your local craft store. If you don't have any candy molds, then pour the liquid chocolate mixture into a parchment-lined glass baking dish. Once it's frozen, you can cut it into small squares using a sharp knife. Make sure to store these white chocolates in the freezer or refrigerator; they begin to get soft at room temperature.

1 cup raw cacao butter (about 8 ounces)
¾ cup raw cashew butter
4 to 5 tablespoons raw honey
1 teaspoon raw vanilla powder
Pinch of sea salt

OPTIONAL FILLING:
2 tablespoons raw almond butter
1 tablespoon raw cacao powder
2 to 3 teaspoons raw honey

1. Melt the cacao butter in a small saucepan over the lowest heat possible. Add to a blender along with the cashew butter, honey, vanilla, and salt. Blend on high until smooth.

2. Place the candy molds onto a baking sheet (this way you can easily transfer it to the freezer).

3. If using the filling, place the ingredients in a small bowl and stir together with a fork until combined. Roll ½-teaspoon-size portions in your hands. Fill the candy molds three-fourths full with the white chocolate mixture. Drop a ball of filling into each candy mold, then fill each the rest of the way with the white chocolate.

4. Freeze the candy molds for 30 minutes. Remove from the freezer and pop the white chocolates out of the molds.

fresh strawberries with lemon avocado custard

FREE OF

MAKES 4 TO 6 SERVINGS

This slightly sweet, creamy custard is bright green! The flavor is lemony, just perfect for spooning over fresh berries in the spring or summer. The coconut milk helps to thicken it once it chills.

AVOCADO CUSTARD

2 small ripe avocados

¼ cup fresh lemon juice

¼ cup coconut nectar

¼ cup coconut milk

½ teaspoon organic lemon flavoring

1 to 2 pints fresh strawberries, rinsed, hulled, and halved

Unsweetened shredded coconut (optional)

1. Place the custard ingredients into a blender and blend for 60 seconds, scraping down the sides and blending again, if necessary, until thick and creamy. Transfer to a glass container with a lid and chill in the refrigerator for at least 1 hour, though 6 hours works better.

2. Place the strawberries in individual serving bowls or small, clear juice glasses. Place a large dollop of the custard atop the berries and sprinkle with a little shredded coconut, if desired.

> **NUTRITION TIP**
> Avocados are a rich source of phytosterols and carotenoids, both of which help keep inflammation in check. Additionally, avocados are a rich source of oleic acid, a fatty acid that helps prevent heart disease.

berry parfaits with orange cashew cream

FREE OF

MAKES 4 TO 6 SERVINGS

This is a favorite recipe to make during the summer months when berries are in abundance. Serve it for breakfast, a healthy snack, or dessert. Use any berries that are fresh and available. Try blueberries, strawberries, blackberries, and raspberries. Note that the cashews need to be soaked for three hours before you begin this preparation.

CASHEW CREAM

1 cup raw cashews, soaked for 3 hours

½ cup fresh orange juice

2 medjool dates, pitted

½ teaspoon grated orange zest

Pinch of sea salt

Dash of pure maple syrup (optional)

4 cups fresh berries

Hemp seeds

1. Drain and rinse the cashews, then place into a blender along with the orange juice, dates, orange zest, and salt. Blend on high until very smooth and creamy. You might need to turn off your blender, scrape down the sides, and blend again a few times. Taste and add a dash of maple syrup for a sweeter cream and blend again, if needed.

2. Place a layer of berries on the bottoms of 4 to 6 parfait cups or clear juice glasses. Add a thin layer of the cashew cream, then another layer of berries, then a final layer of the cashew cream. Sprinkle the tops with the hemp seeds.

NUTRITION TIP

Making your own orange juice from fresh oranges is much more nutritious than buying store-bought pasteurized orange juice. Pasteurization kills harmful bacteria so as to prolong shelf life, but it also destroys live enzymes and certain vitamins. Freshly squeezed orange juice contains all the enzymes, vitamin C, and antioxidants in the orange, which makes the juice far more digestible and easier to assimilate.

---

dark chocolate coconut custard

MAKES 6 SERVINGS

This thick and rich custard can help alleviate any chocolate cravings you might be having! It's really not designed for children—ours think it is far too rich. You'll need six small ramekins for this recipe, which can be purchased at most kitchen stores or online. I use Dagoba organic bittersweet chocolate, though any brand will do—just make sure it's organic and gluten-free. Serve with a dollop of Whipped Coconut Cream (page 443) and sliced fresh strawberries. You can cover and refrigerate any leftover custard for up to a week.

1 (14.5-ounce) can coconut milk
4 ounces bittersweet chocolate
½ to ¾ cup coconut sugar

2 teaspoons vanilla extract
Pinch of sea salt
2 large organic eggs, lightly beaten

1. Preheat the oven to 350°F. Fill a 9 by 13-inch baking pan halfway with water.

2. Heat the coconut milk, chocolate, and coconut sugar in a small saucepan over very low heat. Whisk continuously until the chocolate has melted. Add the vanilla and salt; whisk again. Remove from the heat and let cool for about 10 minutes. Add the eggs and vigorously whisk to incorporate.

3. Evenly pour the custard into six ½-cup ramekins. Carefully place the ramekins into the pan with the water. Bake for approximately 30 minutes. Let cool completely.

> **INGREDIENT TIP**
> We use Native Forest organic coconut milk, which comes in BPA-free cans.

sweet potato custard

FREE OF

MAKES 6 TO 8 SERVINGS

This custard can be baked in a 10-inch deep-dish pie plate or in individual ramekins. Serve with Whipped Coconut Cream (page 443) and a dusting of cinnamon. Store any leftover custard in the refrigerator for up to a week.

2 pounds orange sweet potatoes

1 cup coconut milk

6 large organic egg yolks

¼ cup honey or pure maple syrup

1 teaspoon vanilla extract

1 to 2 teaspoons ground cinnamon

½ to 1 teaspoon ground ginger

Pinch of sea salt

1. Bake the sweet potatoes, with their skins on, in a 350° F oven for about 1 hour, or until soft. Let cool. (The sweet potatoes can be baked 1 to 2 days in advance.)

2. Remove the skins from the sweet potatoes and place the flesh into a food processor fitted with the "s" blade. Mash the potatoes, pulsing until smooth; you should have about 3 cups mashed. Add the remaining ingredients and process until smooth.

3. Pour the sweet potato custard into a greased 10-inch deep-dish pie plate or into six ½-cup ramekins. Bake for about 1 hour for the large custard or 40 to 45 minutes for the ramekins, until the custard is slightly golden on top and is cooked through. Serve warm or cold.

VARIATION: If you tolerate dairy products, replace the coconut milk with organic raw cream.

mango coconut pudding

FREE OF

MAKES 6 SERVINGS

The kudzu root powder here helps the ingredients to come together into a thick pudding. Sometimes called Japanese arrowroot, the powder is extracted from the root of the kudzu plant. It's soothing to the digestive system and can also be used to thicken sauces and gravies in place of cornstarch. You can use either fresh or frozen mangos in this recipe; you'll need about five large fresh ones or two 10-ounce bags of frozen, plus another fresh one for the topping. This recipe can be used in lieu of a cake for a child's first birthday party.

CUSTARD
4 to 6 tablespoons kudzu powder
½ cup water
4 cups diced fresh or frozen mango
1 (14.5-ounce) can coconut milk

¼ cup honey or coconut nectar
2 teaspoons vanilla extract

TOPPING
Diced fresh mango
Unsweetened shredded coconut

1. Place the kudzu powder and water in a 3-quart saucepan. Use the 4 tablespoons if you like a softer pudding or 6 tablespoons if you like it firmer. Whisk to dissolve the kudzu. In a blender, combine the mango, coconut milk, and honey until very smooth and creamy.

2. Pour the mango puree into the saucepan with the kudzu. Turn the heat to medium-high and whisk constantly until the mixture boils. Reduce the heat to low and simmer, still whisking, for 6 to 10 minutes. When the custard changes from a creamy yellow to an egg-yolk yellow, remove from the heat and whisk in the vanilla.

3. Pour or ladle the custard into 6 small 1-cup bowls and chill in the refrigerator to set, 1 to 2 hours. Top with the diced fresh mango and shredded coconut, and serve.

vanilla chia pudding

This raw pudding is similar to tapioca pudding. The chia seeds expand and release their gelatinous substance when they are soaked in a liquid. Serve the pudding in small bowls topped with fresh raspberries or sliced fresh strawberries. If you do not have a high-powered blender, soak the cashews for about three hours before blending them with the remaining ingredients. Also, a regular blender will not pulverize the vanilla bean, so use 1 tablespoon of vanilla extract instead.

½ cup raw cashews

1½ cups water

¼ cup coconut nectar or pure maple syrup

1 vanilla bean

Pinch of sea salt

5 tablespoons chia seeds

Fresh berries, for serving

1. Place the cashews, water, coconut nectar, vanilla bean, and salt into a high-powered blender and blend until smooth and ultra-creamy. Pour into a medium bowl or glass container. Add the chia seeds and whisk well. Let soak on the counter at room temperature for about 1 hour. Then cover and transfer to the refrigerator to thicken for at least 2 hours more.

2. To serve, scoop portions into serving bowls and top with fresh berries.

avocado fudge pops

FREE OF

MAKES 8 SERVINGS

This recipe is quite a treat for anyone, young or old. I think you'll like how healthy they are, too! I use a raw Ecuadorian cacao powder that makes them extra tasty as well as Dagoba chocolate products, which are gluten-free, though not raw. After blending the ingredients, you can serve this pudding immediately or pour it into your icepop molds and freeze for fudge pops.

8 medjool dates, pitted
½ cup water, or more as needed
3 avocados
1 cup coconut milk
¼ cup raw honey

5 to 7 tablespoons raw cacao powder or unsweetened cocoa powder
2 teaspoons vanilla extract
Pinch of sea salt

1. Place the dates into a blender and add the water. Pack the dates down in the blender jar so they are covered, for the most part, with the water. Let soak for about 30 minutes, then add the avocados, coconut milk, honey, cacao powder, vanilla, and salt and blend until very smooth and creamy. Depending on your blender, you may need to add a little extra coconut milk or water to achieve a smooth blend.

2. Pour the pudding into small bowls and serve, or pour them into molds and freeze for at least 6 hours. Run under hot water to release.

dark chocolate ice cream

FREE OF

MAKES 8 SERVINGS

Having an ice cream maker to make your own fresh, dairy-free, and sugar-free ice cream is such a treat! The avocado makes this ice cream extra rich and creamy, yet doesn't detract from the chocolate flavor. We also like to add finely chopped frozen pitted cherries while it is churning. Chilling the coconut milk helps speed the formation of the "ice cream" in the ice cream maker.

2 (14.5-ounce) cans coconut milk, chilled for 3 hours or overnight

1 avocado (optional)

½ cup honey, pure maple syrup, or coconut nectar

¾ cup raw cacao powder

1 tablespoon vanilla extract

¼ teaspoon almond extract

OPTIONAL ADDITIONS

Finely chopped organic dark chocolate bar

Sliced almonds

Chopped frozen cherries

1. Pour the cold coconut milk into a blender. Add the avocado, if using, the honey, cacao powder, and the vanilla and almond extracts; blend until smooth, about 30 seconds.

2. Transfer the mixture to your ice cream maker and process according to the manufacturer's instructions. If adding any extras, stop after about 15 minutes and stir them in, then continue until the ice cream is thick and creamy. It will be the consistency of soft serve ice cream. To harden it, scoop it out and place in a large container, then freeze for about 2 hours. Let stand for about 10 minutes before serving.

mint chocolate chip ice cream

FREE OF

MAKES 8 SERVINGS

Our children love the combination of mint and chocolate chips, and I feel good serving them this ice cream knowing that it is providing healthy fats and a slew of antioxidants. The avocados give the ice cream a light green color and help make it very creamy. Our oldest daughter strongly dislikes avocado, but she likes this recipe because she cannot detect the avocado flavor. Be sure to use a high-powered blender, as the avocados and coconut milk thicken immediately after you start the blender. You'll have to chill the coconut milk in advance of preparing this ice cream.

2 (14.5-ounce) cans coconut milk, chilled for 3 hours or overnight

2 small avocados

¼ to ½ cup raw honey or coconut nectar

1 to 2 teaspoons organic peppermint flavoring

½ cup organic dark chocolate chips

1. Place the coconut milk, avocados, honey, and peppermint flavoring into a high-powered blender and blend on medium to high, until smooth and creamy. Be careful about blending it too long, or the mixture will heat up and will be too warm to turn into ice cream.

2. Transfer to your ice cream maker and process according to the manufacturer's instructions.

After about 15 minutes, add the chocolate chips and continue according to the instructions. The ice cream will be the consistency of soft serve ice cream. To harden it, place in a large container and freeze for about 2 hours. Let stand for about 10 minutes before serving.

strawberry coconut ice cream

FREE OF

MAKES 8 SERVINGS

If you may have a little extra ice cream custard that won't fit into your machine, simply pour it into icepop molds and freeze. Serve this ice cream with sliced fresh strawberries and fresh mint leaves for a cooling summer dessert. Remember to chill the coconut milk well in advance.

2 (14.5-ounce) cans coconut milk, chilled for 3 hours or overnight

2 to 2½ cups frozen strawberries (about 1 pound)

¼ to ½ cup raw honey or coconut nectar

1 tablespoon vanilla extract

½ teaspoon organic lemon flavoring

Pour the coconut milk into a blender. Add the strawberries, honey, vanilla, and lemon flavoring. Blend until smooth and creamy. Pour the custard into your ice cream maker and process according to the manufacturer's instructions. The ice cream will be the consistency of soft serve ice cream. To harden it, place in a large container and freeze for about 2 hours. Let stand for about 10 minutes before serving.

> **INGREDIENT TIP**
>
> Adding a tablespoon or two of alcohol to the ice cream, such as an alcoholic vanilla extract or brandy, helps keep the ice cream from crystallizing in the freezer.

white nectarine ice cream

This off-white ice cream is flecked with little bits of pink from the diced nectarine. It is sweet, rich, and scoops perfectly. Definitely a crowd pleaser! I use a Cuisinart Ice Cream Maker, which can be found at most kitchen supply stores or online. Use either fresh or frozen nectarines; if frozen, your blended cream will turn into "ice cream" much quicker. Remember to chill the coconut cream and soak the cashews and dates in advance of making the ice cream.

¾ cup raw cashews

5 medjool dates, pitted

1 (14.5-ounce) can coconut milk

2 large white nectarines, pitted, plus
1 white nectarine, diced

¼ to ½ cup raw honey or coconut nectar

1 tablespoon vanilla extract

1 to 2 teaspoons almond extract

½ cup slivered almonds (optional)

1. Place the cashews and dates in a small bowl and cover with water; let soak for about 3 hours. Chill the coconut milk for 3 hours.

2. Drain and rinse the cashews and place into a high-powered blender. Add the dates, cold coconut milk, the 2 pitted nectarines, the honey, vanilla extract, and almond extract. Blend on high until very smooth and creamy.

3. Transfer the mixture to your ice cream maker and process according to the manufacturer's instructions. After about 15 minutes, stir in the diced nectarine and slivered almonds, if using. The ice cream will be the consistency of soft serve ice cream. To harden it, place in a large container and freeze for about 2 hours. Let stand for about 10 minutes before serving.

> **INGREDIENT TIP**
>
> If you cannot find large nectarines, use 5 small ones in place of the 3, with 3 for blending into the cream and the remaining 2 for the add-in.

peach blackberry sorbet

MAKES 6 TO 8 SERVINGS

Making your own sugar-free sorbet is easy! We like to pick pounds of local fruit in the summer and store it in an extra freezer so we can have fruit treats all year long! This is one of our favorites, created by our daughter Lily and her friend Kaia when they were eight years old.

2 large frozen peaches, chopped

2 cups frozen blackberries

Juice of 1 lemon

2 to 4 tablespoons raw honey or coconut nectar

Place all the ingredients into a food processor fitted with the "s" blade. Pulse until the fruit is broken down and you have a smooth sorbet. You may need to stop the processor to scrape down the sides, then continue pulsing. Serve this sorbet right away or scoop it into a container and freeze for a few hours.

VARIATION: Use frozen blueberries in place of the blackberries.

watermelon sorbet

FREE OF

MAKES 6 SERVINGS

This is the perfect refreshing dessert or snack on a hot summer's afternoon. The lycopenes in the watermelon give this sorbet a beautiful pink hue that is attractive to children. To make this recipe at a moment's notice, have your freezer stocked with chopped watermelon. Then all you need do is toss everything into a food processor to have a healthy, refreshing dessert in minutes! Just be sure you are using seedless watermelon.

4 to 5 cups frozen seedless watermelon chunks

Juice of 1 lime

4 to 6 tablespoons raw honey or coconut nectar

1. Place the watermelon, lime juice, and 4 tablespoons of the honey into a food processor fitted with the "s" blade. Pulse until the fruit is broken down and you have a smooth sorbet. You may need to stop the processor to scrape down the sides, then continue pulsing.

2. Taste and add the remaining 2 tablespoons of honey, if necessary. Serve right away or transfer to a container and freeze for a few hours.

frozen banana coconut cream pie

FREE OF

MAKES 8 SERVINGS

This luscious pie gets its sweetness mainly from the bananas. It is nutritious enough to have a slice for breakfast along with a green smoothie! Or, serve with a warm chocolate sauce for a divine dessert! For the coconut cream, chill a can of full-fat coconut milk overnight, then use the layer of fat on top.

CHOCOLATE COOKIE CRUMB CRUST

1½ cups blanched almond flour

¼ cup arrowroot powder

¼ cup coconut sugar

3 tablespoons raw cacao powder

¼ teaspoon sea salt

¼ cup coconut oil

1 to 2 tablespoons water

COCONUT CREAM FILLING

4 frozen bananas

½ cup coconut cream (see Headnote)

2 to 4 tablespoons raw honey or coconut nectar

1 teaspoon raw vanilla powder

1. Preheat the oven to 350°F. Place the almond flour, arrowroot powder, coconut sugar, cacao powder, and salt into a food processor fitted with the "s" blade. Pulse a few times to mix well. Add the coconut oil and process again until crumbly. While the motor is running, slowly add the water, starting with 1 tablespoon. Process until the dough begins to form a ball, adding the remaining water, if necessary. Press into a 9-inch deep-dish pie plate.

Bake for 15 to 20 minutes. Cool completely or freeze.

2. Place the filling ingredients into a food processor fitted with the "s" blade. Pulse to break down the bananas, then continue to process until you have a smooth creamy filling. Scoop into the chilled crust. Freeze for 2 to 4 hours, or until firm. Slice and serve.

lime avocado tart
with a macadamia nut crust

This is one of our favorite raw desserts. I love giving my children a slice, knowing it is full of healthy fats, antioxidants, and protein. Serve this with candles in lieu of a birthday cake.

MACADAMIA NUT CRUST

1 cup raw macadamia nuts

½ cup unsweetened shredded coconut

4 medjool dates, pitted

Pinch of sea salt

FILLING

4 small ripe avocados

6 tablespoons melted coconut oil

6 tablespoons fresh lime juice

4 tablespoons raw honey

1 to 2 teaspoons grated lime zest

1. Cut out a 9-inch circle of parchment or waxed paper to line the bottom of a 9-inch springform pan. Place the macadamia nuts into a food processor fitted with the "s" blade. Process until finely ground, then add the coconut, dates, and salt; process again until the dates are ground and the mixture is well combined. Press into an even layer on the bottom of the pan.

2. Rinse out the food processor and then add the filling ingredients. Process until smooth and creamy. Pour into the crust and spread with a spatula or the back of a spoon to make an even layer. Sprinkle with the lime zest. Freeze for 2 hours or until set. Remove from the freezer 30 minutes before serving. (If the whole pie isn't eaten in one sitting, return it to the freezer for storage.)

VARIATION: If desired, add another layer to the pie. Spread some freshly made ice cream or soften some frozen ice cream and spread evenly on top of the avocado layer.

raw blueberry cheesecake

This raw cheesecake is dairy-free and still ever so rich and creamy! The combination of raw soaked cashews and coconut oil is what makes the "cheese" filling. I use hazelnuts and almonds for the crust, but just about any nut will work. If you would like to savor this cheesecake, then slice it and freeze the pieces in serving-size containers. When ready to serve, put a container of frozen cheesecake in the fridge to thaw for a day before serving. Count on soaking the cashews for at least three hours before preparing this.

CRUST
¾ cup raw hazelnuts
¾ cup raw almonds
Pinch of sea salt
6 to 8 medjool dates, pitted
1 tablespoon coconut oil

FILLING
1½ cups raw cashews, soaked in water for 3 hours

¾ cup melted coconut oil
¼ cup fresh lemon juice
4 to 6 tablespoons coconut nectar or raw honey
2 teaspoons vanilla extract
½ teaspoon almond extract
1 cup fresh or frozen blueberries, thawed if frozen

1. Place the hazelnuts, almonds, and salt into a food processor fitted with the "s" blade. Pulse until finely ground. Add the dates and coconut oil; process until finely ground. Line a 9-inch springform pan with parchment paper. Add the crust mixture and press it firmly and evenly into the bottom of the pan. Chill in the refrigerator or freezer while preparing the filling.

2. Drain and rinse the cashews. Place into a high-powered blender along with the coconut oil, lemon juice, coconut nectar, vanilla extract, and almond extract. Blend on high, stopping to scrape the sides down, until very smooth and creamy. The mixture will be somewhat thick, so you may need to stop the blender, stir, and continue to blend. Add the blueberries and blend until incorporated.

3. Pour the filling into the crust. Chill in the freezer for about 1 hour, then transfer to the refrigerator and chill until set and firm, 2 to 3 hours more. To serve, unlatch the springform pan to release the edge, then slice and serve.

raw chocolate pie

FREE OF

MAKES 8 TO 12 SERVINGS

This pie requires a food processor; a regular blender will not work, nor will a high-powered blender. Top each slice with a simple raspberry sauce made by combining 2 tablespoons arrowroot powder, ½ cup water, 1 cup fresh raspberries, and 1 to 3 tablespoons honey or coconut nectar; whisk together and simmer over low heat until translucent. This pie makes a lovely treat for Valentine's Day or a birthday party. The pie can also be frozen for longer storage, if desired.

CRUST
2 cups raw pecans
8 to 10 medjool dates, pitted
1 tablespoon coconut oil
1 tablespoon ground cinnamon
Pinch of ground cardamom (optional)

FILLING
1 cup raw cashew butter
1 small avocado

½ cup plus 2 tablespoons raw cacao powder, or to taste
½ cup coconut nectar or raw honey
½ cup softened coconut butter
¼ cup water, or more as needed
1 teaspoon raw vanilla powder

Fresh berries (optional)

1. Place the pecans into food processor fitted with the "s" blade and pulse until finely ground. Add the remaining crust ingredients and pulse until thoroughly ground and mixed. Press the crust into the bottom of a 9½-inch deep-dish pie plate. Place into the refrigerator to chill.

2. Put the filling ingredients into the food processor and process until smooth and creamy. Add a little more water for a thinner filling, 1 tablespoon at a time. (It will take longer to set if you do this.) Pour the filling into the chilled crust and spread out evenly with a rubber spatula. Place the cheesecake into the refrigerator to chill for 3 to 4 hours. Slice and serve with fresh berries, if desired.

> **INGREDIENT TIP**
> Coconut butter is different from coconut oil. The butter is made from the whole coconut—the flesh and the oil. Be sure to just barely warm the coconut butter on very low heat, as it can quickly burn. You can also place the jar of coconut butter in a bowl filled with hot water to soften it.

flaky grain-free pie crust

FREE OF

MAKES ENOUGH DOUGH FOR 2 SINGLE-CRUST OR 1 DOUBLE-CRUST PIE

This recipe has two versions, one for a single crust and one for a double crust, useful for either a regular 9-inch pie plate or a 9-inch deep-dish pie plate. Be sure the butter or shortening is very cold; in fact, I often freeze it and then grate it into the flour using a cheese grater, which helps to create a very flaky crust.

SINGLE CRUST

1 cup packed blanched almond flour

1 cup arrowroot powder or tapioca flour

¼ to ½ teaspoon sea salt

4 to 5 tablespoons cold unsalted butter or organic shortening

1 large organic egg

DOUBLE CRUST

2 cups packed blanched almond flour

2 cups arrowroot powder or tapioca flour

¾ teaspoon sea salt

8 to 10 tablespoons cold unsalted butter or organic shortening

2 large organic eggs

1. In a medium bowl, whisk together the almond flour, arrowroot powder, and salt. Cut in the butter using your fingers or a pastry cutter until small pea-size crumbs form. Make a well in the center and crack the egg into it, then stir, using a fork, to gradually incorporate the flour. Knead a few times until the mixture forms a ball. If the dough seems too dry, then add a tablespoon of cold water. If making a double crust, divide the dough into two balls. Wrap the dough in parchment or waxed paper and chill in the refrigerator for 1 to 2 hours or in your freezer for about 20 minutes. The dough is now ready for use.

2. *If pre-baking your bottom crust:* Preheat the oven to 350°F. Place one dough ball on a piece of parchment or waxed paper, place another sheet on top, and then roll out to desired size. Remove the top sheet of paper and carefully flip the dough circle into a pie plate. Remove the second sheet of paper. Flute the edges and prick the bottom of the crust with a fork a few times. Pre-bake the crust for 8 to 10 minutes, then fill with your favorite filling, and bake according to your recipe; or roll out and add the top crust, if using, and bake as your recipe directs.

gluten-free pie crust

FREE OF

MAKES ENOUGH DOUGH FOR 2 SINGLE-CRUST OR 1 DOUBLE-CRUST PIE

This gluten-free, egg-free pie crust makes a great replacement for regular wheat-based recipes. It's flaky and tender, as any pie crust should be. The key is to use the "superfine" flours, as listed below. These are very finely ground, much more than regular gluten-free grain flours. Authentic Foods is my supplier. Their products can be found online or possibly at your local health food store.

SINGLE CRUST

½ cup superfine brown rice flour

½ cup superfine sweet rice flour

¼ cup quinoa flour or millet flour

½ teaspoon sea salt

½ cup organic palm shortening or butter

4 to 6 tablespoons ice water

DOUBLE CRUST

1 cup superfine brown rice flour

1 cup superfine sweet rice flour

½ cup quinoa flour or millet flour

1 teaspoon sea salt

1 cup organic palm shortening or butter

8 to 10 tablespoons ice water

1. In a medium bowl, whisk together the flours and salt. Cut in the shortening with your fingers or a pastry cutter until small crumbs form. Freeze the mixture for 10 to 15 minutes if you've used palm shortening and 20 minutes if you've used butter. Then add the water, beginning with the lesser amount and using a spoon or fork to mix the dough until it forms a ball. (If necessary, knead ever so slightly to get a uniform texture.) If making a double crust, divide the dough into two balls. The dough is now ready for use.

2. *If pre-baking your bottom crust:* Preheat the oven to 350°F. Place the dough ball on a piece of parchment or waxed paper, place another sheet on top, and then roll out to desired size. Remove the top sheet of paper and carefully flip the crust over and into a pie plate. Remove the second sheet of paper. Flute the edges and prick the bottom of the crust with a fork a few times. Pre-bake the crust for 10 to 12 minutes. Fill the crust as desired and bake according to your recipe; or top with the second crust, if using, and bake as directed in your recipe.

deep-dish apple pie

FREE OF

MAKES 8 SERVINGS

Enjoy a little slice of autumn with this fresh double-crust apple pie. My favorite baking apple for pie is McIntosh, although Granny Smiths work well, too. Core the apples and slice them as thin as possible for a perfect pie. Or, use the slicing disk on your food processor and you'll have all the apples sliced in about 60 seconds.

Gluten-Free Pie Crust (page 408) or Flaky Grain-Free Pie Crust (page 407), double crust, not pre-baked

6 to 8 apples, cored and very thinly sliced

½ cup coconut sugar, plus a little for sprinkling the top

2 tablespoons arrowroot powder

1 tablespoon fresh lemon juice

2 teaspoons ground cinnamon

½ teaspoon grated nutmeg

Hemp milk

1. Preheat the oven to 425°F. Roll out one ball of dough and fit into a 9-inch deep-dish pie plate. Combine the apples, sugar, arrowroot powder lemon juice, cinnamon, and nutmeg in a large bowl and toss well. Add the filling, then roll out the top crust and add to the pie. Flute the edges, cut steam vents, and brush the top with hemp milk and sprinkle with sugar, if desired.

2. Place the pie on a baking sheet to catch any drips and bake for about 15 minutes, then reduce the heat to 350°F and bake for about 45 minutes more, or until the apple filling is bubbling and the crust is slightly golden around the edges. Cool for about 1 hour before cutting and serving.

classic pumpkin pie

FREE OF

MAKES 8 SERVINGS

I love pumpkin pie, whether as a bedtime snack or a quick breakfast. In autumn, we like to harvest sugar pumpkins from our own garden or get them at local farms. I store the pumpkins, along with other winter squashes, in cardboard boxes in our garage. They last for many months this way. You can use any variety of winter squash in this recipe if you don't happen to have a sugar pumpkin sitting around.

Flaky Grain-Free Pie Crust (page 407), single crust, not pre-baked

1¾ cups cooked and mashed sugar pumpkin, or 1 (15-ounce) can pumpkin puree

½ cup pure maple syrup

½ cup raw cream or Cashew Milk (page 453)

2 large organic eggs

¼ cup arrowroot powder

1 tablespoon pumpkin pie spice

1. Preheat the oven to 350°F. Roll out one dough ball between two pieces of waxed paper, then remove the top layer, flip the dough over, and place in a 9-inch deep-dish pie plate. Remove the second piece of waxed paper. Flute the edges and prick the bottom crust with a fork a few times. Pre-bake for 10 to 12 minutes. Keep the oven set at 350°F.

2. Place the pumpkin, maple syrup, cream, eggs, arrowroot powder, and pie spice into a blender and blend until smooth. Pour the filling into the crust. Bake for 50 to 60 minutes. Let cool at room temperature for about 1 hour, then chill in the refrigerator until set, about 3 hours.

> **INGREDIENT TIP**
>
> I prefer to use homemade cashew milk in this recipe. For best results, use a rich, fatty milk such as full-fat coconut milk, raw cream, or homemade cashew milk.

maple pecan pie

FREE OF

MAKES 8 SERVINGS

Pecan pie is a delicacy around the holidays. It is always the first to disappear from the dessert table, yet nobody ever knows that it is gluten-free and made with natural sweeteners!

Flaky Grain-Free Pie Crust (page 407) or Gluten-Free Pie Crust (page 408), single crust, not pre-baked

3 cups raw pecans

¼ cup arrowroot powder

1½ teaspoons ground cinnamon

⅛ teaspoon baking soda

¼ teaspoon sea salt

½ cup pure maple syrup

¼ cup brown rice syrup

¼ cup unsweetened applesauce

¼ cup melted coconut oil or butter

1. Preheat the oven to 350°F. Roll out the dough between two pieces of waxed paper, then remove the top layer, flip over, and place into a 9-inch pie plate. Remove the second piece of waxed paper. Flute the edges and prick the bottom crust with a fork a few times. Pre-bake for 10 to 12 minutes. Keep the oven at 350°F.

2. Place 2 cups of the pecans into a food processor fitted with the "s" blade. Process until a coarse meal is formed. Transfer to a large bowl and add the arrowroot powder, cinnamon, baking soda, and salt. Mix well, then add the maple syrup, brown rice syrup, applesauce, and oil. Mix again until well combined. Pour the filling into the pie crust and spread out with a spoon. Arrange the remaining 1 cup pecans on top. Bake for about 45 minutes. The filling will set completely when cooled. Chill in the refrigerator until serving, then bring it to room temperature before slicing.

> **INGREDIENT TIP**
> I use Lundberg Organic brown rice syrup.

fig-pear tart with a hazelnut crust

FREE OF

MAKES 16 SERVINGS

This scrumptious, nutritious grain-free tart can be served as an elegant dessert or a healthy after-school snack. I like to offer it during the winter holidays. I prefer to use Bob's Red Mill hazelnut flour, but you can also grind your own from raw hazelnuts and then sift it to remove any large bits. Figure on at least 12 hours to soak the figs before you prepare this tart.

2 cups dried Black Mission figs

1 cup fresh orange juice

½ cup port wine

2 tablespoons honey (optional)

2 ripe pears, cored and sliced

CRUST

2 cups hazelnut flour

½ cup arrowroot flour

¼ cup coconut sugar

½ teaspoon sea salt

¼ cup butter or coconut oil, chilled

2 tablespoons hemp milk or coconut milk

CHOCOLATE SAUCE

½ cup organic dark chocolate chips

2 to 3 tablespoons honey or pure maple syrup

2 to 3 tablespoons hemp milk or coconut milk

1 teaspoon organic orange flavoring

1. Place the figs, orange juice, and port wine into a quart jar and soak the figs for 12 to 24 hours at room temperature.

2. Preheat the oven to 325°F. Lightly grease an 8-inch square tart pan. Place the hazelnut flour, arrowroot powder, sugar, and salt into a food processor fitted with the "s" blade. Pulse a few times to combine, then add the butter and process until completely combined. Add the hemp milk and process until the dough forms a ball. Press the dough into the tart pan on both the bottom and up the sides. Place on a baking sheet and bake for 20 to 25 minutes. Let cool completely before filling.

3. Drain the figs, but reserve the soaking liquid. Place the figs into a food processor fitted with the

"s" blade. Add a few tablespoons of the reserved soaking liquid and the 2 tablespoons honey, if you think the fig paste needs to be a little sweeter. Process until a smooth paste forms. Spread evenly in the tart crust. Arrange the pear slices on top.

4. Heat a small saucepan over low heat. Add the sauce ingredients and whisk until just melted, being careful that the chocolate doesn't burn. Drizzle the sauce over the pear slices.

5. Cut the tart into squares. Serve at room temperature with small glasses of port wine.

apple plum crisp

FREE OF

MAKES 8 TO 10 SERVINGS

In late August through early September here in the Pacific Northwest, the plum trees are drooping with their succulent purple fruit. We often have so many boxes of Italian prune plums at that time of year that I cannot process them fast enough. I slice the plums in half, pit them, and freeze them so we can use them the rest of the year. This recipe combines the plums with fresh apples. Early-season baking apples and plums are in season at the same time. But, if desired, this crisp can be made entirely of apples or include other fruits as well.

FILLING

2 apples, cored and chopped

2 to 3 cups halved Italian prune plums

3 to 4 tablespoons arrowroot powder

3 to 4 tablespoons pure maple syrup or honey

1 tablespoon fresh lemon juice (optional)

TOPPING

1½ cups gluten-free rolled oats

½ cup sweet rice flour

½ to ¾ cup coconut sugar or Sucanat

1 teaspoon ground cinnamon

½ teaspoon ground cardamom

¼ teaspoon sea salt

½ to ¾ cup melted coconut oil or butter

1 teaspoon vanilla extract

1. Preheat the oven to 375°F. Place all the filling ingredients in a 7 by 11-inch baking pan. Gently stir together with a large spoon. A good gauge for having sufficient fruit is to fill your pan almost to the top. It will cook down quite a bit.

2. In a small bowl, stir together the oats, rice flour, sugar, cinnamon, cardamom, and salt. Add ½ cup of the oil and the vanilla; stir together with a fork. If the topping seems a little dry, add the remaining melted oil. Using your hands, crumble the topping evenly over the filling.

3. Bake the crisp for about 40 minutes, or until the juices are bubbling up and the topping is lightly browned.

VARIATION: Add 1 cup coarsely chopped pecans, almonds, or hazelnuts to the topping for added flavor and nutrition.

blueberry peach crisp

FREE OF

MAKES 6 TO 8 SERVINGS

Blueberries and peaches are highlights of the summer, available from mid-July through September, though if fresh fruit is unavailable, frozen berries and peaches work just fine. This oat-free crisp is easy to make and is always a crowd pleaser!

FILLING

2 cups fresh blueberries

2 ripe peaches, thinly sliced

2 tablespoons fresh lemon juice

2 tablespoons arrowroot powder

2 tablespoons pure maple syrup

¼ teaspoon grated nutmeg

TOPPING

1 cup blanched almond flour

¾ cup sprouted brown rice flour

¼ cup arrowroot powder or tapioca flour

¼ teaspoon sea salt

¼ cup butter, palm shortening, or coconut oil

¼ cup pure maple syrup

½ teaspoon almond extract

1. Preheat the oven to 375°F. Place the filling ingredients in an 8-inch square baking pan. Stir together with a large spoon.

2. In a medium bowl, combine the almond flour, rice flour, arrowroot powder, and salt. Whisk well, then add the butter and maple syrup. Begin to mix the topping with a fork and then finish the mixing with your fingers. Crumble it over the filling. Bake the crisp for 30 to 35 minutes, or until the juices are bubbling up and the topping is lightly browned.

banana coconut cookies

FREE OF

MAKES ABOUT 15 TWO-INCH COOKIES

These cookies are crisp on the outside and soft on the inside. They are only slightly sweet and are high in protein, making them a nutritious after-school snack with carrot and celery sticks. You can add organic chocolate chips to some of them if desired, though this will add a bit of cane sugar.

WET INGREDIENTS

⅓ cup mashed ripe banana (about 1 medium)

⅓ cup melted coconut oil

2 tablespoons pure maple syrup

1 teaspoon vanilla extract

½ teaspoon almond extract

DRY INGREDIENTS

2 cups blanched almond flour

1 cup unsweetened shredded coconut

½ teaspoon baking soda

¼ teaspoon sea salt

1. In a medium bowl, whisk together the wet ingredients. Add the dry ingredients and mix using a fork. Form the dough into a ball and refrigerate for 30 to 60 minutes.

2. Preheat the oven to 350°F. Form the dough into small balls (about 15) and place on an ungreased baking sheet. Flatten each cookie ball with the palm of your hand. Bake for about 15 minutes. The cookies will be soft straight out of the oven but will firm up when cool. You can place them onto a wire rack to cool and then move them into your freezer for quick cooling.

INGREDIENT TIP

Use very finely ground blanched almond flour in this recipe. It can be found at www.Nuts.com or www.LucysKitchenShop.com.

cashew ginger cookies

FREE OF

MAKES ABOUT 1½ DOZEN COOKIES

This grain-free cookie recipe doesn't require any flour. The cookies are high in protein, and can be used as a healthy after-school snack for children or packed into their school lunchboxes.

1 cup roasted cashew butter

2 large organic eggs

2 tablespoons blackstrap molasses

¾ cup coconut sugar

2 teaspoons ground ginger

1 teaspoon ground cinnamon

½ teaspoon baking soda

¼ teaspoon sea salt

1. Preheat the oven to 350°F. Lightly grease a baking sheet with coconut oil.

2. Place all the ingredients in a medium bowl and beat using an electric mixer. Drop by tablespoonfuls onto the baking sheet. Bake for approximately 15 minutes. Use a thin spatula to transfer the slightly fragile cookies to a wire rack to cool.

healthy lactation oatmeal raisin cookies

FREE OF

MAKES 2 DOZEN COOKIES

These cookies are the perfect nutrient-dense treat for a breastfeeding mother. Oats help promote breast milk production (for more foods that promote lactation, see "Foods to Increase Milk Production," page 23). Enjoy a cookie or two along with a cup of fennel tea when you sit down to nurse your baby. Plus, my children absolutely love these cookies! I have no problem giving them one for breakfast with a green smoothie. They are packed with healthy fats and fiber. New moms should omit the chocolate—it can be irritating to some babies.

WET INGREDIENTS

¼ cup ground chia seeds

½ cup hot water

½ cup melted coconut oil

½ cup unsweetened applesauce

1 cup almond butter

1 cup coconut sugar

1 tablespoon vanilla extract

DRY INGREDIENTS

5 cups gluten-free rolled oats

¾ teaspoon baking soda

¾ teaspoon sea salt

1 tablespoon ground cinnamon

ADD-INS

½ to 1 cup raisins, chopped

½ to 1 cup organic dark chocolate chips (optional)

1. Preheat the oven to 325°F. Lightly grease a baking sheet. Place the chia seeds into a large bowl and pour the hot water over them; immediately whisk together (otherwise they will clump up). Let rest for a few minutes.

2. Add the coconut oil, applesauce, almond butter, sugar, and vanilla. Whisk well.

3. Add the oats, baking soda, salt, and cinnamon. Stir well with a large wooden spoon. Add the raisins and chocolate, if using. Stir again. Drop by large spoonfuls onto the baking sheet. Gently press each cookie down with the palm of your hand. Bake for 12 to 15 minutes. Cool on a wire rack.

chocolate chip almond butter cookies

FREE OF

MAKES 1 DOZEN COOKIES

My daughter Grace created this recipe when she was eight years old—they are our favorite cookies and we make them a few times per month! These cookies can be made with either raw or roasted almond butter—the former yields thinner, flatter cookies, while the latter produces thicker cookies. You can add chocolate chips or replace them with dried cranberries or raisins, if desired!

¾ cup creamy almond butter

½ cup coconut sugar

1 large organic egg

1 to 2 teaspoons vanilla extract

½ teaspoon baking soda

¼ teaspoon sea salt

¼ cup organic dark chocolate chips

1. Preheat the oven to 350°F. Line a large baking sheet with parchment paper.

2. Place all the ingredients except the chocolate chips in a medium bowl and vigorously mix with a wooden spoon. Drop the dough by tablespoonfuls onto the baking sheet. Bake for 12 to 14 minutes. Cool on a wire rack.

chocolate sunflower seed butter cookies

FREE OF

MAKES 12 TO 15 COOKIES

I love being able to serve these cookies to my children, knowing they are getting some good nutrition with every bite! Sunflower seed butter is made from ground roasted sunflower seeds. It's a great high-protein alternative to nut butters. Serve these grain-free vegan cookies with a glass of Raw Almond Milk (page 451) or a green smoothie for a healthy afternoon treat!

WET INGREDIENTS

1 cup organic sunflower seed butter

⅓ cup coconut nectar

1 tablespoon ground chia seeds

3 tablespoons water

1 teaspoon vanilla extract

DRY INGREDIENTS

¼ cup raw cacao powder

½ teaspoon baking soda

¼ teaspoon sea salt

OPTIONAL ADD-IN

½ cup organic dark chocolate chips

1. Preheat the oven to 350°F. Lightly grease a baking sheet with coconut oil. In a medium bowl, using an electric mixer, beat the wet ingredients until light and fluffy. Add the dry ingredients and beat until thickened and combined. Mix in the chocolate chips, if using.

2. Roll small balls of dough in your hands. You should have between 12 to 15 balls. Place them on the baking sheet and press down using the tongs of a fork into a crisscross pattern. Bake for 12 to 15 minutes. Cool on a wire rack. The cookies will be fragile and crumbly when hot so be careful when you remove them from the sheet. They will firm up when cool.

gingerbread hazelnut cutout cookies

FREE OF

MAKES 2 DOZEN COOKIES

Use currants, raisins, sliced almonds, natural sprinkles, dried goji berries, and shredded coconut to decorate these lovely holiday cutout cookies. I find the dough is easiest to roll out and cut if it has been refrigerated overnight.

DRY INGREDIENTS

2 cups hazelnut meal

1 cup sweet rice flour

½ teaspoon baking soda

½ teaspoon sea salt

2 teaspoons ground cinnamon

1 teaspoon ground ginger

⅛ teaspoon grated nutmeg

WET INGREDIENTS

1 cup coconut sugar

½ cup softened butter

¼ cup blackstrap molasses

1 large organic egg

2 teaspoons vanilla extract

ICING

½ cup powdered coconut sugar (see Tip)

2 to 3 teaspoons almond milk or coconut milk

½ teaspoon vanilla extract

1. In a large bowl, whisk together the dry ingredients. In a smaller bowl, beat the wet ingredients with an electric mixer or vigorously by hand. Add the wet to the dry and mix until well combined. Form the dough into a ball, cover, and place in the refrigerator for a couple of hours or overnight.

2. Preheat the oven to 350°F. Lightly grease a baking sheet. Place a large piece of parchment or waxed paper on a clean work surface and lightly dust with a bit of sweet rice flour. Roll out some of the dough to a little less than ¼ inch thickness. (Put the remaining dough in the fridge to stay chilled.) Cut out the dough using your favorite holiday cookie cutters.

3. Carefully peel away the dough around the cutouts, then use a thin spatula to transfer the cookies to the baking sheet. Bake for 12 to 15 minutes, depending on how crisp you like them. Just watch them so they don't overbake. Transfer the cookies to a wire rack to cool. Repeat with the remaining dough. Let the cookies cool completely before icing.

> **KITCHEN TIP**
>
> To make powdered coconut sugar, place 1 cup coconut sugar and 1 tablespoon arrowroot powder into a high-powered blender and blend for 60 to 90 seconds, or until light and powdery. Leave the blender lid on until the sugar dust settles, then pour into a jar for storage.

orange hazelnut thumbprint cookies

FREE OF

MAKES 2 DOZEN COOKIES

Hazelnuts grow throughout the Pacific Northwest. Our children like to pick them up off the ground and use them in their play. You can make your own hazelnut meal by grinding whole hazelnuts in a food processor or buy it from Bob's Red Mill. Store the hazelnut meal in the freezer or refrigerator to keep it fresh. Any jam will work in this thumbprint cookie. I make honey-sweetened jams from all the fruit we harvest in the summer. We also like Bionaturae's fruit juice–sweetened jams; try apricot, raspberry, blackberry, or sour cherry.

DRY INGREDIENTS

2½ cups hazelnut meal

2 cups brown rice flour

½ cup tapioca flour

2 teaspoons baking powder

½ teaspoon sea salt

WET INGREDIENTS

⅔ cup melted coconut oil

⅔ cup pure maple syrup

¼ cup fresh orange juice

2 tablespoons ground flax seeds

2 teaspoons vanilla extract

1 to 2 teaspoons finely grated orange zest

Sugar-free jam

1. Preheat the oven to 350°F. Lightly grease a baking sheet with coconut oil. In a large bowl, whisk together the dry ingredients. In a small bowl, whisk together the wet ingredients. Add the wet to the dry and mix with a fork or large spoon until the dough thickens.

2. Roll large spoonfuls of the dough into balls with the palms of your hands. Place evenly onto the baking sheet. Gently press your thumb into the middle of each cookie, making a small indent. Place a small spoonful of jam in each indent. Bake for 15 to 20 minutes. Place the cookies on a wire rack to cool.

VARIATION: Replace the hazelnut flour with finely ground raw almonds or use Bob's Red Mill Almond Meal Flour. Replace the orange juice with unsweetened applesauce and omit the zest. You can add a dash of almond extract, if desired.

peanut butter monster cookies

FREE OF

MAKES 1½ DOZEN COOKIES

These healthy, high-protein, flourless cookies make a great late-afternoon snack. You can also pack them into your child's lunchbox as part of a balanced lunch.

1 cup creamy peanut butter

1 cup coconut sugar

2 large organic eggs, lightly beaten

1 tablespoon vanilla extract

½ teaspoon baking soda

½ teaspoon sea salt

½ cup unsweetened shredded coconut

½ cup raisins

½ cup organic dark chocolate chips

1. Preheat the oven to 350°F. Grease a large baking sheet with a little coconut oil. In a medium bowl, beat together the peanut butter, coconut sugar, eggs, vanilla, baking soda, and salt. Add the coconut, raisins, and chocolate chips. Stir together.

2. Drop the dough by the spoonful onto the baking sheet. Gently press each down with the palm of your hand. They won't spread much at all, so you can place them close together.

3. Bake for 10 to 15 minutes, depending on the size of the cookie. Cool on a wire rack.

sunflower seed cookies

MAKES 1 DOZEN COOKIES

These cookies make the perfect nutritious toddler snack cookie. They are free from all major allergens, so even a one-year-old can enjoy them. Use the cornstarch-free baking powder recipe (see page 50) if you are avoiding corn products. To make these cookies more nutritious and easier to digest, use *sprouted* brown rice flour and soak and dehydrate the sunflower seeds before using them (see the "Getting Started" chapter).

DRY INGREDIENTS

1 cup raw sunflower seeds

1 cup brown rice flour

¼ cup tapioca flour

1 teaspoon ground cinnamon

1 teaspoon baking powder

¼ teaspoon sea salt

WET INGREDIENTS

½ cup melted coconut oil

½ cup pure maple syrup

2 tablespoons unsweetened applesauce

1 tablespoon ground flax seeds

1 teaspoon vanilla extract

¼ to ½ cup chopped raisins

1. Preheat the oven to 350°F. Lightly grease a baking sheet with coconut oil. Grind the sunflower seeds in a food processor, coffee grinder, or the dry container of a high-powered blender until finely ground. You should have 1¼ cups.

2. Place the ground sunflower seeds in a large bowl and add the remaining dry ingredients. Whisk well. In a separate bowl or liquid glass measure, whisk together the wet ingredients. Add the wet to the dry, mix, then stir in the raisins. Continue to mix with a wooden spoon until the dough thickens, another 60 seconds or so.

3. Roll the dough into 1-inch balls and place on the baking sheet. Gently flatten each ball with the bottom of an oiled glass. Bake for 15 to 20 minutes. The cookies won't brown on top but will on the bottom. Cool on a wire rack.

chocolate chip cookie bars

FREE OF

MAKES 12 BARS

I like to keep a few jars of organic unsalted Sunbutter in my pantry for quick snacks and for use in healthy baking recipes such as this one. These bars make an excellent nut-free, vegan treat for including in your child's lunchbox!

DRY INGREDIENTS

1½ cups sprouted brown rice flour

¼ cup tapioca flour

½ teaspoon baking powder

½ teaspoon baking soda

¼ teaspoon sea salt

WET INGREDIENTS

2 tablespoons ground chia seeds

¼ cup hot water

½ cup softened coconut oil

½ cup organic sunflower seed butter

½ cup unsweetened applesauce

¾ cup coconut sugar

1 to 2 teaspoons vanilla extract

¼ to ½ cup organic dark chocolate chips

1. Preheat the oven to 350°F. Grease an 8-inch square or 8 x 10-inch baking dish with coconut oil.

2. Place the dry ingredients in a small mixing bowl; whisk well. Place the ground chia and hot water in a medium bowl and let stand for 1 minute. Add the remaining wet ingredients and beat using an electric mixer. Add the dry ingredients to the wet, and beat again until combined. Stir in the chocolate chips.

3. Scoop the dough into the prepared pan and press down evenly. Bake for approximately 30 minutes. Let cool completely before cutting into bars.

VARIATION: Replace the sunflower seed butter with either unsalted peanut butter or almond butter. You could also substitute currants or raisins for the chocolate chips.

chocolate chip teff brownies

FREE OF

MAKES 12 BROWNIES

These brownies are designed for the gluten, dairy, and egg sensitive chocoholic, though your non-gluten-free friends might agree that they are quite divine. The fudge-like consistency from the pureed dates and coconut oil, combined with the rich buttery flavor of the teff flour, makes these a real treat. Add extra chocolate chips for pure decadence!

DRY INGREDIENTS

1 cup teff flour

¼ cup tapioca flour

⅓ cup unsweetened cocoa powder

1 teaspoon baking powder

½ teaspoon baking soda

¼ teaspoon sea salt

WET INGREDIENTS

½ cup medjool dates, pitted

¼ cup ground flax seeds

1¼ cups boiling water

½ cup coconut oil

½ cup coconut sugar or maple sugar

2 teaspoons vanilla extract

½ cup organic dark chocolate chips

1. Preheat the oven to 350°F. Oil a 7 by 11-inch baking dish; an 8-inch square pan works too, although the brownie will be much thicker and more cake-like.

2. In a medium bowl, whisk together the dry ingredients. Place the dates and ground flax into a blender, pour the boiling water over them, then let them sit for 5 to 10 minutes. Add the remaining wet ingredients and blend until smooth and creamy. Add the wet ingredients to the dry and quickly whisk to combine. Add the chocolate chips, and continue to whisk until everything is well mixed. Pour the batter into the pan and bake for 20 to 25 minutes.

chocolate walnut brownies

FREE OF

MAKES 16 SERVINGS

This grain-free brownie recipe can be whipped up in a snap! Only a food processor is needed, meaning not too many dishes to wash! There is no need to add any oil or butter because the ground walnuts provide plenty of fats—and heart healthy ones at that. Serve these brownies with one of our coconut ice cream recipes (see page 399) for a decadent dessert treat.

DRY INGREDIENTS
2 cups raw walnuts
⅓ cup raw cacao powder
½ teaspoon baking soda
¼ teaspoon sea salt

WET INGREDIENTS
2 large organic eggs
½ cup pure maple syrup
1 tablespoon vanilla extract

1. Preheat the oven to 350°F. Grease an 8-inch square glass baking dish with coconut oil.

2. Place the walnuts into a food processor fitted with the "s" blade. Process until very finely ground, stopping just before they turn into nut butter. Add the remaining dry ingredients and pulse again to combine. Add the wet ingredients and process until

smooth. You will still have tiny chunks of walnuts visible, and this is fine.

3. Pour the batter into the baking dish. Spread evenly with a rubber spatula or spoon. Bake for 25 minutes. Cool for about 20 minutes before slicing.

gingerbread

FREE OF

MAKES ABOUT 8 SERVINGS

I love making this healthy, high-protein, grain-free treat for my children as an after-school snack during the winter months. It is also the perfect holiday dessert served with a dollop of the Whipped Coconut Cream (page 443). The smell is intoxicating while it is baking. Serve with apple or pear slices and warm spice tea.

1½ cups creamy roasted almond butter

½ cup mashed cooked sweet potatoes

¼ cup blackstrap molasses

¼ cup pure maple syrup

2 large organic eggs

1 teaspoon baking soda

½ teaspoon sea salt

1 tablespoon ground cinnamon

1 to 2 teaspoons ground ginger

¼ teaspoon grated nutmeg

1. Preheat the oven to 325°F. Grease an 8-inch square glass baking dish with coconut oil.

2. Place all the ingredients into a food processor fitted with the "s" blade and process until smooth and combined. You can also use a hand-held mixer, but the food processor is easier and creates a smoother batter. Pour the batter into the baking dish. Bake for about 35 minutes. Cool and slice. The gingerbread will be fragile while still hot but will firm up when cool.

carrot orange spice cupcakes

FREE OF

MAKES 1 DOZEN CUPCAKES

These grain-free cupcakes are moist and light with a mild, natural sweetness that comes from the carrots, maple syrup, and coconut flour. Serving one of these for breakfast along with a green smoothie is actually quite nutritious! We like to top them with a dollop of the Whipped Coconut Cream (page 443) or Coconut Orange Buttercream Frosting (page 440) and a sprinkling of finely chopped walnuts. They are also delicious topped with the Dairy-Free Cream Cheese Frosting (page 441).

DRY INGREDIENTS

¾ cup coconut flour

¾ cup arrowroot powder

1 teaspoon baking soda

¼ teaspoon sea salt

2 teaspoons ground cinnamon

1 teaspoon ground ginger

½ teaspoon grated nutmeg

2 teaspoons finely grated orange zest

WET INGREDIENTS

5 large organic eggs

½ cup full-fat coconut milk

½ cup pure maple syrup

⅓ cup melted coconut oil

2 teaspoons vanilla extract

ADD-INS

2 cups packed grated carrots

½ cup currants or raisins

1. Preheat the oven to 350°F. Line a 12-cup muffin pan with paper liners.

2. Place the dry ingredients in a medium bowl and whisk well. Place the wet ingredients into a blender fitted with the "s" blade and blend until smooth. Pour the wet ingredients into the dry, and vigorously whisk until well combined. Add the carrots and currants; whisk again.

3. Scoop the batter into the muffin cups, filling each to the top. Bake for about 30 minutes, or until a toothpick inserted into the center comes out clean. Remove the cupcakes from the pan and cool on a wire rack. Serve warm or let cool completely before frosting.

> **KITCHEN TIP**
>
> I've found that specific brands of coconut flour work well in grain-free baking recipes while others do not. My favorite brand of coconut flour is Nutiva. Do not use Bob's Red Mill coconut flour—it won't work! Also, use full-fat coconut milk at room temperature, and shake it well before using.

chocolate brownie cupcakes

FREE OF

MAKES 1 DOZEN CUPCAKES

When making these, use a finely ground blanched almond flour. Coarser flour, such as Bob's Red Mill, will not work here. Once cooled, these cupcakes can be frosted with the Chocolate Ganache Frosting (page 438) and sprinkled with shredded coconut or chopped nuts.

DRY INGREDIENTS

3 cups blanched almond flour

½ cup unsweetened cocoa powder

¼ cup arrowroot powder

2 teaspoons baking powder

½ teaspoon sea salt

WET INGREDIENTS

1 cup coconut milk

½ cup raw honey or coconut nectar

¼ cup melted coconut oil

2 teaspoons vanilla extract

½ teaspoon almond extract

1. Preheat the oven to 350°F. Line a 12-cup muffin pan with paper liners.

2. In a medium bowl, whisk together the dry ingredients. Use your fingers to break up any lumps from the cocoa or almond flour. In another bowl, whisk together the wet ingredients. Add the wet to the dry and whisk well.

3. Spoon the batter into the muffin cups. Bake for approximately 30 minutes. Let cool in the pan for 10 to 15 minutes, then transfer to a wire rack to cool. Handle the cupcakes carefully, as they are very fragile when hot; they will firm up when cool.

molasses spice cupcakes

MAKES 1 DOZEN CUPCAKES

This recipe uses unrefined ingredients to create a delicious, moist, gluten-free vegan cupcake. Reduce the spices and use this for your child's first birthday cake. I like to frost them with the Dairy-Free Cream Cheese Frosting (page 441) and decorate with finely chopped walnuts.

DRY INGREDIENTS

1½ cups teff flour

¼ cup arrowroot powder

2 teaspoons baking powder

½ teaspoon baking soda

½ teaspoon sea salt

2 to 3 teaspoons ground cinnamon

1 to 2 teaspoons ground ginger

¼ to ½ teaspoon grated nutmeg

WET INGREDIENTS

1½ cups boiling water

½ cup pitted medjool dates

½ cup pitted prunes

2 tablespoons ground chia seeds

½ cup plus 2 tablespoons coconut oil

¼ cup pure maple syrup

¼ cup blackstrap molasses

2 teaspoons vanilla extract

1. Preheat the oven to 350°F. Line a 12-cup muffin pan with paper liners. In a large bowl, whisk together the dry ingredients. In a medium bowl, combine the boiling water, dates, prunes, and chia seeds. Give it all a little stir and then let soak for 20 minutes.

2. Pour the date mixture into a high-powered blender and add the remaining wet ingredients.

Blend on high until smooth. Pour the wet ingredients into the dry and whisk well. Spoon the batter into the muffin cups, filling each to the top. Bake for 30 to 35 minutes. Cool completely on a wire rack before frosting, if desired.

pumpkin cupcakes

FREE OF

MAKES 1 DOZEN CUPCAKES

These moist and spicy grain-free cupcakes are made with coconut flour and are sweetened only with medjool dates. You'll need a high-powered blender to make these. Because the dates are not soaked first, a regular blender just wouldn't be able to puree them. Use fresh, homemade pumpkin puree (see page 480) or canned organic puree. You can also puree any winter squash if sugar pumpkins are unavailable. I like to bake and puree a lot of pumpkins in autumn and then freeze the puree in 2-cup containers to use throughout the year. Frost these with the Dairy-Free Cream Cheese Frosting (page 441).

DRY INGREDIENTS

½ cup coconut flour

½ cup arrowroot powder

1 teaspoon baking soda

½ teaspoon sea salt

2 teaspoons ground cinnamon

1 teaspoon ground ginger

½ teaspoon grated nutmeg

WET INGREDIENTS

1¼ cups sugar pumpkin puree (see Tip on page 168)

1 cup soft medjool dates, pitted

½ cup melted coconut oil

4 large organic eggs

1 tablespoon raw apple cider vinegar

1. Preheat the oven to 350°F. Grease a 12-cup muffin pan or line with paper liners.

2. In a medium bowl, whisk together the dry ingredients. Place the wet ingredients into a high-powered blender and blend until smooth and creamy, pulsing if needed. Scoop out the pumpkin mixture with a rubber spatula and whisk into the dry ingredients until well combined.

3. Scoop the batter into the muffin cups, filling each to the top. Gently smooth the tops with your fingertips. Bake for 30 minutes. Remove the cupcakes and cool on a wire rack. If frosting them, wait until they are completely cooled, then top each with a little freshly grated nutmeg, if desired.

almond apricot snack cake

FREE OF

MAKES 9 TO 12 SERVINGS

With only a few basic ingredients and no sweeteners, this cake tastes decadent rather than nutritious. Use only organic, unsulfured dried apricots— they will be a dark orange-brown, not bright orange as is the case with the sulfured ones. Serve this cake for dessert topped with the Whipped Coconut Cream (page 443). It is also makes a great after-school snack for children along with apple slices and herbal tea.

1 cup dried apricots

1 cup creamy roasted almond butter

½ cup unsweetened applesauce

2 large organic eggs

2 teaspoons vanilla extract

½ to 1 teaspoon almond extract

½ teaspoon baking soda

½ teaspoon sea salt

1. Preheat the oven to 350°F. Grease an 8-inch square glass baking dish with coconut oil.

2. Place the apricots into a food processor fitted with the "s" blade. Process until finely chopped. Add the remaining ingredients and process until well combined, about 20 seconds. Be careful not to overprocess the mixture, or the apricots will turn into a puree. You want the mixture to be a little chunky.

3. Pour the batter into the baking dish and smooth the top with a rubber spatula. Bake for 25 to 30 minutes. Cool slightly before cutting.

apricot-almond skillet cake

FREE OF

MAKES 8 TO 10 SERVINGS

Serve this as part of a holiday brunch or breakfast. It's also delicious served with tea in the afternoon. If apricots are out of season, try Italian prune plums, sliced peaches, or blueberries!

DRY INGREDIENTS

1 cup blanched almond flour

1 cup sprouted brown rice flour

½ cup arrowroot powder

2 teaspoons baking powder

½ teaspoon sea salt

WET INGREDIENTS

2 large organic eggs

⅓ cup melted butter or coconut oil

⅓ cup pure maple syrup

¾ cup raw cream or coconut milk

1 tablespoon vanilla extract

1 teaspoon almond extract

6 ripe apricots, halved and pitted

Melted butter or coconut oil, for cooking

1. Preheat the oven to 350°F. Place a 10-inch cast-iron skillet on the stove over low heat.

2. In a medium bowl, whisk together the dry ingredients. Add the wet ingredients and whisk until well combined. Pour about 1 tablespoon butter into the skillet and swirl it around. Pour in the batter and gently place the apricot halves on top (but don't press them in; they will sink some during baking). Remove from the heat and bake for 30 to 35 minutes. Let cool for about 10 minutes, then cut into wedges and serve.

blackberry buckwheat cake

FREE OF

MAKES 9 SERVINGS

When the blackberries are in season, our children take small baskets on our trail hikes or walks through the green spaces in our neighborhood, and fill them with blackberries. Most of them get eaten right away, but sometimes there are enough left to bake with. Serve this healthy cake for a weekend brunch or after a light evening meal. For a more decadent cake, top with the Dairy-Free Cream Cheese Frosting (page 441) or the Coconut Orange Buttercream Frosting (page 440).

DRY INGREDIENTS

2 cups raw buckwheat flour (see Tip on page 98)

2 teaspoons baking powder

½ teaspoon baking soda

¼ teaspoon sea salt

1 teaspoon ground cinnamon

¼ teaspoon ground allspice or cardamom

WET INGREDIENTS

2 tablespoons ground chia seeds

½ cup hot water

¾ cup hemp milk or coconut milk

¾ cup coconut sugar

½ cup melted coconut oil or extra-virgin olive oil

2 teaspoons vanilla extract

1 cup fresh or frozen blackberries

1. Preheat the oven to 350°F. Grease an 8-inch baking dish with coconut oil.

2. In a medium bowl, whisk together the dry ingredients and set aside. Place the chia seeds in a blender, add the hot water, and blend for a few seconds to combine. Let rest for about 2 minutes to form a gel.

3. Add the remaining wet ingredients and blend again to combine. Pour the wet ingredients into the dry and whisk well. Fold in the blackberries. Pour the batter into the baking dish and bake for 35 to 40 minutes. Cool slightly before cutting into squares and serving. If you want to frost the cake, cool it completely before doing so.

VARIATION: Use any variety of berries in place of the blackberries or a combination of a few.

vanilla coconut cake

FREE OF

MAKES 8 SERVINGS

This moist, spongy grain and dairy-free cake is quick and easy to make. Use full-fat canned coconut milk for best results. You can double this recipe and make it into a beautiful layer cake. Frost with the Chocolate Avocado Frosting (page 439) or drizzle individual slices with the Chocolate Ganache Frosting (page 438) and top with fresh berries.

DRY INGREDIENTS

¾ cup coconut flour

¾ cup arrowroot powder

1 teaspoon baking soda

¼ teaspoon sea salt

WET INGREDIENTS

5 large organic eggs

½ cup full-fat coconut milk, at room temperature

½ cup pure maple syrup

⅓ cup melted coconut oil

1 tablespoon vanilla extract

½ teaspoon almond extract

1. Preheat the oven to 350°F. Grease a 9-inch cake pan with coconut oil and dust with coconut flour. Add the dry ingredients to a medium bowl and whisk together. Place the wet ingredients into a blender and blend until smooth. Pour the wet ingredients into the dry and vigorously whisk until well combined.

2. Pour the batter into the cake pan; tap the pan on the counter to spread out the batter and release some of the air bubbles. Bake for 35 to 40 minutes, or until a toothpick inserted in the center comes out clean. Cool for at least 15 minutes in the pan

before flipping out onto a wire rack to cool. If desired, frost the cake when completely cool.

VARIATION: If you can tolerate dairy, replace the coconut milk with raw cream, and replace the melted coconut oil with melted butter. The cake will not have a strong coconut flavor using this variation, which some people prefer.

> **KITCHEN TIP**
> Do not use Bob's Red Mill coconut flour; it won't work here! Also, shake the coconut milk well before using.

warm chocolate cake

FREE OF

MAKES 12 SERVINGS

Decadent yet nutritious, this cake will probably become a family favorite. Nobody will ever know that it is gluten-free! It is best served warm, 20 to 30 minutes out of the oven. Any leftover cake will stay moist for days from the layer of frosting. I like to use Dagoba organic baking chocolate because it comes in 6-ounce bars that are easily divided into 2-ounce squares.

DRY INGREDIENTS

1 cup sorghum flour

½ cup sweet rice flour

1 cup coconut sugar

¼ cup ground chia seeds

¼ cup raw cacao powder

¾ teaspoon baking soda

½ teaspoon sea salt

WET INGREDIENTS

¾ cup plain kefir (cow's, goat's, or coconut milk)

½ cup water

½ cup melted butter or coconut oil

2 large organic eggs

2 teaspoons vanilla extract

FROSTING

¼ cup butter or coconut oil

2 ounces organic bittersweet chocolate

½ cup coconut sugar

2 tablespoons arrowroot powder

¼ cup plain kefir (cow's, goat's, or coconut milk)

1. Preheat the oven to 350°F. Grease an 8-inch square glass baking dish.

2. In a large bowl, whisk together the dry ingredients. In a smaller bowl, whisk together the wet ingredients. Pour the wet into the dry and whisk to combine well. Pour the batter into the baking dish and spread with the back of a spoon. Bake for 35 to 40 minutes. Remove from the oven and let cool slightly.

3. In a small saucepan, combine the butter, chocolate, and coconut sugar. Whisk over very low heat until just melted. Stir in the arrowroot powder and whisk well. Pour into a blender and then add the kefir. Blend on high for about 60 seconds. Immediately pour over the still-warm cake. Let the cake rest for 10 to 20 minutes, then serve warm.

cashew date frosting

FREE OF

MAKES ABOUT 2 CUPS

This luscious frosting is actually nutritious, too! You will need a high-powered blender to make this recipe. Use it to frost your favorite cupcakes or layer cake. It will frost one dozen cupcakes, but will need to be doubled for a layer cake. Note that the cashews and dates have to soak for three hours before you begin this recipe, and the frosting is chilled for six hours before you can use it.

1 cup raw cashews
½ cup medjool dates, pitted
¾ cup water

¾ cup melted coconut oil
1 teaspoon raw vanilla powder
Pinch of sea salt

1. Place the cashews, dates, and water into a blender. Let them soak for about 3 hours. (After soaking they will be soft and blend easily into a creamy frosting.)

2. Blend the cashew mixture on high for 30 to 60 seconds, or until very smooth. Add the coconut oil, vanilla powder, and salt. Blend again until smooth, scraping down the sides if necessary. The

frosting will seem a little thin, but will solidify once chilled.

3. Pour the frosting into a bowl and chill uncovered in the refrigerator for 6 hours or overnight before using. When chilled, whip it by hand using a spoon or beat with an electric beater. Also, make sure your cake or cupcakes are cool before using this frosting.

chocolate ganache frosting

FREE OF

MAKES ABOUT ¾ CUP

This frosting is easy to make—just be sure not to cook it at too high a temperature or the chocolate will burn. Drizzle it over your favorite cake, cupcakes, raw pie, ice cream, or fresh fruit.

½ cup organic dark chocolate chips (about 3 ounces)

¼ cup coconut milk

2 tablespoons pure maple syrup or raw honey

Place all the ingredients in a small saucepan and warm over low heat. Stir continuously until melted and thickened, just about 2 minutes. Remove from the heat and let cool for about 5 minutes. Do not chill! Drizzle over a cake or cupcakes.

VARIATION: If you prefer a thick, creamy, spreadable frosting, let the ganache thicken at room temperature for about 3 hours.

chocolate avocado frosting

FREE OF

MAKES ABOUT 2 CUPS

This heart-healthy frosting is full of monounsaturated fats from the avocado and is rich and creamy despite the lack of saturated fat. Avocados contain oleic acid, a monounsaturated fat that has been shown to lower cholesterol. Use this frosting for your favorite cupcakes or cookies. It makes enough to frost a dozen cupcakes; double the recipe for a layer cake.

3 small ripe avocados, mashed (1 cup)

6 to 8 tablespoons raw honey or pure maple syrup

6 to 8 tablespoons unsweetened cocoa powder

4 tablespoons melted coconut oil

1 tablespoon vanilla extract

½ teaspoon almond extract (optional)

1 teaspoon fresh lemon juice

Place all the ingredients into a food processor fitted with the "s" blade. Process until very smooth and creamy. Transfer to a container and chill in the refrigerator for about 2 hours before using.

coconut orange buttercream frosting

MAKES ABOUT 2 CUPS

I use this nutritious dairy-free frosting to top just about anything from brownies to cupcakes. Make a double batch for a layer cake. To naturally color this frosting for a child's birthday party, add a few teaspoons of beet powder for pink, spirulina for green, or turmeric for yellow.

1 cup coconut butter
½ cup coconut oil
¼ cup raw honey or coconut nectar

¼ cup fresh orange juice
¼ to ½ teaspoon organic orange flavoring

Place all the ingredients in a small saucepan and warm over very low heat, whisking, until the coconut butter and oil have melted. The mixture will look thick and gelatinous. Pour it into a bowl and place the bowl into your freezer for no more than 20 minutes. When you pull it out you'll notice some of the frosting has hardened on the side of the bowl and the rest is still sort of gelatinous and clear. Use an electric mixer to vigorously whip it up. It should quickly turn into a thick, creamy, cream-colored frosting. Use immediately to frost your cupcakes or cake. Make sure your cupcakes have completely cooled before using. The frosting will melt on warm cupcakes or in very warm temperatures.

VARIATION: For a vanilla frosting, replace the orange juice with either coconut milk or almond milk and omit the orange flavoring; add 1 teaspoon raw vanilla powder.

INGREDIENT TIP

Coconut butter is different from coconut oil in that it is made from pureed coconut meat, rather than the pressings of the coconut meat to extract the oil. Our favorite brand of coconut butter is Artisana.

dairy-free cream cheese frosting

FREE OF

MAKES ABOUT 2 CUPS

I like to drizzle this frosting, while it's still warm, over freshly baked cinnamon rolls. When chilled, it has the consistency of a spreadable cream cheese frosting. Double the recipe to frost a cake or use a single batch for a dozen cupcakes. If you want your frosting to be white, use white sweet potatoes.

¾ cup mashed, peeled, cooked sweet potatoes (still warm)

6 tablespoons coconut oil

¼ cup pure maple syrup

2 tablespoons unsweetened applesauce

2 tablespoons arrowroot powder

2 teaspoons vanilla extract

Pinch of sea salt

Place all the ingredients into a high-powered blender and blend until smooth and creamy. Scrape the frosting into a container and chill in the refrigerator until firm, or in the freezer for 30 to 40 minutes, stirring every so often. Spread onto your favorite cupcakes.

simple lemon icing

MAKES ABOUT 1 CUP

This icing is great for cookies or cupcakes. You can color the icing with natural food colorings. I use ground turmeric for yellow, beet juice for pink, and spirulina powder for green. I also use Seelect brand plant-based food coloring, which works beautifully. Note that the cashews are soaked for six hours before you begin this recipe, and the coconut cream comes from one can of chilled full-fat coconut milk.

6 tablespoons melted coconut oil

¼ cup raw cashews, soaked for 6 hours, then drained and rinsed

¼ cup coconut cream

2 tablespoons raw honey

1 tablespoon arrowroot powder

½ to 1 teaspoon vanilla extract

¼ teaspoon organic lemon flavoring

2 to 3 teaspoons fresh lemon juice

Place all the ingredients into a high-powered blender and blend until ultra-smooth, stopping the machine if necessary to scrape down the sides. (If coloring, spoon the icing into individual small bowls and add a tiny amount of natural food coloring, as desired.) Use to ice cookies or cupcakes; then to set the icing, freeze the iced cookies or cupcakes for 20 minutes before serving.

VARIATION: For an almond-flavored icing, replace the lemon flavoring with 1 teaspoon almond flavoring and omit the lemon juice.

whipped coconut cream

FREE OF

MAKES ABOUT 1 CUP

Use this simple recipe as a replacement for whipped heavy cream. You can dollop it on top of fresh strawberries and blueberries, or use to frost cupcakes. The coconut cream begins to soften as it sits at room temperature, and certainly will soften quickly on a hot summer afternoon, so be sure to keep it chilled. It can be stored in a covered glass container in the refrigerator for up to a week. You can easily rewhip the cream when you're ready to use it. Bear in mind, though, that the coconut milk has to be chilled for 12 hours before you begin this recipe.

2 (14.5-ounce) cans coconut milk, chilled for 12 hours

1 to 2 tablespoons coconut nectar, raw honey, or pure maple syrup
Pinch of sea salt

Scoop out the thick white cream from the top of the coconut milk. Pour the watery milk into a jar and use it for another purpose, such as a fruit smoothie. Place the coconut cream, coconut nectar, and salt in a bowl. Use an electric mixer to whip the cream into soft peaks. Serve immediately.

beverages

Our family enjoys purified water as our primary liquid. Sometimes we add lemon and lime slices for a nice zing and extra flavor. We all also enjoy herbal teas on most days. One of the healthiest swaps you can make when upgrading your family's diet is to ditch the juice, soda, and other sweetened beverages in favor of pure water. Get a water filter or begin purchasing filtered water from your local health food store on a weekly basis. This way you can avoid consuming tap water, which is full of potentially damaging chemicals like chlorine (kills beneficial gut bacteria), pharmaceutical medications (you'd be surprised how many drugs are found in municipal drinking water), and heavy metals.

Homemade nut milks, teas, and sodas require simple ingredients and are easy to prepare. Nut milks are made using soaked nuts, water, and a touch of sweetener. We make our herbal teas with a creative combinations of dried herbs—some of which we regularly harvest and dehydrate ourselves, such as nettles and spearmint. And our natural sodas, which we enjoy sparingly, are made from sparkling mineral water and organic fruit juices.

> Our favorite water filter to use at home is the Berkey Water Filter. This filter pulls out the heavy metals, pharmaceuticals, and harmful microbes in addition to the chlorine. You can learn more at www.BerkeyFilters.com.

HOMEMADE BEVERAGES
Dairy-Free Milks

Homemade nut and seed milks can be used in place of cow's milk in all recipes calling for milk. Commercial dairy-free milks often have ingredients that our bodies don't need, such as "natural" flavorings, stabilizers, and too much sugar. In making your own nut milks, you reduce and regulate ingredients while eliminating excess packaging from going to the landfill. Using homemade nut and seed milks will help your diet be cleaner and greener.

Herbal Teas

Making dried herbal tea blends is a wonderful way to preserve the harvest and benefit your health. Herbs often work very efficiently on children to calm digestion, sooth anxiety, or aid in sleep. Our children love to come up with their own herb combinations using the many different jars of dried herbs we have in our kitchen cabinet.

Natural Sodas

Drinking a lot of juice early on in childhood sets the stage for blood sugar imbalances that lead to cravings for sugary, starchy foods. It's much healthier not to begin this pattern with your child by offering only pure water, herbal teas, and homemade nut milks or raw dairy. Natural, homemade sodas can be used for special occasions or to wean your child off a liquid sugar addiction.

All commercial sodas, diet or otherwise, cause weight gain and inflammation in the body. Studies show that diet sodas actually cause even more

10 Tips for Making Homemade Beverages

1. Soak almonds, Brazil nuts, and hazelnuts for at least 8 hours, though they can be soaked for up to 24 hours. If you live in a warm climate, or if your kitchen is very warm, you may need to drain and add new soaking water once or twice to keep the nuts from spoiling.

2. Softer nuts—such as cashews—don't need to be soaked unless you are not using a powerful blender. Then, soaking these nuts for at least 3 hours will help them to blend properly.

3. Seeds can also be blended with nuts for added nutrition—pumpkin seed–almond milk is a delicious combination.

4. Nut and seed milks can be stored in a covered glass container, such as a pitcher or mason jar, in the refrigerator for three to four days.

5. Nut milks can be frozen in ice cube trays and then stored in a sealed container in the freezer. Use to make a refreshing fruit smoothie.

6. Use a nut milk bag to strain out the pulp to make the process of creating your own nut milks very easy!

7. Find a local herb store selling dried bulk organic and wild-crafted herbs. Bring in your glass jars to fill up.

8. Store dried herbs in labeled clean glass jars in a cool, dark, dry location.

9. Leftover herbal teas can be stored in glass jars in the refrigerator and then reheated in a small pot when ready to drink.

10. To make a quick and easy natural soda, take any organic, sugar-free fruit juice concentrate and add to sparkling mineral water in a large pitcher. Use a large glass bowl with a ladle and float thinly sliced oranges, lemons, and limes in the soda for a beautiful presentation.

weight gain and obesity problems than sugar-laden sodas do! If this isn't enough, the phosphoric acid in soda leaches precious minerals from your bones. If you are craving something fizzy and sweet, consider gulping down some sort of fermented drink like kombucha or cultured coconut water, or try some of our homemade soda recipes in this chapter.

coconut kefir

I use the kefir starter from Body Ecology Diet (www.BodyEcology.com) to make this recipe and a quart mason jar with a plastic lid. Add this kefir to smoothies, pour it over granola, or use it to soak whole grains before baking. If you have an allergy to almonds, use another seed milk, such as hemp milk, though the end result won't be as tasty; I use the Quick Rich Almond Milk (page 450).

2 cups coconut milk

2 cups almond milk

1 teaspoon honey or pure maple syrup

1 package kefir starter

1. Pour the coconut milk, almond milk, and honey into a small saucepan. Heat over low to about 92°F, or until barely warm to the touch. Pour the warm milk into a clean quart jar, then add the starter. Cover with a plastic lid and gently shake. Make sure the lid isn't screwed on too tightly, as this will prevent gasses formed during fermentation from escaping.

2. Place the jar in a warm, undisturbed place on your kitchen counter. Let it sit for 24 to 48 hours, or until soured and slightly bubbly.

3. If desired, stir in flavorings such as vanilla extract, almond extract, stevia, or honey.

4. Store in the refrigerator for up to 1 week. The coconut fat will separate from the other liquids at refrigerated temperatures—just shake it vigorously before using.

NUTRITION TIP

Kefir contains trillions of probiotics. These beneficial bacteria line your digestive tract, helping to break down and assimilate your food while keeping guard against pathogenic bacteria and toxins. A balanced digestive tract full of beneficial bacteria is vital to modulate immune system function, improve digestion, heal food allergies, and reduce exposure to potentially toxic substances.

homemade coconut milk

FREE OF

MAKES 1 QUART

Making your own coconut milk is simpler than you think. All you need is water and unsweetened shredded coconut, a high-powered blender, and a few minutes. Use this coconut milk in smoothies or curries—anytime canned coconut milk is called for. You'll need a thin flour-sack dish towel or nut milk bag and a quart mason jar with a lid.

2½ cups unsweetened shredded coconut
3 to 4 cups boiling water

Place the coconut in a glass bowl and cover with 3 cups boiling water; whisk well, adding the remaining cup boiling water if you want a thinner milk. Let rest for 30 to 60 minutes on your counter. Pour the coconut mixture into a high-powered blender and puree on high for 60 to 90 seconds. Lay a thin dish towel across a 4-cup glass measuring cup. Pour the milk through it. Bundle up the sides of the towel and squeeze the excess liquid from the pulp. Pour the resulting milk into a quart jar, cover with a lid, and place into your refrigerator. The fat and water will separate, as does canned coconut milk. Just bring to room temperature and shake well before using.

quick rich almond milk

FREE OF

MAKES 3 CUPS

If I need milk for baking muffins or making pancakes in the morning, I make this because it does not require presoaked nuts. You can use either finely ground blanched almond flour or almond meal, such as from Bob's Red Mill. Use less water or more almond flour if you prefer a richer, creamier milk.

½ cup almond flour

3 cups water

Pinch of sea salt

1. Place all the ingredients into a blender, cover, and blend on high for 60 to 90 seconds.

2. Use a nut milk bag or cheesecloth to strain out the pulp, squeezing out any remaining liquid. Store in a covered glass jar or pitcher in the refrigerator for up to 4 days.

raw almond milk

FREE OF

MAKES 3½ CUPS

Raw almond milk can be used for fresh fruit smoothies or as a nutritious beverage with meals. Add it to tea in place of cow's milk or pour it over chia seeds, hemp seeds, and fresh fruit for a morning "cereal." I usually make a double or triple batch of this and store it in a glass pitcher with a lid in the refrigerator. Note that the almonds are soaked for at least eight hours prior to making the milk.

½ cup raw almonds

3 cups water

1 to 2 tablespoons pure maple syrup

Pinch of sea salt

1. Place the almonds in a small bowl and cover with some purified water. Soak at room temperature for 8 to 12 hours or overnight.

2. Rinse the almonds well under warm running water. Place them in a blender with the 3 cups water, maple syrup to taste, and salt. Blend on high for 2 to 3 minutes, or until you have a very smooth milk. Pour the milk through a cheesecloth or nut milk bag into a container and squeeze out the liquid. (You can add the leftover pulp to make muffins or pancakes with extra fiber and protein.) Store in a covered glass jar or pitcher in the refrigerator for up to 3 days.

hemp milk

Use this dairy-free milk for baking, for pancakes, as a base for smoothies, over whole-grain breakfast porridge, or just for drinking. I always strain the hemp milk using a nut milk bag, though it isn't necessary. You can add more or less water for a thicker or thinner milk, too.

½ cup shelled hemp seeds

3 cups filtered water

1 tablespoon pure maple syrup

Pinch of sea salt

Place all the ingredients into a high-powered blender and blend for 60 to 90 seconds, or until ultra-smooth. Put a nut milk bag into a large jar or pitcher and pour the hemp milk through the bag; squeeze out the milk and leave the pulp behind. (I compost the leftover pulp.) Store in a covered glass jar or pitcher in the refrigerator for up to 4 days.

> **NUTRITION TIP**
>
> Hemp is the second highest source of plant protein after soy. If you need additional protein in your diet, hemp is a fantastic vegan source.

cashew milk

FREE OF

MAKES 2½ CUPS

Cashews are a softer nut and therefore do not need to be soaked overnight to blend smoothly for extracting this milk. Use fresh cashew milk over a cooked whole-grain cereal for breakfast or to make fruit smoothies. I sometimes like to make this a little thicker by reducing the amount of water to 1 cup, and use it like a coffee creamer in my spice tea for a late night warming drink.

½ cup raw cashews

2 cups water

1 to 2 tablespoons pure maple syrup

Pinch of sea salt

Place cashews, water, 1 tablespoon of the maple syrup, and the salt into a high-powered blender. Blend on high until very smooth. Taste and adjust the sweetness, adding the remaining tablespoon maple syrup, if desired. Store in a covered glass jar or pitcher in the refrigerator for up to 4 days.

> **KITCHEN TIP**
>
> If you do not have a high-powered blender, soak the cashews in filtered water for about 3 hours, then drain the nuts and follow the recipe.

creamy macadamia nut milk

FREE OF

MAKES ABOUT 4 CUPS

This recipe is such a treat, as macadamia nuts can be pricy. Pour the milk over granola or drizzle over cooked brown rice cereal. I love to use this poured over a bowl of sliced bananas and topped with a little ground golden flax seed as a calming bedtime snack. Note that the nuts have to be soaked for three hours before you make the milk.

1 cup raw macadamia nuts

3 to 4 cups water

1 to 2 tablespoons honey or pure maple syrup

Pinch of sea salt

1. Place the macadamia nuts in a bowl and cover with some water. Let them soak for at least 3 hours.

2. Rinse and drain the nuts, then place into a blender. Add the 3 cups water, 1 tablespoon of the honey, and the salt. Blend on high for 1 to 2 minutes, until ultra-smooth and creamy. Add the additional cup of water to reach desired consistency, and adjust the sweetness by adding the remaining tablespoon honey, if desired. Store in a covered glass jar or pitcher in the refrigerator for up to 4 days.

NUTRITION TIP

Although macadamia nuts are known to have a high fat content, around 80 percent of the fats are monounsaturated. Having more monounsaturated and less polyunsaturated fats in your diet is healthier. One of the monounsaturated fats in macadamia nuts is palmitoleic acid, which helps lower cholesterol, curb appetite, and burn more body fat for fuel.

---

mineral tea

MAKES ABOUT 2½ CUPS DRY TEA BLEND

Because of our modern diet and our depleted soils, many people are deficient in essential minerals. This herbal tea blend can be used daily to naturally increase the minerals in your diet. People often find that they sleep better, are less anxious, have greater clarity, and, for women, have far less menstrual cramping when their diets have an adequate amount of minerals. This tea is also beneficial to drink all throughout pregnancy—growing a baby requires extra minerals!

½ cup dried oatstraw
½ cup dried nettles
½ cup dried red raspberry leaf
½ cup dried alfalfa
¼ cup dried peppermint
2 tablespoons dried horsetail

OPTIONAL ADDITIONS
¼ cup dried chamomile
2 to 3 tablespoons dried rose petals
1 to 2 tablespoons dried licorice root

1. Place all the dried herbs in a large glass jar. Cover with a lid and shake to blend the herbs. Store in a cool, dry place until ready to use.

2. To make the tea, place 2 to 3 tablespoons of the herb mixture into a quart jar and pour 4 cups of boiling water over the herbs. Cover and steep for 20 to 30 minutes. You can also steep it overnight for best extraction of minerals and then reheat the tea in the morning.

3. Strain the herbs with a small fine-mesh tea strainer and enjoy plain or with a touch of raw honey. Drink up to 1 quart a day.

INGREDIENT TIP
Check your local herb store or health food store for bulk dried herbs. If you can't find them locally, you can always order them online.

nettle mint tea

MAKES 6 CUPS

Here in the Pacific Northwest, from February through April, we go out as a family and harvest nettles. All you need is a pair of gardening gloves, scissors, and a large paper bag. Nettles are best harvested when they are young, just a few inches high. This is the time when the energy and nutrients of the plant are going into the leaves; later in the summer, energy is directed toward seed production. We dry our fresh nettles in a dehydrator and then place them in a food processor to break them up further. I store the pulverized nettles in glass jars. We do the same for all the mint growing in our garden in the summertime.

6 cups water
3 tablespoons dried nettles

3 tablespoons dried mint

1. Place the water in a medium pot, cover, and bring to a boil. Turn off the heat and add the dried herbs. Cover and steep for about 30 minutes.

2. Strain though a fine-mesh strainer into mugs for serving. Store any leftover tea in glass jars in the refrigerator.

> **NUTRITION TIP**
>
> Nettles are a fabulous blood tonic and purifier, being especially helpful for those with anemia or women who have just given birth.

tummy comfort tea

FREE OF

MAKES 6 CUPS

This tea is great for children who may have eaten food that hurts their stomachs. We dilute this tea with water for our children—the younger they are, the more dilution. The licorice root makes the tea naturally sweet, but you could add a touch of honey to each cup, if desired.

6 cups water

2 to 4 tablespoons sliced fresh ginger

1½ tablespoons dandelion root

1 tablespoon licorice root

2 tablespoons dried spearmint

1 tablespoon dried chamomile

1. Place the water, the ginger according to your taste, dandelion root, and licorice root in a medium pot. Cover and simmer for 20 to 25 minutes. Remove from the heat and add the spearmint and chamomile. Cover and steep for 10 to 15 minutes more.

2. Strain, pour into small tea cups, and dilute to desired taste. Store in a large glass jar in the refrigerator for up to 5 days.

NUTRITION TIP

Chinese medicine appropriately lists ginger as a "warming food." The warming effect is obvious after consuming it, as you can sense the heat in your mouth, esophagus, and stomach. It has long been known to calm seasickness and nausea of all types. Beyond calming the stomach, studies have also noted the amazing ability of ginger to reduce inflammation in arthritis.

rooibos rose iced tea

FREE OF

MAKES 10 CUPS

This tea is delicious served hot or cold over ice. It has a flavor akin to black tea, only milder, with rose-flavored undertones. Use organic dried rose petals, as roses are normally sprayed with pesticides. Bulk herbs can be found at your local health food store or a local herb store.

10 cups water
¼ cup loose rooibos tea
¼ cup dried rose petals

2 tablespoons dried rose hips
Raw honey
Ice cubes

1. Bring the water to a boil. Place the dried herbs in an 8-cup glass measuring cup, gallon glass jar, or large bowl. Pour the boiling water over the herbs and let steep for about 20 minutes, or until most of the herbs have fallen to the bottom of the container.

2. Carefully strain the tea into a large glass pitcher using a small fine-mesh strainer. Sweeten to taste with honey, if desired. Let cool completely if serving over ice.

warming raspberry leaf almond drink

MAKES ABOUT 6 CUPS

This drink is intended to nourish breastfeeding mothers immediately following birth and in the early postpartum stage. The fennel seeds and raspberry leaves help contract the uterus after childbirth and also promote the flow of breast milk. The almonds are very rich and nourishing, providing healthy protein and fats to the new mother. The ginger, cinnamon, and cloves are warming spices that aid the digestive systems of both mother and baby. It will keep in the fridge for about one week.

6 cups water

1 cup raw almonds, ground to a fine powder

A 2-inch piece of fresh ginger, peeled and sliced

3 cinnamon sticks

4 whole cloves

2 teaspoons fennel seeds

3 tablespoons dried raspberry leaves

⅓ cup honey, or to taste

1. Place 4 cups of the water in a medium pot with the almond powder, cover, and simmer over low heat for 30 minutes. Be careful not to let the heat get too high, or it will boil over, which can make quite a mess! Remove from the heat and let cool.

2. Place the almond mixture in a blender and blend on high until smooth. Place a fine-mesh strainer over a liquid 4-cup glass measure. Pour the almond milk through it to remove the pulp, then pour the almond milk into a 3-quart pot.

3. Place the remaining 2 cups water in a small pot with the ginger, cinnamon, cloves, and fennel seeds and simmer for 30 minutes, covered. Take the pot off the stove and add the raspberry leaves; let steep for 10 to 20 minutes with the lid on.

4. Strain the herb mixture into the pot with the almond milk and discard the herbs; whisk in the honey. Taste and adjust the sweetness, if necessary. Serve immediately, or pour into jars for future use. Reheat as needed.

warm cranberry orange cider

FREE OF

MAKES 11 CUPS

I like to make this for Thanksgiving and Christmas with a dash of dark rum in each mug for the adults and a cinnamon stick in each child's mug. The spicy cinnamon-orange aromas fill the house with lasting memories. Use less sweetener for a tarter flavor or more for a sweeter one. Store any remaining cider in glass quart jars in the refrigerator for up to one week.

4 cups fresh orange juice

6 cups apple cider

1 (8-ounce) jar cranberry juice concentrate

¼ to ½ cup honey or coconut nectar

6 cinnamon sticks

Place all the ingredients in an 8-quart stockpot. Cover and simmer for about 1 hour. When ready to serve, turn the heat to low and place a ladle in the pot for serving.

strawberry-honey lemonade

A glass of refreshing homemade strawberry lemonade in the summertime creates a memory that will last a lifetime. We love to go strawberry picking in June and bring home container after container of small organic strawberries so full of flavor you wouldn't dare want to cook with them. Fresh strawberries for breakfast, lunch, and dinner are always on the menu! This is one of our favorite ways to use them. Have your children make mint ice cubes by placing a few fresh spearmint leaves in each ice cube section after adding the water, then freeze. These are especially fun to add to the lemonade.

2 to 3 cups fresh strawberries
5 cups water
¼ cup raw honey
1 cup fresh lemon juice

Fresh mint leaves
Sliced strawberries
Lemon wedges

1. Place the strawberries, 1 cup of the water, and the honey into a blender. Puree until smooth. Pour into a large pitcher and add the remaining 4 cups water and the lemon juice. Stir with a long-handled spoon. Taste, and adjust the sweetness, if necessary. (Strawberries can be very sweet so you may not need to add anymore honey.) Add more water if you would like a thinner lemonade.

2. Garnish each glass with a sprig of fresh mint, a strawberry slice, and a lemon wedge, if desired.

> **NUTRITION TIP**
>
> Chock-full of potent antioxidant chemicals, strawberries have been shown to lower the CRP (C-reactive protein) marker that is associated with increased heart attack risk. Consuming at least three servings a week can help decrease inflammation in your body. You may wonder, "Aren't strawberries high in sugar?" Yet when consumed along with table sugar, strawberries have been shown to lessen the sugar's negative effect on the body.

citrus spritzer

FREE OF

MAKES 4 CUPS

Our daughter will occasionally make us breakfast in bed—scrambled eggs, greens, and this spritzer. So, serve it with a special-occasion breakfast, brunch, or holiday meal. We've also made this recipe using blood oranges, which is quite delicious and a real treat. The recipe can easily be doubled or tripled as needed.

2 cups sparkling mineral water

2 cups fresh orange juice

2 tablespoons Meyer lemon juice

Fresh orange slices

Place the mineral water in a glass pitcher and then add the orange and lemon juice. Gently stir and add a few orange slices (or use blood orange slices for a beautiful presentation). Serve within an hour.

INGREDIENT TIP

Use Valencia oranges for juicing, as they contain more juice than other varieties. Meyer lemons are sweeter and more flavorful than regular lemons.

grape soda

MAKES 8 CUPS

This natural grape soda is free of added sugars and is fun to serve at a child's birthday party or other gathering such as a baby or wedding shower. As we generally never have juice in the house, treats such as this recipe are reserved for special occasions. You can use any organic fruit juice in place of the grape. For a party, make a double batch and place in a large bowl with a ladle. Float thin slices of oranges and limes to make a fruit punch! Have your children make raspberry or blackberry ice cubes by placing a berry in each ice cube section and then filling with filtered water and freezing. You can float the berry ice cubes in the grape soda.

4 cups organic Concord grape juice
1 liter sparkling mineral water

Mix all the ingredients in a large pitcher. Serve immediately.

NUTRITION TIP

Unsweeetened organic Concord grape juice is a rich source of the antioxidant flavonoids catechin, epicatechin, quercetin, and anthocyanins. A research article in the *American Journal of Clinical Nutrition* showed that consumption of Concord grape juice can decrease oxidative damage to proteins and lipids in the body.

preservingtheharvest

Only in the last sixty years or so have we been able to buy any vegetable or fruit at any time of the year. Historically, people ate what was available seasonally and preserved the rest. Our great-grandparents were adept at pickling, canning, and dehydrating. Food wasn't wasted. These basic survival skills have been lost in recent generations, but are now making a comeback. Home food preservation not only saves you money but also benefits your health and allows you and your family to connect with the wonderful foods that grow where you live.

We enjoy taking our children berry picking and then coming home to make honey-sweetened jam. By preserving food we are able to more fully connect with the rhythms of the seasons. We know that once the produce starts to become available in the spring, we must get busy. Our children see the first salmonberry as a sure sign of summer and many more berries to come. Peaches represent the heat of summer and apples the fading of summer into autumn.

By preserving your own food you save on packaging and shipping as well—and reduce the use of fossil fuels. Since the equipment and materials needed to store food are reusable, you'll produce much less waste, which would otherwise end up in a landfill. Growing and preserving your own foods ensures that you have a wholesome, chemical-free food source that can feed your family.

FOOD PRESERVATION METHODS

As we're all aware, most produce is highly perishable. Many things work together in the decaying process. Since fresh produce has a high water content, enzymes can begin to break it down and oxygen can react with it and cause spoilage. Also, bacteria, yeasts, and molds can grow and destroy fresh produce. Food can be preserved in a variety of ways to stop or slow this process of natural decay.

Canning

Canning food destroys enzymes, removes oxygen, and prevents the growth of harmful bacteria, yeasts, and molds. The process of canning, or, rather, heating foods in glass jars in a hot water bath or pressure cooker, forms a tight vacuum seal, which keeps the liquid in and the air out. It is important to follow USDA canning guidelines to ensure safe home-canned food. For example, acidic foods such as most fruits can be canned in a boiling water bath. Foods like squash and green beans, however, need to be canned using a pressure canner to achieve the necessary higher temperature.

Because canning destroys the vitality of food, we prefer to can only things like applesauce, jam, and tomato sauce. Freezing and dehydrating are our preferred methods for long-term food storage. Canned food should be stored in a cool, dark place and used within a year.

Pickling

Pickling, or brining, is the process of preserving food by anaerobic fermentation, also called lacto-fermentation. Salt is used to inhibit harmful microbes from growing while the lactic acid bacteria take over. Lactobacilli naturally present on the skins of vegetables begin to flourish by consuming the starches and sugars in the vegetables. They produce enough acid to inhibit harmful microbes from growing and properly preserve the food for many months.

10 Tips for Preserving Food

1. Always start with fresh food that has not begun to spoil.

2. Use in-season produce to capture the maximum nutrients.

3. Search out local, organic farms that offer u-pick fruits and vegetables. You'll save money by picking your own, and it is a fun activity to do with children, which educates them about the seasons and how their food is grown.

4. Follow USDA guidelines for canning to prevent harmful organisms, such as botulism, from growing.

5. Reduce, reuse, recycle. Save glass containers from products you buy and use to store fermented vegetables or dehydrated fruits and vegetables.

6. Place fermenting foods in a warm place where they can rest undisturbed. I like to use the top of the refrigerator for this purpose.

7. Using a large ceramic crock makes fermentation easy and reliable. Plus, you'll be able to make larger batches at once, saving time.

8. Consider purchasing an extra freezer. You'll save money and reduce waste by freezing berries, cherries, peaches, corn, peas, squash puree, and local meats when they are in season.

9. Consider investing in a food dehydrator to preserve food you have grown or harvested.

10. Be sure that your dehydrated foods are completely free of moisture before storing them; otherwise mold will begin to grow.

Pickling is thought to have originated over 4,000 years ago in India using cucumbers. Cultures all over the world have used lacto-fermentation to preserve food naturally. Unlike canning, pickling does not require the food and jars to be sterile. Some examples of naturally pickled foods include kimchi from Korea, pickled radish from China, sauerkraut from Germany, and the famous cucumber-dill pickle from North America. Naturally pickled foods should be stored in a cool, dark place, such as a refrigerator or root cellar, where they will stay good for up to six months.

Vinegar is another way to pickle foods. Vinegar's high acidity inhibits harmful microbes such as botulism from growing in home-canned pickled vegetables. Be sure to use a vinegar with a 5 percent acidity or greater.

Dehydrating
Dehydration of food is probably the oldest method of food preservation known. There is evidence that since before recorded history, people have been dehydrating meats, vegetables, fruits, and herbs to store and use at a later time. Microorganisms need

moisture to grow and survive. Proper food dehydration removes 80 to 90 percent of the moisture, so microbes are unable to function.

Dehydrating is much easier and more effective if you are living in a warm, dry climate. If not, you will need a food dehydrator to assist in the process. Dehydrating at or below 118°F keeps the enzymes and nutrients intact, retaining the food as a viable source of nutrition when fresh foods are unavailable. Store your dehydrated food in tightly sealed glass jars in a cool, dark place. We store our jars in the back of our pantry.

Freezing

Freezing is an ancient form of food preservation that originated in extreme northern latitudes. We use an upright deep freezer in our garage for food storage. Some foods can be frozen fresh, such as berries, peaches, pears, peas, and onions, while others, such as corn, green beans, kale, carrots, and asparagus, need to be blanched for 2 to 4 minutes before freezing.

I freeze whole Roma (plum) tomatoes in large containers, and then when I need a few cups of diced tomatoes for soup, I take out two or three tomatoes and let them thaw on the counter for about 20 minutes, and then dice them with a sharp knife. We freeze our berries, pitted cherries, halved peaches, and quartered pears in large reusable plastic containers. I don't like using plastic for anything but freezing. Plastic bags need to be thrown away once they have served their purpose, but plastic containers can be used over and over until they crack, at which point they can be recycled. We try to use our frozen foods within a year of freezing them. Usually in June most of our frozen produce has been used, at which point we defrost and clean the deep freezer to get ready for the next season's produce.

four thieves vinegar

MAKES ABOUT 1 QUART

The legend of Four Thieves Vinegar dates back to the 1600s, during the Black Plague in Europe. The story has it that a group of thieves were wandering through homes and businesses robbing the sick and dead. Four thieves were apprehended, but rather than punish them the judge offered them a deal. He offered to let them go if they gave him the secret of their resistance to the plague. Rather than be hung, they gave away their secret—a vinegar made from thyme, rosemary, sage, and lavender; herbs that offer powerful antiviral, antibacterial, antifungal, and immune-boosting chemicals.

Preserved in vinegar, they create the perfect medicine to drizzle over a plate full of summer greens or sip by the tablespoonful. I prefer to use either raw apple cider vinegar or raw coconut vinegar for this recipe, though white wine vinegar is typically used for its sweeter flavor. Although garlic was added to the mixture later, this basic infusion became famous and was used for hundreds of years in Europe. You can add a variety of herbs to the basic recipe. Try parsley, marjoram, mint, lemon balm, chives, and hyssop, too. Whisk together a few tablespoons of this Four Thieves Vinegar with a few tablespoons extra-virgin olive oil and a pinch or two of sea salt, and drizzle over fresh salad greens. It can also be taken by the tablespoonful as a medicine for the common cold or flu.

5 large sprigs fresh rosemary

5 large sprigs fresh thyme

5 large sprigs fresh sage

2 sprigs fresh lavender

4 or 5 garlic cloves, crushed

Raw apple cider vinegar or coconut vinegar

1. Place the herbs and garlic in a clean quart jar. Cover with vinegar, leaving at least 2 inches of space at the top. Place the lid on the jar and tightly close. Let the vinegar infuse in a cool, dark place for 6 weeks.

2. After 6 weeks, strain out and discard the herbs and garlic using a fine-mesh strainer. Pour the vinegar into a clean glass jar or bottle. Label and date your vinegar. Store in your pantry or kitchen cabinet for up to a year.

black currant vinegar

MAKES ABOUT 3 CUPS

We have a black currant bush in our garden that produces so many berries. Our children pick the berries by the handful and bring them into the kitchen for me to deal with. We simply cannot eat them all right away. We like to toss them into our green smoothies, put them in our strawberry-currant-honey jam, and make this nourishing vinegar. You can use this beautiful purple vinegar in salad dressings or eat it by the spoonful as daily medicine.

3 cups fresh black currants
Raw coconut vinegar or white wine vinegar

1. Place the black currants in a wide-mouth quart jar and fill the jar with vinegar, leaving about 2 inches at the top. Cover with a plastic lid and place in a kitchen cabinet or pantry. Let it sit for 6 to 12 weeks. A few times a week, gently shake the jar.

2. Place a fine-mesh strainer over a 4-cup liquid glass measure and pour the vinegar through it, mashing the berries in the strainer with the back of a spoon. Pour the vinegar into another jar or glass bottle for storage. The vinegar will keep for a year in a cool, dark place.

NUTRITION TIP

Studies indicate that anthocyanins, which create that dark purple color you see in black currants and other foods, show promising benefit as antioxidants, anti-inflammatories, and antimicrobials. As a result, they are being examined for their potential in combating cancers, neurodegenerative diseases (early stage cognitive decline and Alzheimer's), eye diseases, and high blood pressure. The food industry is even considering using antioxidants from black currant extract as a preservative in processed meats.

cayenne hot sauce

FREE OF

MAKES ABOUT 1½ CUPS

In the Northwest, chiles and peppers are grown in greenhouses because our summer temperatures are fairly mild but chiles need drier, hotter weather. Nonetheless, our farmers' markets brim with chiles of all kinds from late summer through early autumn. Making your own hot sauce takes very little time and is a wonderful way to preserve the harvest. I've kept bottles in the fridge through the winter. This hot sauce can also be canned in small jars using the water bath method. I use sweet Italian frying peppers to add sweetness and body without sugar—red bell peppers can also be used. Normally you are advised to wear rubber gloves when cutting up chiles, but I have designed the recipe in such a way that it isn't necessary. By trimming the stems and not cutting into the chile itself you won't need to wear gloves.

½ pound fresh cayenne chiles

¾ pound sweet Italian frying peppers or red bell peppers

3 or 4 garlic cloves

2 teaspoons sea salt

1½ cups raw apple cider vinegar

1. Trim the stem ends of the chiles. If they are large, cut in half (leaving the seeds in). Cut the sweet peppers in half, remove the seeds and stems, and chop into large chunks. Place the chiles and sweet peppers into a blender along with the remaining ingredients. Blend on high until smooth.

2. Pour the sauce into a 3-quart stainless steel pot. Cover and simmer for 20 to 30 minutes, whisking occasionally, until thickened and translucent. Transfer to a glass jar and store in the refrigerator for up to 6 months. (If you prefer to store some of the sauce for a longer time, can the sauce in small, sterilized glass jars for 10 minutes in a boiling water bath.)

> **NUTRITION TIP**
>
> People who live in hot climates have been known to eat cayenne and other hot chiles to help combat the heat and regulate body temperature. Cayenne chiles are high in capsaicin, which helps increase thermogenesis and fat burning. Many companies are now using capsaicin in weight-loss supplements.

raw sauerkraut

FREE OF

MAKES 1 QUART

Raw sauerkraut originated in China over 2,000 years ago and eventually made its way to Europe, where it became a staple food, especially in Germany. Captain James Cook kept thousands of pounds of raw sauerkraut—which contains a good dose of vitamin C—aboard his ships to prevent scurvy among his crew during the long voyages. I like to keep a few crocks going at once so we always have an ample supply of sauerkraut. Our children love the salty, crisp cabbage atop beans and quinoa for lunch or breakfast! This recipe uses a quart jar. Once you acquire a taste (and craving) for it, you might want to consider investing in a ceramic fermenting crock.

10 to 12 cups shredded green or red cabbage (see Tip)

1 to 1½ tablespoons sea salt
Cabbage leaf

1. Place the cabbage in a large bowl and sprinkle the sea salt over; toss well, then pound it with a wooden mallet or other blunt object that won't break or damage the bowl—I use a wooden kraut pounder. Keep pounding—this can take up to 10 minutes—until the cabbage has released its juices.

2. Spoon the kraut into a wide-mouth quart jar. Firmly press it into the jar to push out the air as you add more cabbage. I use the wooden pestle for this. Pack it in, leaving about 2 inches space from the top of the jar. Fold up the cabbage leaf and press it on top of the kraut. Use the pestle to firmly press it down so the juices rise above it. You want your kraut to stay below the juices to properly ferment.

3. Put a plastic lid on the jar but don't tighten it all the way; this leaves room for gasses to be released. Place the jar in a bowl or small glass dish to catch any juices that leak out. Place in a warm spot. I like to put the jar on the top of my refrigerator. Keep it out of direct sunlight. Let it ferment for 5 to 10 days, or longer if your house is on the cooler side. (I ferment sauerkraut in my ceramic crock for about 4 weeks in a cool place.) When done, it should taste tangy and sour. If not, place the lid back on and let it ferment for a few more days. Remove the large cabbage leaf on top of the jar, screw the lid back on, and store in your refrigerator for up to 6 months.

> **KITCHEN TIP**
>
> To shred the cabbage, remove the outer leaves and save one good-looking leaf for the top. Cut the cabbage into chunks, then use the slicing disk on a food processor to shred it.

beet sauerkraut

MAKES 1 QUART

My children call this "purple kraut." They absolutely love to help make it. The flavor is tangy like regular sauerkraut, with earthy undertones from the beet and carrots. You might want to make a few jars at once while you are at it. I find we go through it so fast that it is easier to make more than the yield here. Serve this with a meat main dish or bean soup to make it more digestible. I also like to serve this over poached eggs for breakfast.

8 cups shredded cabbage (about 1 small head)

1 beet, peeled and shredded

2 large carrots, shredded

1 to 1½ tablespoons sea salt

Cabbage leaf

1. Place the cabbage in a large bowl and add the beet and carrots. Sprinkle the sea salt over and toss well. Pound the vegetables with a wooden mallet or other blunt object that won't break or damage the bowl—I use a wooden kraut pounder. Keep pounding—this can take up to 10 minutes—until the veggies have released their juices.

2. Spoon the kraut into a wide-mouth quart jar. Firmly press it into the jar to push out the air. I use the wooden pestle for this. Pack it all in there leaving about 2 inches of space from the top of the jar. Fold up the cabbage leaf and press it on top of the kraut. Use the pestle to firmly press it down so the juices rise above it. You want your kraut to stay below the juices to properly ferment.

3. Put a plastic lid on the jar but don't tighten it all the way; this leaves room for gasses to be released. Place the jar in a bowl or small glass dish to catch any juices that leak out. Place in a warm spot. I like to place the jar on the top of my refrigerator. Keep it out of direct sunlight.

4. Let it ferment for 5 to 10 days, or longer if your house is on the cooler side. When done, it should taste tangy and sour. Remove the large cabbage leaf on top, screw the lid back on, and store in your refrigerator for up to 6 months.

chile-garlic fermented green beans

FREE OF

MAKES 1 QUART

This preparation uses lacto-fermentation to preserve raw green beans—no canning and no subsequent loss of nutrients! Usually it takes anywhere from five to ten days to properly ferment, but can take as little as three, depending on the season and temperature in your home. Fermentation happens quickly in very warm weather! I've used small dried whole chiles, red pepper flakes, and chopped fresh chiles—use whatever you have on hand. Be sure to keep the liquid above the beans. Any beans, garlic, or chiles exposed to air could mold and spoil the whole batch!

3 to 4 garlic cloves, chopped

3 to 6 dried red chiles

½ to ¾ pound green beans, trimmed and cut in half

1½ tablespoons sea salt

2 cups purified water

Cabbage leaf (optional)

1. Place the garlic and red chiles at the bottom of a clean wide-mouth quart jar. Place all the green beans in vertically as will fit, packing them in tightly. (Placing them vertically prevents their floating to the top and also keeps the garlic and chiles at the bottom.) Allow 2 inches of space from the top of the jar.

2. Dissolve the salt in the water, then pour over the beans. Add a touch more water, if needed, to submerge the beans. Fold the cabbage leaf and press down on top of the beans. This keeps the beans submerged; you could also place a small lid

with a weight or boiled rock on top to keep the beans submerged. Cover the jar with a plastic lid and set somewhere in your kitchen out of reach of direct sunlight.

3. After 3 days, you should see little bubbles rising to the top. Use a fork to pull a bean out and taste it. It should be sour, salty, and crispy; if not, let it ferment longer. Keep checking until the beans are soured to your liking. For me, this is usually 5 to 7 days. Place the jar in the refrigerator where it will keep for up to 6 months.

dilly radishes

This method of preservation is called lacto-fermentation. A salt brine is used to inhibit the growth of unfriendly microorganisms while letting the lactobacilli bacteria normally present on the vegetables flourish and grow. Eating fermented foods daily keeps our digestive system strong and healthy. Serve these tasty radishes with baked salmon and sautéed kale for a balanced meal.

1 to 2 bunches radishes

Small handful of fresh dill

3 garlic cloves, coarsely chopped

1 tablespoon red peppercorns

2 cups filtered water

1 to 1½ tablespoons sea salt

Cabbage leaf

Rinse the radishes and trim the ends. Cut into ¼-inch slices. Place the dill, garlic, and peppercorns at the bottom of a wide-mouth quart jar. Add enough radish slices to fill the jar, leaving about 1 inch of space from the top. In a small bowl or liquid glass measure, whisk the filtered water and salt, dissolving the salt. Pour over the radishes; don't shake or stir the jar because you want to make sure the dill stays at the bottom

(otherwise it can float to the top and mold during the fermentation). Fold and press a cabbage leaf into the jar so the liquid rises above it and all of the radishes are submerged beneath. If you need to, add a little more brine. Cover the jar with a plastic lid and set it out of direct sunlight. Let it sit for 5 to 10 days. Remove the cabbage leaf and store in your refrigerator for up to 6 months.

pickled carrots and cauliflower

FREE OF

MAKES 1 QUART

This is one of our favorite fermentation recipes. We make a few jars of it a week. In some of the jars we add hot chiles and in others we simply add herbs and garlic so our children will eat them. If you grow cauliflower in your garden, this is a fabulous way to preserve it.

4 garlic cloves, chopped

1 teaspoon black peppercorns

4 sprigs fresh dill or tarragon

3 or 4 large carrots, finely chopped

2 to 3 cups finely chopped cauliflower florets

2 cups filtered water

1 to 1½ tablespoons sea salt

Cabbage leaf

1. Place the garlic, peppercorns, and herbs at the bottom of a wide-mouth quart jar. Add layers of carrots and cauliflower, leaving about 1 inch of space at the top. In a small bowl or liquid glass measure, whisk the filtered water and salt to dissolve the salt. Pour over the vegetables to submerge them. Fold and press a cabbage leaf into the jar so the liquid rises above it and the vegetables are submerged beneath. If necessary, add a little more brine.

2. Tightly cover the jar with a plastic lid and set it out of direct sunlight. Let it sit for 5 to 10 days. Taste to see if it has soured (fermented) enough; if not, let sit a few more days, checking and tasting daily. Fermentation happens much faster in warmer temperatures, so the timing can vary widely. Remove the cabbage leaf and store the pickled vegetables in your refrigerator for up to 6 months.

raw sour dill pickles

FREE OF

MAKES 1 GALLON

This uses lacto-fermentation and is one of the easiest ways to preserve some of the summer harvest. Lactobacilli bacteria normally present on the skins of cucumbers are allowed to grow in a salt brine, creating an acidic, sour flavor that is not only tasty but also beneficial for your gut. I prefer to use small to medium pickling cucumbers. They can be found at your local farmers' market in the summer; I also buy them by the case from organic farms. Pickles made this way can be stored in your refrigerator for up to six months!

4 pounds whole pickling cucumbers

2 or 3 bunches flowering dill

¼ to ½ cup pickling spice

1 or 2 garlic heads, chopped

6 tablespoons sea salt

2 quarts filtered water

1 fresh grape leaf or sour cherry leaf (optional)

Cabbage leaf

1. Rinse a 1-gallon glass jar or ceramic fermenting crock with very hot water. Wash the cucumbers, rubbing them to remove any dirt or debris. Place the dill sprigs, pickling spice, and garlic at the bottom of the jar. Add the cucumbers until they reach to within a few inches of the top of the jar. Dissolve the salt in the water. Pour over the cucumbers until submerged. If you need more liquid, add 2 teaspoons of salt per cup of filtered water until the water covers the cucumbers. Add a grape leaf, if desired, which helps keep the pickles crisp. Fold and press a large cabbage leaf onto the cucumbers, then add a glass weight or boiled rock to keep them beneath the brine. This is very important! Your pickles will begin to mold if they are exposed to air.

2. Cover the jar tightly with the lid and place in an undisturbed spot away from direct sunlight. Let ferment for 1 to 2 weeks, depending on the temperature. If it is very warm in your house, it may take less than a week. In the Pacific Northwest, without air conditioning, the cucumbers ferment for almost 2 weeks, sometimes longer. The brine will get cloudy, and this is what you want to see. Cover and refrigerate for up to 6 months.

> **INGREDIENT TIP**
>
> Pickling spice usually contains hot chiles, which are a nightshade vegetable. If you are avoiding nightshades, you can easily make your own pickling spice and omit the chiles.

fresh tomato-basil marinara sauce

MAKES 5 TO 6 QUARTS

This is a great way to use an abundant tomato harvest. Instead of removing the skins and seeds, I simply puree the tomatoes, making this one of the easiest sauce recipes imaginable! If you want to make a smaller batch, cut the quantities by two-thirds; for example, use 6 to 7 pounds of tomatoes and 1 large onion. This sauce can be frozen in quart jars or canned in a hot water bath according to the USDA guidelines.

½ cup extra-virgin olive oil

3 large onions, minced

1 garlic head, minced

20 pounds ripe tomatoes, trimmed of stem ends

½ cup red wine vinegar

2 to 4 tablespoons coconut sugar or raw honey

2 to 3 tablespoons Italian seasoning

2 tablespoons sea salt, or more as needed

2 to 3 cups packed fresh basil, chopped

1. Heat a 12-quart or larger stockpot over medium. Add the olive oil and then the onions and garlic. Sauté for about 10 minutes. Process the tomatoes in batches in a food processor, leaving them a little chunky, and add to the stockpot. (You can also blend the remaining tomatoes until smooth in a blender.). Add the vinegar, coconut sugar, Italian seasoning, and salt. Cook, uncovered, for 3 to 4 hours, or until the sauce has cooked down and thickened to desired consistency. Stir it occasionally and keep it on a rapid simmer. Taste and add more salt, if needed. Stir in the basil and simmer a few minutes more.

2. Pour the sauce into clean wide-mouthed quart jars, leaving at least 1 inch of space from the top. Let cool completely, then place in a freezer without the lids. After the jars have frozen, screw on the lids. (Or follow USDA guidelines for canning.)

homemade applesauce

FREE OF

MAKES 6 TO 8 PINTS; 3 TO 4 QUARTS

Making your own applesauce is so easy—and what better way is there to preserve the apple harvest? Applesauce is best made from sweet apples; that way you won't need to add any sweetener. Galas, Jonagold, Jonathon, Yellow Delicious, and Fuji are all great choices. Use one variety or a combination. If you are not picking your own apples, then buy seconds from a local organic farmer. Imperfect apples are cheaper and well-suited for applesauce. The sauce can then be frozen or, as here, can be processed in a water bath and stored in your pantry for about two years.

10 pounds apples, washed

1. You can make this applesauce two ways: by peeling, coring, and chopping the apples and cooking them, or by chopping them and using a food mill. When I first began making my own sauce, I peeled and cored them all and cooked the applesauce in my largest pot at the time, an 8-quart stockpot. Now I have a large canning pot and a food mill, which makes the process go much faster and smoother. If you don't have a food mill, then core, peel, and chop the apples. If you do have one, simply chop the apples—no need to peel or core them.

2. Add about 1 inch of water to a heavy-bottomed 8-quart stockpot. Then add the chopped apples. Cover the pot. Turn the heat to medium-high and bring to a boil. Stir, and reduce the heat to medium, cooking the apples. They will release more water; continue to cook for 10 to 15 minutes, or until the apples are cooked through and soft, stirring occasionally.

3. Fill a canning pot with water. Set a rack inside, and bring to a boil.

4. If not using a food mill, process the apples in a food processor or use a potato masher or large slotted spoon to mash them into sauce. If using a food mill, process in the mill to remove the skins and seeds, and make the sauce.

5. Pour the applesauce into clean, sterilized pint or quart jars to within ¼ inch of the top. Wipe away any spills, then screw on sterilized canning lids. Carefully, using a jar grabber, lower the jars into the boiling water. Process pint jars for 15 minutes or quart jars for 20 minutes at sea level. (Add about 5 minutes for every 3,000 feet above sea level.) Remove the jars from the canning pot and let cool gradually on a rack. The canning lids will be depressed in the centers if the seal is made.

6. Or, if you do not want to process the jars, you can refrigerate the sauce for 2 weeks or freeze for up to a year.

VARIATION: Add fresh or frozen cranberries to the stockpot for a beautiful ruby-red sauce that is a little tart and tangy. You can also add pears, peaches, plums, or berries.

homemade pumpkin puree

FREE OF

MAKES ABOUT 4 CUPS

Making your own pumpkin puree is easy and tastes so much better than pumpkin from a can! You can use any type of winter squash, but sugar pumpkins are by far our favorite. They can be found at your local health food store or farmers' market in autumn. Once you have made your puree, you can freeze it to use throughout the year. If you want to can it instead, you'll need a pressure cooker; follow the USDA guidelines.

A 3- to 4-pound sugar pumpkin

1. Preheat the oven to 400°F. Place the pumpkin on a large cutting board and use a sharp heavy-duty knife to cut it in half cross-wise. Scoop out the seeds. Place the seeds in a bowl to sort out later and roast, if desired. Roasted pumpkin seeds with sea salt and coconut oil are a favorite snack at our house!

2. Cut the pumpkin halves in half again, and then into eighths. Place the pumpkin pieces in a shallow baking dish, skin side down, cover with a lid, and roast for about 1 hour.

3. Scoop the pumpkin flesh into a food processor fitted with the "s" blade and process until a smooth puree forms. Scoop the puree into glass jars or storage containers, cover, and refrigerate for up to 1 week or freeze for a year. (Note: If you are using a very moist squash you may need to drain off any excess water by placing the puree in a fine-mesh strainer fitted over a bowl. Let drain for 1 to 2 hours before storing.)

vanilla plum butter

MAKES ABOUT 3½ CUPS

Italian prune plums are one of our favorite fruits to pick. Our children eat them like candy. I can't imagine a more perfect snack food. Once ripe, though, these plums spoil quickly. We like to cut them in half, remove the pits, and dehydrate most of them, then freeze the rest. In the midst of freezing and dehydrating, I like to make a few batches of this fruit butter. Unripe apples, which are very high in pectin, help to naturally thicken the butter. There should be plenty of unripe apples available on trees in your area when the plums are in season. (To check if the apples are still unripe, cut them in half—if the seeds are white it's in the perfect stage to use in this recipe; if the seeds are brown, it's too ripe.) Stir the plum butter into plain yogurt or spread on warm buttered bread.

4 cups pureed Italian prune plums

1 small unripe apple, cored

1 teaspoon raw vanilla powder

1 cup coconut sugar

1. Place the prune puree into a blender and add the apple and vanilla powder; blend well, until the apple is completely pureed. Pour the puree into a large, wide pot or deep skillet and bring to a boil. Add the coconut sugar, whisk again, then reduce the heat to low and simmer for 20 to 40 minutes. Stir frequently to avoid any burning on the bottom. Cook until reduced and thickened. When cool, it will be even thicker.

2. Fill a canning pot with water and bring to a boil. Fill sterilized half-pint or 12-ounce jam jars to within ¼ inch of the top with the puree. Cover with sterilized lids. Place in the hot water bath and process for 10 minutes. (Add 1 minute for every 1,000 feet above sea level.) Remove the jars and let cool on a rack. When the centers of the lids are depressed, the jars will have sealed properly.

KITCHEN TIP

If you do not want to can the puree, place the jars in the refrigerator, where they will last for about 3 weeks. You can also freeze the cooled plum butter in small jars.

PRESERVING THE HARVEST

481

sun-dried tomatoes

MAKES 4 TO 5 CUPS

Making true sun-dried tomatoes can be done in a very dry, hot climate in the summer, such as in parts of the Southwest. Here in the Northwest, it is far too moist to dry anything out in the open, so we use a food dehydrator. Roma (plum) tomatoes work best for this because of their low moisture content. Dried tomatoes can be rehydrated with hot water to make tomato sauce or pizza sauce. They are great added to soups that will be pureed. I also use them to make savory crackers and biscuits. You will need a food dehydrator with at least five trays to make this recipe.

10 pounds ripe Roma (plum) tomatoes
Sea salt

1. Cut the tomatoes in half and arrange cut side up on the dehydrator sheets so they are not touching each other. They need enough airflow to properly dehydrate. Sprinkle the tomatoes with a little salt. Dehydrate for 12 to 48 hours at 130°F. The timing depends on the size and moisture content of the tomatoes; they should feel leathery when done, with no soft mushy spots. If some are underdone, simply leave those pieces to dehydrate a few hours longer.

2. Store the tomatoes in a tightly sealed glass jar in a cool, dark place for up to a year. We store our dehydrated fruit and vegetables in the back of our pantry.

kale-herb seaweed sprinkle

FREE OF

MAKES ABOUT ½ CUP

This is a good way to use the extra kale growing in your garden. We have so much sometimes we don't know what to do with it all, and have called in friends to take some of it away—of course, they don't mind at all! Dehydrating kale is a fantastic way to preserve it, however. Use this sprinkle over popcorn, soups, stews, mashed potatoes, steamed vegetables, grilled fish, or fresh salads. You will need a food dehydrator to make this recipe.

1 bunch kale

2 to 4 tablespoons kelp granules (see Tip)

1 tablespoon dried dill

1 tablespoon dried rosemary

1. Remove the thick inner rib that runs up each leaf of the kale. Tear the kale into small pieces and place them onto 3 or 4 racks of your food dehydrator; set the temperature to 118°F. Dehydrate until dry and crisp, 3 to 6 hours.

2. Place the dried kale pieces into a food processor fitted with the "s" blade. Add the kelp, dill, and rosemary and process to a fine powder. Carefully pour into a glass jar and close tightly with a lid. Store in a cool, dark place for up to a year.

VARIATION: Use any combination of dried herbs you have on hand. Dried thyme, chives, parsley, garlic powder, onions granules, or red pepper flakes all work well.

> **NUTRITION TIP**
>
> Kelp, like many sea vegetables, is a concentrated source of iodine, which is needed to produce the thyroid hormones T3 and T4. Thyroid hormones are composed of a tyrosine amino acid attached to either three or four iodine molecules, so it is absolutely essential that we consume enough iodine to produce enough thyroid hormones. These hormones control our metabolism, which regulates our body temperature, body weight, and energy production. Did you know every single cell in the body has a receptor for thyroid hormones? People with food sensitivities often have elevated autoantibodies in their thyroid gland. If you have food sensitivities and low thyroid function, you might want to consider having your thyroid autoantibodies tested.

homemade herbed sea salt

MAKES ABOUT 1¾ CUPS

Throughout this book I use a sea salt and herb blend called Herbamare; it can be found at your local health food store or ordered online. It's a fabulous replacement for sea salt as it lends more flavors with the added benefit of less sodium per teaspoon. If you can't find Herbamare, then you can create your own at home using some sea salt and dehydrated herbs and vegetables—most of which can be found in the bulk herb and spice section at your local health food store. If you can't find an ingredient then just leave it out. Use this flavorful herbed sea salt anywhere sea salt is called for in a savory recipe!

1 cup fine sea salt

¼ cup kelp pieces, or 1 tablespoon kelp powder

4 tablespoons dried chives

4 tablespoons dried parsley

3 to 4 tablespoons celery powder (see Tip)

3 to 4 tablespoons dried nettles

2 tablespoons dried marjoram

2 tablespoons dried thyme

1 tablespoon dried rosemary

1 tablespoon dried basil

1 tablespoon onion powder

1 tablespoon garlic powder

OPTIONAL ADDITIONS

3 to 4 tablespoons dehydrated leeks

3 to 4 tablespoons dehydrated lovage

2 to 3 tablespoons dehydrated wild bittercress

2 to 3 tablespoons dehydrated lamb's quarters

1. Place all the ingredients, including any optional ingredients, into a food processor fitted with the "s" blade or a high-powered blender and chop for a few minutes, or until very finely ground and combined. It should be a pale green color. Spoon it into a clean, dry pint-size jar and cover tightly with a lid. It will last for a year in your cabinet or pantry.

2. For daily use, I suggest reusing a small, clean, dry spice jar with a shaker lid and filling it with some of your herbed sea salt. This will keep your pint jar from getting too much moisture in it.

> **KITCHEN TIP**
>
> It's very easy to make your own celery powder! Simply chop up some fresh organic celery (leafy tops included) and add it to your dehydrator. Set the temperature to the fruits and vegetables setting (about 120° to 140°F). Dehydrate until completely dry and crispy, 24 to 48 hours. Then transfer the celery to a high-powered blender (I use the dry container) and blend until powdered. You can do this with any vegetable or herb—leeks, onions, or kelp!

Resources and Recommendations

Alternative Sweeteners

Coconut sugar: Essential Living Foods, www
.essentiallivingfoods.com

Coconut nectar: Coconut Secret, www.coconutsecret
.com

Maple syrup, grade B: Coombs, www
.coombsfamilyfarms.com

Stevia: Sweet Leaf Liquid Stevia, www.sweetleaf.com

Oils

Organic extra-virgin olive oil: Napa Valley Naturals,
www.worldpantry.com

Virgin coconut oil: Nutiva, www.nutiva.com

Organic palm shortening: Spectrum, www
.spectrumorganics.com

Gluten-Free Flours

Coconut flour: Nutiva, www.Nutiva.com

Blanched almond flour: Lucy's Kitchen Shop, www
.lucyskitchenshop.com

Organic blanched almond flour: Nuts, www.nuts.com

Almond meal: Bob's Red Mill, www.bobsredmill.com

Hazelnut meal: Bob's Red Mill, www.bobsredmill
.com

Organic GF cornmeal: Arrowhead Mills, www
.arrowheadmills.com

Whole-grain flours gluten-free: Bob's Red Mill, www
.bobsredmill.com

Sprouted brown rice flour: Planet Rice, www
.planetricefoods.com

Sprouted gluten-free flours: To Your Health Sprouted
Flour Co., www.organicsproutedflour.net

Superfine flours: Authentic Foods, www.authenticfoods
.com

Arrowroot powder: Bob's Red Mill, www.bobsredmill
.com

Nut and Seed Butters

Raw sprouted nut and seed butters: Better Than
Roasted, www.bluemountainorganics.com

Sunflower seed butter: Organic Sunbutter, www
.sunbutter.com

Organic raw almond butter: Once Again, www
.onceagainnutbutter.com

Organic roasted almond butter: Zinke Orchards, www
.zinkeorchards.com

Organic peanut butter: Once Again, www
.onceagainnutbutter.com

Nondairy Milks

Coconut milk: Native Forest Organic, www
.edwardandsons.com

Meats

Pastured meats: Tropical Traditions, www
.tropicaltraditions.com

Whole Grains

Organic gluten-free whole grains: Bob's Red Mill,
www.bobsredmill.com

Sea Vegetables

Organic nori, sound sea vegetables, kombu, hijiki:
Arame Eden Foods, www.edenfoods.com

Salts and Seasonings

Herbamare: A. Vogel, www.avogel.com

Sea salt: Real Salt, www.realsalt.com

Coconut aminos: Coconut Secret, www.coconut secret.com

Wheat-free tamari: San-J, www.san-j.com

Food Buying

Bulk natural foods: Azure Standard, www .azurestandard.com

Food buying clubs: UNFI, www.unitedbuying clubs.com

Farmers' markets: Local Harvest, www.localharvest.com

Food co-ops: Co-op Directory Service, www .coopdirectory.org

References

Introduction

CDC website for Autism Spectrum Disorders. Data and Statistics. Retrieved March 20, 2012, www.cdc.gov/ncbddd/autism/index.html

Branum AM, Lukacs SL. (Oct 10, 2008). Food Allergy Among U.S. Children: Trends in Prevalence and Hospitalizations. NCHS Data Brief Number 10. Retrieved February 16, 2012, www.cdc.gov/nchs/data/databriefs/db10.htm

CDC Diabetes Public Health Resource website. 2011 National Diabetes Fact Sheet. Retrieved February 16, 2012, www.cdc.gov/diabetes/pubs/factsheet11.htm

CDC Attention-Deficit/Hyperactivity Disorder (ADHD) website. Data and Statistics. Retrieved February 16, 2012, www.cdc.gov/NCBDDD/adhd/data.html

Why Whole Foods?

Demmig-Adams B, Adams WW III. Antioxidants in photosynthesis and human nutrition. *Science*. 2002 Dec 13;298(5601):2149–53. PMID: 12481128

Subbiah MT. Understanding the nutrigenomic definitions and concepts at the food-genome junction. OMICS. 2008 Dec;12(4):229–35. PMID: 18687041

Hanhineva K, Törrönen R, Bondia-Pons I, et al. Impact of dietary polyphenols on carbohydrate metabolism. Int J Mol Sci. 2010 Mar 31;11(4):1365–402. PMID: 20480025

Hardy TM, Tollefsbol TO. Epigenetic diet: impact on the epigenome and cancer. *Epigenomics*. 2011 Aug;3(4):503–18. PMID: 22022340

Javierre BM, Hernando H, Ballestar E. Environmental triggers and epigenetic deregulation in autoimmune disease. Discov Med. 2011 Dec;12(67):535–45. PMID: 22204770

Barbeau WE. What is the key environmental trigger in type 1 diabetes—Is it viruses, or wheat gluten, or both? Autoimmun Rev. 2012 May 22. [Epub ahead of print] PMID: 22633932

Masala S, Paccagnini D, Cossu D, et al. Antibodies recognizing Mycobacterium avium paratuberculosis epitopes cross-react with the beta-cell antigen ZnT8 in Sardinian type 1 diabetic patients. *PLoS One*. 2011; 6(10):e26931. Epub 2011 Oct 27. PMID: 22046415

Abhilash M, Sauganth Paul MV, Varghese MV, et al. Long-term consumption of aspartame and brain antioxidant defense status. Drug Chem Toxicol. 2012 Mar 2. [Epub ahead of print] PMID: 22385158

Abdel-Salam OM, Salem NA, Hussein JS. Effect of aspartame on oxidative stress and monoamine neurotransmitter levels in lipopolysaccharide-treated mice. Neurotox Res. 2012 Apr;21(3):245–55. PMID: 21822758

Pisarik P, Kai D. Vestibulocochlear toxicity in a pair of siblings 15 years apart secondary to aspartame: two case reports. Cases J. 2009 Sep 15;2:9237. PMID: 20181217

Rommens CM, Shakya R, Heap M, et al. Tastier and healthier alternatives to French fries. J Food Sci. 2010 May;75(4):H109–15. PMID: 20546404

Roberts HJ. (Jan 7, 2004) Aspartame Disease: An FDA-Approved Epidemic. Mercola.com. Retrieved on January 11, 2012, from http://articles.mercola.com/sites/articles/archive/2004/01/07/aspartame-disease-part-two.aspx

Ellis WG. Uncured rice as a cause of Beriberi. Br Med J. 1909 Oct 2;2(2544):935. PMID: 20764688

Lanou AJ, Svenson B. Reduced cancer risk in vegetarians: an analysis of recent reports. Cancer Manag Res. 2010 Dec 20;3:1–8. PMID: 21407994

Crinnion WJ. Organic foods contain higher levels of certain nutrients, lower levels of pesticides, and may provide health benefits for the consumer. Altern Med Rev. 2010 Apr;15(1):4–12. Review. PMID: 20359265

Roberts EM, English PB, Grether JK, et al. Maternal residence near agricultural pesticide applications and autism spectrum disorders among children in the California Central Valley. Environ Health Perspect. 2007 Oct;115(10):1482–9. PMID: 17938740

Rauh V, Arunajadai S, Horton M, et al. Seven-year neurodevelopmental scores and prenatal exposure to chlorpyrifos, a common agricultural pesticide. Environ Health Perspect. 2011 Aug;119(8):1196–201. PMID: 21507777

Bouchard MF, Chevrier J, Harley KG, et al. Prenatal exposure to organophosphate pesticides and IQ in 7-year-old children. Environ Health Perspect. 2011 Aug;119(8):1189–95. PMID: 21507776

Engel SM, Wetmur J, Chen J, et al. Prenatal exposure to organophosphates, paraoxonase 1, and cognitive development in childhood. Environ Health Perspect. 2011 Aug;119(8):1182–8. PMID: 21507778

Eskenazi B, Rosas LG, Marks AR, et al. Pesticide toxicity and the developing brain. Basic Clin Pharmacol Toxicol. 2008 Feb;102(2):228–36. Pesticide toxicity and the developing brain. PMID: 18226078

Rosas LG, Eskenazi B. Pesticides and child neurodevelopment. Curr Opin Pediatr. 2008 Apr;20(2):191–7. PMID: 18332717

Why Gluten-Free?

Volta U, De Giorgio R. New understanding of gluten sensitivity. Nat Rev Gastroenterol Hepatol. 2012 Feb 28;9(5):295–9. PMID: 22371218

Di Sabatino A, Corazza GR. Nonceliac gluten sensitivity: sense or sensibility? Ann Intern Med. 2012 Feb 21;156(4):309–11. PMID: 22351716

Sapone A, Bai JC, Ciacci C, Dolinsek J, et al. Spectrum of gluten-related disorders: consensus on new nomenclature and classification. BMC Med. 2012 Feb 7;10:13. PMID: 22313950

Hollén E, Högberg L, Stenhammar L, et al. Antibodies to oat prolamines (avenins) in children with coeliac disease. Scand J Gastroenterol. 2003 Jul;38(7):742–6. PMID: 12889560

Drago S, El Asmar R, Di Pierro M, et al. Gliadin, zonulin and gut permeability: Effects on celiac and non-celiac intestinal mucosa and intestinal cell lines. Scand J Gastroenterol. 2006 Apr;41(4):408–19. PMID: 16635908

García-Manzanares A, Lucendo AJ. Nutritional and dietary aspects of celiac disease. Nutr Clin Pract. 2011 Apr;26(2):163–73. PMID: 21447770

Visser J, Rozing J, Sapone A, et al. Tight junctions, intestinal permeability, and autoimmunity: celiac disease and type 1 diabetes paradigms. Ann N Y Acad Sci. 2009 May;1165:195–205. PMID: 19538307

Malterre T. Digestive and nutritional considerations in celiac disease: could supplementation help? Altern Med Rev. 2009 Sep;14(3):247–57. PMID: 19803549

Rostami K, Steegers EA, Wong WY, et al. Coeliac disease and reproductive disorders: a neglected association. Eur J Obstet Gynecol Reprod Biol. 2001 Jun;96(2):146–9. PMID: 11384797

Hwang C, Ross V, Mahadevan U. Micronutrient deficiencies in inflammatory bowel disease: From A to zinc. Inflamm Bowel Dis. 2012 Apr 5. PMID: 22488830

Gimenez MS, Oliveros LB, Gomez NN. Nutritional deficiencies and phospholipid metabolism. Int J Mol Sci. 2011;12(4):2408–33. PMID: 21731449

Alvarez-Jubete L, Arendt EK, Gallagher E. Nutritive value and chemical composition of pseudocereals as gluten-free ingredients. Int J Food Sci Nutr. 2009;60 Suppl 4:240–57. PMID: 19462323

Why the Rise in Food Allergies and Sensitivities?

Gruzieva O, Bellander T, Eneroth K, et al. Traffic-related air pollution and development of allergic sensitization in children during the first 8 years of life. J Allergy Clin Immunol. 2012 Jan;129(1):240–6. Epub 2011 Nov 21. PMID: 22104609

Genuis SJ, Sears M, Schwalfenberg G, et al. Incorporating environmental health in clinical medicine. J Environ Public Health. 2012;2012:103041. Epub 2012 May 17. PMID: 22675371

Genuis SJ. What's out there making us sick? J Environ Public Health. 2012;2012:605137. Epub 2011 Oct 24. PMID: 22262979

Genuis SJ. Sensitivity-related illness: the escalating pandemic of allergy, food intolerance and chemical sensitivity. Sci Total Environ. 2010 Nov 15;408(24):6047–61. PMID:20920818

Uddin R, Huda NH. Arsenic poisoning in bangladesh. Oman Med J. 2011 May;26(3):207. PMID: 22043419

Daley CA, Abbott A, Doyle PS, et al. A review of fatty acid profiles and antioxidant content in grass-fed and grain-fed beef. Nutr J. 2010 Mar 10;9:10. Review. PMID: 20219103

Aljada A, Mohanty P, Ghanim H, et al. Increase in intranuclear nuclear factor kappaB and decrease in inhibitor kappaB in mononuclear cells after a mixed meal: evidence for a proinflammatory effect. Am J Clin Nutr. 2004 Apr;79(4):682–90. PMID: 15051615

Demmig-Adams B, Adams WW 3rd. Antioxidants in photosynthesis and human nutrition. Science. 2002 Dec 13;298(5601):2149–53. PMID: 12481128

Cotter PD, Stanton C, Ross RP, et al. The impact of antibiotics on the gut microbiota as revealed by high throughput DNA sequencing. Discov Med. 2012 Mar;13(70):193–9. PMID: 22463795

Pistiner M, Gold DR, Abdulkerim H, et al. Birth by cesarean section, allergic rhinitis, and allergic sensitization among children with a parental history of atopy. J Allergy Clin Immunol. 2008 Aug;122(2):274–9. PMID: 18571710

Turpin W, Humblot C, Thomas M, et al. Lactobacilli as multifaceted probiotics with poorly disclosed molecular mechanisms. Int J Food Microbiol. 2010 Oct 15;143(3):87–102. PMID: 20801536

Liu AH. Hygiene theory and allergy and asthma prevention. Paediatr Perinat Epidemiol. 2007 Nov;21 Suppl 3:2–7. PMID: 17935569

Aris A, Leblanc S. Maternal and fetal exposure to pesticides associated to genetically modified foods in Eastern Townships of Quebec, Canada. Reprod Toxicol. 2011 May;31(4):528–33. PMID: 21338670

de Vendômois JS, Roullier F, Cellier D, et al. A comparison of the effects of three GM corn varieties on mammalian health. Int J Biol Sci. 2009 Dec 10;5(7):706–26. PMID: 20011136

Dean, A., Armstron, J. (May 8, 2009). Genetically Modified Foods, American Academy of Environmental Medicine Position Paper. http://aaemonline.org/gmopost.html

Nourishing Your Growing Child

Dovey TM, Staples PA, Gibson EL, et al. Food neophobia and 'picky/fussy' eating in children: a review. Appetite. 2008 Mar-May;50(2–3):181–93. PMID: 17997196

Mennella JA, Jagnow CP, Beauchamp GK. Prenatal and postnatal flavor learning by human infants. Pediatrics. 2001 Jun;107(6):E88. PMID: 11389286

Varendi H, Porter RH, Winberg J. Attractiveness of amniotic fluid odor: evidence of prenatal olfactory learning? Acta Paediatr. 1996 Oct;85(10):1223–7. PMID: 8922088

Forestell CA, Mennella JA. Early determinants of fruit and vegetable acceptance. Pediatrics. 2007 Dec;120(6):1247–54. PMID: 18055673

Disantis KI, Collins BN, Fisher JO, et al. Do infants fed directly from the breast have improved appetite regulation and slower growth during early childhood compared with infants fed from a bottle? Int J Behav Nutr Phys Act. 2011 Aug 17;8:89. PMID: 21849028

Sevenhuysen GP, Holodinsky C, Dawes C. Development of salivary alpha-amylase in infants from birth to 5 months. Am J Clin Nutr. 1984 Apr;39(4):584–8. PMID: 6608871

Clifford SM, Bunker AM, Jacobsen JR, et al. Age and gender specific pediatric reference intervals for aldolase, amylase, ceruloplasmin, creatine kinase, pancreatic amylase, prealbumin, and uric acid. Clin Chim Acta. 2011 Apr 11;412(9–10):788–90. PMID: 21238443

Sawasdivorn S, Taeviriyakul S. Are infants exclusively breastfed up to 6 months of age at risk of anemia? J Med Assoc Thai. 2011 Aug;94 Suppl 3:S178–82. PMID: 22043773

Georgieff MK. Nutrition and the developing brain: nutrient priorities and measurement. Am J Clin Nutr. 2007 Feb;85(2):614S-620S. PMID: 17284765

Fiese BH, Schwartz M. Reclaiming The Family Table: Mealtimes and Child Health and Wellbeing. Social Policy Report. 2008. Vol 22, Number 4. Retrieved on April 24, 2011, www.yaleruddcenter.org/resources/upload/docs/what/reports/ReclaimingFamilyTable.pdf

Pearson N, Biddle SJ, Gorely T. Family correlates of fruit and vegetable consumption in children and adolescents: a systematic review. Public Health Nutr. 2009 Feb;12(2):267–83. PMID: 18559129

Shibuya-Saruta H, Kasahara Y, Hashimoto Y. Human serum dipeptidyl peptidase IV (DPPIV) and its unique properties. J Clin Lab Anal. 1996;10(6):435–40. PMID: 8951616

Shattock P, Whiteley P. Biochemical aspects in autism spectrum disorders: updating the opioid-excess theory and presenting new opportunities for biomedical intervention. Expert Opin Ther Targets. 2002 Apr;6(2):175–83. PMID: 12223079

Grant EC. Developmental dyslexia and zinc deficiency. Lancet. 2004 Jul 17–23;364(9430):247–8. PMID: 15262100

Hambidge M. Human zinc deficiency. J Nutr. 2000 May;130(5S Suppl):1344S-9S. PMID: 10801941

Dórea JG. Zinc deficiency in nursing infants. J Am Coll Nutr. 2002 Apr;21(2):84–7. PMID: 11999547

Caulfield LE, Zavaleta N, Shankar AH, et al. Potential contribution of maternal zinc supplementation during pregnancy to maternal and child survival. Am J Clin Nutr. 1998 Aug;68(2 Suppl):499S-508S. PMID: 9701168

Wiklund I, Norman M, Uvnäs-Moberg K, et al. Epidural analgesia: breast-feeding success and related factors. Midwifery. 2009 Apr;25(2):e31–8. PMID: 17980469

Scott KD, Klaus PH, Klaus MH. The obstetrical and postpartum benefits of continuous support during childbirth. J Womens Health Gend Based Med. 1999 Dec;8(10):1257–64. PMID: 10643833

Johnston M, Landers S, Noble L, et al. Breastfeeding and the use of human milk. Pediatrics. 2012 Mar;129(3):e827–41. PMID: 22371471

Jantscher-Krenn E, Bode L. Human milk oligosaccharides and their potential benefits for the breast-fed neonate. Minerva Pediatr. 2012 Feb;64(1):83–99. PMID: 22350049

Gao Y, Zhang J, Wang C, et al. [Fatty acid composition of mature human milk in three regions of China]. Wei Sheng Yan Jiu. 2011 Nov;40(6):731–4. PMID: 22279667 [Article in Chinese]

Uriu-Adams JY, Keen CL. Zinc and reproduction: effects of zinc deficiency on prenatal and early postnatal development. Birth Defects Res B Dev Reprod Toxicol. 2010 Aug;89(4):313–25. PMID: 20803691

King JC. Determinants of maternal zinc status during pregnancy. Am J Clin Nutr. 2000 May;71(5 Suppl):1334S-43S. PMID: 10799411

Yasuda H, Yoshida K, Yasuda Y, et al. Infantile zinc deficiency: association with autism spectrum disorders. Sci Rep. 2011;1:129. Epub 2011 Nov 3. PMID 22355646

Grant EC. Developmental dyslexia and zinc deficiency. Lancet. 2004 Jul 17–23;364(9430):247–8. PMID: 15262100

Botero-López JE, Araya M, Parada A, et al. Micronutrient deficiencies in patients with typical and atypical celiac disease. J Pediatr Gastroenterol Nutr. 2011 Sep;53(3):265–70. PMID: 21865972

Holick MF. Vitamin D deficiency. N Engl J Med. 2007 Jul 19;357(3):266–81. PMID: 17634462

Thorne-Lyman A, Fawzi WW. Vitamin D During Pregnancy and Maternal, Neonatal and Infant Health Outcomes: A Systematic Review and Meta-analysis. Paediatr Perinat Epidemiol. 2012 Jul;26 Suppl 1:75–90. PMID: 22742603

Wei SQ, Audibert F, Hidiroglou N, et al. Longitudinal vitamin D status in pregnancy and the risk of pre-eclampsia. BJOG. 2012 Jun;119(7):832–9. PMID: 22462640

Hollis BW, Wagner CL. Vitamin D and Pregnancy: Skeletal Effects, Nonskeletal Effects, and Birth Outcomes. Calcif Tissue Int. 2012 May 24. [Epub ahead of print] PMID: 22623177

Hollis BW. Vitamin D requirement during pregnancy and lactation. J Bone Miner Res. 2007 Dec;22 Suppl 2:V3944. PMID: 18290720

Cannell JJ, Vieth R, Willett W, et al. Cod liver oil, vitamin A toxicity, frequent respiratory infections, and the vitamin D deficiency epidemic. Ann Otol Rhinol Laryngol. 2008 Nov;117(11):864–70. PMID: 19102134

Vermeer C. Vitamin K: the effect on health beyond coagulation—an overview. Food Nutr Res. 2012;56. PMID: 22489224

Houston M. The role of magnesium in hypertension and cardiovascular disease. J Clin Hypertens (Greenwich). 2011 Nov;13(11):843–7. PMID: 22051430

Chacko SA, Sul J, Song Y, et al. Magnesium supplementation, metabolic and inflammatory markers, and global genomic and proteomic profiling: a randomized, double-blind, controlled, crossover trial in overweight individuals. Am J Clin Nutr. 2011 Feb;93(2):463–73. PMID: 21159786

Zhang Q, Ananth CV, Li Z, et al. Maternal anaemia and preterm birth: a prospective cohort study. Int J Epidemiol. 2009 Oct;38(5):1380–9. PMID: 19578127

Allen LH. Anemia and iron deficiency: effects on pregnancy outcome. Am J Clin Nutr. 2000 May;71(5 Suppl): 1280S-4S. PMID: 10799402

Scholl TO. Iron status during pregnancy: setting the stage for mother and infant. Am J Clin Nutr. 2005 May;81(5):1218S-1222S. PMID: 15883455

Skeaff SA. Iodine deficiency in pregnancy: the effect on neurodevelopment in the child. Nutrients. 2011 Feb;3(2):265–73. PMID: 22254096

Zimmermann MB. Iodine deficiency in pregnancy and the effects of maternal iodine supplementation on the offspring: a review. Am J Clin Nutr. 2009 Feb;89(2):668S-72S. PMID: 19088150

Vermiglio F, Lo Presti VP, Moleti M, et al. Attention deficit and hyperactivity disorders in the offspring of mothers exposed to mild-moderate iodine deficiency: a possible novel iodine deficiency disorder in developed countries. J Clin Endocrinol Metab. 2004 Dec;89(12):6054–60. PMID: 15579758

Higdon J. (2002). Updated by Drake VJ (2007). The OSU Linus Pauling Institute website. Micronutrient Information Center. Retrieved on January 19, 2012, http://lpi.oregonstate.edu /infocenter/vitamins/fa/

Scholl TO, Johnson WG. Folic acid: influence on the outcome of pregnancy. Am J Clin Nutr. 2000 May;71(5 Suppl):1295S-303S. PMID: 10799405

Villamor E, Rifas-Shiman SL, Gillman MW, et al. Maternal intake of methyl-donor nutrients and child cognition at 3 years of age. Paediatr Perinat Epidemiol. 2012 Jul;26(4):328–35. PMID: 22686384

Untersmayr E, Bakos N, Schöll I, et al. Antiulcer drugs promote IgE formation toward dietary antigens in adult patients. FASEB J. 2005 Apr;19(6):656–8. Epub 2005 Jan 25. PMID: 15671152

7 Ways to Help Your Child THRIVE!

Peraza MA, Ayala-Fierro F, Barber DS, et al. Effects of micronutrients on metal toxicity. Environ Health Perspect. 1998 Feb;106 Suppl 1:203–16. PMID: 9539014

Binns HJ, Brumberg HL, Forman JA, et al. Chemical-management policy: prioritizing children's health. Pediatrics. 2011 May;127(5):983–90. PMID: 21518722

Johnston M, Landers S, Noble L, et al. Breastfeeding and the use of human milk. Pediatrics. 2012 Mar;129(3):e827–41. PMID: 22371471

Dufault R, Schnoll R, Lukiw WJ, et al. Mercury exposure, nutritional deficiencies and metabolic disruptions may affect learning in children. Behav Brain Funct. 2009 Oct 27;5:44. PMID: 19860886

Packing a Healthy School Lunch

Turner L, Chaloupka FJ. Slow Progress in Changing the School Food Environment: Nationally Representative Results from Public and Private Elementary Schools. J Acad Nutr Diet. 2012 Jun 4. [Epub ahead of print] PMID: 22673797

McGray D. A revolution in school lunches. Getting kids to want to eat healthy food isn't easy. Serving wholesome fare at fast-food prices is even harder. How Revolution Foods is helping school cafeterias swear off frozen pizza and fries. Time. 2010 Apr 26;175(16):50–3. PMID: 20429247

Getting Started

Daley CA, Abbott A, Doyle PS, et al. A review of fatty acid profiles and antioxidant content in grass-fed and grain-fed beef. Nutr J. 2010 Mar 10;9:10. PMID: 20219103

Manning, R. (April/May 2009). The Amazing Benefits of Grass-fed Meat. Mother Earth News. Retrieved

Dec 12, 2011, www.motherearthnews.com
/Sustainable-Farming/Grass-Fed-Meat-Benefits
.aspx

Alterman, T. (Oct 15, 2008). Relish blog. Eggciting
News!!! Mother Earth News. Retrieved on Nov
19, 2011, www.motherearthnews.com/Relish
/Pastured-Eggs-Vitamin-D-Content.aspx

Ebbeling CB, Swain JF, Feldman HA, et al. Effects
of dietary composition on energy expenditure
during weight-loss maintenance. JAMA. 2012 Jun
27;307(24):2627–34. PMID: 22735432

Datta N, Hayes MG, Deeth HC, et al. Significance
of frictional heating for effects of high pressure
homogenisation on milk. J Dairy Res. 2005
Nov;72(4):393–9. PMID: 16223453

Michalski MC, Januel C. Does homogenization affect
the human health properties of cow's milk?
Trends Food Sci Tech 2006 Aug;17(8):423–37.

Lee SJ, Sherbon JW. Chemical changes in bovine milk
fat globule membrane caused by heat treatment
and homogenization of whole milk. J Dairy Res.
2002 Nov;69(4):555–67. PMID: 12463693

Bhatnagar S, Aggarwal R. Lactose intolerance. BMJ.
2007 Jun 30;334(7608):1331–2. PMID: 17599979

Macdonald LE, Brett J, Kelton D, et al. A systematic
review and meta-analysis of the effects of
pasteurization on milk vitamins, and evidence for
raw milk consumption and other health-related
outcomes. J Food Prot. 2011 Nov;74(11):1814–32.
PMID: 18588554

Roth-Walter F, Berin MC, Arnaboldi P, et al.
Pasteurization of milk proteins promotes allergic
sensitization by enhancing uptake through Peyer's
patches. Allergy. 2008 Jul;63(7):882–90. PMID:
18588554

Gregory JF 3rd. Denaturation of the folacin-binding
protein in pasteurized milk products. J Nutr. 1982
Jul;112(7):1329–38. PMID: 7097350

Haug A, Høstmark AT, Harstad OM. Bovine milk in
human nutrition —a review. Lipids Health Dis.
2007 Sep 25;6:25. PMID: 17894873

Kilshaw PJ, Heppell LM, Ford JE. Effects of heat
treatment of cow's milk and whey on the
nutritional quality and antigenic properties.
Arch Dis Child. 1982 Nov;57(11):842–7. PMID:
6983327

Perkin MR. Unpasteurized milk: health or hazard?
Clin Exp Allergy. 2007 May;37(5):627–30. PMID:
17456210

Said HM, Ong DE, Shingleton JL. Intestinal
uptake of retinol: enhancement by bovine
milk beta-lactoglobulin. Am J Clin Nutr. 1989
Apr;49(4):690–4. PMID: 2929489

Shah NP. Effects of milk-derived bioactives: an
overview. Br J Nutr. 2000 Nov;84 Suppl 1:S3–10.
PMID: 11242440

Urbano G, López-Jurado M, Aranda P, et al. The
role of phytic acid in legumes: antinutrient or
beneficial function? J Physiol Biochem. 2000
Sep;56(3):283–94. PMID: 11198165

Ibrahim SS, Habiba RA, Shatta AA, et al. Effect of
soaking, germination, cooking and fermentation
on antinutritional factors in cowpeas. Nahrung.
2002 Apr;46(2):92–5. PMID: 12017999

Mensah P, Tomkins A. Household-level technologies
to improve the availability and preparation of
adequate and safe complementary foods. Food
Nutr Bull. 2003 Mar;24(1):104–25. PMID:
12664529

Han JR, Deng B, Sun J, et al. Effects of dietary
medium-chain triglyceride on weight loss and
insulin sensitivity in a group of moderately
overweight free-living type 2 diabetic Chinese
subjects. Metabolism. 2007 Jul;56(7):985–91.
PMID: 17570262

Kasai M, Nosaka N, Maki H, et al. Effect of dietary
medium- and long-chain triacylglycerols (MLCT)
on accumulation of body fat in healthy humans.
Asia Pac J Clin Nutr. 2003;12(2):151–60. PMID:
12810404

St-Onge MP, Bosarge A. Weight-loss diet that includes
consumption of medium-chain triacylglycerol
oil leads to a greater rate of weight and fat mass
loss than does olive oil. Am J Clin Nutr. 2008
Mar;87(3):621–6. PMID: 18326600

Smoothies

Lacombe A, Wu VC, White J, et al. The antimicrobial
properties of the lowbush blueberry (Vaccinium
angustifolium) fractional components against
foodborne pathogens and the conservation
of probiotic Lactobacillus rhamnosus. Food

Microbiol. 2012 May;30(1):124–31. PMID: 22265292

Vendrame S, Guglielmetti S, Riso P, et al. Six-week consumption of a wild blueberry powder drink increases bifidobacteria in the human gut. J Agric Food Chem. 2011 Dec 28;59(24):12815–20. PMID: 22060186

Wang SY, Chen CT, Sciarappa W, et al. Fruit quality, antioxidant capacity, and flavonoid content of organically and conventionally grown blueberries. J Agric Food Chem. 2008 Jul 23;56(14):5788–94. PMID: 18590274

Lohachoompol V, Srzednicki G, Craske J. The Change of Total Anthocyanins in Blueberries and Their Antioxidant Effect After Drying and Freezing. J Biomed Biotechnol. 2004;2004(5):248–252. PMID: 15577185

Müller D, Schantz M, Richling E. High Performance Liquid Chromatography Analysis of Anthocyanins in Bilberries (Vaccinium myrtillus L.), Blueberries (Vaccinium corymbosum L.), and Corresponding Juices. J Food Sci. 2012 Apr;77(4):C340–5. PMID: 22394068

Dunjic BS, Svensson I, Axelson J, et al. Green banana protection of gastric mucosa against experimentally induced injuries in rats. A multicomponent mechanism?. Scand J Gastroenterol 1993 Oct;28(10):894–8. PMID: 8266018

Hills BA, Kirwood CA. Surfactant approach to the gastric mucosal barrier: Protection of rats by banana even when acidified. Gastroenterology 1989;97:294–303. 1 PMID: 2744353

Rabbani GH, Teka T, Saha SK, et al. Green banana and pectin improve small intestinal permeability and reduce fluid loss in Bangladeshi children with persistent diarrhea. Dig Dis Sci. 2004 Mar;49(3):475–84. PMID:15139502

Thurnham DI, Northrop-Clewes CA, McCullough FS, et al. Innate immunity, gut integrity, and vitamin A in Gambian and Indian infants. J Infect Dis. 2000 Sep;182 Suppl 1:S23–8. PMID: 10944481

Krajka-Kuźniak V, Szaefer H, Ignatowicz E, et al. Beetroot juice protects against N-nitrosodiethylamine-induced liver injury in rats.

Food Chem Toxicol. 2012 Jun;50(6):2027–33. PMID: 22465004

Jin F, Nieman DC, Sha W, et al. Supplementation of Milled Chia Seeds Increases Plasma ALA and EPA in Postmenopausal Women. Plant Foods Hum Nutr. 2012 Jun;67(2):105–10. PMID: 22538527

Kensler TW, Egner PA, Agyeman AS, et al. Keap1-Nrf2 Signaling: A Target for Cancer Prevention by Sulforaphane. Top Curr Chem. 2012 Jul 3. [Epub ahead of print] PMID: 22752583

McCann JC, Ames BN. Vitamin K, an example of triage theory: is micronutrient inadequacy linked to diseases of aging? Am J Clin Nutr. 2009 Oct;90(4):889–907. PMID: 19692494

Breakfast

de Castro JM. The time of day of food intake influences overall intake in humans. J Nutr. 2004 Jan;134(1):104–11. PMID: 14704301

Keim NL, Van Loan MD, Horn WF, et al. Weight loss is greater with consumption of large morning meals and fat-free mass is preserved with large evening meals in women on a controlled weight reduction regimen. J Nutr. 1997 Jan;127(1):75–82. PMID: 9040548

USDA SR-21 Nutrient Data (2010). "Nutrition Facts for Seeds, chia seeds, dried" Nutrition Data. Retrieved Nov 11, 2010

Sharafetdinov KhKh, Gapparov MM, Plotnikova OA, et al. [Influence of breads with use of barley, buckwheat and oat flours and barley flakes on postprandial glycaemia in patients with type 2 diabetes mellitus]. Vopr Pitan. 2009;78(4):40–6. PMID: 19999818 [Article in Russian]

Li SQ, Zhang QH. Advances in the development of functional foods from buckwheat. Crit Rev Food Sci Nutr. 2001 Sep;41(6):451–64. PMID: 11592684

Jensen HH, Batres-Marquez SP, Carriquiry A, et al. Choline in the diets of the US population: NHANES, 20032004. The FASEB Journal 2007;21:lb219

Egli I, Davidsson L, Juillerat MA, et al. Phytic Acid Degradation in Complementary Foods Using Phytase Naturally Occurring in Whole Grain Cereals. J Food Sci 2003 June 68;5:1855–59

Fernandes AA, Novelli EL, Okoshi K, et al. Influence of rutin treatment on biochemical alterations in experimental diabetes. Biomed Pharmacother. 2010 Mar;64(3):214–9. PMID: 19932588

Li L, Seeram NP. Further investigation into maple syrup yields 3 new lignans, a new phenylpropanoid, and 26 other phytochemicals. J Agric Food Chem. 2011 Jul 27;59(14):7708–16. PMID: 21675726

Breads and Muffins

Kasim S, Moriarty KJ, Liston R. Nonresponsive celiac disease due to inhaled gluten. N Engl J Med. 2007 Jun 14;356(24):2548–9. PMID: 17568042

Vuksan V, Whitham D, Sievenpiper JL, et al. Supplementation of conventional therapy with the novel grain Salba (Salvia hispanica L.) improves major and emerging cardiovascular risk factors in type 2 diabetes: results of a randomized controlled trial. Diabetes Care. 2007 Nov;30(11):2804–10. PMID: 17686832

Skrabanja V, Liljeberg Elmstahl HG, Kreft I, et al. Nutritional properties of starch in buckwheat products: studies in vitro and in vivo. Agric Food Chem 2001 Jan;49(1):490–6. PMID: 11170616

Kawa JM, Taylor CG, Przybylski R. Buckwheat concentrate reduces serum glucose in streptozotocin-diabetic rats. J Agric Food Chem. 2003 Dec 3; 51(25): 7287–91. PMID: 14640572

Middleton E, Kandaswami C. Effects of flavonoids on immune and inflammatory cell functions. Biochem Pharmacol 1992;43(6):1167–1179. PMID: 1562270

Gabrovska D, Fiedlerova V, Holasova M et al. The nutritional evaluation of underutilized cereals and buckwheat. Food Nutr Bull 2002 Sep;23(3 Suppl):246–9. PMID: 12362805

Alvarez P, Alvarado C, Puerto M, et al. Improvement of leukocyte functions in prematurely aging mice after five weeks of diet supplementation with polyphenol-rich cereals. Nutrition. 2006 Sep;22(9):913–21. PMID: 16809023

Soups and Stews

Siebecker, A. (Feb/March 2005). Traditional Bone Broths in Modern Health and Disease. Townsend Letter for Doctors and Patients. Retrieved on Oct 18, 2011, www.townsendletter.com /FebMarch2005/broth0205.htm

Klentrou P, Cieslak T, MacNeil M, et al. Effect of moderate exercise on salivary immunoglobulin A and infection risk in humans. Eur J Appl Physiol. 2002 Jun;87(2):153–8. PMID: 12070626

Gleeson M, McDonald WA, Pyne DB, et al. Salivary IgA levels and infection risk in elite swimmers. Med Sci Sports Exerc 1999, 31:67–73. PMID: 9927012

Jeong SC, Koyyalamudi SR, Pang G. Dietary intake of Agaricus bisporus white button mushroom accelerates salivary immunoglobulin A secretion in healthy volunteers. Nutrition. 2012 May;28(5):527–31. PMID: 22113068

Hernández-Salazar M, Osorio-Diaz P, Loarca-Piña G et al. In vitro fermentability and antioxidant capacity of the indigestible fraction of cooked black beans (Phaseolus vulgaris L.), lentils (Lens culinaris L.) and chickpeas (Cicer arietinum L.). J Sci Food Agric. 2010 Jul;90(9):1417–22. 2010. PMID: 20549791

Environmental Working Group. (March 2007). EWG Research. A Survey of Bisphenol A in U.S. Canned Foods. Retrieved on Nov 11, 2011, www .ewg.org/reports/bisphenola

Salads and Vegetables

Chainy GB, Manna SK, Chaturvedi MM, et al. Anethole blocks both early and late cellular responses transduced by tumor necrosis factor: effect on NF-kappaB, AP-1, JNK, MAPKK and apoptosis. Oncogene 2000 Jun 8;19(25):2943–50. 2000. PMID:12930.

Lu QY, Zhang Y, Wang Y, et al. California Hass Avocado: Profiling of Carotenoids, Tocopherol, Fatty Acid, and Fat Content During Maturation and From Different Growing Areas. J Agric Food Chem. 2009; 57:10408–13. PMID: 19813713

USDA Agricultural Research Service. (Modified April 8, 2005). Phytonutrient FAQ's. Retrieved on Sept 22, 2011, www.ars.usda.gov/aboutus/docs .htm?docid=4142

Morrow, M., Morrow, R. (Aug 11, 2010) California Avocado Commission. California Avocado

Aommission Spreads the Word on Avocado Nutrition. Retreived on Nov 9, 2011, www .avocado.org/california-avocado-commission -spreads-the-word-on-avocado-nutrition/

Aga M, Iwaki K, Ueda Y, et al. Preventive effect of Coriandrum sativum (Chinese parsley) on localized lead deposition in ICR mice. J Ethnopharmacol. 2001 Oct;77(2–3):203–8. PMID: 11535365

Zava TT, Zava DT. Assessment of Japanese iodine intake based on seaweed consumption in Japan: A literature-based analysis. Thyroid Res. 2011 Oct 5;4:14. PMID: 21975053

D'Orazio N, Gemello E, Gammone MA, et al. Fucoxantin: a treasure from the sea. Mar Drugs. 2012 Mar;10(3):604–16. PMID 22611357

Thompson CA, Habermann TM, Wang AH, et al. Antioxidant intake from fruits, vegetables and other sources and risk of non-Hodgkin's lymphoma: the Iowa Women's Health Study. Int J Cancer. 2010 Feb 15;126(4):9921003. PMID: 19685491

Kijlstra A, Tian Y, Kelly ER, et al. Lutein: More than just a filter for blue light. Prog Retin Eye Res. 2012 Jul;31(4):303–15. PMID: 22465791

Morris MC, Evans DA, Tangney CC, et al. Associations of vegetable and fruit consumption with age-related cognitive change. Neurology. 2006 Oct 24;67(8):1370–6. PMID: 17060562

Park WT, Kim JK, Park S, et al. Metabolic Profiling of Glucosinolates, Anthocyanins, Carotenoids, and Other Secondary Metabolites in Kohlrabi (Brassica oleracea var. gongylodes).J Agric Food Chem. 2012 Jun 28. [Epub ahead of print] PMID: 22742768

Dinkova-Kostova AT. Chemoprotection Against Cancer by Isothiocyanates: A Focus on the Animal Models and the Protective Mechanisms. Top Curr Chem. 2012 Jul 3. [Epub ahead of print] PMID: 22752581

Ryan E, Galvin K, O'Connor TP, et al. Fatty acid profile, tocopherol, squalene and phytosterol content of brazil, pecan, pine, pistachio and cashew nuts. Int J Food Sci Nutr. 2006 May-Jun;57(3–4):219–28. PMID: 17127473

Sikora E, Bodziarczyk I. Composition and antioxidant activity of kale (Brassica oleracea L. var. acephala) raw and cooked. Acta Sci Pol Technol Aliment. 2012 Jul 1;11(3):239–48. PMID: 22744944

Keck AS, Finley JW. Cruciferous vegetables: cancer protective mechanisms of glucosinolate hydrolysis products and selenium. Integr Cancer Ther. 2004 Mar;3(1):5–12.

Whole Grains and Noodles

Hurrell RF, Reddy MB, Juillerat MA, et al. Degradation of phytic acid in cereal porridges improves iron absorption by human subjects. Am J Clin Nutr. 2003 May;77(5):1213–9. PMID: 12716674

Famularo G, De Simone C, Pandey V, et al. Probiotic lactobacilli: an innovative tool to correct the malabsorption syndrome of vegetarians? Med Hypotheses. 2005;65(6):1132–5. Epub 2005 Aug 10. PMID: 16095846

Vucenik I, Shamsuddin AM. Cancer inhibition by inositol hexaphosphate (IP6) and inositol: from laboratory to clinic. J Nutr. 2003 Nov;133(11 Suppl 1):3778S-3784S. PMID: 14608114

Zhang H, Onning G, Oste R, et al. Improved iron bioavailability in an oat-based beverage: the combined effect of citric acid addition, dephytinization and iron supplementation. Eur J Nutr. 2007 Mar;46(2):95–102. PMID: 17225920

Vega-Gálvez A, Miranda M, Vergara J, et al. Nutrition facts and functional potential of quinoa (Chenopodium quinoa willd.), an ancient Andean grain: a review. J Sci Food Agric. 2010 Dec;90(15):2541–7. PMID: 20814881

Brown Rice is Recommended for Breast Cancer. (n.d.). FoodforBreastCancer.com. Retrieval on Feb 20, 2012, http://foodforbreastcancer.com/foods /brown-rice

Jackson BP, Taylor VF, Karagas MR, et al. Arsenic, organic foods, and brown rice syrup. Environ Health Perspect. 2012 May;120(5):623–6. PMID: 22336149

Cebrian D, Tapia A, Real A, et al. Inositol hexaphosphate: a potential chelating agent for uranium. Radiat Prot Dosimetry. 2007;127(1–4):477–9. PMID: 17627956

Greiner R, Konietzny U, Jany K-D. Phytate—an undesirable constituent of plant-based foods? Journal für Ernährungsmedizin 2006; 8 (3): 18–28

Pallauf J, Rimbach G. Nutritional significance of phytic acid and phytase. Arch Tierernahr. 1997;50(4):301–19. PMID: 9345595

Guallar-Castillón P, Rodríguez-Artalejo F, Tormo MJ, et al. Major dietary patterns and risk of coronary heart disease in middle-aged persons from a Mediterranean country: the EPIC-Spain cohort study. Nutr Metab Cardiovasc Dis. 2012 Mar;22(3):192–9. PMID: 20708394

Thacher TD, Aliu O, Griffin IJ, et al. Meals and dephytinization affect calcium and zinc absorption in Nigerian children with rickets. J Nutr. 2009 May;139(5):926–32. PMID: 19321589

Fretham SJ, Carlson ES, Georgieff MK. The role of iron in learning and memory. Adv Nutr. 2011 Mar;2(2):112–21. PMID: 22332040

Jonnalagadda SS, Harnack L, Liu RH, et al. Putting the Whole Grain Puzzle Together: Health Benefits Associated with Whole Grains— Summary of American Society for Nutrition 2010 Satellite Symposium. J Nutr. 2011 May; 141(5): 1011S–1022S. PMID: 21451131

Topping DL, Clifton PM. Short-chain fatty acids and human colonic function: roles of resistant starch and nonstarch polysaccharides. Physiol Rev. 2001 Jul;81(3):1031–64. PMID: 11427691

Main Meals

Hernández-Ramírez RU, Galván-Portillo MV, Ward MH, et al. Dietary intake of polyphenols, nitrate and nitrite and gastric cancer risk in Mexico City. Int J Cancer. 2009 Sep 15;125(6):1424–30. PMID: 19449378

Kumar V, Sinha AK, Makkar HP, et al. Dietary roles of non-starch polysachharides in human nutrition: a review. Crit Rev Food Sci Nutr. 2012 Oct;52(10):899–935. PMID: 22747080

Riso P, Klimis-Zacas D, Del Bo' C, et al. Effect of a wild blueberry (Vaccinium angustifolium) drink intervention on markers of oxidative stress, inflammation and endothelial function in humans with cardiovascular risk factors. Eur J Nutr. 2012 Jun 26. [Epub ahead of print] PMID: 22733001

Wedick NM, Pan A, Cassidy A, et al. Dietary flavonoid intakes and risk of type 2 diabetes in US men and women. Am J Clin Nutr. 2012 Apr;95(4):925–33. PMID: 22357723

Rhone M, Basu A. Phytochemicals and age-related eye diseases. Nutr Rev. 2008 Aug;66(8):465–72. PMID: 18667008

Hurrell RF, Juillerat MA, Reddy MB, et al. Soy protein, phytate, and iron absorption in humans. Am J Clin Nutr. 1992 Sep;56(3):573–8. PMID: 1503071

Aithal BK, Kumar MR, Rao BN, et al. Juglone, a naphthoquinone from walnut, exerts cytotoxic and genotoxic effects against cultured melanoma tumor cells. Cell Biol Int. 2009 Oct;33(10):1039–49. PMID: 19555768

Vinson JA, Cai Y. Nuts, especially walnuts, have both antioxidant quantity and efficacy and exhibit significant potential health benefits. Food Funct. 2012 Feb;3(2):134–40. PMID: 22187094

Urwin HJ, Miles EA, Noakes PS, et al. Salmon Consumption during Pregnancy Alters Fatty Acid Composition and Secretory IgA Concentration in Human Breast Milk. J Nutr. 2012 Jun 27. [Epub ahead of print] PMID: 22739373

Kiecolt-Glaser JK, Belury MA, Porter K, et al. Depressive Symptoms, omega-6:omega-3 Fatty Acids, and Inflammation in Older Adults. Psychosom Med. 2007 Apr;69(3):217–24. PMID:17401057

Mazza M, Pomponi M, Janiri L, et al. Omega-3 fatty acids and antioxidants in neurological and psychiatric diseases: an overview. Prog Neuropsychopharmacol Biol Psychiatry. 2007 Jan 30;31(1):12–26. PMID:16938373

Chua B, Flood V, Rochtchina E, Wang JJ, et al. Dietary fatty acids and the 5-year incidence of age-related maculopathy. Arch Ophthalmol. 2006 Jul;124(7):981–6. PMID:16832023

Seddon JM, George S, Rosner B. Cigarette smoking, fish consumption, omega-3 fatty acid intake, and associations with age-related macular degeneration: the US Twin Study of Age-Related Macular Degeneration. Arch Ophthalmol. 2006 Jul;124(7):995–1001. PMID:16832023.

Erkkila A, Lichtenstein A, Mozaffarian D, et al. Fish intake is associated with a reduced progression of coronary artery atherosclerosis in postmenopausal women with coronary artery disease. Am J Clin Nutr, Sept. 2004; (80(3):626–32. PMID:15321802

Harris WS, Pottala JV, Sands SA, et al. Comparison of the effects of fish and fish-oil capsules on the n 3 fatty acid content of blood cells and plasma phospholipids. Am J Clin Nutr. 2007 Dec;86(6):1621–5. PMID:18065578

Caturla N, Funes L, Pérez-Fons L, et al. A randomized, double-blinded, placebo-controlled study of the effect of a combination of lemon verbena extract and fish oil omega-3 fatty acid on joint management. J Altern Complement Med. 2011 Nov;17(11):1051–63. PMID: 22087615

Harris WS, Pottala JV, Sands SA, et al. Comparison of the effects of fish and fish-oil capsules on the n 3 fatty acid content of blood cells and plasma phospholipids. Am J Clin Nutr. 2007 Dec;86(6):1621–5. PMID: 18065578

Karimi R, Fitzgerald TP, Fisher NS. A Quantitative Synthesis of Mercury in Commercial Seafood and Implications for Exposure in the U.S. Environ Health Perspect. 2012 Jun 25. [Epub ahead of print] PMID: 22732656

Bernhoft RA. Mercury toxicity and treatment: a review of the literature. J Environ Public Health. 2012;2012:460508. Epub 2011 Dec 22. PMID: 22235210

Lasky T, Sun W, Kadry A,et al. Mean total arsenic concentrations in chicken 1989–2000 and estimated exposures for consumers of chicken. Environ Health Perspect. 2004 Jan;112(1):18–21. PMID: 14698925

Silbergeld EK, Nachman K. The environmental and public health risks associated with arsenical use in animal feeds. Ann N Y Acad Sci. 2008 Oct;1140:346–57. PMID: 18991934

Harris, G., Grady, D. (June 8, 2011). Pfizer Suspends Sales of Chicken Drug With Arsenic. NewYorkTimes.com. Retrieved on March 16, 2012, www.nytimes.com/2011/06/09/business /09arsenic.html? r=3

Cima G. Drug's sale halted over arsenic concerns. J Am Vet Med Assoc. 2011 Aug 1;239(3):290–1. PMID: 21916049

Wallinga, D. (April 2006) Playing Chicken: Avoiding Arsenic in Your Meat. Institute for Agriculture and Trade Policy. Retrieved on March 16, 2012, www.iatp.org/files/421 2 80529.pdf

Vahter ME. Interactions between arsenic-induced toxicity and nutrition in early life. J Nutr. 2007 Dec;137(12):2798–804. PMID: 18029502

Reviewed by Seidu, L. (May 12, 2012) Allergies and Sulfite Sensitivity. WebMD.com. Retrieved on May 24, 2012, www.webmd.com/allergies/guide /sulfite-sensitivity

Pauling L. Orthomolecular psychiatry. Varying the concentrations of substances normally present in the human body may control mental disease. Science. 1968 Apr 19;160(3825):265–71. PMID: 5641253

Kumar N. Acute and subacute encephalopathies: deficiency states (nutritional). Semin Neurol. 2011 Apr;31(2):169–83. PMID: 21590622

Le Floc'h N, Otten W, Merlot E. Tryptophan metabolism, from nutrition to potential therapeutic applications. Amino Acids. 2011 Nov;41(5):1195–205. PMID: 20872026

Daley CA, Abbott A, Doyle PS, et al. A review of fatty acid profiles and antioxidant content in grass-fed and grain-fed beef. Nutr J. 2010 Mar 10;9:10. PMID: 20219103

Manning, R. (April/May 2009) The Amazing Benefits of Grass-Fed Meat. MotherEarthNews .com. Retrieved on Nov 16, 2011, www .motherearthnews.com/Sustainable-Farming /Grass-Fed-Meat-Benefits.aspx

Dressings, Dips, and Sauces

Victor L. Fulgoni, III, Mark L Dreher, et al. Avocado consumption is associated with better nutrient intake and better health indices in U.S. adults (19+ years): NHANES 2001–2006 FASEB J. April 2010;24 (Meeting Abstract Supplement) lb350

Dailey OD Jr, Wang X, Chen F, et al. Anticancer activity of branched-chain derivatives of oleic acid. Anticancer Res. 2011 Oct;31(10):3165–9. PMID: 21965723

Pauwels EK. The protective effect of the Mediterranean diet: focus on cancer and cardiovascular risk. Med Princ Pract. 2011;20(2):103–11. PMID: 21252562

Ashton OB, Wong M, McGhie TK, et al. Pigments in avocado tissue and oil. J Agric Food Chem. 2006 Dec 27;54(26):10151–8. PMID: 17177553

Kontogianni MD, Panagiotakos DB, Chrysohoou C, et al. The impact of olive oil consumption pattern on the risk of acute coronary syndromes: The CARDIO2000 case-control study. Clin Cardiol. 2007 Mar;30(3):125–9. PMID: 17385704

Masella R, Varì R, D'Archivio M, et al. Extra virgin olive oil biophenols inhibit cell-mediated oxidation of LDL by increasing the mRNA transcription of glutathione-related enzymes. J Nutr. 2004 Apr;134(4):785–91. PMID: 15051826

Covas MI, Nyyssönen K, Poulsen HE, et al. The effect of polyphenols in olive oil on heart disease risk factors: a randomized trial. Ann Intern Med. 2006 Sep 5;145(5):333–41. PMID: 16954359

Ruano J, Lopez-Miranda J, Fuentes F, et al. Phenolic content of virgin olive oil improves ischemic reactive hyperemia in hypercholesterolemic patients. J Am Coll Cardiol. 2005 Nov 15;46(10):1864–8. PMID: 16286173

Wraps and Rolls

Whfoods.com. (n.d.). Pumpkin Seeds. In-depth Nutrient Analysis. Retrieved on January 23, 2012, www.whfoods.com/genpage.php?tname =nutrientprofile&dbid=117

Trumbo P, Yates AA, Schlicker S, et al. Dietary reference intakes: vitamin A, vitamin K, arsenic, boron, chromium, copper, iodine, iron, manganese, molybdenum, nickel, silicon, vanadium, and zinc. J Am Diet Assoc. 2001 Mar;101(3):294–301. PMID: 11269606

Baquer NZ, Sinclair M, Kunjara S, et al. Regulation of glucose utilization and lipogenesis in adipose tissue of diabetic and fat fed animals: effects of insulin and manganese. J Biosci. 2003 Mar;28(2):215–21. PMID: 12711814

Snacks and Treats

Zhang Y. Allyl isothiocyanate as a cancer chemopreventive phytochemical. Mol Nutr Food Res. 2010 Jan;54(1):127–35. PMID: 19960458

Dinkova-Kostova AT. Chemoprotection Against Cancer by Isothiocyanates: A Focus on the Animal Models and the Protective Mechanisms. Top Curr Chem. 2012 Jul 3. [Epub ahead of print] PMID: 22752581

Mauskop A, Varughese J. Why all migraine patients should be treated with magnesium. J Neural Transm. 2012 May;119(5):575–9. PMID: 22426836

Cunha AR, Umbelino B, Correia ML, et al. Magnesium and vascular changes in hypertension. Int J Hypertens. 2012;2012:754250. Epub 2012 Feb 29. PMID: 22518291

USDA. National Nutrient Database for Standard Reference Release 24. (March 30, 2012) Nutrient Data for 12036, Seeds, Sunflower Seed Kernels, Dried. Retrieved on April 16, 2012, http://ndb .nal.usda.gov/ndb/foods/show/3688

Tucker JM, Townsend DM. Alpha-tocopherol: roles in prevention and therapy of human disease. Biomed Pharmacother. 2005 Aug;59(7):380–7. PMID: 16081238

Wiser J, Alexis NE, Jiang Q, et al. In vivo gamma-tocopherol supplementation decreases systemic oxidative stress and cytokine responses of human monocytes in normal and asthmatic subjects. Free Radic Biol Med. 2008 Jul 1;45(1):40–9. PMID: 18405673

Lee DH, Iwanski GB, Thoennissen NH. Cucurbitacin: ancient compound shedding new light on cancer treatment. *ScientificWorldJournal*. 2010 Mar 5;10:413–8. PMID: 20209387

Milder IE, Arts IC, van de Putte B, et al. Lignan contents of Dutch plant foods: a database including lariciresinol, pinoresinol, secoisolariciresinol and matairesinol. Br J Nutr. 2005 Mar;93(3):393–402. PMID: 15877880

Ríos JL, Recio MC, Escandell JM, et al. Inhibition of transcription factors by plant-derived compounds and their implications in inflammation and cancer. Curr Pharm Des. 2009;15(11):1212–37. PMID: 19355962

Thoennissen NH, Iwanski GB, Doan NB, et al. Cucurbitacin B induces apoptosis by inhibition of the JAK/STAT pathway and potentiates antiproliferative effects of gemcitabine on pancreatic cancer cells. Cancer Res. 2009 Jul 15;69(14):5876–84. PMID: 19605406

Desserts

Taubs, G. (April 13, 2011). Is Sugar Toxic. NewYorkTimes.com. Retrieved on Dec 14, 2011, www.nytimes.com/2011/04/17/magazine/mag-17Sugar-t.html?pagewanted=all

Cassileth B. Lycium (Lycium barbarum). Oncology (Williston Park). 2010 Dec;24(14):1353. PMID: 21294484

Potterat O. Goji (Lycium barbarum and L. chinense): Phytochemistry, pharmacology and safety in the perspective of traditional uses and recent popularity. Planta Med. 2010 Jan;76(1):7–19. Epub 2009 Oct 20. PMID: 19844860

Gross PM, Zhang R, Zhang X. (2006). Wolfberry: Nature's Bounty of Nutrition and Health. BookSurge Publishing. ISBN 978–1-4196–2048–5

Victor L. Fulgoni, III, Mark L Dreher, et al. Avocado consumption is associated with better nutrient intake and better health indices in U.S. adults (19+ years): NHANES 2001–2006 FASEB J. April 2010;24 (Meeting Abstract Supplement) lb350

Dailey OD Jr, Wang X, Chen F, et al. Anticancer activity of branched-chain derivatives of oleic acid. Anticancer Res. 2011 Oct;31(10):3165–9. PMID: 21965723

Ashton OB, Wong M, McGhie TK, et al. Pigments in avocado tissue and oil. J Agric Food Chem. 2006 Dec 27;54(26):10151–8. PMID: 17177553

Baldwin EA, Bai J, Plotto A, et al. Effect of extraction method on quality of orange juice: hand-squeezed, commercial-fresh squeezed and processed. J Sci Food Agric. 2012 Aug 15;92(10):2029–42. PMID: 22290491

Josse AR, Kendall CW, Augustin LS, et al. Almonds and postprandial glycemia —a dose-response study. Metabolism. 2007 Mar;56(3):400–4. 2007. PMID:17292730

Beverages

Fung TT, Malik V, Rexrode KM, et al. Sweetened beverage consumption and risk of coronary heart disease in women. Am J Clin Nutr. 2009 Apr;89(4):1037–42. PMID: 19211821

de Koning L, Malik VS, Rimm EB, et al. Sugar-sweetened and artificially sweetened beverage consumption and risk of type 2 diabetes in men. Am J Clin Nutr. 2011 Jun;93(6):1321–7. PMID: 21430119

Fowler SP, Williams K, Resendez RG, et al. Fueling the obesity epidemic? Artificially sweetened beverage use and long-term weight gain. Obesity (Silver Spring). 2008 Aug;16(8):1894–900. PMID: 18535548

Bellisle F, Drewnowski A. Intense sweeteners, energy intake and the control of body weight. Eur J Clin Nutr. 2007 Jun;61(6):691–700. PMID: 17299484

Hadisaputro S, Djokomoeljanto RR, Judiono, et al. The effects of oral plain kefir supplementation on proinflammatory cytokine properties of the hyperglycemia wistar rats induced by streptozotocin. Acta Med Indones. 2012 Apr;44(2):100–4. PMID: 22745139

Grice EA, Segre JA. The Human Microbiome: Our Second Genome. Annu Rev Genomics Hum Genet. 2012 Jun 6. [Epub ahead of print] PMID: 22703178

House JD, Neufeld J, Leson G. Evaluating the quality of protein from hemp seed (Cannabis sativa L.) products through the use of the protein digestibility-corrected amino acid score method. J Agric Food Chem. 2010 Nov 24;58(22):11801–7. PMID: 20977230

Matthan NR, Dillard A, Lecker JL, Effects of dietary palmitoleic acid on plasma lipoprotein profile and aortic cholesterol accumulation are similar to those of other unsaturated fatty acids in the F1B golden Syrian hamster. J Nutr. 2009 Feb;139(2):215–21. Erratum in: J Nutr. 2009 Apr;139(4):793. J Nutr. 2010 Feb;140(2):419. PMID: 19106316

Griel AE, Cao Y, Bagshaw DD, et al. A macadamia nut-rich diet reduces total and LDL-cholesterol in mildly hypercholesterolemic men and women. J Nutr. 2008 Apr;138(4):761–7. PMID: 18356332

Borrelli F, Capasso R, Aviello G, et al. Effectiveness and safety of ginger in the treatment of pregnancy-induced nausea and vomiting. Obstet Gynecol. 2005 Apr;105(4):849–56. 2005. PMID: 16135602

Srivastava KC, Mustafa T. Ginger (Zingiber officinale) in rheumatism and musculoskeletal disorders.

Med Hypotheses. 1992 Dec;39(4):342–8. PMID: 1494322

Srivastava KC, Mustafa T. Ginger (Zingiber officinale) and rheumatic disorders. Med Hypotheses. 1989 May;29(1):25–8.PMID: 2501634

Törrönen R, Sarkkinen E, Tapola N, et al. Berries modify the postprandial plasma glucose response to sucrose in healthy subjects. Br J Nutr. 2010 Apr;103(8):1094–7. PMID: 19930765

Sesso HD, Gaziano JM, Jenkins DJ, et al. Strawberry intake, lipids, C-reactive protein, and the risk of cardiovascular disease in women. J Am Coll Nutr. 2007 Aug;26(4):303–10. PMID: 17906180

O'Byrne DJ, Devaraj S, Grundy SM, et al. Comparison of the antioxidant effects of Concord grape juice flavonoids alpha-tocopherol on markers of oxidative stress in healthy adults. Am J Clin Nutr. 2002 Dec;76(6):1367–74. PMID: 12450905

Preserving the Harvest

USDA Complete Guide to Home Canning, 2009 revision. National Center for Home Food Preservation website. Retrieved on January 10, 2012, http://nchfp.uga.edu/publications /publications usda.html

Four Theives Vinegar. (Last Modification May 11, 2012) Wikipedia.org. Retrieved on October 16, 2011, http://en.wikipedia.org/wiki/Four Thieves Vinegar

Gopalan A, Reuben SC, Ahmed S, et al. The health benefits of blackcurrants. Food Funct. 2012 Jun 6. [Epub ahead of print] PMID: 22673662

Yoshioka M, St-Pierre S, Drapeau V, et al. Effects of red pepper on appetite and energy intake. Br J Nutr. 1999 Aug;82(2):115–23. PMID: 10743483

Yoshioka M, St-Pierre S, Suzuki M, et al. Effects of red pepper added to high-fat and high-carbohydrate meals on energy metabolism and substrate utilization in Japanese women. Br J Nutr. 1998 Dec;80(6):503–10. PMID: 10211048

Zava TT, Zava DT. Assessment of Japanese iodine intake based on seaweed consumption in Japan: A literature-based analysis. Thyroid Res. 2011 Oct 5;4:14. PMID: 21975053

Index

ABOUT THE AUTHORS

Alissa Segersten is a cooking instructor and author of the food blog www.NourishingMeals.com, empowering people with cooking skills and knowledge of whole foods so they may reconnect with pleasure in eating delicious, nourishing food.

Tom Malterre, MS, CN, is a certified nutritionist who holds two degrees in nutritional sciences and is a faculty member of the Autism Research Institute. He coaches physicians and other health-care practitioners on using functional medicine principles in their clinical practices.